Picture
HISTORY
OF THE
WORLD

Contributors
Brian Adams
Christopher Fagg
Frances Halton
Robert Knox
Keith Lye
W. D. Townson

General Editor
Frances M. Clapham

Consultant Editors
Lionel Butler (Middle Ages)
Amélie Kuhrt (Ancient World)
W. D. Townson (Age of Discovery and Modern World)

Copyright © 1986, 1981, 1980, 1979
by Grisewood & Dempsey Limited.
First published in the United States of America
in 1986 by Grosset & Dunlap,
a member of The Putnam Publishing Group, New York.
All rights reserved.
Published simultaneously in Canada.
Printed and bound in Italy.
Library of Congress Catalog Card Number: 86-80404
ISBN 0-448-18988-7

The material in this book has previously been
published by the Longman Group Limited in four
separate volumes: *Atlas of the Ancient World* (1979),
Illustrated Atlas of the World in the Middle Ages
(1980), *Illustrated Atlas of the World in the Age of
Discovery* (1981), and *Illustrated Atlas of the
Modern World* (1981).

Picture
HISTORY
OF THE
WORLD

Publishers • GROSSET & DUNLAP • New York
A member of The Putnam Publishing Group

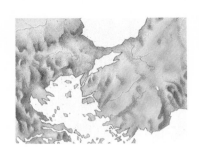

Contents

THE ANCIENT WORLD

The pyramids of Giza, west of the river Nile, were built by the pharaohs of the Old Kingdom (c.2686–2181 B.C.).

Looking at the Past

The way in which people live has always been influenced by the sort of country they live in: by the climate, the crops they can grow, and the animals they can rear; by the building materials and the ease of getting from place to place. Looking at the history of the world by regions, instead of by periods of time, helps us to understand the sort of places in which ancient people lived and how these influenced their civilizations.

Hunting and Farming
The first men fed themselves on seeds and fruit, and by hunting. They moved about, often following herds of animals and going to places where they knew food would be plentiful. They lived in caves, or built themselves very simple huts or tents of branches and skins. Some parts of the world were particularly suitable for this way of life and the people there lived in the same way for thousands of years.

We can learn a great deal about the past from objects dug up at places where people lived long ago. These places are usually known as "sites." They must be very carefully dug so that the exact place where each object is found can be noted down. The picture on the left shows part of a site where a "dig" is going on. Finds are placed in the labeled boxes; all the earth is taken away to be sieved in case any small find has been missed. The grid of string helps to map the site at different stages.

This picture of dogs hunting a wild boar has been reconstructed from a wall painting at Tiryns in Greece. The darker parts are the original fragments, found in the position in which they are shown here. The artist who painted in the rest has followed what he thought was on the original, from studying similar paintings. These reconstructions are a great help in imagining what ancient places looked like, but sometimes dreadful mistakes are made. An artist doing a reconstruction at Knossos in Crete filled in the figure of a boy picking crocuses. Later researchers decided that the picture showed not a boy, but a monkey!

But in other places, perhaps where the climate was different and food was not so easy to get, people learned to domesticate animals like goats and sheep, cattle and pigs. Instead of harvesting wild grain crops they planted their own, and they developed plants which gave more and better grain.

This kind of life is very hard and needs a lot of continuous work, so men had to stop moving around and build settled homes. They started to adapt the country around them to suit their needs. They cleared the land to make fields for their crops, and they cut down trees for fires and to build houses. They dug water channels to irrigate their crops and turned land that was semidesert into good farming land. Once all Europe was covered with thick forests, where today there are open fields. Around the Mediterranean coast forests were cut down and olive trees planted. But their deep roots did not hold the topsoil together and it was blown away by the wind and washed away by the rain. People have not always improved the land.

Sites and Trade
When people became dependent on the food they grew, it became important for them to live in places which they could easily defend and which provided the things they needed. These included not only grazing ground, reasonable soil, and enough water but also, as the settlements grew, access to essential materials for building and for making tools. Some, like the Greeks, liked to center their settlements on a hill which they could fortify. The ancient Chinese built their towns and cities beside rivers, which not only provided water for the crops but also defended them from at least one side. The rivers were also a good way of traveling and of carrying goods. Many important cities grew up because they were on trade routes.

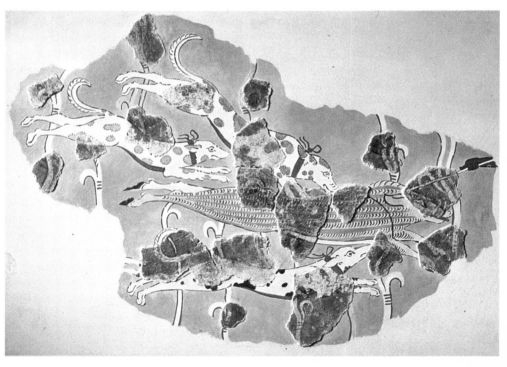

This relief shows the pharaoh Ramses II holding Nubian prisoners by the hair. The inscription around the picture tells of his campaigns. But inscriptions like these can be unreliable, and historians have learned not to trust them. Often they paint a falsely glorious picture of a ruler's deeds.

This bronze horse bit is from Luristan, in the Zagros mountains of Persia. It is one of a number of strange and wonderful bronze articles which began to appear in antique markets in 1928. Because they had been dug up without any scientific knowledge no one has been able to say exactly where each object was found or which were older than others. But by comparing them with other bronze work which can be dated, archaeologists have worked out that they were made from the 10th to the 7th centuries B.C.

Discovering the Past

We can learn a great deal about the past from the remains of ancient peoples and the things they made, and by studying their written records. But the distant past is like a vast jigsaw puzzle with most of the pieces lost. Although archaeologists have discovered and studied large numbers of fascinating sites there must be many, many others still unknown to us which would help to fill in the picture. Every few years we read of discoveries which teach us new facts and which sometimes show that a piece of the "puzzle" has been put into the wrong place and that our previous ideas were quite wrong. This is one reason why new history books sometimes disagree with other, earlier books.

The written records of the past are very valuable, but they do not always tell the true story of what actually happened. For every country tends to write records which show it coming out on top – in skills, in learning, in wealth, and in war. In the 14th century B.C. the pharaoh Ramses II described how he was cut off from his army by the Hittites, saying he rode at the gallop and charged the enemies, having no one with him: "I found that 2,500 enemy chariots in whose midst I had been lying were broken in pieces before my steeds." His account does not mention that he had a division of soldiers with him, and that it was his own fault that they were cut off. The Hittites recorded this battle as a draw!

In Roman times we read of good emperors who worked wisely with the Senate, and bad ones who ruled without it; but were these records perhaps written from the Senate's point of view? This is the sort of thing which historians must always remember when they are trying to find out what really happened.

However hard they try to be objective,

Below: Maiden Castle, in Dorset in southwest England. This ridge overlooking the countryside was a good place to live. In the 2000s B.C. Stone Age people built huts and a ditched enclosure for their animals there. At this time the country around was wooded marshes, and the ridge provided farmland. About 2000 B.C. a vast long barrow (burial mound) was built on the highest point. A little later Bronze Age people settled there. By about 1500 B.C. the bogs and swamps below had dried out and the land could be farmed. The ridge was deserted until the 5th century B.C. when a fort was built there, surrounded by walls of earth and chalk and outside them a wide, deep ditch.

historians always see the past from the point of view of their own times. If we look at pictures of the past drawn by 19th-century artists, we can tell almost at once that they were painted at that date. In rather the same way a history written then praises what people admired at the time. We always tend to praise what we ourselves like; so in looking at the jigsaw puzzle of the past it is always tempting to put a piece where we think it would go well, and to think that the whole picture is far simpler and tidier than, so far as we can tell, it was.

The First Men

Who were the first "men"? No one can answer this question exactly. Scholars have traced our ancestors right back to small, furry, tree-living creatures who were also ancestors of apes and monkeys. But at some time Man's ancestors split off from the others. They became able to walk upright and their brains became larger. They began to make and use tools and they learned to speak.

All we know about the earliest men is what we can learn from their bones and from the objects they made. So far only a few early sites have been studied. But more and more skeletons are being found which help to build up a picture of our ancestors' gradual development from creatures little different from apes to people who, though primitive cave-dwelling hunters, were physically just like us.

2 People living at Terra Amata in southern France about 300,000 years ago built camps with huts made from wooden poles and stones, roofed with hide or branches. They used stone "hand axes" and were skilled hunters, killing elephants, wild boats, and rhinoceroses.

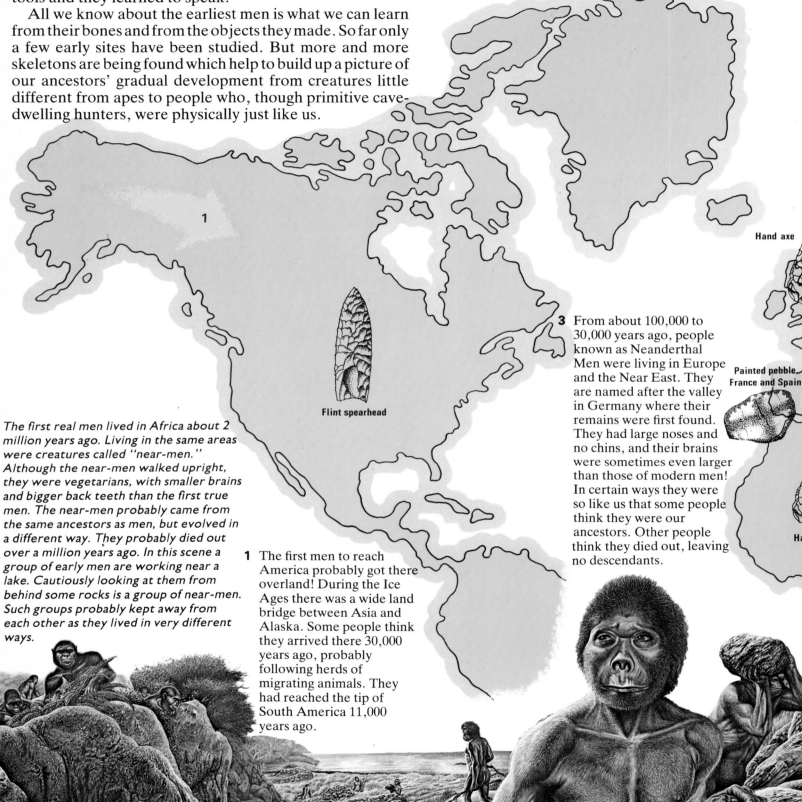

Hand axe

Flint spearhead

3 From about 100,000 to 30,000 years ago, people known as Neanderthal Men were living in Europe and the Near East. They are named after the valley in Germany where their remains were first found. They had large noses and no chins, and their brains were sometimes even larger than those of modern men! In certain ways they were so like us that some people think they were our ancestors. Other people think they died out, leaving no descendants.

Painted pebble, France and Spain

6

Hand a

The first real men lived in Africa about 2 million years ago. Living in the same areas were creatures called "near-men." Although the near-men walked upright, they were vegetarians, with smaller brains and bigger back teeth than the first true men. The near-men probably came from the same ancestors as men, but evolved in a different way. They probably died out over a million years ago. In this scene a group of early men are working near a lake. Cautiously looking at them from behind some rocks is a group of near-men. Such groups probably kept away from each other as they lived in very different ways.

1 The first men to reach America probably got there overland! During the Ice Ages there was a wide land bridge between Asia and Alaska. Some people think they arrived there 30,000 years ago, probably following herds of migrating animals. They had reached the tip of South America 11,000 years ago.

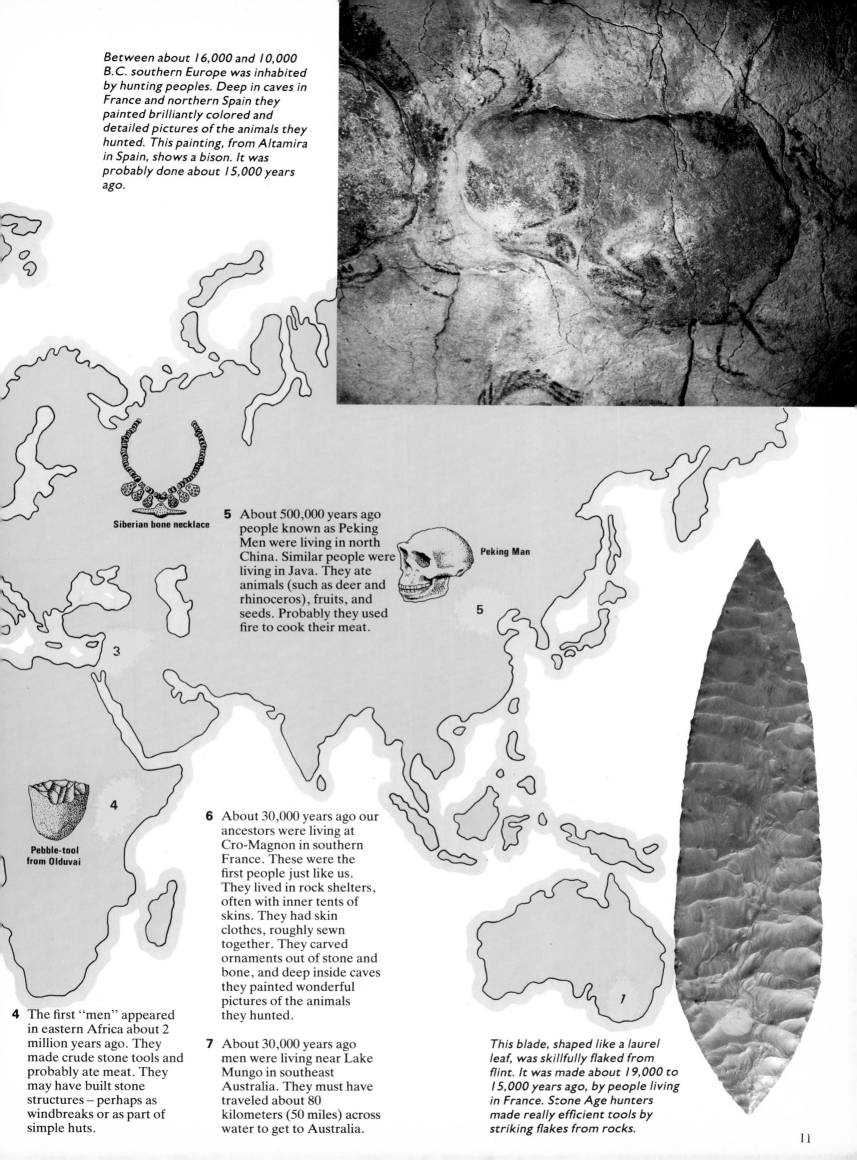

Between about 16,000 and 10,000 B.C. southern Europe was inhabited by hunting peoples. Deep in caves in France and northern Spain they painted brilliantly colored and detailed pictures of the animals they hunted. This painting, from Altamira in Spain, shows a bison. It was probably done about 15,000 years ago.

Siberian bone necklace

5 About 500,000 years ago people known as Peking Men were living in north China. Similar people were living in Java. They ate animals (such as deer and rhinoceros), fruits, and seeds. Probably they used fire to cook their meat.

Peking Man

Pebble-tool from Olduvai

6 About 30,000 years ago our ancestors were living at Cro-Magnon in southern France. These were the first people just like us. They lived in rock shelters, often with inner tents of skins. They had skin clothes, roughly sewn together. They carved ornaments out of stone and bone, and deep inside caves they painted wonderful pictures of the animals they hunted.

4 The first "men" appeared in eastern Africa about 2 million years ago. They made crude stone tools and probably ate meat. They may have built stone structures – perhaps as windbreaks or as part of simple huts.

7 About 30,000 years ago men were living near Lake Mungo in southeast Australia. They must have traveled about 80 kilometers (50 miles) across water to get to Australia.

This blade, shaped like a laurel leaf, was skillfully flaked from flint. It was made about 19,000 to 15,000 years ago, by people living in France. Stone Age hunters made really efficient tools by striking flakes from rocks.

The First Religions

From very early times people have had to come to terms with happenings which they could not explain but which deeply affected their lives – events like the seasons, disease, birth, and death, and the migrations of animals they hunted. In all parts of the world, religions have grown up based on efforts to understand the unknown.

Early Gods

Neanderthal Men, who lived between 100,000 and about 30,000 years ago, carefully buried their dead. Sometimes they put flowers, or animal bones and flint tools, with them. The Cro-Magnon people who followed them in Europe made skillfully carved and modeled figures of animals and women. Deep inside their caves they painted pictures of the animals they hunted. People think that these early communities already had ceremonies to do with death, and to bring them success in hunting.

Perhaps during that time people were already thinking that all sorts of things, such as the sun and moon and special places and objects, had their own spirits, or gods and goddesses. These spirits could be influenced if they were approached in the right way, and with the right sort of ceremony. This is certainly the way in which many simple peoples, who lived in places cut off from developing civilizations, have thought until the present day.

Unfortunately, we can know very little for sure. Early religious practices were not written down, but handed on from generation to generation by example. In areas where people settled down to a way of life which depended on farming, customs and ceremonies must have gradually changed. Ceremonies designed to make sure of good hunting, for instance, would slowly have given way to others meant to produce a good harvest.

Organized Religion

The earliest religion of which we have definite knowledge is that of the city-states of Sumer. Here religious ceremonies became especially important and closely linked to the ways in which the states were governed.

In Sumer there was an ancient tradition of building temples to local nature gods who protected the crops from flood and drought. Some of these temples became the centers around which the first cities grew up. The god of the temple grew in importance to become the protector of the city. The ruler of a Sumerian city kept the city god friendly by building more temples, and by performing the ceremonies the god required.

The cat was considered a sacred animal by the ancient Egyptians. In this papyrus from Thebes, made about 1300 B.C., a cat cuts up the serpent Apophis who had attacked the sun-god Ra.

This female figure, dating from about 5750 B.C., was found at Çatal Hüyük in Anatolia. Figures like these are found at ancient sites far away from one another. They suggest that some sort of mother goddess was worshiped by early people.

This seal is from the Indus Valley civilization of northern India (about 2500–1750 B.C.). It shows Pashupali, lord of the animals, seated in a cross-legged position. This posture and the three faces of the god remain elements in the Hindu tradition of a thousand years later.

In Egypt, too, early farmers worshiped local nature gods. Later, after Upper and Lower Egypt were joined together, these gods became associated with the power and glories of the Egyptian kings. One local nature god, Amun of Thebes, rose in importance to become the king of the gods – this was because a family of kings from Thebes came into power.

Myths and Legends

All over the world, early peoples made up stories to explain how the world and the things in it began. These stories are usually called "myths," from a Greek word meaning "a story of the gods."

The Near East produced many myths. This was the region where the change from village farming to highly organized states first took place. Old religious traditions were altered to fit a world in which warfare between states, and violent invasions by peoples outside the civilized areas, were common events.

This complicated world also showed in stories of gods and goddesses, who quarreled among themselves for power just like human rulers. Over 2,000 years such myths built up and overlapped: often different countries had very similar myths about their own gods.

Greek and Roman Mythology

The Greeks borrowed stories from Near Eastern and Egyptian myths and peopled them with the Greek family of gods and goddesses. In the 7th century B.C. a Greek writer called Hesiod wrote a long poem in which he explained how all the gods came to be born and what each god did.

The Greeks thought that their gods, like the thunder-god Zeus, the sea-god Poseidon, and the moon-goddess Artemis, must have shown themselves to different peoples in different forms. So to the Greeks the Egyptian god Amun was a form of Zeus, and the Great Goddess of the Ephesians was a form of Artemis.

The Romans were deeply attracted by the beautiful stories of the Greek gods, and they adapted their own gods to the Greek system. So the Roman Jupiter became identified with Greek Zeus, Roman Neptune with Greek Poseidon, and so on.

Eastern Ways of Life

In India and China, conditions were right for the growth of great systems of thought (*philosophies*) in which every kind of belief and practice had a place. One reason for this was the sheer size of the areas involved. With so many people having different beliefs it was impossible to impose a single set of beliefs upon them. Instead, such systems accepted that people must continue to worship in their own ways.

Hinduism, the first great religion of India, dates back to well before 1000 B.C. It teaches of a single world spirit, Brahman, of which all gods, people, and things are part. All sorts of gods and beliefs come within its framework. Its law of *Dharma* teaches that people must obey the divine order of the universe. Each person is born into a certain position in life, and must work to fulfill the tasks laid down for him. If he does so, he will be rewarded by being born again into a higher position.

In the 6th century B.C., three great philosophies developed in the East. They were Buddhism, Confucianism, and Taoism, and they taught that people must accept things as they are and work hard to live correctly.

Buddhism was developed by a great Indian teacher, Gautama, who lived from about 563 to 483 B.C. Gautama was known as the Buddha (the Enlightened One), and he taught that men could only escape the pain and suffering of life on earth by obeying certain great rules. One of the rules was that people should not harm any living thing. This rule was called *Ahimsa*.

The Chinese philosopher Confucius, who lived in the 6th century B.C. He taught that, in dealing with other people: "What you do not want done to yourself, do not do to others."

A row of sculptured lions on the island of Delos. They guard the lake where the god Apollo was said to have been born. This island was one of the most sacred places of ancient Greece, and had temples to Apollo and several other gods.

China, too, had great spiritual teachers. The two greatest were Confucius, born about 551 B.C. and Lao-Tze, who lived about the same time. Confucius said that order, good conduct toward people of higher rank, and setting a good example were very important. In this way, he thought, society would be made perfect.

Lao-Tze wrote down the basic ideas of Taoism. The word Tao means "the Way," or the principle on which nature works. By following the Way, people can live in peace and harmony with the world.

All these philosophies, in one form or another, have survived into the modern world. All of them were rooted in the unchanging nature of life in the East where the most important fact was the unceasing round of planting and harvesting the crops.

One God

Of all the religions of the ancient world only one – Judaism – developed the idea of a single, all-powerful god. This being revealed himself to Abraham, the ancestor of the Jewish people. God entered into an agreement with his people. If they would obey certain laws, he would protect them.

Judaism was the ancestor of Christianity. Christians accept the great Jewish religious writings called the Old Testament. But they believe, as Jews do not, that Jesus Christ was the promised Son of God, born into the world to save mankind. Christianity soon spread through the Roman world.

Another great religion with close links to Judaism is Islam, or Submission to the Will of God, or Allah. Muslims (as the followers of Islam are known) respect the Jewish scriptures and the teachings of Jesus, whom they regard as a prophet. Islam was founded in Arabia by Muhammad, in the 7th century A.D. It spread rapidly to divide the old Mediterranean world into Christian Europe and Islamic Africa and Asia.

A Peruvian gold figure of a puma, dating from the 4th to 9th centuries A.D. On its back is a design of sacred two-headed snakes. The "Cult of the Cat," shown in snarling fanged masks of pumas and jaguars, began in Peru in the last few centuries B.C.

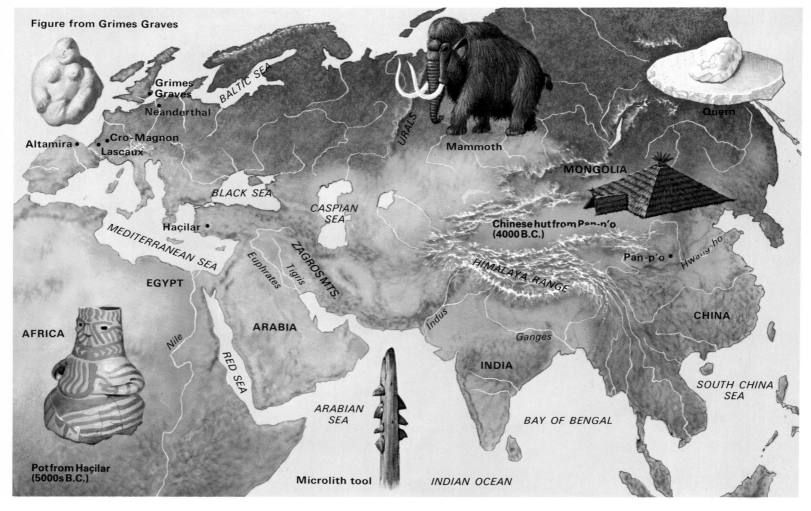

Figure from Grimes Graves

Grimes Graves
Neanderthal
Altamira •
• Cro-Magnon
Lascaux
BALTIC SEA
URALS
Mammoth
MONGOLIA
Quern
BLACK SEA
CASPIAN SEA
Chinese hut from Pan-p'o
(4000 B.C.)
MEDITERRANEAN SEA
Haçilar •
Euphrates
Tigris
ZAGROS MTS.
HIMALAYA RANGE
Pan-p'o • Hwang-ho
EGYPT
Nile
ARABIA
RED SEA
AFRICA
Indus
Ganges
CHINA
INDIA
SOUTH CHINA SEA
ARABIAN SEA
BAY OF BENGAL
Pot from Haçilar
(5000s B.C.)
Microlith tool
INDIAN OCEAN

From Hunters to Farmers

More than 35,000 years ago the world was deep in the grip of the last great Ice Age. In the northern hemisphere, vast ice sheets stretched from the North Pole to cover much of what is now Britain and northern Europe. The huge area of ice meant that the climate of the world was very different from that of today. Central Europe, for example, was a type of semifrozen treeless desert, called tundra, which today is only found within the Arctic Circle. Even the shape of the land was different. So much water was locked up in the ice that the sea level was much lower. Areas of land now separated by the sea were then joined by land bridges.

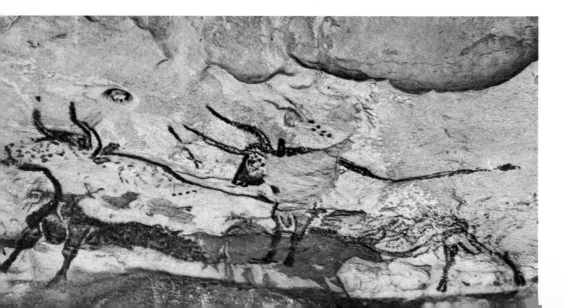

Man in the Ice Age

The people who lived in the Ice Age were hunters. They used tools and weapons made of flint, skillfully chipped into shape. With these they hunted down and killed the big game animals which wandered in great herds over the earth. In the cold lands of the north, herds of woolly mammoth, caribou, mastodon, and moose provided meat for food and skins for clothing and shelter. Further south were herds of elephant, tapir, wild pig, and deer.

The hunters of these times had no settled homes, so that we have very little knowledge of them. What we do know is based on scattered finds of tools and food remains left behind at temporary encampments. A camp might be occupied for a few days or a few months, and when the wild herds moved on in search of new feeding grounds, the hunters followed.

One site at Cro-Magnon in France has given its name to a group of hunters who spread westward from the Near East about 30,000 B.C. The Cro-Magnons may have been the first modern men – our direct ancestors. As they moved westward across Europe they may have met a different type of man. This type, called Neanderthal Man after the site in Germany where the first remains were found, may have died out.

Paintings of animals from a cave at Lascaux, in southern France. They date from 16,000 to 10,000 B.C.: in those times people lived by hunting.

Left: Even today there are still people who depend on migrating animals for food, clothing, and shelter. These Lapps follow herds of reindeer as they move through northern Scandinavia.

The Cro-Magnon people were skilled hunters and toolmakers. They fashioned fine tools and weapons out of flint, stone, bone, ivory, and the antlers of deer. The animals they hunted gave them meat for food and skins for clothes and tents. These, of course, have not survived, but we *can* get an idea of how advanced the Cro-Magnon people were. Deep in special caves at sites like Lascaux and Altamira (see page 11) they painted extraordinary pictures of the animals they hunted.

A woman's head, delicately carved from mammoth ivory as early as 22,000 B.C. She may be wearing a type of headdress, or perhaps some special hairstyle. It was found in France.

Left: The Fertile Crescent – the region in the Near East where farming first developed, about 8000 B.C.

Mammoth hunters in the cold wastes of eastern Europe, 25,000 years ago. Evidence suggests that hunters made tents and clothing from animal hides, and used coal (from surface outcrops) for campfires.

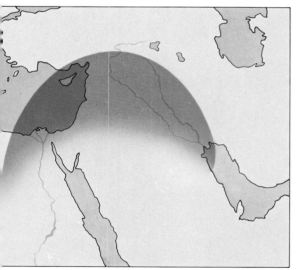

The End of the Ice Age

Toward 10,000 B.C. the Ice Age came to an end. The great ice sheets slowly melted and shrank northward, bringing enormous changes to the world. Europe, which had been an arctic desert, became covered with thick forest and woodland. North Africa became an area with heavy rainfall, before drying up into the great deserts of today. The melting ice caused enormous amounts of water to flow into the oceans and the sea level rose. Many parts of the world were cut off by the rising oceans, leaving people and animals in those areas to develop in very different ways.

In Europe and Asia, many of the big mammals which had survived the Ice Age were slowly hunted to extinction. Others, like bison, elk, and reindeer, moved farther north to stay with the tundra. By 10,000 B.C., hunters had to depend on smaller game – fish, deer, wild pig, and wildfowl. They developed a great variety of weapons and tools, such as the bow and arrow, for hunting different kinds of animals. They also added to their food supply by gathering wild fruits and berries in the forests. Some peoples made permanent homes by shallow coastal waters where there was a plentiful supply of shellfish.

THE FIRST FARMERS

In many parts of the world people carried on a hunting and gathering life for thousands of years. But about 8000 B.C., important developments took place in the Near East. Here men learned first to harvest the wild grains that grew in the area, and then to sow them. The early farmers made flint sickles to cut the wild grain, and primitive millstones (called querns) to separate the grain from the husks. For the first time, men began to rely on food that they grew themselves, and to domesticate wild sheep, goats, pigs, and cattle.

The World in 3000 B.C.

By now, settled farming has developed in many parts of the world. Villages have grown up whose people often make beautifully painted pottery. Metalworking – first of natural copper and gold, and then of copper smelted from ores and bronze – is spreading out from Anatolia (Asia Minor) where it developed. The two most advanced areas are Mesopotamia and Egypt; in both regions cities and temples are being built, writing systems have been developed, and skills including sculpture and metalworking are increasing rapidly.

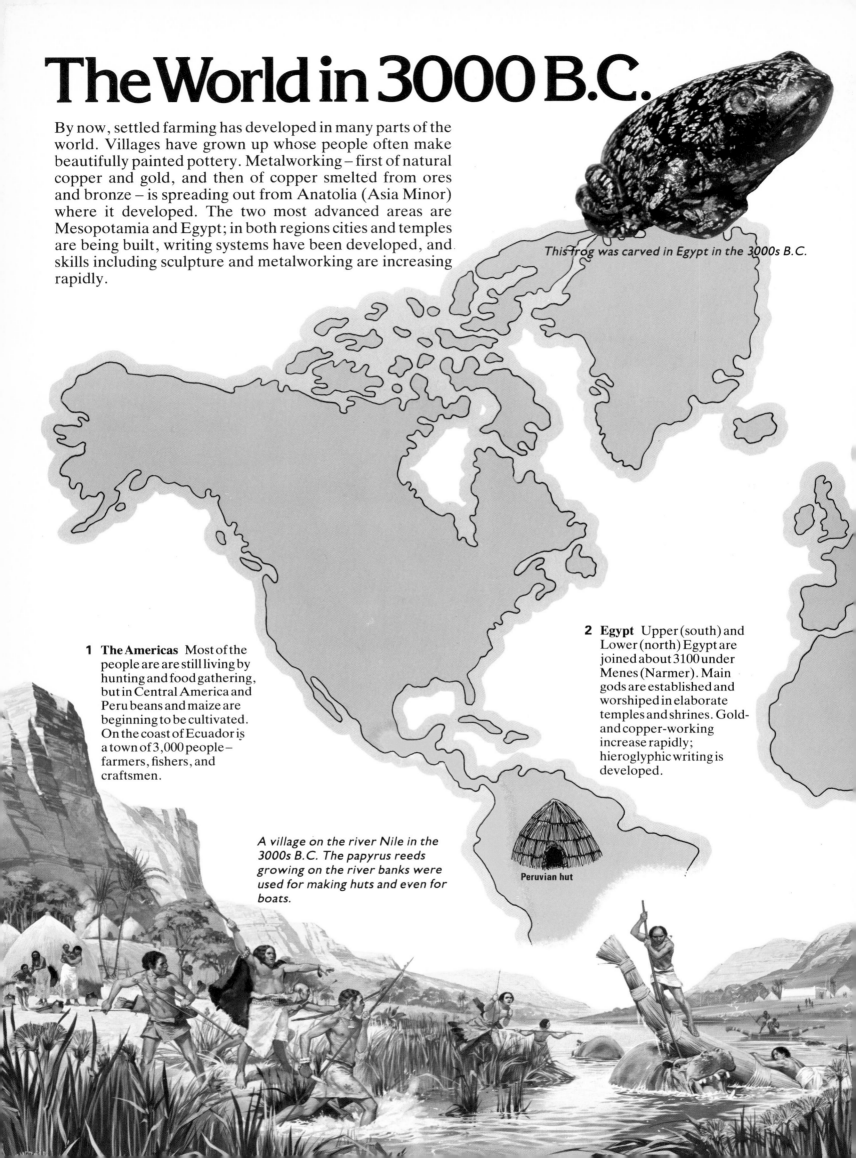

This frog was carved in Egypt in the 3000s B.C.

1 The Americas Most of the people are are still living by hunting and food gathering, but in Central America and Peru beans and maize are beginning to be cultivated. On the coast of Ecuador is a town of 3,000 people – farmers, fishers, and craftsmen.

2 Egypt Upper (south) and Lower (north) Egypt are joined about 3100 under Menes (Narmer). Main gods are established and worshiped in elaborate temples and shrines. Gold- and copper-working increase rapidly; hieroglyphic writing is developed.

A village on the river Nile in the 3000s B.C. The papyrus reeds growing on the river banks were used for making huts and even for boats.

Peruvian hut

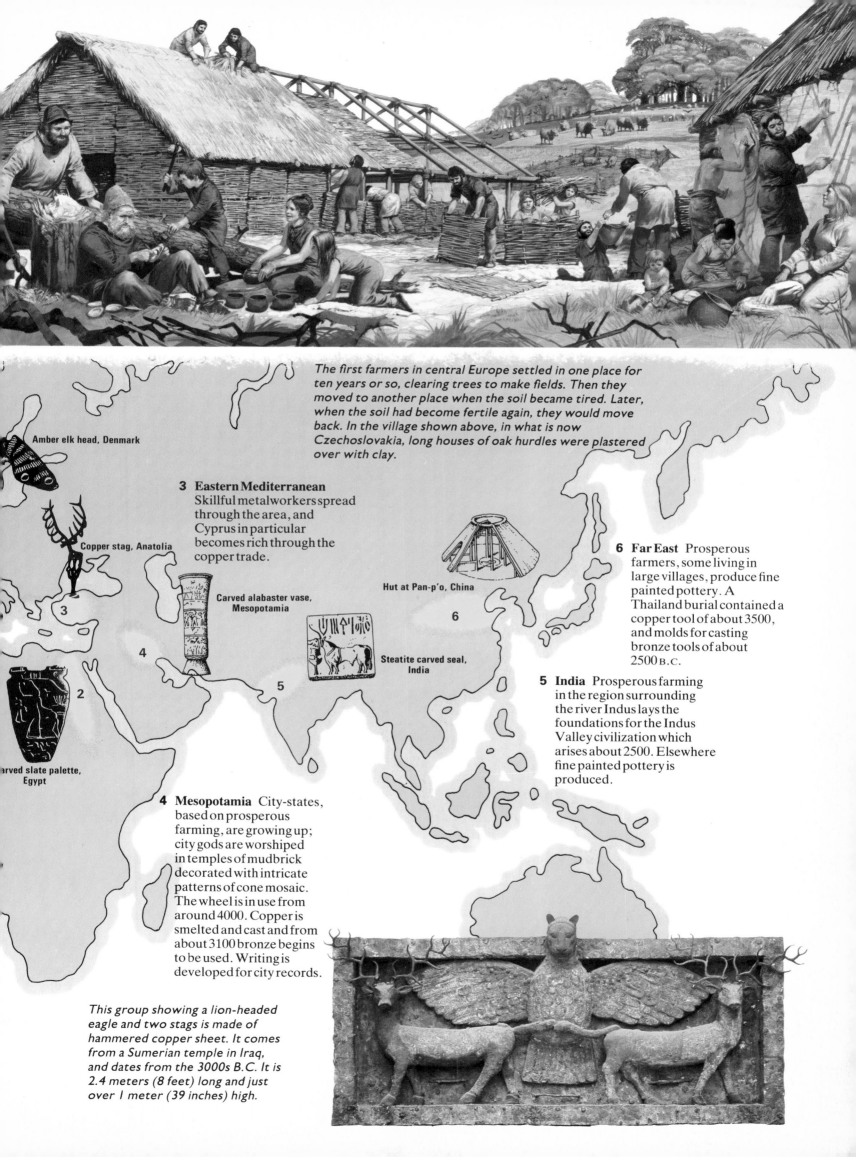

The first farmers in central Europe settled in one place for ten years or so, clearing trees to make fields. Then they moved to another place when the soil became tired. Later, when the soil had become fertile again, they would move back. In the village shown above, in what is now Czechoslovakia, long houses of oak hurdles were plastered over with clay.

Amber elk head, Denmark

Copper stag, Anatolia

3 Eastern Mediterranean Skillful metalworkers spread through the area, and Cyprus in particular becomes rich through the copper trade.

Carved alabaster vase, Mesopotamia

Hut at Pan-p'o, China

Steatite carved seal, India

6 Far East Prosperous farmers, some living in large villages, produce fine painted pottery. A Thailand burial contained a copper tool of about 3500, and molds for casting bronze tools of about 2500 B.C.

5 India Prosperous farming in the region surrounding the river Indus lays the foundations for the Indus Valley civilization which arises about 2500. Elsewhere fine painted pottery is produced.

Carved slate palette, Egypt

4 Mesopotamia City-states, based on prosperous farming, are growing up; city gods are worshiped in temples of mudbrick decorated with intricate patterns of cone mosaic. The wheel is in use from around 4000. Copper is smelted and cast and from about 3100 bronze begins to be used. Writing is developed for city records.

This group showing a lion-headed eagle and two stags is made of hammered copper sheet. It comes from a Sumerian temple in Iraq, and dates from the 3000s B.C. It is 2.4 meters (8 feet) long and just over 1 meter (39 inches) high.

Mastering Skills

When we look at ancient history, we usually look at each area of the world in turn. We see how its civilization grew up, how it became powerful, and how it eventually fell. This is an easy way to learn about things. But another way of looking at the past is to study developments that were common to many different civilizations. Examples of such things are metalworking, pottery, the use of money, and writing systems.

These developments did not happen overnight. They were the results of perhaps thousands of years of experience. Sometimes, as in the case of metalworking, the same discoveries were made separately in quite different parts of the world. Sometimes a similar need led to very different developments, such as the variety of writing systems worked out by different civilizations.

Metalworking

Wherever metalworking developed, it became important to people in controlling their surroundings. Once metal tools were invented, it was easier and quicker to clear and cultivate land, and to work a wider range of materials. Metal weapons, produced in large quantities, allowed rulers to equip great armies.

The earliest metals to be worked were copper, silver, and gold in the Near East – especially in Anatolia (Asia Minor), which had rich sources of these metals. As early as the 7000s B.C., nuggets of metal found on the ground surface were hammered into small pins, fishhooks, and trinkets.

True metalworking in the Near East did not begin until about 4500 B.C. Only then did people learn how to heat copper-bearing rock to a temperature high enough to melt out the pure metal. Molten copper was then poured into molds to make tools like axheads, spearheads, chisels, and so on. But copper is a rather soft metal; it needs frequent hammering and reheating if it is to keep a sharp edge. Copper tools were not as good as tools and weapons made of flint and obsidian (volcanic glass) which were already in existence.

Not until about 3000 B.C. did the Near Eastern metalworkers learn how to make copper much harder, by adding a small amount of a much rarer and more expensive metal – tin. The mixture that resulted is called bronze.

Copper- and bronze-working spread only slowly from centers in the Near East. It cost a lot to make tools from the metals and only the highly organized and wealthy societies of the region could afford to employ skilled craftsmen. In undeveloped northern Europe, for example, bronze-working did not begin until about 1000 B.C.

In other parts of the world, metalworking began later than in the Near East. It spread to the Indus Valley after 2500 B.C. In China, bronze-working had developed independently by 1500 B.C. But in the Americas true metalworking was unknown until the 4th century B.C.

Iron

In the Near East, it was more than 1,500 years from the start of the Bronze Age to the start of iron production. This was because iron was very difficult to work. One problem was that iron-bearing rocks had to be heated to very high temperatures in order to separate the metal from the rock. The result was still not molten iron, but a spongy mass which had to be heated and hammered for a long time.

In the eastern Mediterranean area skilled craftsmen were working iron by about 1200 B.C.; iron implements are found in Europe dating from about 1000 B.C. Iron-working developed independently in the Ganges Valley of India (about 1000 B.C.) and in China (about 600 B.C.). The Chinese developed cast iron (melting the ore and pouring it into molds) about 1,800 years before the Europeans.

Money

It is hard for us today to think of buying anything without paying for it in coins of a fixed value. Yet coinage did not develop until about 700 B.C. in the Near East, long after the beginning of civilization. Until then people paid for goods in a variety of ways. Some used tokens, such as shells or beads. Others used ingots of metals like copper, bronze, and iron, or even paid with livestock, such as cattle and horses. This still happens in parts of the world today.

This wallpainting from an Egyptian tomb shows metalworkers. They are using bellows worked by foot to get a hot enough fire to melt the copper and tin for bronze. It dates from about 1500 B.C.

This pot, shaped like an animal, was made in China around 2000 B.C. It is much like a pot made in South America in about A.D. 500 by the Mochica people (see page 56).

An early coin from Phrygia in Anatolia (Asia Minor). It is made of electrum, an alloy (mixture) of gold and silver.

This huge storage jar, or pithos, was found at Knossos in Crete. Jars like this were used for storing grain, oil, and wine. For thousands of years jars of many sizes were used as containers, and many of them were sent abroad when they contained exports.

An oracle bone from China. It dates from the Shang period, about 1500 B.C. Oracle bones were used for telling the future. The drawings on them are a very early form of modern Chinese writing. The Shang script had characters like small pictures, but over the centuries these have changed so that now Chinese characters are not usually at all like the objects or ideas they represent.

The Sumerian cuneiform script was adapted to write many Near Eastern languages. The writing on this seal is in the Elamite language. It comes from the 6th or 5th century B.C.

A tablet from Knossos showing writing in the Linear B script, used by the Mycenaeans. Until 1952 no one could read this script. Then a British architect named Michael Ventris worked out that it was used for writing a very early form of Greek.

Right: An Egyptian papyrus of the 13th century B.C. The written language of the Egyptians is called hieroglyphic. It was made up of picture symbols which sometimes represented objects or ideas, and sometimes represented consonants. A simplified form of hieroglyphic called "hieratic" was developed about 1900 B.C. About 700 B.C. a popular ("demotic") script was developed which was much faster to write.

The first known use of money was in the kingdom of Lydia, in Anatolia, in the 7th century B.C. The Lydian "coins" were thick oval pieces of precious metal, stamped with a symbol showing their fixed weight.

From Lydia their use spread to the Greek cities of the Anatolian coasts, and from there to mainland Greece itself. These early coins were too valuable for everyday use – just one might have paid for a whole boatload of goods. But by the 5th century B.C. it was becoming usual to issue coins of smaller value for day-to-day use, and payment in money was becoming common.

Pottery

Even 25,000 years ago, hunters made small clay models of the animals they hunted. But wandering hunters and food gatherers could not carry heavy, breakable clay pots with them. The first pottery vessels were not made until the 7000s B.C., when village life developed in the Near East. Everywhere in the world, pottery is linked to the growth of settled, village communities.

Early pots were made by pressing a slab of sandy clay over a rounded object, or by coiling a long roll of clay on top of a flat base. The sides were then smoothed, and the finished pots dried in the sun before being baked hard in a fire. Later, special ovens called kilns were made, in which pots could be fired at controlled temperatures.

In the 4000s B.C. came another important development – the potter's wheel. Rotating the clay on a simple turntable made it easier to shape. The potter's wheel was in use in the Aegean area by 2000 B.C. – but it only reached Europe after 1000 B.C.

Writing

Even though there are thousands of different spoken languages in the world, only a very few writing systems have developed.

The first known writing system came about in Sumer in about 3000 B.C. It developed to meet the need to make records of the complicated transactions of huge landowning organizations like temples and palaces. In the beginning Sumerian "writing" was no more than a number of simplified picture symbols of the objects that they stood for. They were pressed into tablets of soft river clay with reed "pens." The clay was then dried in the sun.

As time went on, however, the Sumerian picture-writing developed until it could record not only simple lists of objects, but the language that people actually spoke. An important change came about when a picture symbol could stand not only for an object, but the *sound* of the word for that object. The first picture symbols gave way to a kind of shorthand version of them, which was quicker and easier to write. It was made up of triangular marks in the clay tablets. It is called *cuneiform* (wedge-shaped) script, from the Latin word *cuneus*, a wedge.

In Egypt, a rather different form of picture writing developed about 3000 B.C. Not long afterward the Egyptians invented a kind of paper made from the split and flattened stems of the papyrus reed. This meant that from early on the Egyptians painted their *hieroglyphic* script on a smooth surface, and it became flowing and decorative.

The Alphabet

Between 1600 and 1000 B.C. a new writing system grew up in the Near East. This was the alphabetic system. Although there were various forms, all had the advantage that they needed fewer signs to write a language.

Scripts like Egyptian hieroglyphic and cuneiform were *syllabic*: each sign stood for the sound of a whole word, or part of a word. The alphabet, on the other hand, used a single sign for each sound in a word. Egyptian and cuneiform systems had many hundreds of signs, but an alphabetic system needed fewer than 30.

By the 10th century B.C. a fully alphabetic system was in use in the Phoenician city of Tyre. It may have been from the Phoenicians that the ancient Greeks adopted the alphabet in the 8th or early 7th century B.C. Our word "alphabet" itself is made up of the first two signs of the Greek alphabet, alpha (α) and beta (β). Because the Greeks used the alphabet, all modern European languages are written with the alphabetic system.

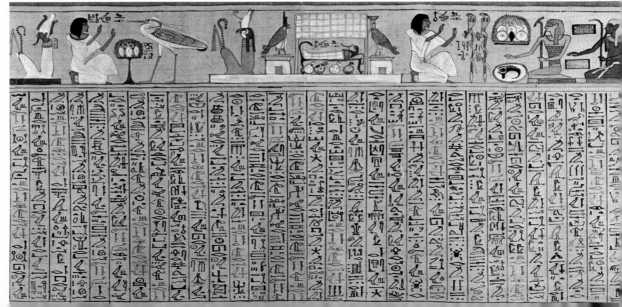

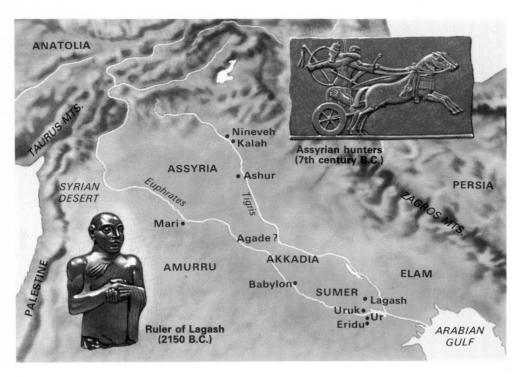

ANATOLIA

TAURUS MTS.

Nineveh
Kalah

Assyrian hunters
(7th century B.C.)

ASSYRIA

SYRIAN
DESERT

Euphrates

Ashur

PERSIA

Tigris

ZAGROS MTS.

Mari

Agade?

AMURRU

AKKADIA

ELAM

PALESTINE

Babylon

SUMER
Lagash
Uruk
Ur
Eridu

Ruler of Lagash
(2150 B.C.)

ARABIAN
GULF

Mesopotamia

B.C.	CHRONOLOGY
c.3100	Great temples built in Sumer. Earliest writing at Uruk
c.2700–2400	Sumerian cities fortified and ruled by kings. Constant warfare
2371–2255	Akkadian empire, founded by Sargon
2113–2006	Third Dynasty of Ur rules Sumer

Mesopotamia is a Greek word which means "the land between the rivers." It is used to describe the region between the rivers Tigris and Euphrates, the southern area of which is mainly low-lying swamp and marshland. It was here, in what is now the southern part of the state of Iraq, that one of the world's first civilizations grew up between 4000 and 3000 B.C.

The fertile lands of Mesopotamia lie between the desert and the mountains. To the west are the vast Arabian and Syrian deserts: to the east the Zagros Mountains rise to 3,000 meters (10,000 feet). Mesopotamia itself falls into two main regions. The northern part has a regular rainfall. The south, stretching down to the Arabian Gulf, suffers dry, scorching summers from May to October. This area, once called Sumer, is a flat plain built up from layers of mud carried there by the rivers when they flooded. The soil is fertile, but needs to be watered (irrigated) if it is to grow crops. Because the area is so flat, it is often threatened by violent floods.

The marshlands of ancient Sumer (now southern Iraq) saw the growth of the world's first cities. Today communities of Marsh Arabs (right) live lives that may not be very different from those of the early Sumerians. The Marsh Arabs use reeds to build houses and boats and even as food: fish and dates are important sources of food today, just as they were 6,000 years ago. Some people think that the Marsh Arabs may be the descendants of the ancient Sumerians.

From Villages to Cities

Farming spread slowly all over western Asia. By 5000 B.C. there were many large, prosperous villages – almost towns. Between 4000 and 3500 B.C., however, the farming peoples of Sumer made the greatest step forward of all. From living in villages they developed to build the world's first true cities at sites like Ur and Eridu.

Sumer is a flat, swampy area of southern Mesopotamia about the size of the Netherlands. Although the soil is fertile river mud, the ancient Sumerian farmers faced many difficulties. There was no rainfall, so they had to dig irrigation canals to water their fields. For seven months the sun was burning hot: it drew the moisture from the ground, leaving it salty and infertile. In the spring, just as the crops were ripe, the rivers often flooded disastrously, swamping the fields and threatening the harvest.

But Sumer had important natural resources. Date palms grew well, even in salty ground. In the marshes were wild pig and wildfowl, and there were fish from the rivers. These extra sources of food could support a large population. The more people there were, the better they could dig and clean the canals, and build dams to control the floods.

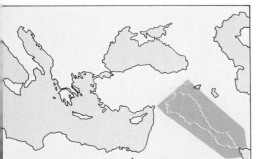

Trade and Empire

Between 2800 and 2400 B.C., the city-states of Sumer were at their strongest and most wealthy. At different times, one city or another became powerful enough to rule the others. Sumer became the richest market in the world, attracting trade from the eastern Mediterranean to the Indus Valley.

But the wealth of Sumer also attracted greedy eyes. Just to the north, in the area of Agade, the ruler Sargon had become very powerful through his control of the trade routes to the north, west, and east. In about 2350 B.C., Sargon attacked Sumer and made it part of his huge empire. His capital, Agade, gives us the name by which Sargon's empire is known – the Akkadian empire.

The Akkadian empire was the first attempt to unite a huge area under the rule of one man. From now on Mesopotamia was nearly always dominated by one, or at the most two, powerful states.

At the same time local centers, including temples, grew up. The temples were dedicated to the local god, who protected the people from floods and gave them a good harvest. The temples stored produce, either for food or for replanting at the start of the new growing season in October. They kept herds of animals, like the oxen and donkeys needed to draw plows. It is possible that the temples hired out these animals to farmers in return for a part of the crop.

The temples grew rich, and some cities were ruled by a temple official with the help of a staff of officials and scribes. Writing and counting systems were developed in order to keep track of the goods passing into and out of the storehouses. Two of the ruler's tasks were to build new temples to the god, and to maintain the irrigation system. These temples became the starting point for growing cities. Not only temple officials lived there but also the craftsmen who built and maintained the temples, merchants, and scribes. Sumer became a patchwork of independent cities, each supplied with food by its surrounding area of countryside.

Part of the so-called "Standard of Ur," perhaps the base of a harp, from about 2500 B.C. The scenes show a society already divided into classes. At the top the rich sit at a feast. In the middle, servants drive cattle, sheep, and goats. At the bottom, laborers carry heavy loads. The figures are of shell and red limestone, set into a background of lapis lazuli with bitumen. Lapis lazuli, a semiprecious blue stone, was traded over long distances from sources in Afghanistan.

Right: A bronze head of an Akkadian king. The Akkadian empire grew to include all of Mesopotamia and parts of North Syria and Elam (in southwest Iran). It was the first recorded attempt to administer such a large area.

NATURAL RESOURCES

The Sumerians had no metal, stone, or wood of their own. These materials, together with precious metals, gemstones, and other luxuries, were imported by way of the Arabian Gulf or overland from the north. The main resources of Sumer were deposits of clay and the river mud itself. Clay was used to make decorative bricks and pottery. Sumerian scribes wrote with reed "pens" on soft clay writing tablets. The river mud was shaped into bricks and allowed to dry naturally in the scorching sun. Mudbrick was the main building material. Reeds were plentiful in the marshlands, and they were also useful: tied into bundles, they could be made into houses, boats, and rafts, as well as being woven into baskets and reed mats. Bitumen, a kind of tar, was also important: it was used to fill cracks and make them watertight, and as a glue for inlay work.

The Sumerian city-states were often at war. This inscribed stone was put up to celebrate a great victory by the city of Lagash, under its ruler Eannatum (about 2500 B.C.), over its rival city of Umma. Two scenes are shown: at the top, Eannatum, in a garment of animal skins, leads a close formation of troops. Below: Eannatum, in his four-wheeled chariot, aims his lance at the enemy.

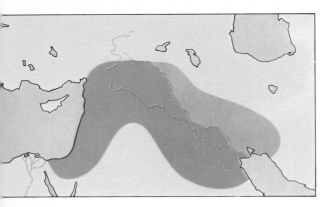

The map above shows the two Babylonian empires. The brown area is that ruled over by Hammurabi : 1792–1750 B.C.) and later by the Kassites. The orange area is the Neo- (New) Babylonian empire, created by Nabopolassar (626–605 B.C.) and his son Nebuchadrezzar (605–562 B.C.). Between the two Babylonian empires came the period when Mesopotamia was ruled by the Assyrians. The map below shows their empire at its greatest extent, during the 7th century B.C.

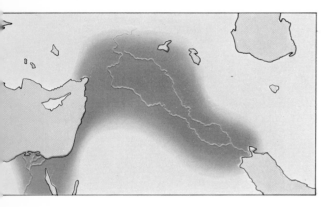

The First Empire

Sargon of Agade and his successors ruled the first empire that we know of. But size brought its own problems. Sargon's grandson, Naram-Sin, had to deal with many revolts by the peoples that he ruled. The Akkadian empire was also threatened by desert nomads in the west and hostile and warlike peoples of the Zagros Mountains to the east.

The herders on the edge of the desert were not always hostile. But in times of severe drought they moved into the cultivated areas of the empire in search of grazing for their flocks. This naturally led to conflict.

In 2230 B.C. the Akkadian empire fell, because of these difficulties. For a while, part of south Mesopotamia was dominated by the Gutians, a mountain people the Sumerians called "the Vipers from the Hills." After a century of confusion Sumer, led by the kings of Ur's Third Dynasty, regained much of its former glory. But after only a hundred years, Ur was sacked by the strong state of Elam, to the east. At the same time, Sumer was invaded from the north by a Semitic people, the *amurru*, groups of whom settled in all the old Sumerian cities. Once again, Sumer suffered a period of weakness and confusion.

The Amorites

The *amurru*, or Amorites, were nomads living on the edge of the desert. Gradually some of them took over large areas of Mesopotamia, settling in cities like Mari, Ashur, and Babylon. When they became city-dwellers they absorbed the ways of Mesopotamia, and adapted the cuneiform script of the Sumerians and Akkadians (see page 19) to write their own language.

About 1760 B.C., the great Hammurabi, the Amorite ruler of Babylon, attacked Mari and Ashur and became overlord of most of the city-states of northern and southern Mesopotamia. By the end of his reign in 1750 B.C., he could describe himself as "Mighty king, King of Babylon, King of the whole country of Amurru, King of Sumer and Akkad, King of the Four Quarters of the World."

The Kassites

About 1600 B.C. Babylon was sacked by an Indo-European people, the Hittites, of central Anatolia to the northwest. In the confusion that followed, the Kassites – whose original home may have been in the Zagros Mountains – seized the throne of Babylonia. Their power had much to do with their expert knowledge of horses: their two-wheeled horse-drawn chariots were the most advanced weapons of the time.

The Kassites ruled peacefully for 400 years. Under them, the cities of Babylonia came under central rule, but they were still thought of as important centers of religion, art, and literature. Babylonia developed into a national state, with Babylon as its administrative capital. But in 1150 Babylonia was devastated by a terrible raid by the Elamites. With great difficulty, new rulers in Babylon drove out the invaders, only to face a new threat from the warlike Assyrians to the north.

A black stone weight in the form of a duck. Setting up standard weights and measures was a way of carrying the power of a ruler into distant parts of his empire. This weight dates from the Third Dynasty of Ur.

A boundary stone, or "kudurru," of the Kassite period in Babylonia (1590–1245 B.C.). Such stones were carved with prayers asking the gods to protect the owner's land.

A winged "pazuzu" – a type of desert demon. The desert was the home of nomads who, from time to time, threatened the stability of the Mesopotamian states.

The Assyrians

The Assyrian homeland lay between the cities of Ashur and Nineveh on the river Tigris. From here, important trade routes led to Syria and Anatolia. For a long time the powerful rule of Babylonia to the south and the Hittites to the northwest prevented Assyria from expanding. But in the centuries following the collapse of the Hittite empire the Assyrians began to expand into the space left behind.

Under a strong king, Tiglathpileser III, in the 8th century, the Assyrian army was turned into a permanent, highly trained force. Over the next 50 years, the Assyrians conquered most of Syria, Palestine, and Phoenicia and invaded Egypt as far as Thebes (Luxor). Some regions became provinces; others were allowed to rule themselves under pro-Assyrian kings. The tribute and taxes that the Assyrians demanded led to terrible hardship. There were frequent revolts – which were savagely crushed. Land was left uncultivated, allowing hostile Aramaean herders to devastate whole areas of the empire.

An Assyrian king watches prisoners of war dragging a huge statue of a winged, human-headed bull from the stone quarries to his capital. Nearly every Assyrian king built himself a palace, or added greatly to an existing one. The wealth and labor needed to do so were drawn from the provinces of the Assyrian empire. This policy made the provinces poor and encouraged revolts. All the details in this reconstruction, including the sled, dragged along on rollers, and the raft, buoyed with inflated animal skins, are taken from Assyrian carvings.

THE NEO-BABYLONIAN EMPIRE

In Babylonia, a number of groups waged a desperate struggle to free themselves from Assyrian domination. Babylon itself was sacked by the Assyrian king Sennacherib, and the population murdered. But the Babylonians fought on. Then about 631 civil war broke out in Assyria and after the death of King Ashurbani-pal. Under Nabopolassar the Babylonians joined forces with the Medes of western Iran. Between 614 and 612 Assyria was invaded and the major cities Nineveh, Ashur, and Kalah were captured and destroyed. Nabopolassar's son Nebuchadrezzar II went on to conquer much of the Assyrian empire. But after less than a century his Neo- (New) Babylonian empire surrendered to Persia.

This reconstruction of the Ishtar Gate of Babylon uses the original glazed bricks. It dates from the Neo-Babylonian period, when Babylon was splendidly rebuilt.

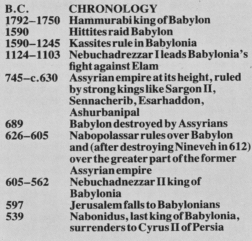

B.C.	CHRONOLOGY
1792–1750	Hammurabi king of Babylon
1590	Hittites raid Babylon
1590–1245	Kassites rule in Babylonia
1124–1103	Nebuchadrezzar I leads Babylonia's fight against Elam
745–c.630	Assyrian empire at its height, ruled by strong kings like Sargon II, Sennacherib, Esarhaddon, Ashurbanipal
689	Babylon destroyed by Assyrians
626–605	Nabopolassar rules over Babylon and (after destroying Nineveh in 612) over the greater part of the former Assyrian empire
605–562	Nebuchadnezzar II king of Babylonia
597	Jerusalem falls to Babylonians
539	Nabonidus, last king of Babylonia, surrenders to Cyrus II of Persia

Egypt

The pyramids at Giza, seen across the green strip of the Cultivation. Farmland was so valuable in Egypt that great monuments like these were built in the desert, which begins where the fertile "black earth" ends.

An Egyptian king was regarded as a god. This silver coffin of King Psusennes (about 1000 B.C.) shows him with a crook and a flail, symbols of his power to care for and punish.

B.C.	CHRONOLOGY
3100	Menes (?Narmer) unites Egypt
2686–2181	Old Kingdom
2650	Death of Zoser for whom first pyramid was built
2180–2040	First Intermediate Period. Absolute rule of kings disrupted by civil war
2040–1633	Middle Kingdom. Egyptian power extended southward. Widespread trade with the Aegean and Levant
1633–1567	Second Intermediate Period. Egypt invaded by Hyksos peoples using horse-drawn chariots
1567–1085	New Kingdom. Hyksos driven from Egypt
1504–1450	Reign of Thutmosis III, who wins a vast empire. Egyptian power at its greatest
1087–751	Third Intermediate Period. Egypt ruled by Libyan, then Ethiopian invaders
751–332	Late Period. Times of independence alternate with conquest by Assyrians, then Persians, finally Alexander the Great (332). After his death Egypt is ruled by Alexander's general Ptolemy and his heirs
30	Egypt becomes a Roman province

Egypt is a hot, desert land, divided by the fertile valley of the river Nile. Hardly any rain falls there, and the summers are scorching hot. Even today, more than 90 percent of Egypt is arid desert, where nothing can grow. But the strip of land, called the Cultivation, on each side of the Nile is one of the most fertile places in the world. Although it is no more than 20 kilometers (12½ miles) wide, it runs for about 1,000 kilometers (620 miles) from Aswan in the south to the broad farmlands of the Delta, where the river runs into the Mediterranean.

The rich black soil of the Cultivation was laid down over thousands of years by the regular flooding of the Nile. The river used to burst its banks every year between June and October until modern dams were built to control it. The sticky black mud that the floodwaters left behind was so rich that two or even three crops could be grown in one season, as long as the soil was well-watered.

The Ancient Egyptians
Its fertile soil was the reason why, more than 5,000 years ago, the Nile Valley saw the development of the brilliant civilization of the Ancient Egyptians. The earliest Egyptians had learned to farm the land along the banks, using water from the river to water their crops. The villages along the Nile grew rich and began to join to help one another dig the ditches and dams needed to control the annual flooding.

In about 3100 B.C. a king called Menes united the whole of Egypt under his rule. He and his descendants were Egypt's first ruling family, or dynasty. The earliest period we know much about is called the Old Kingdom (2686–2181 B.C.). By this time the kings had become immensely powerful. Writing, painting, architecture, and crafts were highly developed. Egyptian power and influence flourished for almost 2,000 years, despite two periods of civil war and foreign invasion.

At its greatest, under strong rulers like Thutmosis III (1504–1450 B.C.), Egypt controlled Palestine and Syria and reached southward to the African state of Nubia. But by 1150 B.C. Egypt was surrounded by powerful enemies. In 935 a Libyan invader, Sheshonk I, seized the throne. Except for a period between 664 and 525 B.C., Egypt was ruled by foreign kings until it was finally conquered by Rome in 30 B.C.

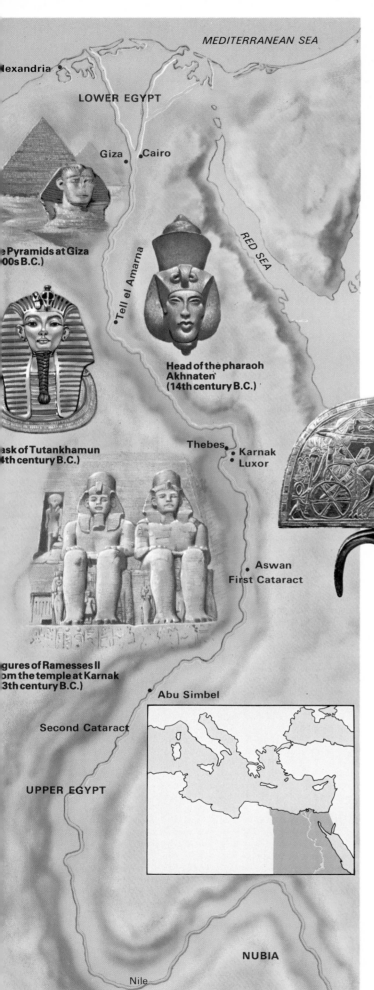

Head of the pharaoh Akhnaten (14th century B.C.)

Mask of Tutankhamun (14th century B.C.)

Figures of Ramesses II from the temple at Karnak (13th century B.C.)

Egypt stretches for some 1,000 kilometers (620 miles) north to south. In Lower Egypt, around the Delta, a few centimeters of rain fall each year. But the land watered by the Nile is astonishingly fertile.

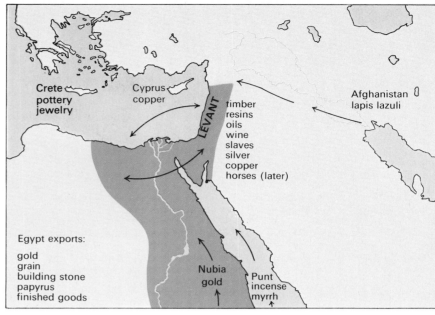

Egypt exports:

gold
grain
building stone
papyrus
finished goods

Trade by land and sea linked Egypt with the rest of the Near East. There were contacts, too, with Crete. To the south, Egypt exploited the gold of Nubia and imported frankincense and myrrh from the land of Punt (?Somalia).

Egypt traded over a wide area. In return for grain, gold, copper, gemstones, and building stone, it imported the things that it did not have. From Lebanon came timber, resins, oils, silver, and slaves. Later, horses were imported from Syria and Anatolia, and the blue stone called lapis lazuli through Mesopotamia. Overland trade routes were protected by strong forts. During the empire, trade in Palestine and Syria was firmly controlled by Egypt. To the south, Nubia remained in Egyptian hands almost continuously for 800 years. It was Egypt's most important source of gold and slaves.

The golden fan-holder of Tutankhamun. The fan itself was made of imported ostrich feathers, and the gold came from Nubia.

The kings of Egypt were absolute rulers. The king owned all the land, and farmers had to give the king part of what the land produced. An army of officials and scribes (see the pictures above and right; had the task of fixing the exact amount due to the king from each farmer. Crops and livestock were carried off to the storehouses surrounding the royal palaces. Out of this vast tribute, the king paid his officials and provided funds for huge irrigation projects.

Cult of the Dead

The early people of the Nile Valley buried their dead in pits in the hot dry sand, which dried out the bodies and preserved them. When, later on, the dead were buried in rock tombs, the corpses decayed. So the Egyptians worked out ways of preserving (*mummifying*) them. Kings built massive pyramid tombs during their lifetime and later, to try to prevent robbery, hidden tombs were cut into cliffs in the Valley of the Kings near Thebes.

The Egyptians believed in eternal life in the Next World, and spent a lot of time preparing for it. Burial chambers were decorated with beautiful paintings and writings which recorded the dead man's life, his family and his servants, and happy days spent hunting. The Egyptians believed that in the Next World the scenes would come to life through prayer. Food and drink and little models of people were also placed there, with all the dead man's jewelry and personal equipment.

Instructions for the dead man's journey were placed in the tomb, for he faced a difficult journey across the River of Death and into the Next World before he faced Osiris, god of the dead, for the final test – the Weighing of the Heart. The dead person's heart was weighed against the Feather of Truth – a sinful, heavy heart would outweigh the feather and a dreadful monster devoured its owner; a good man would have a light heart, and would spend eternity in the Fields of the Blessed.

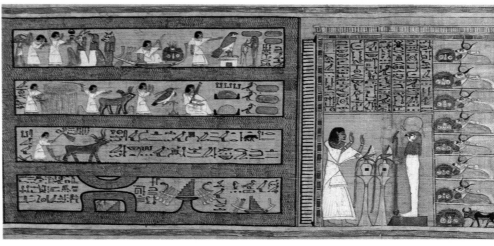

The Egyptians believed that death was only the beginning of a long journey to the Next World. The dead person would be ferried across the river to the kingdom of Osiris, the god of the dead. But there were many hazards to be overcome. To help the dead person on his journey, a book of instructions, the "Book of the Dead," was buried in the tomb along with the body. This papyrus from the tomb of the priest Ani shows some of the stages of the journey. On the left the dead priest crosses the river; below are shown the Blessed Fields of the Next World. To the right, Ani is welcomed by Ra, the sun-god.

A prosperous farm in ancient Egypt. The fields are surrounded by irrigation ditches, one of which is being filled from a larger channel. The laborer uses a "shaduf" to transfer the water; this is a leather bucket attached to a swiveling, counter-weighted pole. The shaduf is used in Egypt to this day. The mudbrick farmhouse has small windows set high in the wall to keep out the sun. Transport is by donkey; camels were introduced much later.

Agriculture

The farmer's year began in September, when the Nile flood, called the Inundation, began to go down, leaving a rich black silt which made the soil very fertile. Then oxen were used to drag wooden plows to till the soil, and by November the farmers had sown their crops – wheat for bread and fattening cattle, barley for beer, and grapes for wine. They also grew fruit and vegetables, and flax for making linen.

The farmers weeded and watered their crops, with the help of specially built irrigation canals. The crops were ready to be harvested in March and April. Then the grain was threshed and stored. The soil was so fertile that sometimes two crops could be grown before April, when the hot season began and when even the river began to dry up. So from April to June the farmers repaired the canals, dikes, and basins needed to irrigate their fields, in time for the new Inundation in June. While the land was flooded the men worked on royal projects, such as building pyramids.

Most of the land watered by the Inundation was used to grow crops. The only pasture land was in the Delta, and so in Upper Egypt cattle to be fattened for food were kept in stalls. The Egyptians also kept sheep, goats, pigs, geese, ducks, donkeys, and later, chickens. Cats and dogs were kept as pets, and horses were introduced during the Hyksos period.

TRAVEL

The river Nile was Egypt's main highway; people traveled by water wherever they could. Travel by land was hard. A rich man traveled in a chair, carried on the shoulders of servants, or very rarely by horse-drawn chariot; no other wheeled vehicles were used. Everyone else walked. Heavy loads were dragged on sledges, while smaller loads were packed into donkey panniers. Camels only began to be used in the Late Period, and the long caravans that crossed the desert before then were made up of donkeys.

Africa

These Stone Age rock carvings from Algeria show a leopard and an ostrich. The place in which they are found is now part of the Sahara. They are evidence of how that part of Africa has changed, for such animals could not possibly live in desert conditions.

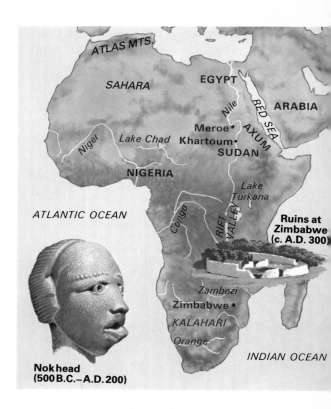

Nok head (500 B.C.–A.D. 200)

Ruins at Zimbabwe (c. A.D. 300)

The vast continent of Africa saw the rise of some of Man's earliest ancestors. Farming and the great civilization of Egypt in North Africa developed in early times. But it was only in the 4th century B.C. that some city-based civilizations appeared farther south and west. Farming developed in some of these areas around 1500 B.C. But in many areas of Africa hunting and herding have continued until very recently to be the most satisfactory way of life. "Civilization" (as we understand it) did not exist in many parts of Africa, but this does not mean that the people were "primitive savages." The complex tribal structures with their rituals, rich store of folktales, music, and art are proof of this.

The deserts, dense tropical forests, and mountains of Africa were all serious barriers to the spread of knowledge and ideas. In the rest of the world trade routes crossed the continents and people from one civilization met and exchanged with men from others. But Africa, apart from the Mediterranean coasts, had almost no contact with the rest of the ancient world.

Between about 15,000 and 10,000 B.C. Africa was much cooler than it is now. Later came warmer and wetter weather, which lasted until about 2500 B.C. Rock carvings have been found in the Sahara which show that many animals lived there, providing good hunting. Lake Chad was about eight times its present size – a sign of how much more fertile the area must have been.

B.C.	CHRONOLOGY
c.30,000– 10,000	Early types of men in Africa displaced by modern hunting peoples
6000–5000	Period of rock carvings and paintings
5000–1500	Agriculture spreads southward from early centers in Egypt and Sudan. Yam (sweet potato) cultivated in West Africa
2000	Black herder-farmers begin to move southward from homelands (?) south of the Sahara
c.1000	Cattle- and sheep-owning peoples populate Rift Valley area of East Africa
500– A.D. 200	Iron-using Nok people in northern Nigeria
300	Mortarless stone structures at Zimbabwe

MEROE

South of Egypt lay the state of Kush. At first it was overshadowed by the greatness of Egypt itself, but after 700 B.C. Kush began to develop as an independent state. Meroe, which became its center, lay at the junction of three rivers at a point where the Nile is still navigable. There were large reserves of iron ore and plenty of trees to provide fuel for smelting. Meroe was also at the end of an easy caravan route to the Red Sea. The region's wealth is shown by its stone temples, decorated with carvings. These, and a type of pyramid used for royal burials, show Egyptian influence.

For a long time Meroe kept up trading contacts with the Roman empire (see page 52). At its greatest it controlled territory as far north as the First Cataract, the southern border of Egypt. But after A.D. 100 Meroe began to decline. In the 4th century it fell under the influence of Axum in Ethiopia, which had close connections through trade with Arabian kingdoms across the Red Sea.

In contrast, traders to the west coast of Africa had almost no contact with the people living there. The Carthaginians traded goods for gold, but left them in piles on the beach, retreating to their ships when the Africans approached!

We know very little about the early people in Africa, apart from their stone tools and some rock engravings and carvings. And there is very little evidence for the change from hunters to farmers. Wheat was cultivated in Egypt about 4,400 years ago, and roughly a thousand years later goats were kept by early farmers near Khartoum. From here, agriculture spread slowly through the continent, taking 2,000 years or more to move down through West Africa. We do not know just what plants were cultivated; yams were probably important in the rain forests, while some people think that rice was grown by farmers round Lake Niger perhaps as early as 1500 B.C. Farther east, cattle and sheep herders may have grown millet.

The Iron Age in Africa

By far the most important widespread change in Africa was the introduction of iron – which happened south of the Sahara about 400 B.C. The Nok people of northern Nigeria lived between 500 B.C. and A.D. 200. They were skilled iron users, and also possessed specialized craftsmen who produced beautiful clay figures.

The use of iron meant that the African peoples had much greater control over their environment. Iron tools helped in timber-cutting and the clearing of new farmland. Iron weapons made men more effective warriors, and could be used for hunting. It is clear that some peoples became very powerful, like the builders of the great stone city of Zimbabwe, who moved into the area about A.D. 300. Although we know little about their way of life, they were skilled builders, potters, and gold miners: but they disappeared long before Europeans first began to explore the interior of Africa.

Crete and Mycenae

The Aegean Sea is an area of the Mediterranean lying between the mainland of Greece and the western coast of Anatolia. In the northeast it is linked to the Black Sea by the narrow channel of the Dardanelles, which divides Europe from Asia. The Aegean is dotted with a great number of mountainous islands. The largest of these is Crete, about 96 kilometers (60 miles) southeast of Greece itself.

The islands and coastal regions of the Aegean have much in common. All have narrow fertile plains which border the sea. Behind these strips rise steep mountains. All over the Aegean, and especially in Greece, there are deep inlets which make fine natural harbors.

The Minoans of Crete

Between 2000 and 1450 B.C., the island of Crete was the most important place in the Aegean. The largest and most fertile island in the area, it was then thickly forested. Wild game, and fish from the sea, added to their crops of grain, grapes for wine, and olives, gave the islanders plenty of food.

This regular food supply gave people time to develop special crafts. As early as 4000 B.C. the inhabitants of Crete (called Minoans, after their legendary King Minos) used obsidian from the island of Melos to make sharp-edged blades for tools and weapons. They may have traded these with North Africa and Egypt in return for pottery. When copper came into use about 3000 B.C. Crete imported copper ingots from Cyprus and exported fine painted pottery, engraved stone seals, and textiles. Later, bronze objects too were made and exported.

Crete grew rich from trade between Egypt, the Aegean, and Anatolia (Asia Minor). Its seamen were among the most experienced and skillful sailors in the

Mediterranean. Great centers, known as palaces, grew up at sites like Knossos, Mallia, and Phaistos. They included rooms for living in, courtyards, storehouses and workshops, and religious shrines. The palaces were centers for storing and distributing produce like grain and olive oil, and perhaps the raw materials with which craftsmen worked.

Whoever lived in these palaces controlled not only life on Crete but also a trading network spread throughout the Aegean. The fact that the palaces were not fortified shows that they felt secure from attack.

But suddenly all this came to an end. Nobody knows quite why this happened, although some people have linked it to a terrific volcanic explosion on the island of Thera in 1450 B.C. The tidal wave which followed could have destroyed most of Crete's merchant ships, on which its wealth depended. Whatever happened, its great palaces were abandoned, except for Knossos, which for a short time was lived in by people from the north Aegean called the Mycenaeans.

B.C.	CHRONOLOGY
c.6000– 5000	Earliest settlements on Crete
c.3000– 2000	Stone-built villages on coasts in Crete. Trading contacts with Egypt, Levant, Cyclades, and Anatolia
1900–1450	Palaces built and extended. Civilization on Crete at its height. Cretan craftsmen produce their finest work
1650–1450	Greeks ("Mycenaeans") grow in power at centers such as Mycenae and Pylos
1450	Collapse of Cretan power. Knossos occupied by Mycenaeans
?1220	Troy destroyed according to legend by mainland Greeks
c.1150– 1100	Collapse of Mycenaean civilization. Linear B writing disappears. Greek "Dark Age" begins

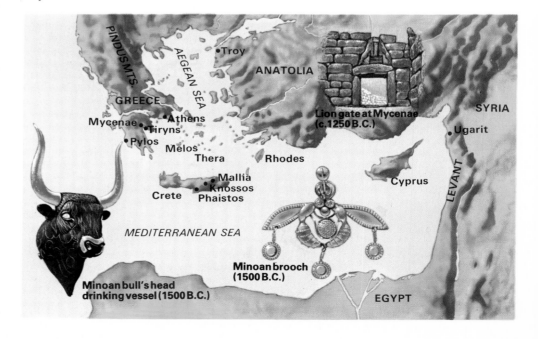

Lion gate at Mycenae (c.1250 B.C.)

Minoan brooch (1500 B.C.)

Minoan bull's head drinking vessel (1500 B.C.)

Left: The palace of Knossos as it may have been – a great area of interconnecting buildings, courtyards, and staircases. Around grand suites of rooms were storage chambers, where rows of giant pottery vases held grain and oil, and the workshops of skilled craftsmen.

Below: The "throne room" at the palace of Knossos; both the throne and the elaborate wall paintings (which have been heavily restored) date from the Mycenaean occupation of Crete, but earlier wall paintings have been found in many Minoan buildings.

The Mycenaeans

While the trading empire of Crete was at its most important, Greek-speaking peoples were living in cities on the coasts of mainland Greece. Historians call these people "Mycenaeans" after the site of Mycenae, where the first traces of them were found.

The Mycenaeans' cities usually grew up near the coasts, for two main reasons. Here, the most fertile land lay in a narrow coastal strip fringing the rugged mountains inland, while the mountains made land travel more difficult than travel by sea. Strong, fortified towns were built which dominated the fertile countryside around. Each town had a central strongpoint (citadel), such as a steep hill. In time of war the whole population could retreat to the safety of the city.

Who were the Mycenaeans? This is a problem. It is possible that people from Anatolia may have moved into Greece about 1900 B.C.; but Mycenaean civilization also had many links with the earlier culture of Greece and probably developed gradually between 1900 B.C. and 1600 B.C. By 1600 B.C. the Mycenaeans were trading in the Aegean, although Crete was still the most important trading power.

After the fall of Crete, Mycenaean trading stations and settlements were set up over a wide area, from Sicily and south Italy to the coast of Syria. There were close links, too, with Troy, at the mouth of the Black Sea, which was a rich grain-growing area.

But after 1300 B.C. trade in the eastern Mediterranean suddenly declined, for reasons we do not know. This must have been a time of growing dangers, for the citadels at Mycenae, Tiryns, and Athens were now strengthened with massive walls of stone. About 1200 B.C., the whole region went through a time of violent upheaval. Centers in Greece, Asia Minor, and the Near East were sacked and burned. At this time small bands of pirates and adventurers (who may be connected with the "Sea Peoples" of Egyptian texts) were raiding in the southeast Mediterranean. They may have played a part in the area's decline, or they may have joined during the economic crisis it caused. Whatever the reasons, a period of chaos followed in which the Bronze Age civilization of the Mycenaeans disappeared to be remembered only dimly in legends.

Right: A mask of beaten gold discovered in a royal tomb at Mycenae. Large numbers of gold and silver objects were buried with the Mycenaean rulers, and their workmanship shows links with the Near East and Crete.

A bronze Mycenaean dagger inlaid with a scene of a lion hunt. The tall shields carried by the hunters are like those described in Homer's "Iliad," a 9th-century poem telling of the legendary destruction of Troy.

The circle of graves at the palace of Mycenae. The palace commanded great stretches of the surrounding country; it was heavily fortified and had its own water supply.

29

The World in 1500 B.C.

In the southeast Mediterranean Egypt is an imperial and trading power of enormous wealth; its trading contacts include the Minoans of Crete and the Mycenaeans of mainland Greece. In Mesopotamia the Kassites are in control of Babylonia while Assyria is just a vassal of the neighboring state of Mitanni. The Hittites control Anatolia (Asia Minor). Bronze spreads through the Old World. In China the first historical period, the Shang dynasty, begins; in northern Europe the last great *megalithic* structures (made of huge stone slabs) are erected. In the Americas cultivation spreads, and the first ceremonial centers are built in Peru.

3 Northern Europe and Scandinavia Early Bronze Age. Smiths produce fine, often highly decorated weapons and ornaments.

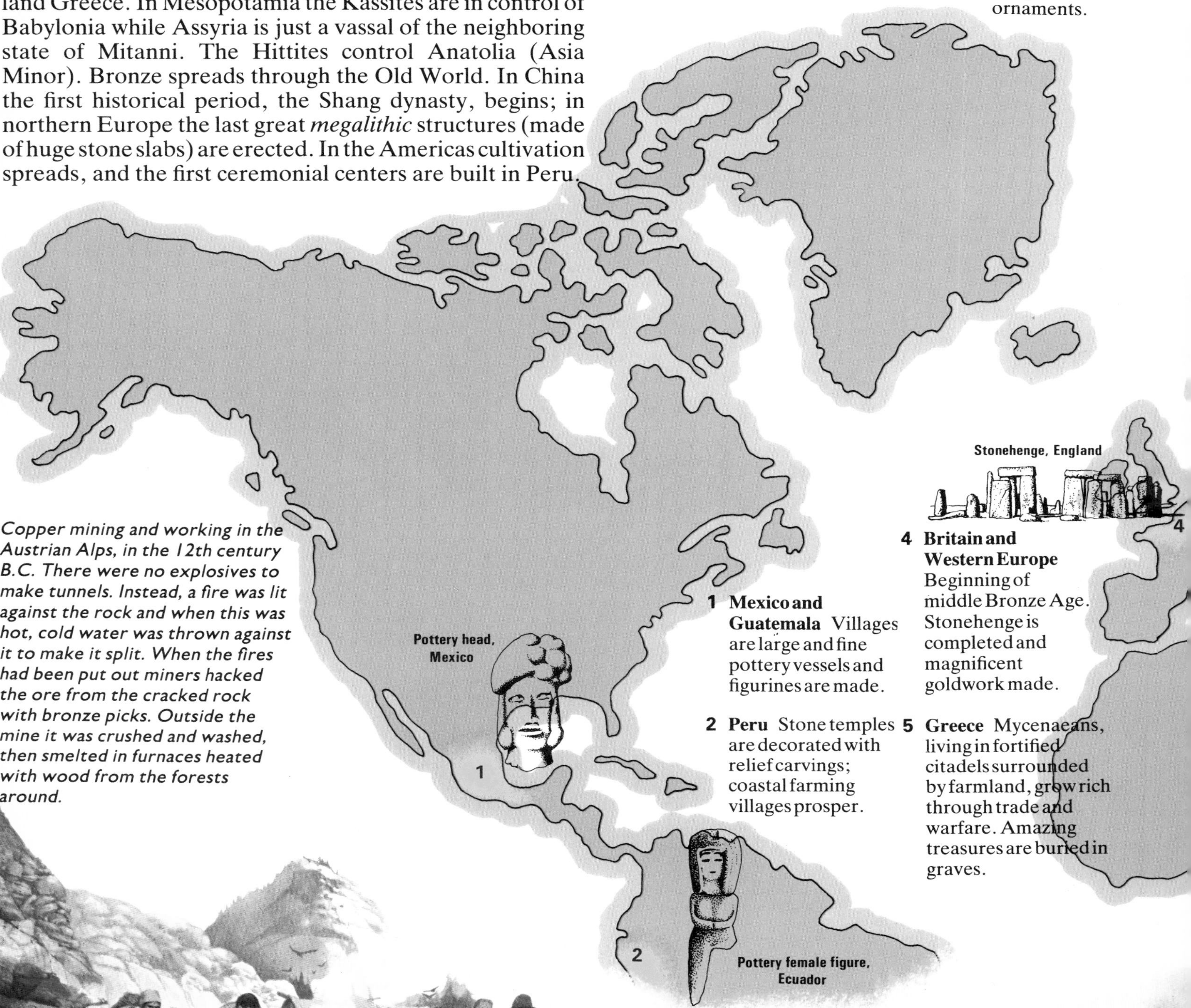

Copper mining and working in the Austrian Alps, in the 12th century B.C. There were no explosives to make tunnels. Instead, a fire was lit against the rock and when this was hot, cold water was thrown against it to make it split. When the fires had been put out miners hacked the ore from the cracked rock with bronze picks. Outside the mine it was crushed and washed, then smelted in furnaces heated with wood from the forests around.

Pottery head, Mexico

Stonehenge, England

1 Mexico and Guatemala Villages are large and fine pottery vessels and figurines are made.

2 Peru Stone temples are decorated with relief carvings; coastal farming villages prosper.

4 Britain and Western Europe Beginning of middle Bronze Age. Stonehenge is completed and magnificent goldwork made.

5 Greece Mycenaeans, living in fortified citadels surrounded by farmland, grow rich through trade and warfare. Amazing treasures are buried in graves.

Pottery female figure, Ecuador

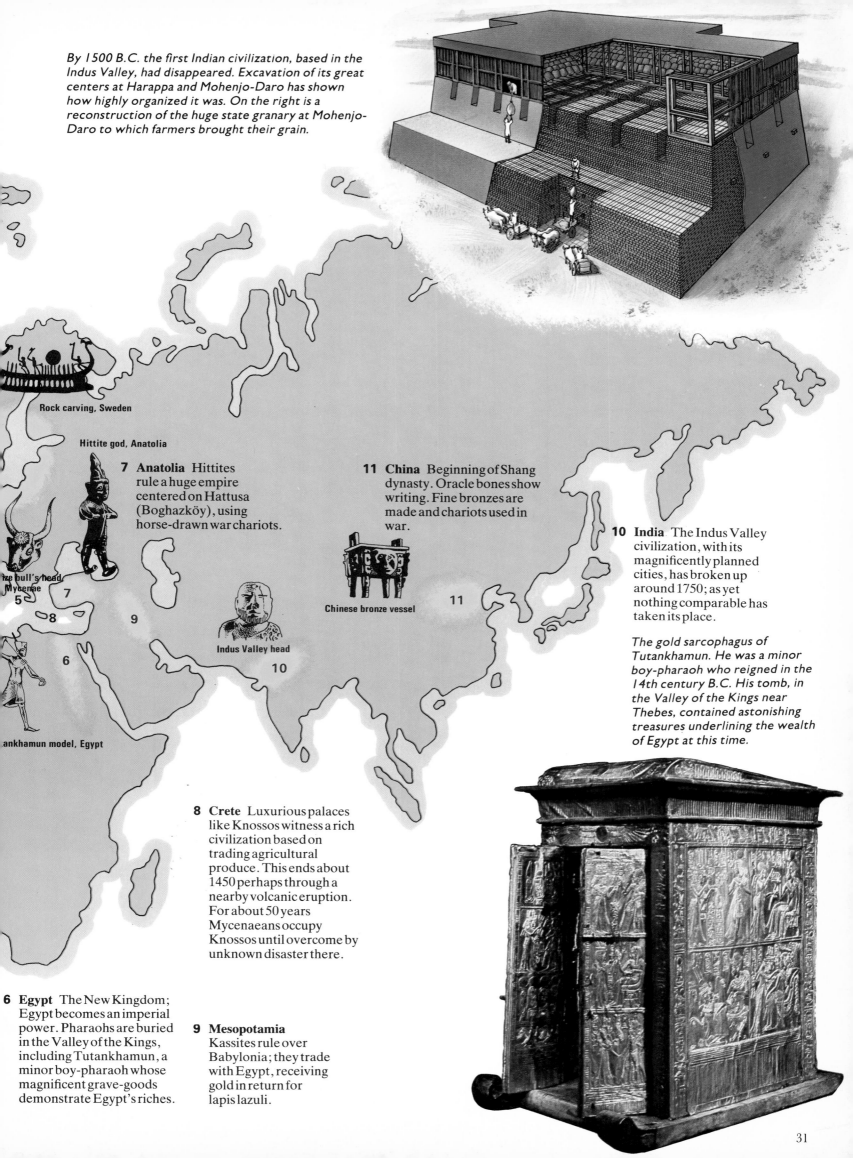

By 1500 B.C. the first Indian civilization, based in the Indus Valley, had disappeared. Excavation of its great centers at Harappa and Mohenjo-Daro has shown how highly organized it was. On the right is a reconstruction of the huge state granary at Mohenjo-Daro to which farmers brought their grain.

Rock carving, Sweden

Hittite god, Anatolia

7 Anatolia Hittites rule a huge empire centered on Hattusa (Boghazköy), using horse-drawn war chariots.

Bronze bull's head, Mycenae

11 China Beginning of Shang dynasty. Oracle bones show writing. Fine bronzes are made and chariots used in war.

Chinese bronze vessel

Indus Valley head

10 India The Indus Valley civilization, with its magnificently planned cities, has broken up around 1750; as yet nothing comparable has taken its place.

The gold sarcophagus of Tutankhamun. He was a minor boy-pharaoh who reigned in the 14th century B.C. His tomb, in the Valley of the Kings near Thebes, contained astonishing treasures underlining the wealth of Egypt at this time.

Tutankhamun model, Egypt

8 Crete Luxurious palaces like Knossos witness a rich civilization based on trading agricultural produce. This ends about 1450 perhaps through a nearby volcanic eruption. For about 50 years Mycenaeans occupy Knossos until overcome by unknown disaster there.

6 Egypt The New Kingdom; Egypt becomes an imperial power. Pharaohs are buried in the Valley of the Kings, including Tutankhamun, a minor boy-pharaoh whose magnificent grave-goods demonstrate Egypt's riches.

9 Mesopotamia Kassites rule over Babylonia; they trade with Egypt, receiving gold in return for lapis lazuli.

India

The subcontinent of India is a great triangle of land jutting southward from the mainland of Asia. To the northeast towers the immense range of the Himalaya Mountains. In the northwest high mountain passes lead to Afghanistan and on to Iran. Much of India is a high tableland, the Deccan, surrounded by mountains. Between the northern mountains and the Deccan lie vast fertile river plains. In the east is the plain of the Ganges, and in the west that of the Indus and its four tributaries, known as the Punjab, or Land of the Five Rivers.

India is a land of great local variations of climate and vegetation, but as a whole, it is very dry for seven months of the year. Most of the rain falls between June and September, carried by a warm wind from the southwest which is called the monsoon.

At Mohenjo-Daro there was a complicated system of water and drainage tanks and channels. This building, known as the Great Bath, may have played some part in religious ceremonies.

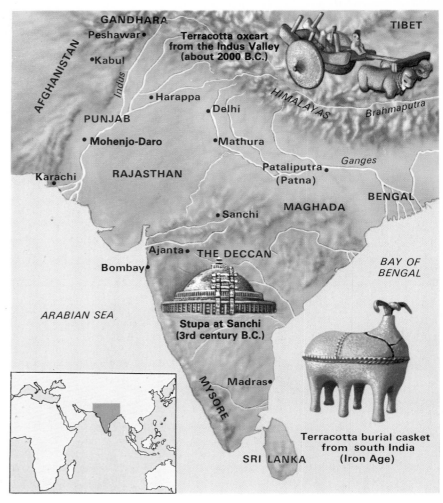

Terracotta oxcart from the Indus Valley (about 2000 B.C.)

Stupa at Sanchi (3rd century B.C.)

Terracotta burial casket from south India (Iron Age)

The Indus Civilization

The first civilization of India grew up in the fertile Indus Valley about 2500 B.C. Until the 20th century nothing was known of it, apart from vague legends written down by the people who lived in this area many centuries later on. Now archaeologists have found the remains of two great cities, Mohenjo-Daro and Harappa, and more than a hundred lesser towns and villages.

The Indus Valley people depended on a large-scale system of dams and canals to control the fierce flooding of the river Indus, and to make the best use of its waters in the dry season. In this way large tracts of land could be farmed and used to feed a large settled population. Farmers grew wheat and barley, and were the first to cultivate cotton. They tended herds of cattle and buffalo, and probably knew how to tame elephants for heavy work. In the cities, craftsmen worked in gold and copper imported from Afghanistan and Rajasthan, made fine pottery, and were expert carvers of ivory. Trade over land and sea linked the Indus Valley with Iran, Mesopotamia, and even the eastern Mediterranean. However, despite all its wealth and its splendid administration, the Indus civilization collapsed about 1750 B.C. Some cities were destroyed, and the population slaughtered.

Below: A carved stone seal showing a domesticated buffalo, and writing which no one can now read. Bottom: Indian civilization grew up in river plains like this. The land is fertile, but flooding is always a danger.

B.C.	CHRONOLOGY
c.2500–1750	Indus Valley civilization
c.1500–1000	Early "Aryan" (Vedic) period in Ganges Valley
c.600	Early cities in Ganges Valley
563	Birth of the Buddha
533	
c.550–342	Persians invade India Maghada empire in northeast India
326	Alexander the Great in India
100s–	Andhras dominate central India
c. A.D. 200	
187–75	Shunga dynasty in northern India
A.D.	
15–300s	Kushans rule northern India
320–535	Guptas rule northern India

THE INDUS CITIES

The two great centers of the Indus Valley civilization were Mohenjo-Daro and Harappa – about 600 kilometers (375 miles) apart. In these cities lived administrators, merchants, craftsmen, and shopkeepers. They were fed by the farmers of the surrounding countryside, who brought grain in two-wheeled ox-carts to store in the huge city granaries. Both cities were laid out in a pattern of rectangular blocks divided by wide roads. Within the blocks were brick houses, opening into central courtyards.

Each city was dominated by a raised, fortified platform on which were built huge mudbrick storehouses for grain, assembly houses, and, perhaps, temples. There were excellent drainage systems, and a large number of public wells provided a constant water supply.

The polished stone capital of one of the many pillars put up at the orders of the great emperor Ashoka in the 3rd century B.C.

The Ganges Valley

Over several hundred years new peoples from the west, often called the Aryans, moved into the Indus area. They may have been responsible for the final breakdown of the Indus civilization about 1750 B.C.

The descendants of the Aryans slowly spread eastward into the Ganges Valley. They spoke an Indo-European language distantly related to Greek, Hittite, and Persian. By about 1000 B.C., men in the Ganges Valley had learned how to smelt iron ore and make iron tools and weapons.

By the 6th century B.C. great cities had grown up on the sites of the Iron Age villages. They were built of brick and stone and were surrounded by high walls and moats. Like the independent city-states of Greece, these cities controlled the farmland around them. The Ganges cities were often at war, but gradually one center, Maghada, became more powerful than its neighbors. It ruled a huge kingdom in the northeast. Later this came under the rule of the Mauryan dynasty, which eventually united nearly all of India. The greatest of the Mauryan emperors was Ashoka (273–232 B.C.) who brought peace and order to his huge empire. But within 50 years of his death, his empire had broken up.

The Andhras

One of the former subject tribes, the Andhras, grew steadily in power in the Deccan. By the 2nd century A.D. they dominated central India from coast to coast. They built splendid stupas – Buddhist monuments – decorated with wonderful stone carvings. They also carved ivory most skillfully, and some of their carvings reached Pompeii in southern Italy. At this time Hindu culture developed in south India and Sri Lanka, which were mostly free from foreign influences.

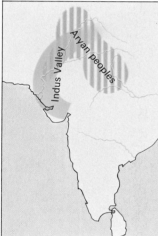

The Indus Valley civilization lasted from about 2500 to 1750 B.C. After its decline, "Aryan" peoples moved westward into the Ganges Valley.

After invasions by Persia (533 B.C.) and Alexander (327), the Mauryan dynasty (324–187) gained control of much of India. It was greatest under Ashoka.

By A.D. 150, India was divided into three main empires: the Kushan, Kshatrapa, and Andhra states. They gave way to the Gupta empire (320–535) based in Maghada.

INVADERS FROM THE WEST

Northern India is hemmed in by mountains. To the east are the almost impassable Himalayas, but to the west high passes lead to Afghanistan and Persia. This means that northwest India has always been more closely in contact with the Western world than with East Asia.

In 533 B.C. King Cyrus II of Persia advanced into the Punjab. Two centuries later Alexander the Great of Greece invaded northwest India. His Greek soldiers were soon driven out, but early in the 2nd century Greeks from the kingdom of Bactria occupied north India as far east as Pataliputra. Next came Scythians (known as Shakas), and then the Kushans from central Asia who conquered northern and much of middle India. Through these passes, too, the White Huns invaded in the 5th century A.D.

This "reliquary" (container for sacred objects) comes from the province of Gandhara, in the northwest of India. It was briefly part of Alexander's empire, but Greek influence lasted long after Alexander's death. Four centuries later, when this reliquary was made, the figures on the sides still show a mixture of Indian and Greek styles. The Gandharan craftsmen were skilled in stone carving, and also famous workers in gold and precious stones. Here, the stones are rubies.

Anatolia

Anatolia, also called Asia Minor, is a broad peninsula jutting westward from the continent of Asia itself. To the north lies the Black Sea, to the south the easternmost part of the Mediterranean. At the entrance to the Black Sea are the narrow straits of the Bosporus and the Dardanelles. Here the old civilizations of Asia come closest to Europe. Because of this, Anatolia has always been the main link between east and west.

Anatolia is a very varied region. The coasts have a Mediterranean climate – warm dry summers, and cool wet winters. But in the mountains inland the winters are very cold and the summers extremely hot. At the center is a high tableland, the Anatolian plateau: to the southeast, the high Taurus Mountains divide Anatolia from Syria.

Early Farmers

The history of Anatolia is confusing because of the different peoples who lived there. Its steep mountain ranges made travel difficult, so that developments in one area could not spread easily to others. Until the Hittites emerged in about 1700 B.C., we can get only brief glimpses of events in the area.

From about 8000 B.C. it is clear that farming was carried on in settled upland villages in eastern Anatolia. Cattle-raising, however, did not begin until nearly 6000 B.C. As well as farming, there was an ancient trade in Anatolian obsidian and Syrian flint. These were rocks used to make tools and weapons. Later on, trade in other natural resources – such as copper and possibly silver – grew up. Between 3000 and 2000 B.C., bronze working was highly developed in Anatolia.

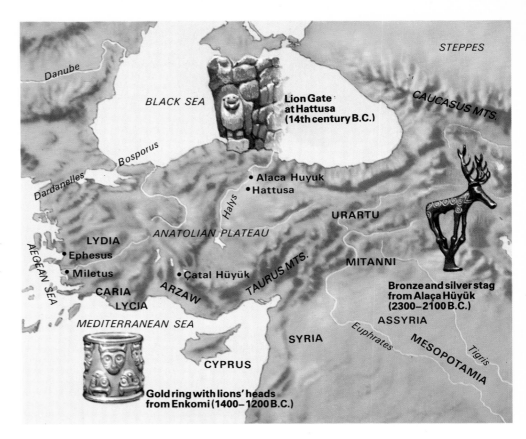

Lion Gate at Hattusa (14th century B.C.)

Bronze and silver stag from Alaça Hüyük (2300–2100 B.C.)

Gold ring with lions' heads from Enkomi (1400–1200 B.C.)

Anatolia was rich in copper, gold, silver, and iron and in the skills to work them. It had strong trade contacts with the rest of the Near East. But the mountainous terrain was a barrier to easy conquest.

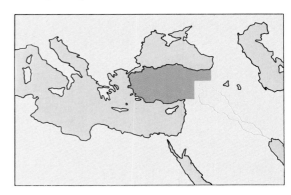

ÇATAL HÜYÜK

Between 6000 and 5000 B.C. more than 5,000 people lived in Çatal Hüyük in central Anatolia. They grew wheat, barley, and vegetables. They kept sheep and goats, and hunted aurochs (wild cattle), deer, and wild pigs. Çatal Hüyük's prosperity was only partly due to agriculture. It probably controlled the trade in obsidian, a hard, volcanic glass which its craftsmen turned into sharp-bladed tools and weapons. Other craftsmen were expert woodworkers and weavers.

Çatal Hüyük is one of the earliest towns we know of, not just in Anatolia but anywhere in the world. But it did not lead to the development of a true city-based civilization. As yet, no one knows why this was.

Houses in Çatal Hüyük were built in terraces around courtyards; there were no streets, and they were entered across the flat roofs and down ladders. The houses were built of mud bricks around a timber frame. Many of these houses may have served as shrines. Their walls were decorated with paintings of vultures and headless men, and with modeled animal figures. These included leopards, which may have been kept as sacred pets.

This view, looking toward the ancient Hittite capital of Hattusa, shows the fertile land which lies among the mountains in this region.

A gold drinking vessel or rhyton made by Thracian craftsmen in the 3rd century B.C. The Thracians lived in southeast Europe and parts of Anatolia. They built no great cities, but their chiefs lived in fortified settlements, surrounded by warriors. They acknowledged a single king who was also their high priest. Their craftsmen were famous for their beautiful and skilled metalwork.

B.C.	CHRONOLOGY
3000–2000	Early Bronze Age in Anatolia. Links with Aegean and North Syria
2000s	City-states recognize a "great prince" as overlord
c.1650–1460	Hittite Old Kingdom. Their armies using horse-drawn chariots conquer North Syria and invade Mesopotamia
1460–1180	Hittite Empire phase
c.1200	Hittites overwhelmed by Phrygians from the north. Hittite provinces in North Syria survive until the 8th century
c.1000	Greek cities founded on Aegean coast. They later colonize Black Sea coasts
c.900	Western Anatolia divided into small kingdoms, among them Lydia, which expands to include much of central Anatolia
545	Cyrus the Great of Persia conquers Lydia and dominates Greek cities on the western Anatolian coasts

The Hittites

About 2000 B.C., a number of Indo-European peoples moved into Anatolia, probably from the northwest. Among them were the Hittites, who eventually settled in Anatolia. Little is known of this period – but by 1700 B.C. the Hittites ruled an area around their capital at Hattusa.

The Hittites expanded westward across Anatolia, and southward into Syria. This brought them into conflict with the Egyptian empire. After a series of wars, Egypt recognized the Hittite empire as *the* great power in the north.

In the east, the Hurrian state of Mitanni and later the Assyrians threatened the Hittites. In the west, the state of Arzawa and the Ahhiyawa (who are thought by some to be Mycenaean Greeks) were challenging Hittite control of the trade routes. In 1200 the whole area was thrown into confusion by the attacks of the "Sea Peoples." The Hittites in Anatolia disappeared from history. Only in Syria did Hittite provinces survive. They lasted for another 500 years before falling to the Assyrians in the 8th century B.C.

New Rulers

After the collapse of Hittite power, Anatolia was occupied first by the Phrygians, and then in about 700 B.C. by the Cimmerians. At the same time the small princedoms of Lydia, Lycia, and Caria, which had been dominated by the Hittites, grew more powerful. The Lydians were rich in river gold and in the 6th century their ruler, Croesus, was legendary for his wealth. But he was defeated by Cyrus the Great of Persia, and Anatolia became part of the Persian empire.

Urartu

In the confusion following the fall of the Hittites, new states were set up. Urartu (the biblical Ararat) was made up of several smaller kingdoms. Its lands reached from eastern Anatolia northeastward to the steppes of southern Russia. Urartian kings built fortified cities to protect them from raids by the Scyths, who were nomads from the steppes. Huge engineering works brought water to irrigate the fields. Urartian farmers raised cattle and grew a wide variety of crops. Linen and cloth weaving were major industries.

For a long time Urartu acted as a strong check against the expansion of the Assyrian empire. But in the 6th century B.C., it finally fell to the Medes and Scyths, who had joined.

GREEK CITIES OF ASIA

On the coasts of the Aegean Sea and on islands off the west coast of Asia Minor there were Greek cities, which had been settled in the 10th century. On the coasts of the Black Sea, too, were Greek colonies, founded in the 8th and 7th centuries. They grew grain in the fertile lands around. Some of the cities, like Miletus and Ephesus, became rich and powerful. They had close links with one another through trade and their common language and traditions. But their independence was often threatened by powerful rulers in Asia Minor – first the Lydians, and then the Persians.

The Greek Cities

Greece is a rugged, mountainous peninsula running southeast from the mainland of Europe into the Mediterranean. The summers are hot and dry, the winters cool and rainy. Today the mountains are bare and rocky, but in Ancient Greece they were covered in thick forest.

In those days Greece was more fertile than it is now. Even so, the fertile areas were cut off from one another by the mountains. There were small pockets of farmland between the sea and the mountains, and in the bottoms of narrow, winding mountain valleys. The best land of all lay in central Greece, between Athens and Thebes, and farther south in the interior of the Peloponnese, the southern peninsula of Greece.

The mountains formed barriers that made overland travel difficult, so small, isolated states grew up. These depended very much on the sea for communication with the outside world. As time went on and populations grew, they relied more and more upon trade, for large numbers of people could not be supported by farming alone.

The Acropolis at Athens. Originally the defensive strongpoint of the city, this rocky outcrop became a symbol of Athenian power and prestige. By the 5th century B.C. the Acropolis was a glittering complex of shrines and temples. The most famous was the Parthenon, sacred to Athene.

The Greek world about 550 B.C. From Spain to the Black Sea, Greek colonists founded new cities. They spread Greek language and culture far from the tiny states of mainland Greece.

The Rise of the City-States

The strong citadels of the Mycenaeans, their society, and culture finally collapsed by about 1100 B.C. For 200 years most of Greece became a land of scattered farming settlements, ruled by local chieftains. The pattern of population changed and the number of people was much smaller: more people were living in Attica, Euboea, and the Cyclades and some people from mainland Greece settled in Cyprus.

By the 10th century B.C., Greeks had settled on most of the Aegean islands and the coasts of Anatolia (Asia Minor) with citadels (*poleis*) to protect their farmland. These settlements traded with the Near East. They were later the homes of some of the greatest Greek thinkers and scientists.

The Greeks probably learned alphabetic writing from the Phoenicians. As this spread, it helped all Greeks to realize that they shared the same language and heritage. Contacts were renewed between the eastern Greeks and the mainland.

Between 800 and 700 B.C., growing populations forced the many Greek states (particularly the eastern ones) to settle new areas. They planted colonies first on the fertile shores of the Black Sea, then far to the west in Sicily and southern Italy. By 550 B.C. there were hundreds of Greek settlements, from Spain to the Black Sea.

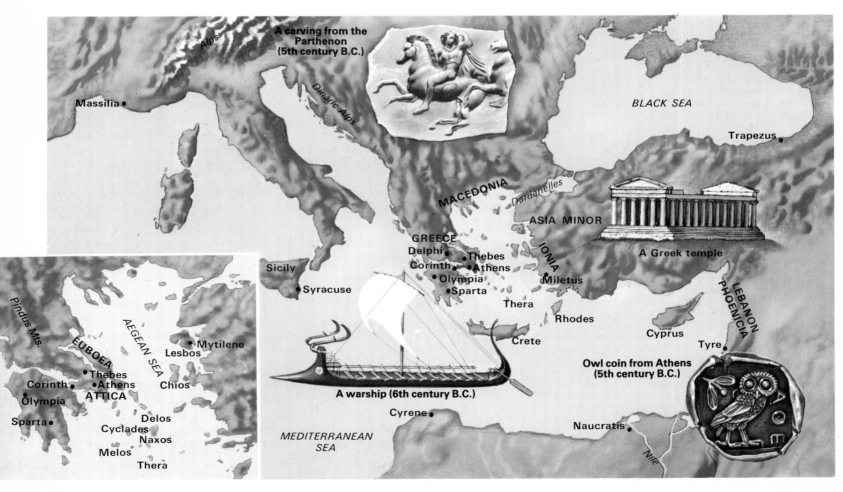

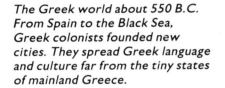

Harvesting olives – an Athenian black-figure vase. The Athenians exported olive oil to pay for foreign grain.

A typical Greek house of the 5th century B.C. The street entrance leads through a passage into an open courtyard. The rooms are simply furnished; even well-to-do citizens frowned on luxury.

B.C.	CHRONOLOGY
c.1000	Greek settlers colonize coasts of Anatolia
850–750	Independent city-states grow up in mainland Greece.
850–550	Eastern and mainland Greeks set up colonies from the Black Sea to Spain
546	Persia begins to take over Greek cities in Anatolia
?507	Athenian democracy begins
490–479	Persia twice unsuccessfully invades mainland Greece
477–405	Athenian navy dominates Aegean. Athens's Golden Age
431–404	Peloponnesian war between Athens and Sparta ends in Athens's defeat.
356–338	Warfare between Greek states allows Philip of Macedon to master Greece

TRADE AND TYRANTS

By the 6th century B.C., mainland Greece was at the center of trade between the western and eastern Mediterranean. The city of Corinth, on the narrow strip or isthmus of land connecting northern and southern Greece, became very powerful. The Corinthians built a slipway, the *diolkos*, across the isthmus. Large ships were dragged across it by teams of oxen – saving several days' sailing around the southern tip of Greece.

The Greeks built merchant ships to carry their trade goods. They also built warships with which they controlled the eastern Mediterranean. When the Persians invaded Greece the Athenian navy played the greatest part in their defeat. This made Athens the powerful leader of an alliance of Greek islands.

A procession of Spartan warriors, from a metal vessel. All male Spartan citizens were trained from childhood to become soldiers. Their toughness and courage were legendary. This cup dates from the 6th century B.C.

Athens v. Sparta

There was always great rivalry between the city-states of Greece. This was partly to do with the cities' own pride in themselves. The worst rivalry of all was between Athens and Sparta in the 5th century. The two could not have been more different. Athens was a democracy – all citizens could vote to say how they should be governed. Sparta was a military state. Every male citizen had to spend his life serving in the army: all work was done by serfs, called *helots*, who were treated cruelly. The Athenians despised the Spartans who seemed barbarians to them: the Spartans thought the Athenians dangerous revolutionaries. In 431 the two cities and their allies went to war – a long, bitter struggle that left Greece weak and divided. In the end Sparta was victorious. The Spartans became leaders of the Greek states, but there were constant revolts. Eventually King Philip of Macedon, to the north, moved in to take control of the country.

A bust of Pericles, who led Athens in the middle of the 5th century B.C. and made it into the most magnificent city in Greece.

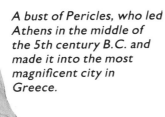

The theater at Delphi, site of the great Greek shrine to the god Apollo. The Greeks believed that at certain places like this the gods came into close contact with the world of men. To all Greeks, the importance of these sacred sites was far above political differences. At festivals like the four-yearly Games to Zeus at Olympia, even Greek states at war joined to pay homage to the gods.

The World in 500 B.C.

By now the first great centers of civilization, Mesopotamia and Egypt, have declined; both have fallen to the Persians, who in less than a century build up an empire from Egypt in the west to India in the east. As they move north, the Persians come into conflict with the Greek city-states, which dominate the eastern Mediterranean. Most important of these are the warlike Sparta and Athens, famous for its art and democracy. The use of iron has spread through much of the old world.

3 Central and Northern Europe From 700 B.C. the iron-using Hallstatt culture has spread out from Austria; hill forts are surrounded by farmland. In 450 the Celtic La Tène culture develops, with its delicate metalwork and splendid gold ornaments.

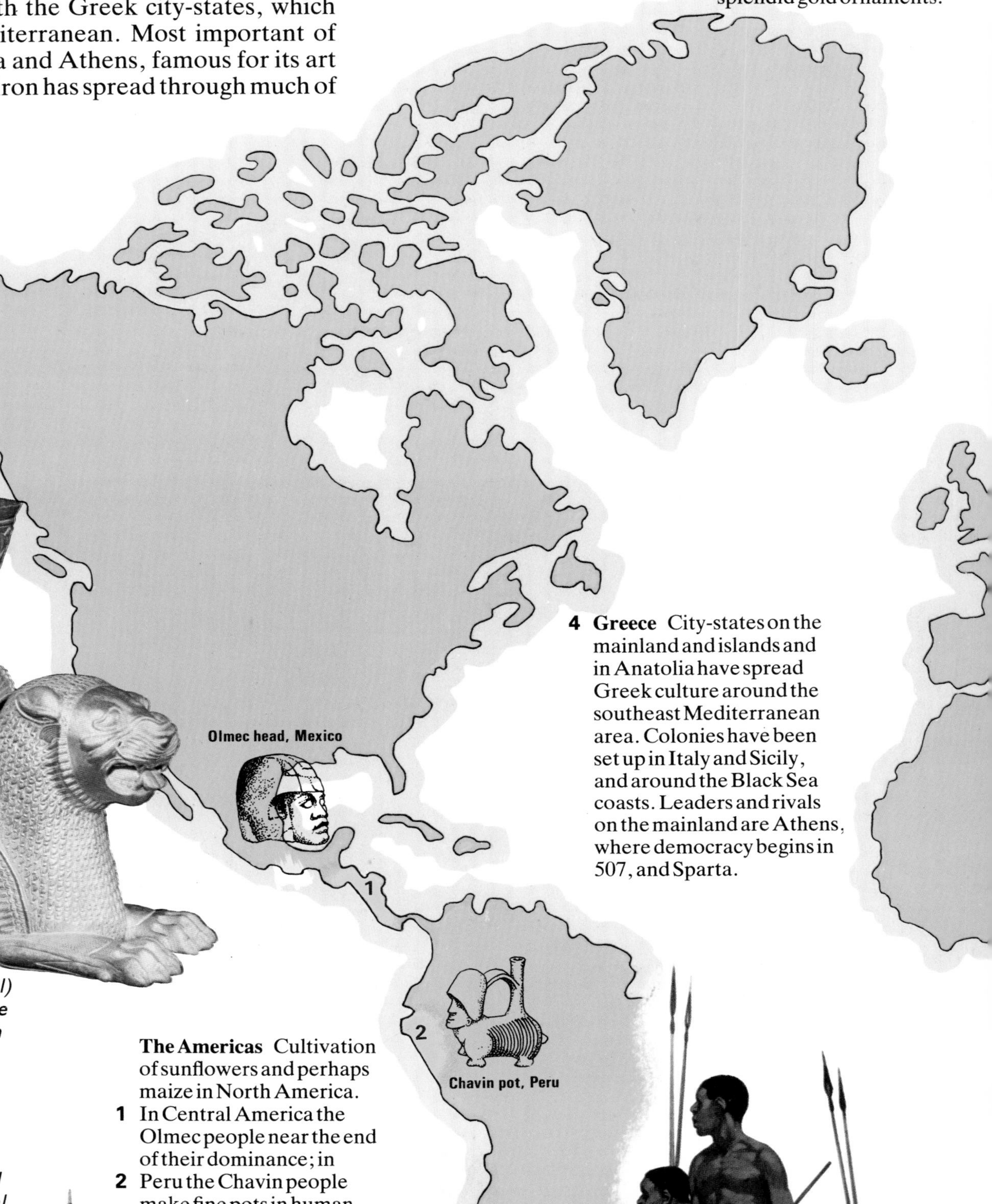

Olmec head, Mexico

4 Greece City-states on the mainland and islands and in Anatolia have spread Greek culture around the southeast Mediterranean area. Colonies have been set up in Italy and Sicily, and around the Black Sea coasts. Leaders and rivals on the mainland are Athens, where democracy begins in 507, and Sparta.

A Persian rhyton (drinking vessel) made of gold. The Persian empire became fabulously rich in the 6th and 5th centuries B.C.

Chavin pot, Peru

The Americas Cultivation of sunflowers and perhaps maize in North America.
1 In Central America the Olmec people near the end of their dominance; in
2 Peru the Chavin people make fine pots in human and animal shapes.

Carthaginians trading with Africans on the island they called "Cerne," off the coast of Senegal. The exchange of trade goods was carried on through some kind of agreed sign language.

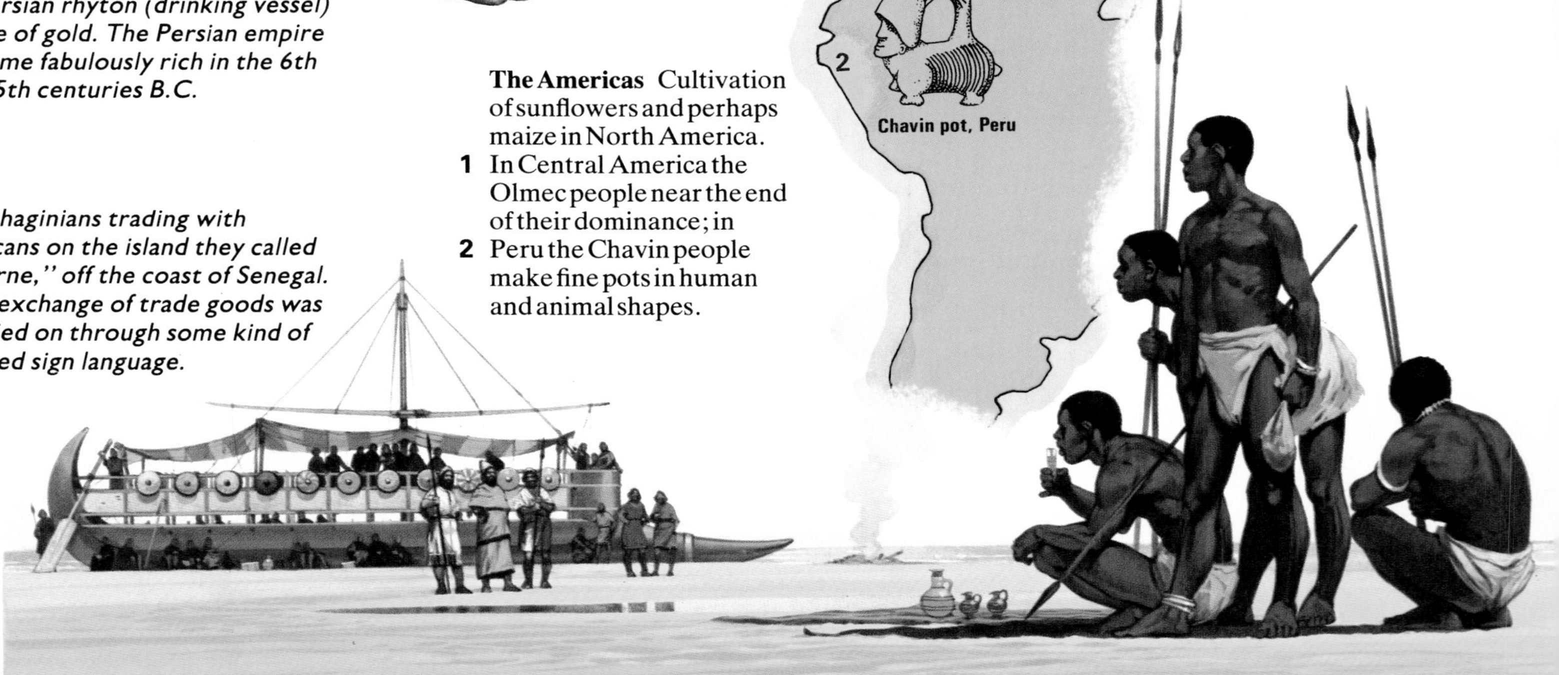

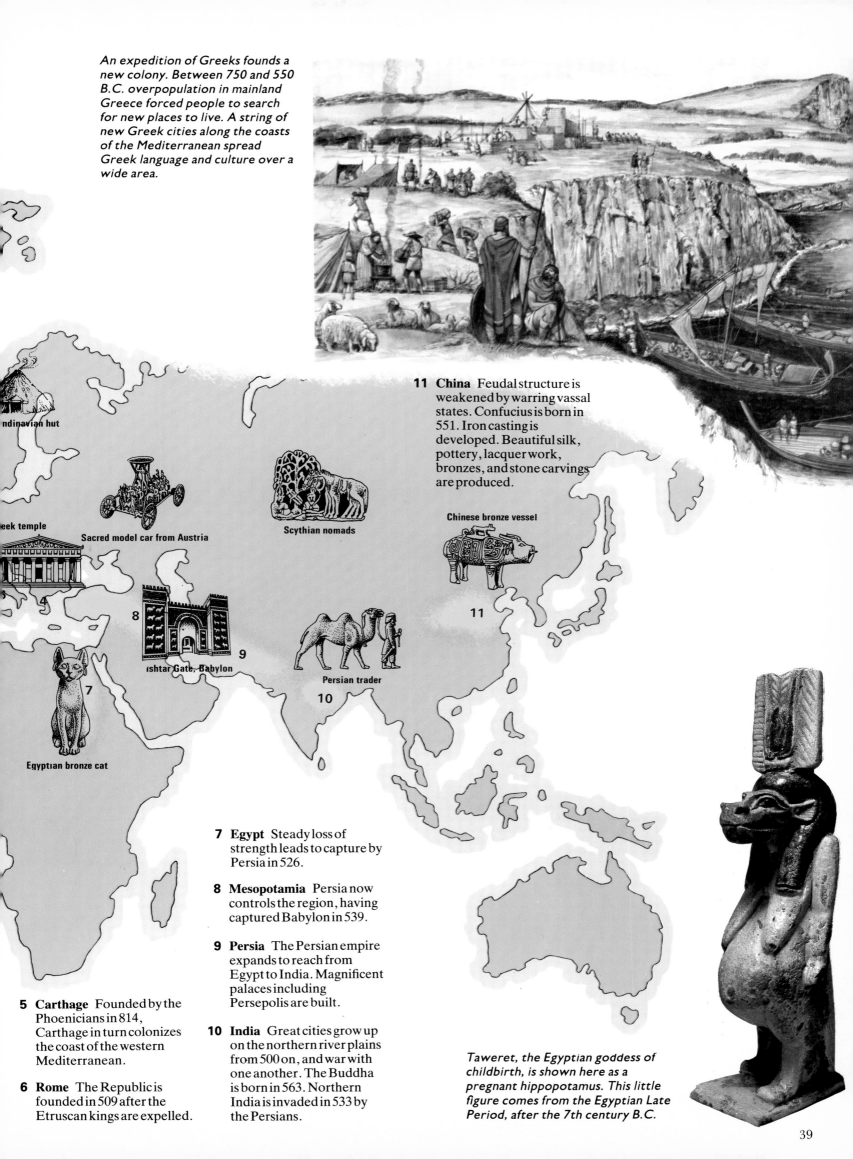

An expedition of Greeks founds a new colony. Between 750 and 550 B.C. overpopulation in mainland Greece forced people to search for new places to live. A string of new Greek cities along the coasts of the Mediterranean spread Greek language and culture over a wide area.

ndinavian hut

eek temple

Sacred model car from Austria

Scythian nomads

11 China Feudal structure is weakened by warring vassal states. Confucius is born in 551. Iron casting is developed. Beautiful silk, pottery, lacquer work, bronzes, and stone carvings are produced.

Chinese bronze vessel

8

Ishtar Gate, Babylon

9

11

Persian trader

10

7

Egyptian bronze cat

7 Egypt Steady loss of strength leads to capture by Persia in 526.

8 Mesopotamia Persia now controls the region, having captured Babylon in 539.

9 Persia The Persian empire expands to reach from Egypt to India. Magnificent palaces including Persepolis are built.

5 Carthage Founded by the Phoenicians in 814, Carthage in turn colonizes the coast of the western Mediterranean.

6 Rome The Republic is founded in 509 after the Etruscan kings are expelled.

10 India Great cities grow up on the northern river plains from 500 on, and war with one another. The Buddha is born in 563. Northern India is invaded in 533 by the Persians.

Taweret, the Egyptian goddess of childbirth, is shown here as a pregnant hippopotamus. This little figure comes from the Egyptian Late Period, after the 7th century B.C.

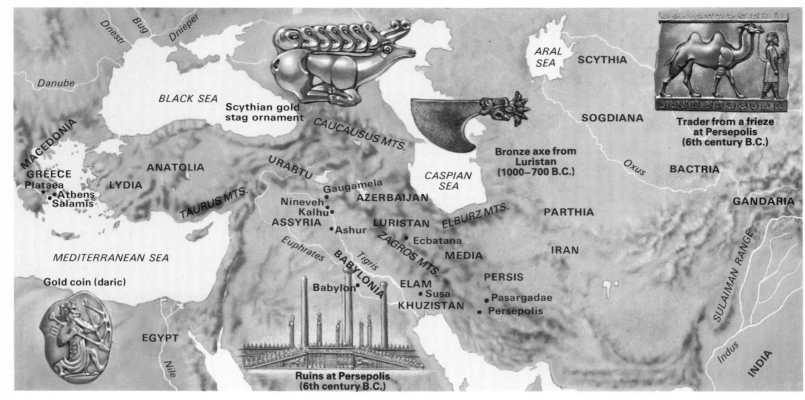

Scythian gold stag ornament

Bronze axe from Luristan (1000–700 B.C.)

Trader from a frieze at Persepolis (6th century B.C.)

Gold coin (daric)

Ruins at Persepolis (6th century B.C.)

The Persian Empire

The land of Persia, or Iran, stretches eastward from the Zagros Mountains almost to northern India. Much of it is a vast, high desert tableland, surrounded by mountains. But around the borders are more fertile regions: Azerbaijan and the Caspian plain in the north, and the wide Khuzistan plain to the south.

Iran has a great range of climate and in many places rainfall is irregular. As a result many groups followed a nomadic way of life, as some still do. During the scorching heat of summer the peoples of Iran took their herds to the pastures of the cool, fertile upland valleys of the mountains. Here they grew wheat, barley, vines, figs, and pomegranates. The lower slopes of the mountains were thickly wooded with wild almond, walnut, and pistachio trees.

Throughout its history Iran was often invaded by nomadic peoples. Some came through the Elburz Mountains, east of the Caspian Sea. Others, like the Medes and Persians, entered Iran through the Caucasus Mountains in the northwest.

By the 9th century B.C. the most powerful group in Iran was the Medes with their Persian vassals. Their kingdom, Media, lay in the northwest: to the west and north it was hemmed in by the strong states of Assyria and Urartu.

In 612 B.C. the Medes, together with the Babylonians, captured Nineveh, Ashur, and Kalhu. The Assyrian empire came to an end and its vast territories were divided between the Medes and the Babylonians.

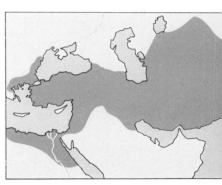

The splendor surrounding the Persian kings drew craftsmen and precious metals from all over the empire. This leaping winged ibex, of partly gilded silver, originally formed the handle of a bowl. It was made in the 4th century B.C.

B.C.	CHRONOLOGY
3000s	Elamite civilization in southwest Iran
1300s	Medes and Persians move into Iran
600	Cyaxares, king of the Medes, destroys Assyria
549	Persians under Cyrus II the Great defeat Medes and conquer Lydia
539	Babylon falls to Persians
533	Cyrus II invades India
526	Cambyses conquers Egypt
490–479	Persians under Darius and Xerxes unsuccessfully invade Greece
331	Alexander of Macedon conquers the Persian empire

Elam was the region between southwest Persia and south Mesopotamia. It developed its own civilization around 3000 B.C. Little is known of its history. Left: King Teumann of Elam and his son Tammaritu fleeing from the conquering Assyrians in the 7th century B.C.

THE PERSIAN WARS

In 495 the Greeks of Anatolia (Asia Minor) revolted against the Persians. The king, Darius, quickly put down the revolt. The cities had had help from mainland Greece, so in 490 Darius sent a seaborne expedition against Greece – only to see it defeated by the Athenians on the coastal plain of Marathon. His son Xerxes began a new invasion in 481. An army was sent to invade Greece from the north, backed by a huge battle fleet. The Persian army captured several cities, including Athens. But the fleet was defeated by a Greek navy at Salamis. Then the Greeks destroyed the Persian army at Plataea. They chased the Persians out of Greece and into Asia Minor, where the Greek cities allied with the mainland once more. The Greek victory was complete.

Right: The ruins of the palace at Pasargadae, in south Persia. It was built by Cyrus the Great. Like all the great Persian palaces, it stood on a vast man-made terrace, and two grand staircases led up to it.

The Rise of the Persians

In about 550 B.C. the king of the Persians, Cyrus the Great, overthrew his Median overlords. From now on the Persians ruled over Iran. Cyrus captured Babylon and gained control of the whole of the former Babylonian empire – virtually all of western Asia was now under Persian rule. The next two kings, Cambyses and Darius, extended Persian rule to Egypt in the south and to the borders of India in the east. Darius organized his vast empire into provinces, ruled by *satraps* (governors) and linked by a network of superb roads.

In spite of revolts in the provinces and plots in the palaces, Persian kings continued to hold most of their empire. The exception was Egypt, which successfully revolted against Artaxerxes II (404–359 B.C.). Artaxerxes III (359–338 B.C.) was able to recapture Egypt. But before he could turn his attention to the problem of Greece, he was poisoned. After two years of confusion, Darius III came to the throne. Before he could establish himself, he was faced with the invasion of Greeks and Macedonians led by Alexander the Great. Alexander defeated Darius's army at the great battle of Gaugamela in Mesopotamia; Darius fled, but was soon murdered by one of his own governors. With his death, the Persian empire came to an end.

Right: Persian kings commanded a personal guard of 10,000 soldiers, like these archers from the palace at Susa.

THE SCYTHIANS

The Persian empire included a number of nomad peoples. Among them were Scyths or Scythians, who had moved west from the Asian steppes in about the 8th century, and had established themselves in south Russia, Armenia, and north Iran. They moved swiftly between grazing grounds, the men on horseback and the women and children in large felt-roofed wagons. They took with them cushions and wall-hangings of brightly decorated felt. Some had ornaments and vessels of beautifully worked gold, like the one in the picture on the left. Much of what we know comes from Scythian tombs at Pazyryk in Siberia, which were preserved by the freezing climate. Men and women were buried with their possessions, the men's bodies tattooed with animal designs.

Alexander the Great from a mosaic found at Pompeii in southern Italy.

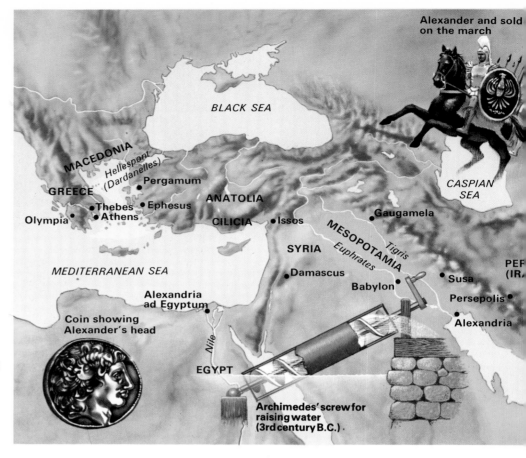

Alexander and sold[ier]s on the march

Archimedes' screw for raising water (3rd century B.C.)

Coin showing Alexander's head

Alexander and After

Alexander of Macedon was one of the greatest generals the world has ever seen. In ten years of constant fighting he conquered the Persian empire and spread Greek domination as far as northwest India. His great conquests mark an important point in history. Before him, the greatest advances in civilization were made in Asia – from the beginnings of farming to the first cities and empires. With Alexander the first European-controlled empire was born. From now on Europe, still largely undeveloped, began to be the center of progress.

Philip of Macedon died in 336 B.C. In a few years he had taken advantage of the quarrels between the Greek city-states to bring them under his power. But at his death the royal treasury was empty.

Philip's son Alexander was only 20 years old, and barely 150 centimeters (5 feet) tall. The Greeks thought him a mere boy, and soon the city of Thebes rebelled against him. Swiftly Alexander and his army attacked the city and captured it, killing the population. After this, no other Greek city dared to revolt.

Alexander still had to find money. For a long time Greeks had envied the fabulous wealth of the Persian empire. They saw too that the empire was weak. Alexander brought together a huge army of 24,000 Greek and Macedonian troops. He made sure that the army was backed up by special battalions of engineers and medical staff.

In 334 B.C., Alexander led his army across the Hellespont into Anatolia. Always fighting at the head of his troops, Alexander wôn a number of small battles before meeting the main Persian army, under Darius III, at Issos. Darius's army was beaten, and he fled, leaving the way open to Syria and Egypt. After conquering Egypt, Alexander turned north and east into the heart of the Persian empire.

The ruins of the Philippeum at Olympia. This building was commissioned by Philip of Macedon to celebrate his victory over the Greeks at Khaironeia in 338 B.C. The victory gave Philip control of Greece. Many Greeks despised Philip, thinking his kingdom was barely civilized.

B.C.	CHRONOLOGY
336	Alexander inherits throne of Macedon. He becomes undisputed master of Greece
334	Alexander with a Greek and Macedonian army invades Anatolia
333	Alexander defeats Persians under Darius III at Issos
331	Battle of Gaugamela. Alexander now controls Persian empire
330–325	Alexander conquers provinces in eastern Iran and northwest India
323	Alexander dies in Babylon
323–319	Struggles between Alexander's generals and their heirs for his empire
188	Syria submits to Rome
168	Macedonia becomes a Roman province
146	Romans combine Greek cities with province of Macedonia
133	Pergamum bequeathed to Rome
65–63	Pompey annexes Cilicia and Lydia for Rome
30	Egypt becomes a Roman province

Part of a diadem (head ornament) made in Hellenistic times. It is in the form of a Herakleian knot. This knot was used to show the descent of the family of Alexander the Great from the legendary hero Herakles (Hercules), and it often appears in Hellenistic ornaments.

GOVERNING THE EMPIRE

Alexander brought few new ideas to governing the former Persian empire, though the Persian provinces were ruled now by Macedonian generals backed up by garrisons of troops. Alexander admired many aspects of Persian civilization and he encouraged his officers and troops to marry Persian wives. He himself married Roxane, a Persian princess. Alexander's vision was of a world ruled by a master race of Greeks, Macedonians, and Persians. Young Persian noblemen were made to join Alexander's army. He insisted on following the Persian court traditions which required that all subjects, including his close friends, *prostrate* themselves (bow down very low) before the king. This was resented by his Macedonian and Greek officers.

Persia and India

At Gaugamela, in Mesopotamia, Alexander once more faced Darius. Again the Persians were beaten and Darius fled – only to be murdered by his own courtiers. Within a short time, Alexander was master of Persia.

Not content with his victory, Alexander led his army on into northwest India. Only when his battle-weary troops refused to go farther did Alexander return. He was planning new campaigns of conquest when he died, perhaps from poison, in Babylon in 323 B.C.

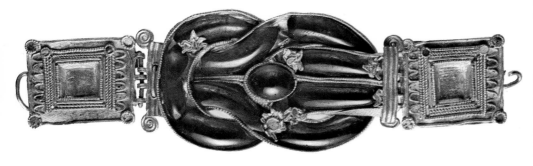

Ruins of the ancient Greek city of Ephesus, in Anatolia. The eastern Greek cities, liberated from the Persians by Alexander in 333 B.C., rose in renewed splendor. The vast wealth of the defeated Persian empire was used for magnificent temples, theaters, and public buildings.

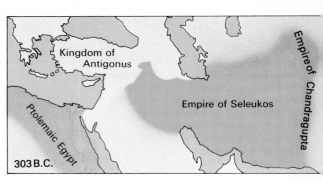

When Alexander died his son by Roxane was too young to rule and was soon murdered. His empire was divided among his generals (above). His shieldbearer Seleukos and his descendants ruled over a vast federation of provinces, stretching eastward to the lands of the Indian ruler Chandragupta. Ptolemy and his descendants ruled over Egypt. Anatolia was ruled by Antigonus. These divisions were arrived at only after bitter warfare.

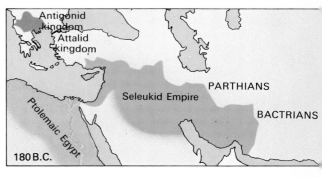

The map above shows the Hellenistic world in about 180 B.C. The Seleukids had lost part of their lands to the Parthians and Bactrians. The Antigonids now ruled only over Macedonia in northern Greece. Anatolia was divided into a number of small kingdoms, the most important of which was Pergamum. These fought among themselves and were soon to be taken over by Rome, the rising Mediterranean power.

ALEXANDRIA

The greatest of the Hellenistic cities was Alexandria in Egypt, founded by Alexander the Great in 322, and chosen by Ptolemy as his capital. He enlarged the harbor and built the Pharos lighthouse, one of the wonders of the ancient world. Alexandria became a naval base and trading port – the largest and richest Greek city in the world. Its library contained about 700,000 rolls of papyrus and parchment by the 1st century B.C., and Alexandria became a center for poets, writers, philosophers, and perhaps above all for scientists. Euclid wrote his geometry book, Eratosthenes showed that the world was round, and Archimedes and Hero invented machines including a steam turbine. Alexandria was captured by Muslim Arabs in the 7th century A.D. Some of them became scientists and learned from the writings of the Greeks.

The Bible Lands

The biblical land of Canaan, the "land of milk and honey," was an area about 160 kilometers (99 miles) wide, running north to south along the east coast of the Mediterranean. In modern times the region includes the states of Israel, Jordan, Lebanon, and part of Syria. The area made up of Israel and Jordan is often known as Palestine.

This is an area of great variety, divided down the middle by high mountains and the deep valley of the river Jordan, which is the lowest point on the earth's surface. In the west lies a narrow, fertile coastal strip. To the east and south a jumble of rocky hills and valleys merges into arid desert wilderness.

Farming began about 8000 B.C., and the land was rich enough to grow wheat, vines, and olives. Mudbrick towns grew up around local water sources. However, away from the coast, fertile areas were scattered and separated by stretches of semidesert. As a result no large-scale food production developed as it did in Egypt or Mesopotamia. But the region was always important. It formed a route between Africa and Asia, along which the armies of many empires marched. It was the crossroads of trade routes from east to west and north to south. It possessed natural resources, like the cedars of Lebanon, which attracted the great powers of Egypt, Mesopotamia, and the Hittites. Desert nomads like the Amorites, Aramaeans, and later the Israelites could move in from the east. In the west there were contacts with seafaring traders from Cyprus, Anatolia (Asia Minor), and the Aegean.

Phoenician glass

The Ark of the Covenant of the Israelites

B.C.	CHRONOLOGY
8000–2000	Farming carried on. Large towns such as Jericho grow up. Later small independent kingdoms emerge
1200	After disruption by raiders much of the region is settled by Israelites, Aramaeans, and Philistines
995	The Israelite King David builds a fortified capital at Jerusalem
722–539	Assyrians, then Babylonians, control region; Jerusalem falls 597 and many exiled to Babylon; from 539 region passes to Persia and exiles return, known from now on as Jews
331–63	Palestine and Syria become part of Alexander's Hellenistic empire and at last fall to Rome

The hill fortress of Masada, near the Dead Sea, was the last stronghold of Jews when they revolted against Roman rule from A.D. 66 to 73.

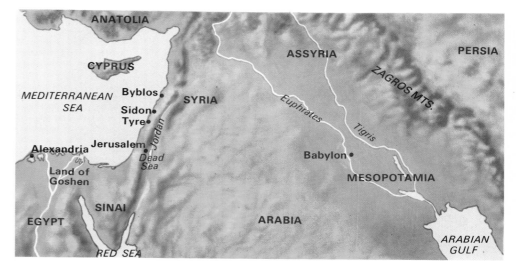

The top map shows the land of Canaan. The map above shows its key position in the Near East, connecting Egypt, Mesopotamia, and Anatolia.

Shifting Peoples
About 2000 B.C. the land was invaded by Semitic desert peoples, the Amorites. The area now had close links with Egypt through trade. Later, Hyksos ("foreign rulers") from Palestine drove into Egypt and controlled much of it until they were finally expelled about 1550 B.C. Soon after 1468 B.C. Palestine and Syria became part of an Egyptian empire. About 1200 B.C., Canaanite civilization was destroyed by raiding bands and was followed by the settlement of Israelites and Aramaeans. By 1150 B.C. the Israelites were farming in the hills west of the Jordan, while the Aramaeans were established in northern Syria, Lebanon, and the area around Damascus. The Philistines, related to the earlier raiders, were occupying the strip from Gaza to Joppa.

The Phoenicians

During the 12th century many coastal cities were destroyed. The few that survived were strung along the narrow, mountainous strip of coast that we call the Lebanon: the main cities were the ancient ports of Byblos, Tyre, and Sidon. The Greeks called the people of Lebanon "Phoenicians."

Their greatest natural resource was the great cedar forests of the high mountain slopes. For 2,000 years cedar timber had been traded through the port of Byblos. Now the Phoenicians built up a great fleet of merchant ships. Exploratory expeditions were probably sent as far as Britain and the west coast of Africa. In the western Mediterranean the Phoenicians founded many colonies, including Carthage on the coast of Africa and Cadiz in Spain.

To the Lebanon came linen from Egypt, and silver, iron, lead, and tin from Spain and Sardinia. From Africa came ivory, slaves, gold, silver, apes, and peacocks. Canaan provided grain, honey, and oils: southeast Anatolia exported horses and mules. Overland routes linked Phoenicia to the Red Sea, Arabia, and Mesopotamia.

But the wealth of the Phoenicians was not only based on buying and selling these goods. They were also famous for their craftsmen, who turned raw materials into finished items which were exported over a wide area from Italy to Mesopotamia. Weavers wove cloth from wool imported from Syria. The cloth, together with Egyptian linen, was dyed with the famous "Tyrian purple." This was a dye made from a kind of shellfish. Phoenician metalsmiths worked in bronze, iron, silver, and gold.

At their greatest, the Phoenicians controlled a vast network of trading colonies from Cyprus to Spain. Even after the Lebanon fell under the domination of great empires, the cities themselves remained wealthy. In the west, the Phoenician empire of Carthage survived to compete with the growing power of Rome.

Part of an Assyrian relief showing cedar logs from the forests of Lebanon being floated downstream to be used in an Assyrian palace.

THE BIBLE AND HISTORY

The Israelites were wandering herdsmen from the edge of the desert west of Mesopotamia. From time to time, small changes in climate seriously affected the grazing on the desert's rim. When this happened some desert peoples moved into the settled, fertile areas of Mesopotamia, Syria, and Palestine. One such migration may have been that of a small group led by Abraham, moving from North Syria into Canaan about 2000 B.C.

A few centuries later a similar nomadic group (according to the Old Testament, descended from Abraham) moved to Egypt in search of new pastures for their flocks. It was not unusual for Egyptians to allow nomadic tribes to graze their flocks on unwanted pasture in the "Land of Goshen," east of the Delta. Generations later, some of these people had become slaves. Under the leadership of Moses they fled into the wilderness of the Sinai Desert, where they joined other similar people. After wandering for many years they reached Canaan (about 1200 B.C.), and established themselves in villages among the hills and valleys west of the Jordan. From now on we can speak of them as the "Israelites."

After many battles the Israelites defeated the neighboring peoples, and under King David they set up a secure kingdom with a capital at Jerusalem. But under his grandson the Israelites divided into two hostile states, Israel and Judah. From now on control of the area changed from one great power to another as empires rose and fell. In A.D. 70 its Roman rulers destroyed Jerusalem after a revolt; in 135, after another uprising, they drove the Jews out of Palestine.

China

The first great civilization of the Far East grew up in China, and spread so widely that it strongly influenced almost all the other Far Eastern countries. This was a civilization that grew up in isolation, for China is cut off from the western world by the mountains of Tibet to the west, and by the Gobi Desert and Manchurian Plain in the northwest and north.

Three great river systems dominate China. In the south is the Si-kiang or West River. Here the climate is tropical and rice is grown all through the year. But this area is rather cut off from the rest of China by mountains that, though not very high, are difficult to cross. Through central China runs the Yangtze River. Here summers are hot and moist, though the short winters can be very cold. And to the north is the Hwang-ho or Yellow River. Its name comes from the fine yellow soil which covers the highlands through which the river flows, and which it carries down to spread over its flood plain. Here the summer rains are slight and unreliable, while the winters are long, dry, and bitterly cold. Northwest winds from the Gobi Desert swirl the soil into dust storms. The Yellow River often floods disastrously, drowning thousands of people and sweeping away villages and crops. But the yellow soil is so fertile that it was along the Yellow River that China's first civilization grew up.

Kneeling pottery figure (3rd century B.C.)

Bronze flying horse (2nd century A.D.)

This red lacquer bowl dates from the Chou period. Lacquer was the sap of an oak tree, which became very hard and black when left in a damp place. The Chinese built up layer upon layer of lacquer on a thin core of wood or cloth, and often colored it and decorated it with gold or silver.

Below: In the north China highlands the yellow soil may be 100 meters (about 325 feet) thick. When dry it blows off in dust storms, but when wet it becomes very fertile. From very early times the Chinese joined together in elaborate irrigation schemes.

B.C.	CHRONOLOGY
c.5000	Village farming communities in the Hwang-ho (Yellow River) Valley
c.1500	Bronze-working begins in An-yang region. Shang dynasty rules an empire with its main capital at An-yang
1027	Chou people from west China defeat Shang and establish a feudal dynasty, ruling many vassal states
771	Chou move capital to Loyang
c.700–500	Vassal states grow in power and Chou are weakened
660	Nomad barbarians ravage north Honan
551	Confucius born
481–221	Warring States period
256–221	State of Ch'in emerges victorious. First Ch'in emperor, Shih Huang-ti, unites China and consolidates Great Wall
206	Ch'in dynasty collapses
206– A.D. 220	Han dynasty
50–A.D. 50 A.D.	Buddhism introduced from India
166	Marcus Aurelius sends embassy to China
220–587	Six Dynasties period

A gilded bronze incense burner dating from the Han dynasty. Chinese bronze workers were very skilled in casting elaborate vessels. They used molds fitted together from a large number of pieces, which allowed them to cover their work with decorations. Bronzes were often gilded and inlaid or lacquered.

Unbroken Traditions

All over the ancient world great civilizations grew up and then died away. But Chinese civilization was never destroyed; instead, it developed without a break until the 20th century. From time to time invaders conquered and settled parts of the north, but they did not change the Chinese way of life; instead, they learned it themselves.

The earliest villages and towns grew up on the banks of the Yellow River and its tributaries. The water was used to irrigate the yellow soil and make it fertile. Cities were surrounded by walls of *hang-t'u* (stamped earth), built up layer by layer and pounded so solid that many are still standing today. The first period of Chinese history we know about is the time when the Shang dynasty ruled in the Yellow River area, from about 1500 B.C. on. Later dynasties spread Chinese rule and ways of life west and south. At its greatest the Chinese empire stretched from North Korea in the east, far west into Central Asia.

The Chinese empire was governed by a vast number of efficient civil servants, some employed by the central government and some by local government. In the name of the emperor, they controlled all aspects of everyday life. Weights and measures, laws and taxes were made the same all over the empire. Only this sort of strong central rule could hold such a vast area together.

Silk was China's most famous export. For centuries only the Chinese knew how to get silk from silkworm cocoons. This piece of silk dates from the Han dynasty.

TRAVEL

China's main link with the rest of the world was the Silk Road. This led from China, through Sinkiang, Turkestan, and Bactria, and then to Persia and Syria. Along this road long caravans of camels carried Chinese goods, especially silk, to the west. China imported little in return except for jade from central Asia and pearls from the south.

Within China itself, the main highways were the rivers and the many canals, which were used by countless boats. Special roads were built for moving armies and their supplies. Government officials were allowed to travel along the imperial highways, but most people used rough tracks.

AGRICULTURE

One of the Han dynasty emperors said "the world is based on agriculture" and most people in ancient China worked on the land. In the north, wheat, millet, and barley were the most important crops; farther south, rice was grown. Orchards of fruit trees were planted around the villages. Pigs and sheep were kept, but few cows – the Chinese have never liked milk or any of its products, and cattle were mainly used to pull carts. Hens and geese were important. Tea and cotton, which are both so common in China today, were not cultivated in ancient times, but hemp, from which cloth was made, was an important crop.

A model of a house, dating from the Han dynasty. Much of our knowledge of ancient China comes from such pottery figures and models found in tombs, showing animals, houses, farms, and servants.

Hunting was a popular pastime in ancient China. In Shang times young men set out in chariots; cheetahs, falcons, and hounds were used to chase the prey.

Europe under the Romans

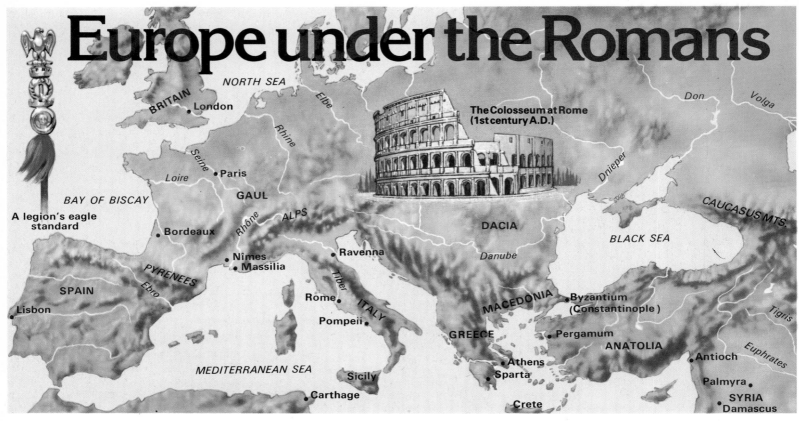

NORTH SEA
BRITAIN • London
Elbe
Rhine
Seine
Loire • Paris
BAY OF BISCAY
GAUL
A legion's eagle standard
Rhône
ALPS
• Bordeaux
Nîmes
Massilia
PYRENEES
Ebro
SPAIN
• Lisbon
• Ravenna
Tiber
Rome • ITALY
Pompeii •
GREECE
• Athens
• Sparta
MEDITERRANEAN SEA
Sicily
• Carthage
Crete
The Colosseum at Rome (1st century A.D.)
Don
Volga
Dnieper
DACIA
Danube
CAUCASUS MTS.
BLACK SEA
MACEDONIA
• Byzantium (Constantinople)
• Pergamum
ANATOLIA
Tigris
• Antioch
Euphrates
Palmyra •
SYRIA
• Damascus

Until 250 B.C., trade in the Mediterranean was controlled by Phoenician and Greek colonies on the coasts. At the same time, however, a new power was growing in Italy – the city-state of Rome. Between 250 and 30 B.C. Rome gained control of the whole Mediterranean region, the Near East, and a large part of western Europe. How did this happen?

Rome's rise to power was based on the position of Italy itself. As trade developed in the western Mediterranean, Italy became an important link between west and east. Just as important were the resources of Italy, which was very fertile, although not yet developed. In the south, Greek colonies grew rich: but central and northern Italy were mountainous regions, inhabited by many warring tribes. Only when Rome had united Italy under its leadership could the full value of Italy's position and resources be seen.

The Growth of Rome

Rome began, perhaps in the 800s B.C., as a group of hilltop settlements which overlooked the river Tiber, and beyond that the fertile plain of Latium. For several hundred years the area was dominated by the Etruscans of north central Italy. In 509 B.C. the native Romans rejected the rule of their Etruscan king, Tarquinius, and set up a republic. Instead of the hated king, they elected two magistrates, the consuls, to rule them. The new republic was a community of farmers, who cultivated the fertile countryside around the city.

B.C.	CHRONOLOGY
900s	Rise of Etruscans in north Italy
753	Traditional date of founding of Rome
509	Founding of Roman republic
343–275	Rome becomes dominant in Italy
264–201	Rome defeats Carthage and gains first overseas provinces
133–60	Aristocratic and popular parties struggle for power
59–52	Caesar conquers Gaul
49–44	Dictatorship of Caesar
44	Caesar assassinated; after conflict with Mark Antony Caesar's nephew Octavian (Augustus) gains power
A.D.	
286	Diocletian divides empire into west and east
476	After barbarians overrun France, Spain, and Italy, last western emperor is deposed

Whenever the need arose, the Roman farmers made tough, disciplined troops, always ready to fight in defense of their lands. Over the next 500 years they had to fight many enemies. By 266 B.C. Rome was the leading power in Italy. Then came two bitter wars with the North African city of Carthage, Rome's greatest rival in the western Mediterranean. Once again, Rome was victorious.

The next challenge came from the wealthy Greek kingdoms of Anatolia, Macedonia, and Syria. By 80 B.C. these had come under Roman rule. Then, in 59 B.C., Rome turned north. An ambitious Roman aristocrat, Julius Caesar, invaded Celtic Europe, which the Romans called Gaul. Caesar conquered all of Europe west of the Rhine. During the next hundred years the Romans won even more territory, including Britain: Rome ruled everything west of the Rhine and Danube rivers except Scotland and Ireland.

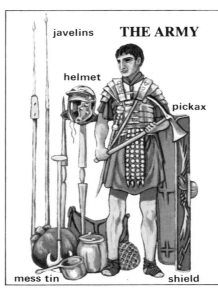

javelins THE ARMY
helmet
pickax
mess tin   shield

Rome's empire was won by the steadiness of the well-disciplined Roman troops. At first, the army was made up of farmer-citizens. But when the army was fighting abroad for long periods, the farms suffered from neglect. Under the consul Marius, just before 100 B.C., the army was changed into a permanent, paid force. The biggest unit of the army was the legion; it was made up of 6,000 (later 4,000) men, divided into ten cohorts. The cohort was made up of six centuries, each numbering 100 troops. Marius's soldiers were issued with standard equipment (see left). As well as fighting, they had to build fortifications, roads, and bridges.

Administering the Empire

Rome's greatest gifts to its empire were orderly government and technical knowledge. The Romans knew that they could not rule their vast empire by force of arms alone. In return for loyalty to Rome, the Romans allowed conquered peoples to keep their own customs and, to a certain extent, to govern themselves. To Europe, still a wilderness, the Romans brought their skills as builders, engineers, and farmers. They built towns and cities, connected by excellent roads. Roman landowners developed organized farming in Europe, draining marshes and clearing woodland to make fertile farmland. Trade and craftsmanship began to flourish, and came to rival even those of Italy itself. The Celtic people of Europe were encouraged to take part in all this. As time went on they settled peacefully into a Romanized way of life.

In Rome itself, luxury and poverty lived close together. Wealthy citizens occupied large ground-floor apartments in blocks ("insulae"). But the upper floors were overcrowded with poor families.

Roman occupation of southern Gaul brought a steady development of trade and agriculture. The Pont du Gard (above) was built to bring water to Nîmes (Nemausus), one of the richest towns of Roman Gaul.

The borders of the Roman empire were defended by a chain of walls and forts. Hadrian's Wall in the north of England was built between 122 and 136. It was part of a defensive zone many miles deep.

Heroic Societies

The peoples of central, northern, and western Europe did not develop cities until long after southeast Europe and the Near East. When Egypt and Crete were at their most powerful and glorious, Stonehenge was just being given its final form.

Before Roman occupation, the peoples of Europe formed what are called "heroic societies." Tribal chiefs and their warriors lived in hill forts surrounded by timber-framed ramparts. They were supported by farmers who worked the country around, herding animals or growing grain. Specialist metal-workers traveled through the countryside, skillfully producing goods first of bronze and later of iron. In the 5th century B.C. the Greeks described all the inhabitants of western Europe, from Spain to the Danube, as *Keltoi* – from which we get our term Celts.

The Celts soon accepted Roman ways. But east and north of the river Rhine were other tribes, together known as "barbarians." They constantly raided and threatened the Roman border, and eventually caused the empire's downfall.

ITALY

Italy had a special position in the Roman empire; at first, for instance, it was not taxed. But although there were many quite flourishing towns it became a problem. One trouble was that the other provinces were soon able to provide more cheaply everything that Italy had supplied, including grain, wine, and strong soldiers. The government asked the rich to invest their money in Italian farms. Low-interest loans were made available to farmers, grants were given to support children, and roads and land reclamation schemes were set up. But Italy declined into a land of large estates, owned by a few rich people, with poor farmers struggling alongside them.

The World in A.D. 117

In A.D. 117 the Roman empire reaches its greatest extent, from Britain in the north and Spain in the west, eastward to Mesopotamia. In the eastern Mediterranean the influence of Greece is still very strong, with Greek culture admired by everyone and Greek the language of educated people. But to the north the empire is threatened by barbarians who are starting to shift southward and westward. In China under the Han dynasty patterns of life become established that will last for 1,800 years, while in Central America the Mayan civilization emerges.

3 Central and Northern Europe west of the Rhine and Danube become rich through trade and accept Roman ways. Across these rivers "barbarian" tribes resist attempts at conquest.

This Celtic bronze shield probably dates from the 1st century A.D. It was found in the river Thames at Battersea in London. The central design includes four owl faces, simplified into a decorative pattern.

1 America In Central America small city-states compete for power. In the low-lying forests the Mayans build ceremonial centers and use their own form of
2 hieroglyphic writing. On the Peruvian coast pottery and textiles are produced.

Pottery figures, Mexico

Celtic bronze head

4 North Africa prospers under the Romans; vines, grain, and olives are grown on irrigated land and cities are built.

Below: A Roman military camp was a miniature city. Built to a standardized pattern, it had special areas set aside for the high command, ordinary soldiers, stabling, and so on. Familiar patterns and routines in unfamiliar surroundings helped keep up the spirits and effectiveness of Roman forces far from home.

Pottery fragment, Peru

5 Eastern Mediterranean Rome allows the old citi to keep their way of life; the area is united by its Greek-derived culture a the Greek language. Th Jews refuse to be govern by Rome and Judaea is eventually annihilated i A.D. 130.

6 Egypt Under Roman ru "river of grain" flows fro Egypt to Rome, while Alexandria is a center of trade and learning.

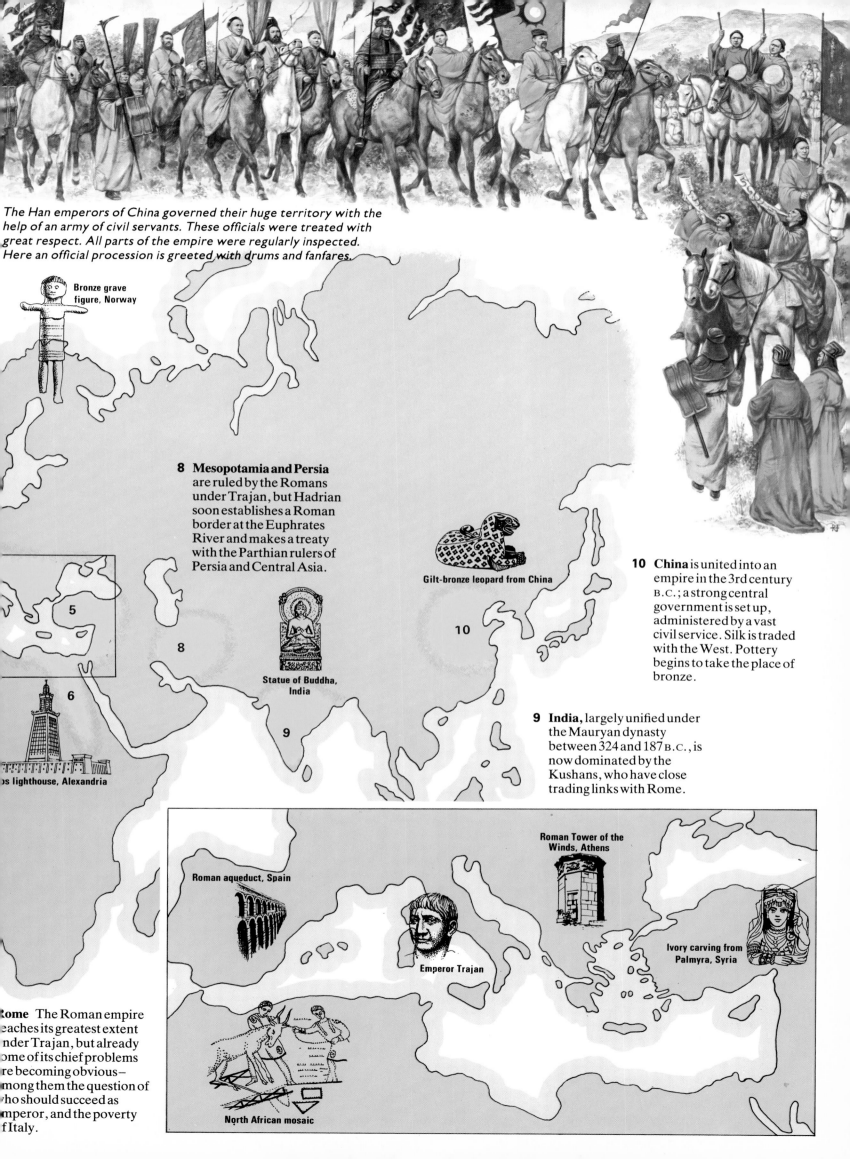

The Han emperors of China governed their huge territory with the help of an army of civil servants. These officials were treated with great respect. All parts of the empire were regularly inspected. Here an official procession is greeted with drums and fanfares.

Bronze grave figure, Norway

8 Mesopotamia and Persia are ruled by the Romans under Trajan, but Hadrian soon establishes a Roman border at the Euphrates River and makes a treaty with the Parthian rulers of Persia and Central Asia.

Gilt-bronze leopard from China

Statue of Buddha, India

os lighthouse, Alexandria

10 China is united into an empire in the 3rd century B.C.; a strong central government is set up, administered by a vast civil service. Silk is traded with the West. Pottery begins to take the place of bronze.

9 India, largely unified under the Mauryan dynasty between 324 and 187 B.C., is now dominated by the Kushans, who have close trading links with Rome.

Roman Tower of the Winds, Athens

Roman aqueduct, Spain

Emperor Trajan

Ivory carving from Palmyra, Syria

Rome The Roman empire reaches its greatest extent under Trajan, but already some of its chief problems are becoming obvious – among them the question of who should succeed as emperor, and the poverty of Italy.

North African mosaic

The Empire Outside Europe

In Anatolia, in the Near East, and in Egypt, civilization had existed for anything from 1,000 to 2,500 years before the Romans came. Through the ages the peoples there had become used to being ruled by great empires, and in many ways were far more civilized than the Romans. They were prosperous and there were many centers of learning. When Rome took control of these areas, it did not try to impose its own way of life on them. Instead it was a matter of carrying on, and growing rich from, an ancient pattern of trade, city life, craftsmanship, and agriculture.

The ruins of Palmyra, in Syria. Under the Romans, it became a very important city. In the late 3rd century A.D. its queen, Zenobia, declared her country independent; she was captured in 272 by the Roman emperor Aurelian and the city was destroyed in 273.

ROMAN RULE IN THE PROVINCES

Until the rule of the first emperor, Augustus (27 B.C.–A.D. 14), Roman provinces were governed by unpaid Roman politicians. They were responsible for law and order and the collection of taxes. Naturally enough, many governors used the opportunity to make their own fortunes. There were often complaints from those they governed. But Augustus changed all that. He employed paid governors, and allowed provinces to appeal directly to Rome if they felt unjustly treated. He allowed the ancient cities of the east to govern themselves according to their own customs. Moreover, Roman emperors were generous in their gifts to the cities–giving money for aqueducts, marketplaces, and amphitheaters.

MAJOR EMPERORS

27 B.C.–A.D. 14	**Augustus**
14–37	**Tiberius**
37–41	**Caius (Caligula)**
41–54	**Claudius**
54–68	**Nero**
69	**Year of the Four Emperors**
69–79	**Vespasian**
79–81	**Titus**
98–117	**Trajan**
117–138	**Hadrian**
161–180	**Marcus Aurelius**
284–305	**Diocletian**
306–337	**Constantine I**

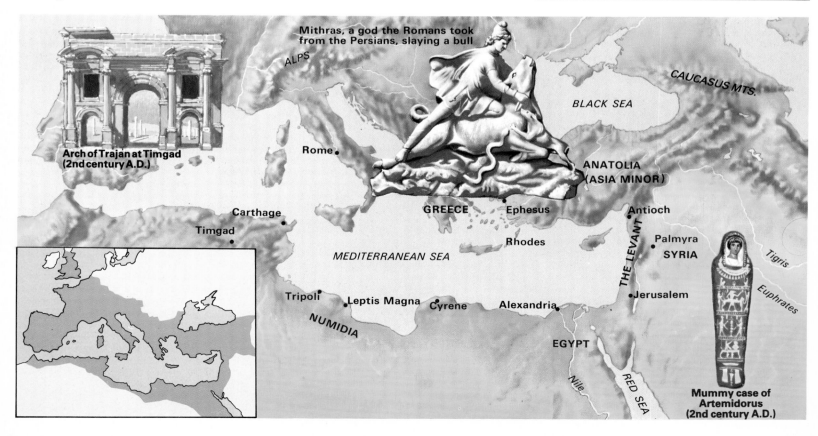

Arch of Trajan at Timgad (2nd century A.D.)

Mithras, a god the Romans took from the Persians, slaying a bull

ALPS

Rome

Carthage

Timgad

Tripoli Leptis Magna Cyrene Alexandria

NUMIDIA

MEDITERRANEAN SEA

GREECE Ephesus

Rhodes

BLACK SEA

CAUCASUS MTS.

ANATOLIA (ASIA MINOR)

Antioch

THE LEVANT

Palmyra
SYRIA

Jerusalem

Tigris

Euphrates

EGYPT

Nile

RED SEA

Mummy case of Artemidorus (2nd century A.D.)

Rome's Empire in the East

Rome gained its first overseas territories by defeating Carthage and taking over its colonies. This made Rome a power to be reckoned with. At this time the eastern Mediterranean was dominated by powerful rival kingdoms ruled by Greek kings. These were the descendants of Alexander's generals who had carved up his empire among them. The kingdoms constantly fought with one another to win new territory. Rome, the great new Mediterranean power, seemed to be a useful ally in the struggle for power.

At different times Rome was called in to deal with the ambitious rulers of Macedonia and Syria, who were threatening the kingdoms of Rhodes and Pergamum. At first, Rome fought simply to keep the balance of powers in the east – and for the rich rewards in loot. But there was so much trouble that the Romans lost patience and took control of the whole area. Finally, in 30 B.C., the Romans invaded Egypt, the wealthiest kingdom of all. With this, the Roman conquest of the east was complete.

The Division of the Empire

The Roman empire soon proved too vast to be kept firmly under control. The army was enlarged to deal with the attacks of warlike people beyond the borders, but new problems arose when powerful army commanders appointed their own candidates as emperor. Weak emperors, barbarian invasions, and economic crises made the empire almost ungovernable. The emperor Diocletian decided to reorganize it completely. In A.D. 286 he split the provinces and the army into smaller units, all firmly controlled by his own civil service. He divided the empire itself into West and East, and set up an emperor in Rome to rule the West; he ruled the East and had supreme power overall. The system did not work for very long, but it showed that the wealthy East was now more important. The strongest emperor of the 4th century, Constantine the Great, moved his capital from Rome to Byzantium, which he renamed Constantinople. Even after the weaker West fell to barbarian invasions in 476, the Eastern empire remained strong for several more centuries.

The Romans' engineering skills brought more wealth to the cities of Africa and the Near East. Emperors made grants toward building essential but expensive constructions, such as the aqueduct below. Aqueducts carried water over long distances to supply cities and irrigate fields.

AFRICA

Roman rule in Africa stretched all along the Mediterranean coast, and inland until mountains or desert formed a natural barrier. Under the Romans, North Africa became very rich. Miles and miles of irrigation pipes were laid to carry water to farms where grain, vines, and olives were grown. Old cities like the Phoenician Carthage and the Greek Cyrene flourished, and new cities like Timgad in Algeria were magnificent. North Africa has never been so prosperous, for since the Romans were defeated in Africa by the Vandals in the 5th century A.D. the desert has spread into the fertile areas.

Egypt was a special case. It had far more in common with the long-established cities of Anatolia than with the rest of Africa. It was also specially important for its grain, which brought great wealth to Rome.

The problems of administering the empire led the Emperor Diocletian to divide it into two units, West and East. He proposed a rule of four – two emperors ("augusti"), with two lieutenants ("caesari") who would succeed them after 20 years. This statue shows the four rulers clasping each other.

The Barbarians

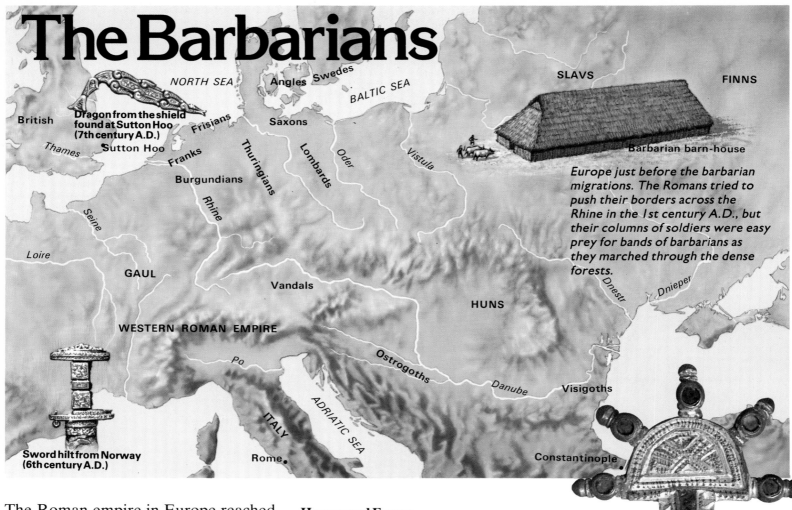

NORTH SEA

Dragon from the shield found at Sutton Hoo (7th century A.D.)

British

Thames

Sutton Hoo

Frisians

Franks

Burgundians

Seine

Rhine

Loire

GAUL

Angles   Swedes

BALTIC SEA

Saxons

Thuringians

Lombards

Oder

Vistula

SLAVS

FINNS

Barbarian barn-house

Europe just before the barbarian migrations. The Romans tried to push their borders across the Rhine in the 1st century A.D., but their columns of soldiers were easy prey for bands of barbarians as they marched through the dense forests.

WESTERN ROMAN EMPIRE

Vandals

HUNS

Dnestr

Dnieper

Po

Ostrogoths

Danube

Visigoths

Sword hilt from Norway (6th century A.D.)

ITALY

ADRIATIC SEA

Rome

Constantinople

The Roman empire in Europe reached east and north to the rivers Rhine and Danube. Within the empire, the Celtic peoples soon took up Roman ways. But across the long borders, in the forests and mountains of central and eastern Europe, lived warlike peoples the Romans called "barbarians" – from the "bar-bar" sounds of their languages.

Who were the barbarians? Even today no one knows. According to their traditions, they came originally from Scandinavia and the Baltic lands. They migrated south, settling for a time before moving on to another region. Between the mid-3rd and mid-6th centuries A.D. they moved around so much that this is called the Age of Migrations.

The Romans scorned the barbarians. However, although they did not live in cities, and had only a simple writing system, they had their own well-organized customs and laws. They were also superb metalworkers, and their minstrels composed long and stirring poems. They were great warriors. They stopped the Roman expansion, and raided and harassed the Roman forts. When tribes became more and more crowded against one another during the Age of Migrations, they eventually broke through the borders, and overthrew the empire in the west.

Houses and Farms
The barbarians lived in farming villages. Even after they had invaded the western Roman empire they kept clear of the stone-built towns and cities.

A barbarian village was built of sturdy wooden-framed houses: the walls were a sort of woven matting of brushwood, thickly plastered with clay (called "wattle and daub"). Inside the house were rows of posts, supporting a thatched roof. A house was divided into two sections, one for the family and one for their livestock – a valuable source of warmth in winter. The largest house in the village belonged to the chief. It was fenced off and surrounded by workshops.

Beyond the village lay fields and pastures. Barbarians kept herds of cattle, for hides, meat, and milk. Some tribes kept sheep and goats, while pigs could be left to root for food in the surrounding woods and forests. Livestock was more important than crops – but farmers grew wheat, barley, rye, peas, and beans.

Barbarian men fastened their cloaks with brooches like this. It is set with garnets. Such precious objects were made by traveling goldsmiths. Far from being primitive and ignorant, the barbarian peoples produced metalwork of the finest quality.

The Nydam boat, discovered in a peat bog in northern Germany. It is the only surviving example of the type of boat used by the Angles, Saxons, Jutes, and Frisians to cross the North Sea to raid England. It is 21 meters (70 feet) long, and needed 30 oarsmen to propel it. The Viking longships of 400 years later were very similar in design.

Trade routes connected even remote areas of northern Europe with the fringes of the Mediterranean world. This beautiful silver bowl is decorated with a variety of human and animal figures. It shows both Celtic and Thracian influences, but was actually discovered in Gundestrop, Denmark, far to the north.

B.C.	CHRONOLOGY
c.200	Peoples living in the Baltic region of northern Europe begin to move south and east, eventually occupying large areas of central and eastern Europe
A.D.	
c.250–550	The Age of Migrations, a confused period of tribal warfare and large-scale movements of peoples
c.370	The Huns, fierce nomads from central Asia, drive into south Russia and central Europe; from there Goths and Vandals flee westward
445	Huns under Attila attack Constantinople. Eastern Roman emperor buys peace. Attila then invades Gaul but is defeated by Western emperor. After his death Attila's empire breaks up
476	Rome falls to German tribes. Southern Britain, Gaul, Spain, and North Africa are overrun by barbarian tribes

The Tribal System

Historians group barbarian tribes into "peoples" like Goths, Vandals, and so on, according to their languages and traditions. But there was no unity about the tribes of any such people. Each tribe was an independent unit which guarded its rights selfishly. Within the tribe were a number of closely knit *kindreds* or family groups.

Tribal affairs were run by an assembly of warriors, and by a council of elders. Chiefs or kings were elected; they had to be skilled war leaders, for the barbarians were ferocious fighters. Many of the poems sung at their feasts were in praise of warriors who had chosen to die rather than retreat.

During the Age of Migrations, the tribal system was weakened as newcomers from the east forced established tribes to leave their lands. In turn these attacked weaker neighbors, or were broken up. Young men grouped together in warbands under a strong leader, who promised treasure in return for loyalty. The rich villas and towns of Roman Gaul were often the targets of warband raids.

The Romans recruited many "friendly" barbarian bands to fight for them; some chiefs rose to be senior commanders in the Roman army. Toward the end of the empire, barbarians were allowed to settle inside the Roman boundaries. But under weak rulers these people were as hard to control as those beyond the borders. One of their commanders, Alaric the Goth, led his people from the lands they had been given down into Italy, to sack Rome itself.

Europe at the time of the fall of Rome, A.D. 476. Once the barbarians had broken through the borders they soon overran Europe and parts of North Africa. The western Roman empire was reduced to a small area of what is now Yugoslavia but 12 years later was taken over by the Ostrogoths.

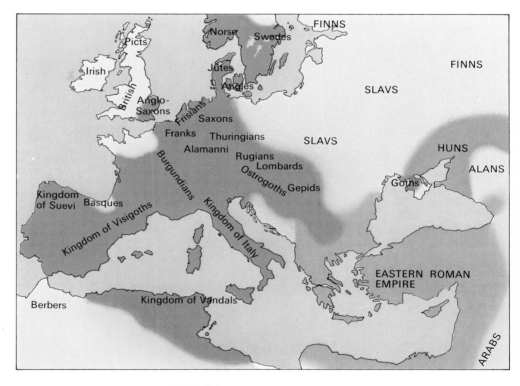

This shoulder clasp is one of a pair found in a ship burial at Sutton Hoo, in eastern England. They date from about A.D. 625 and the king who wore them owned many beautiful pieces of armor and jewelry. They are finely made and set with garnets and glass in divisions of gold. The "barbarian" jewelry found at Sutton Hoo is generally thought to be some of the most beautiful and skillfully worked ever found.

The Americas

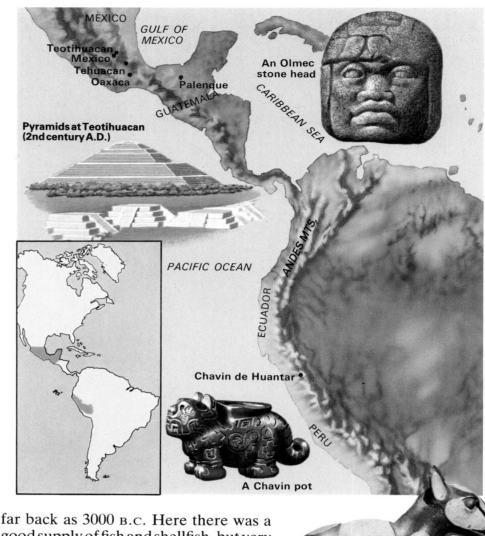

The first men probably crossed into America around 26,000 B.C. At this time there was a land bridge between Asia and Alaska, and it seems likely that hunting Stone Age people crossed it to become the ancestors of all the Americans. A few sites have been found which show that hunters were living in north Alaska around 24,000 B.C. and in Mexico in about 22,000 B.C. By 10,000 B.C. the first peoples had reached the tip of South America.

The Americas were a vast wilderness of forests, deserts, plains, and mountains. Each type of region made different demands on the peoples who lived there. As time went on, each found the best way of adapting to its surroundings. In many areas, groups kept largely to their hunting way of life, adding to their food supply by gathering seeds, nuts, and fruit. They were so successful that this way of life had changed little even by the 19th century A.D., long after the Europeans arrived: there was no need for settled farming when it was easy to find food in this way.

Where agriculture developed, as it did before 3000 B.C. in the Tehuacan Valley in Mexico, three main crops were cultivated: maize, beans, and squashes. Settled villages grew up here around 1500 B.C. In other areas, as on the coast of Peru, villages and even towns grew up as far back as 3000 B.C. Here there was a good supply of fish and shellfish, but very gradually the people turned to farming. Their crops included the potato and sweet potato, which were first cultivated high in the Andes Mountains.

All over the Americas large hunting or agricultural communities grew up. But city-based civilizations developed only in two main regions: Central America, and the northwest coast of South America with the neighboring Andes.

The Mochica culture of the northern Peruvian coast produced excellent pottery during the first 500 years A.D. Pottery was shaped in molds – the potter's wheel was unknown.

This Olmec pavement is shaped like a jaguar's face. It is nearly 3,000 years old but is beautifully preserved since it was covered over by the Olmecs shortly after it was laid. Sometimes the Olmecs showed humans with fangs and claws like a jaguar.

THE OLMECS

The first Central American civilization we know of is that of the Olmecs, which grew up in the swampy tropical forests of the Gulf of Mexico coast around 1300 B.C. The main Olmec sites were not cities, but ceremonial centers; they had carefully planned temples, platforms, and courtyards, but few ordinary houses. Farmers lived in the country around, and there were no large towns. Among the most striking Olmec remains are the giant heads carved from huge blocks of rock; the largest stands about 3 meters (10 feet) high. Their heavy features and thick lips are found in other Olmec carvings. Although there are no Olmec centers outside the coast area, Olmec influence stretched far along the trade routes to east and west.

THE MAYANS

East of the Olmec area, in another low-land region of tropical forests, grew up the Mayan civilization. Like the Olmec, it had elaborate ceremonial centers but no real cities. Each of four main centers ruled over a quarter of the Mayan region, through a network of lesser centers. Most of the Mayans were farmers, living in small villages.

The Mayans built tall pyramid temples and beautiful palaces, decorated with stone carvings and wall paintings. They also carved jade, turquoise, and a greenish rock called serpentine. They produced painted pottery and set up vast, curiously carved stone slabs; they were the most skilled astronomers in Central America. The Mayan civilization began around 1000 B.C. and lasted until about A.D. 900, when it collapsed. No one knows why. Palaces and villages were abandoned. People either died out or moved away, leaving the jungle to grow over the ruins.

Central America

Central America is the relatively narrow strip of land which joins the great continents of North and South America. It is a region of high volcanic mountains bounded to the east and west by narrow coastal plains. The climate changes with altitude: the hot, wet tropical forests of the plains give way to the cooler, drier mountain uplands and finally the cold, dry regions of the high mountains.

The different civilizations which grew up in Central America had several things in common. They shared many of the same gods and had similar myths; they built stepped pyramids and made human sacrifices. They developed hieroglyphic writing systems and an arithmetic based on 20, and they were skilled astronomers. They worked out a very accurate calendar, with the year divided into "months" of 20 days; there was a second, sacred cycle of 260 days. Ball courts were important features of every large city; on them a game was played in which heavily padded players tried to propel a solid rubber ball across a central line.

After the Olmec civilization declined, power moved from the lowlands to the highlands of Mexico. Here growing city-states fought for power among themselves. Among these were Teotihuacan, in a side branch of the Valley of Mexico, which by A.D. 500 had a population of 50,000 and was the most powerful of all the city-states. It had a vast ceremonial section and houses built on a rectangular plan; there were lords and priests, administrators and soldiers. Craftsmen had their own areas according to their trade. Pottery from Teotihuacan was traded over a wide area, and the influence of its art is seen all over Central America.

The palace at Palenque, one of the great centers of the Mayans. Centers like this, built in the tropical lowlands of Central America, were complexes of ball courts, temples, and towers.

After 1800 B.C., the development of irrigation led to intensive agriculture in Peru. The Peruvians soon learned how to terrace steep mountainsides in order to grow their crops.

South America

The northwestern area of South America is very different from Central America. Here the Pacific coast is dry, almost a desert. From it rise the Andes, the second highest mountain range in the world. On the plains, and even in the mountains, irrigation is needed in order to grow crops.

The first civilizations of South America grew up in Peru. Its people developed irrigation systems around 1800 B.C. and soon large settlements appeared. The steep mountain-sides were terraced so that every possible scrap of land could be used. At about the same time pottery began to be made. The first great culture which spread through the region was the Chavin, based on Chavin de Huantar high in the Andes. Here stepped stone platforms, terraces, and sunken courts were decorated with fantastic carvings of man-beasts, often with snarling jaguar-mouths. Sacred images, including jaguars, eagles, and snakes, were also used to decorate pottery and textiles.

Chavin influence lasted from about 1000 to 300. After this there was no one dominant culture, but some six nations have been identified. The best known is the Mochica, on the north coast; its people built temples of mudbrick and huge aqueducts and canals to irrigate their farmland.

THE MIDDLE AGES

"La Dame à la Licorne" or *"The Lady and the Unicorn"* (c.1509–1513) is one of a series of richly colored tapestries which can be seen in the Musée de Cluny in Paris.

After the Romans

During the Middle Ages many pilgrims made long journeys, often on foot, to visit places connected with saints. This pilgrim badge, showing St. Michael, is in Salisbury museum in southwest England.

The religion of Islam, which began in Arabia in the 7th century, soon spread all through the Near East. This picture, painted in Baghdad in 1237, shows a market scene.

The Middle Ages is a term historians use to describe the period in Europe between the fall of the Western Roman empire and the beginning of the modern age of science, exploration, and widespread knowledge. In the rest of the world, too, this was a time of growth and change, which were to some extent connected with what happened in Europe. All settled areas of civilization found themselves threatened by barbaric peoples during this period. By A.D. 500 the Roman empire in western Europe had fallen to Germanic peoples from across the Rhine. India and China had been attacked by the nomadic Huns of Central Asia, some of whom had also threatened Europe.

The Breakup of the Western Empire
At its greatest the Roman empire was well administered, strongly defended, and prosperous. It united millions of people, from Britain to the Near East, in a way of life based on cities, trade, organized agriculture, and a code of laws written in a single language – Latin. From the 4th century Christianity provided another strong link. From the 3rd century, however, this great unified empire began to decay from within. The western provinces, Gaul, Spain, Britain, and Italy, suffered a decline in trade and population. Administering the west, and defending the long Rhine-Danube border, became increasingly difficult.

At the same time, the empire faced increasing threats from outside. In the wild forests and marshlands to the east lived warlike Germanic peoples. Their way of life was based on farming but included constant raiding and warfare: for them, the highest virtues were courage and loyalty in battle. To the Romans they were "barbarians." From the end of the 3rd century these peoples stepped up their raids across the Rhine and the Danube.

Fall of the Empire
The period from the 3rd to the 8th century is often called the Age of Migrations. It was a time of tremendous upheaval as the peoples of eastern and central Europe moved westward toward the frontiers of the Roman empire. The Romans were forced to admit some of these peoples into the empire. They gave them lands and privileges in return for which the barbarians became *foederati* (allies) charged with defending the borders. Shortly after 400, there were new upheavals. The Huns, savage nomads from Central Asia, drove westward across Europe. Germanic Goths, Vandals, Burgundians, and later, Franks crossed into Gaul, pushing deeply into the western provinces. The Romanized populations were forced to give them the lands they needed. The Germanic peoples set up kingdoms in Gaul, Spain, North Africa, and Italy, where a Gothic chieftain, Odoacer, deposed the last Western Roman emperor, Romulus Augustulus, in A.D. 476. The Eastern Roman empire survived to become the Byzantine empire (see page 66).

The "Dark Ages"
Over the next century the barbarian kings struggled to hold on to and expand their territories. This time was once thought of as a Dark Age, when civilization perished. But, however much they had run down, Roman law and administration were too well established to disappear overnight. Rulers still hoped to rebuild a great European empire on Roman lines – even if their ideas of the old empire were rather hazy and inaccurate. The Christian church had not been destroyed and in the next few centuries many more people were converted to Christianity. Churchmen traveled from one country to another. Many monasteries were built. Their monks spent much time studying and they sent missionaries to pagan lands. Christians had a common belief, a spiritual leader in the pope, and a common cause for which they would unite and fight when necessary. In 1054, however, the Christian church split. The Christians of Asia Minor refused to accept the authority of the pope and formed the Eastern Orthodox church centered on Constantinople. The Eastern church spread to many people in eastern Europe.

Nevertheless, Europe was in a bad state. Undoubtedly people continued to work the land and gather the harvest. But old patterns

The Vikings threatened Europe between 800 and 1100. In the 13th and 14th centuries, Mongol hordes under Genghis Khan and Timur the Lame scoured Asia from east to west. But by 1500 a more settled picture had emerged. Europe was beginning to develop into a patchwork of powerful nation-states. Rulers of the Islamic faith controlled North Africa, the eastern Mediterranean countries, and Asia as far as India. In China, the Ming dynasty controlled a splendid empire. Trade routes by land and sea linked Europe and the Far East. As the number of contacts increased, Europeans began to look for new trade routes. The Age of Exploration was about to dawn, which would finally link all the places in the world where settled civilizations existed.

Below: The Catalan map, made in the late 14th century for the king of France. The increase in trade led to the need for, and making of, increasingly accurate maps.

The many great stone cathedrals and churches built in Europe in the Middle Ages remind us of the strength of Christianity at that time. Notre Dame cathedral, Paris (above), was begun in 1163 and was a model for many later French churches.

Below: A gold coin showing Theodoric (454– 526), who founded the Ostrogothic kingdom in Italy. Theodoric had spent nine years in Constantinople, and the Byzantine emperor supported him in Italy. The Roman Senate also gave him its full support.

of trade had been changed and travel was difficult and dangerous. Kings had to hand over local government to their sons and relatives. In return for grants of land barbarian nobles and leading churchmen protected their territory, administered local affairs, and received most of the produce. In this system can be seen the roots of later feudalism, the way of life which dominated Europe during much of the Middle Ages.

The World in A.D. 500

Migrating barbarians over the last few centuries have overthrown the Gupta empire in India and invaded north China. In western Europe they have settled throughout the Western Roman empire; lacking a central organization, they develop a number of small states linked increasingly by their common Christianity. The stronger Eastern Roman (Byzantine) empire remains and Roman laws and learning are upheld there. In the 7th century the new religion of Islam spreads quickly through the Near East and North Africa.

3 Northern Europe Saxons, Angles, and Jutes settle in England; the Celts thrive in Wales, Cornwall, Scotland, Brittany in northwest France, and especially in Ireland. They are converted to Christianity. Scandinavia is dominated by pagan warrior farmers.

Gilded bronze buckle, Sweden

1 The Americas The city of Teotihuacan, in Mexico, now has a population of over 50,000. The Mayans in the Central American lowlands have splendid ceremonial centers but no true cities. In Peru, the
2 Mochica and Nazca Indians of the coast are making fine pottery, goldwork, and textiles.

Mayan carving

4 Western Europe The Western Roman empire is now under barbarian rule. Soon the Franks gain control of much of modern France and parts of Germany. Christianity spreads and missionaries are sent to England, Scotland, and France. St. Bernard of Nursia draws up his rule for monasteries.

Visigothic brooch, Spain

A waterside scene in China. Great canals were built to link the main rivers, and together these formed the most important trading highways. Goods of all sorts were carried along the waterways, and the river people lived in thatched shelters on their boats.

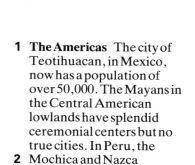

Baked clay figure, Peru

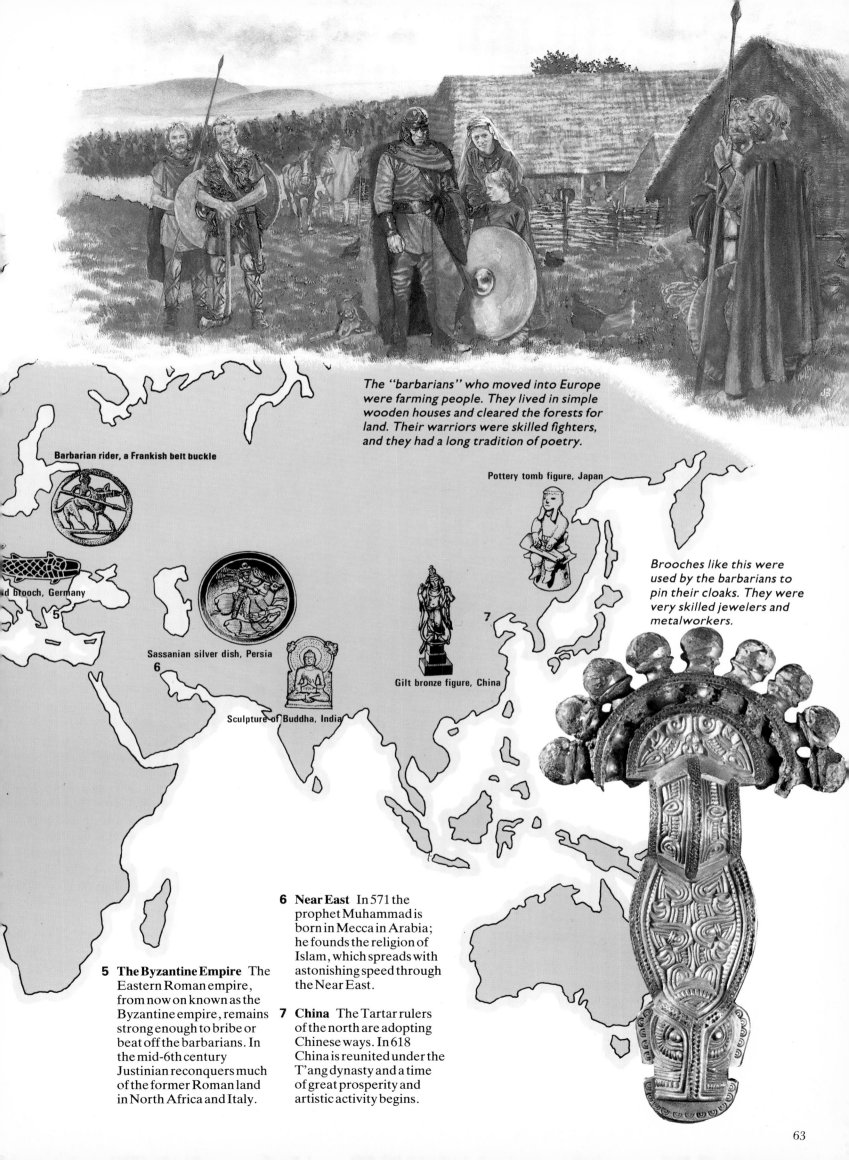

The "barbarians" who moved into Europe were farming people. They lived in simple wooden houses and cleared the forests for land. Their warriors were skilled fighters, and they had a long tradition of poetry.

Barbarian rider, a Frankish belt buckle

Pottery tomb figure, Japan

Brooches like this were used by the barbarians to pin their cloaks. They were very skilled jewelers and metalworkers.

d brooch, Germany

5

Sassanian silver dish, Persia

6

Gilt bronze figure, China

7

Sculpture of Buddha, India

5 The Byzantine Empire The Eastern Roman empire, from now on known as the Byzantine empire, remains strong enough to bribe or beat off the barbarians. In the mid-6th century Justinian reconquers much of the former Roman land in North Africa and Italy.

6 Near East In 571 the prophet Muhammad is born in Mecca in Arabia; he founds the religion of Islam, which spreads with astonishing speed through the Near East.

7 China The Tartar rulers of the north are adopting Chinese ways. In 618 China is reunited under the T'ang dynasty and a time of great prosperity and artistic activity begins.

Technology

This mosque lamp was made in Syria in the 13th century. The Muslims found an old-established glass industry here which they developed. Muslim glass was prized for its beauty.

During the Middle Ages many inventions and discoveries were made, and old ways of doing things were improved. Many new ideas came from the East, and were brought west by traders. The Muslims learned a number of skills, including papermaking, from China and brought to Europe the "Arabic" numbering system learned from the Hindus of India. They were also clever astronomers, chemists, and doctors. Technology in Europe suffered a setback with the barbarian invasions, when many of the Roman techniques were partly or even completely lost. However, the barbarians themselves were immensely skilled metalworkers. As Europe became more settled again, new developments were made which improved agriculture, transport, and manufacture.

Farming

Farming was the most widespread way of life in the Middle Ages. In the East great irrigation schemes allowed new land to be cultivated, and in Europe forests were cleared and marshes drained for plowland and pasture. As iron became common, tools were improved; spades and forks were shod with iron and new tools like the long-handled scythe were developed. A three-year crop rotation system was used in much of Europe instead of the Roman two-year system. Plows were improved by a moldboard to turn over the soil (a device used by the Chinese some 2,000 years earlier). Teams of oxen were used for plowing, and in the late Middle Ages plowhorses were also used.

Right: A page from a Bible printed by Johannes Gutenberg of Mainz, who in the 1450s invented printing with movable metal type. Before this, books had to be copied by hand. This was slow and expensive and mistakes were easily made. Gutenberg made a separate mold for each letter and the letters were then cast in metal. They could be used again and again. He arranged the letters into words, and then clamped them together on a crude wine press. He inked them with a new kind of oil-based ink, and then pressed a sheet of paper against them. He could print up to 300 sheets a day.

The invention of the padded horsecollar was a great advance, as it allowed horses to pull heavy weights. This picture of farming in October comes from a 15th-century book called Les Très Riches Heures du duc de Berry, *and is one of a series showing work on the land in the different months.*

Watermills became more common. The Domesday Book tells us that in 1086 there were 5,624 in England south of the Trent. They were used for milling corn and later for industries; fulling mills were an important part of cloth-processing, and water-power operated hammers and bellows for the metal industry. Windmills were used in Iran in the 7th century. They were used first to pump water and later to grind corn. Windmills became common in Europe in the 13th century.

Travel and transport

At the end of the 9th century three inventions spread rapidly through Europe which had a great effect on travel and transport. One was the stirrup. A little toe stirrup was used in India in about A.D. 100, but stirrups were not used in China until the 5th century. Stirrups not only made riding more comfortable but also made mounted knights more efficient. Now they could stand in the saddle and use their swords over a much wider range, and they were less easily unhorsed by their enemies. Toward the end of the 9th century nailed horseshoes were used in Europe, which meant that horses could travel longer distances and carry heavier burdens. A little later the rigid, padded horsecollar came into use. Before this, the horse had been harnessed with a breastband. When a horse pulled hard this pressed against its windpipe, and choked it. The horsecollar meant that horses could pull much heavier weights, and now wagoners and carters could transport much greater loads over longer distances.

GUNPOWDER

One of the most important inventions of the Middle Ages was that of gunpowder and cannon. Some time in the 10th century the Chinese discovered that crushed niter, sulfur, and charcoal mixed in the right proportions would explode. From there the invention spread to the West.

The use of guns meant the end of medieval warfare. Cannonballs could smash through metal armor, and could break down castle walls. The medieval era of armed knights, based in stone-walled castles, was over.

In about 1321 the first cannon were used in Europe. They were made by Italians and fired by Chinese gunpowder. This picture shows the siege of La Rochelle in France at the end of the 14th century. In the foreground is a primitive cannon. It is made of iron rods welded and bound together.

Clothmaking was one of the most important industries of the Middle Ages, and several inventions helped cloth production. They included the spinning wheel, the horizontal frame loom, and the fulling mill, in which cloth was thickened by being beaten with water-driven mallets. The cloth trade brought great wealth to cities, including those of Flanders and northern Italy. This carving of a weaver, by the 13th-century sculptor Pisano, is in a Florence museum.

BUILDING

The most common material for important buildings in medieval Europe was stone. An architect would draw up plans or sometimes make a model. Over a thousand men would work under him on a cathedral. Stone was cut at the quarry by roughmasons, who also laid and mortared the blocks in place. The important carving was done by freemasons. Wooden scaffolding was used for the building, with cranes operated by donkeys or even men to lift the stones. Masons' tools were much the same as those used today: saws, chisels, wedges, and mallets. Many other craftsmen, including carpenters, glaziers, painters, and metalworkers, all helped to make the great cathedrals that were one of the chief glories of the Middle Ages.

Shipping

Advances in ship building helped traders and fishermen in the Middle Ages and made possible the later explorations. Two such inventions came from the East. One was the lateen (triangular) sail, which made it possible for ships to beat into the wind. It was used from the 9th century on in the Mediterranean. Four centuries later hinged sternpost rudders came into use in the eastern Mediterranean; they made ships much easier to steer. At this time, too, magnetic compasses were becoming common and good charts began to be made.

Metalworking

The barbarian invaders of Europe were skilled metalworkers, producing fine jewelry and weapons. All through the Middle Ages magnificent metal objects were made. Many of them were very elaborate. Bronze was easily cast in molds. Gold and silver were sometimes cast but more often cut from a thin sheet and hammered into shape. A mixture of gold powder and mercury was used for gilding other metals. This liquid was painted on and the object heated until the mercury evaporated and the gold melted into a thin film.

Metal armor was vital to the knights of the Middle Ages. At first they used mail, made of iron wire rings welded together. Later they had plate armor. In Europe the iron had to be forged into shape with continuous heating and hammering, until the end of the Middle Ages. Then furnaces were developed which could reach high enough temperatures to melt the iron so that it could be cast into shape. In China, cast iron had been produced since the 5th century B.C.!

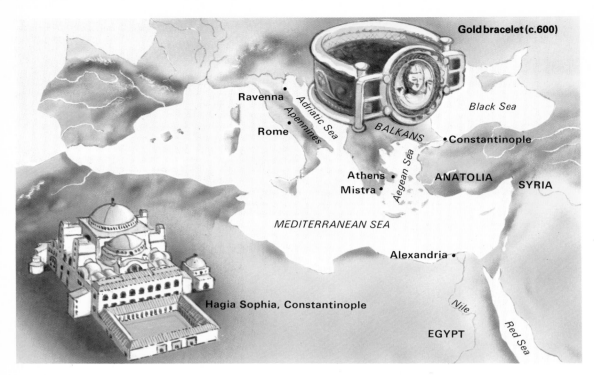

Gold bracelet (c.600)

Ravenna
Rome
Adriatic Sea
Apennines
BALKANS
Black Sea
Constantinople
Athens
Mistra
Aegean Sea
ANATOLIA
SYRIA
MEDITERRANEAN SEA
Alexandria
Nile
Red Sea
EGYPT

Hagia Sophia, Constantinople

The Byzantine Empire

The huge empire built by the Romans did not completely disappear with the fall of Rome and the conquest of western Europe by the "barbarians." The eastern part, including the Balkans, Greece, Turkey, Syria, Palestine, and Egypt, was richer and stronger than the west. It was able to drive off, or buy off, the invaders. It was ruled from Byzantium and for that reason it is known as the Byzantine empire. Byzantium was a small Greek port converted by the Roman emperor Constantine in A.D. 330 into a great capital for the Eastern Roman empire. He called it Constantinople, and Istanbul, its modern name, is the Turkish form of Constantinople.

The emperor had chosen the site for his city very carefully. It is on a promontory or triangle of land and commands the sea route between the Black Sea and the Mediterranean. Trade routes from the mainland of Europe led through Constantinople to the Near East and on to China. Ships from the Mediterranean sea could bring their goods into the safety of the city's excellent natural harbor.

The Romans gave the Byzantine empire its laws and its ways of government. But before Roman times the whole area had come under the Greek rule of Alexander the Great and his successors. Many rich cities on the coast of Anatolia had been founded by Greek colonists centuries earlier. The common language of the area was still Greek. In Constantinople, Ephesus, Alexandria in Egypt, and other centers the learning of the ancient Greeks was kept alive by learned men and women. Side by side with them were the new Christian scholars, for from its beginning Constantinople was a Christian city.

Running the Empire

The emperor's court was run with traditions and ceremonies which never varied. A large number of officials controlled the towns and the trade which passed through them. There was an elaborate customs service. Farther afield, Byzantine power was maintained by well-trained diplomats, who skillfully set the many enemies of the empire against one another.

The Byzantines made a great deal of beautiful jewelry. This gold and enamel pendant, showing St. George, dates from about 1000.

Below: The walls of Constantinople were built in the 4th and 5th centuries to defend the city against the barbarians. They were never stormed until 1203.

Life in the Country

Under Byzantine rule huge areas of land were in the hands of wealthy, often quarrelsome, landowners. In the villages, peasants kept small herds of sheep or cattle. The land they worked varied from the rich fields of Egypt to the dry scrubland of central Anatolia (later Turkey). A drought or plagues of locusts sometimes ruined large areas. Taxes were heavy and it was hard for poor people to save money. They were tied to their land. The only way for them to get a better life was by running away to the towns or, if they were young men, by joining the army. Yet it was possible for a humble man to do well. The emperor Justinian came from a peasant family.

The Shrinking Empire

Persians, Arabs, Avars, Slavs, and finally Turks all conquered large parts of the Byzantine empire. By 1453 only the area around Constantinople was left. On Monday, May 28th that year, the Ottoman Turks led by Sultan Mehmet II captured the city (see page 109). The last Greek emperor, called Constantine like the founder of the city, died during the final attack. His body was never found.

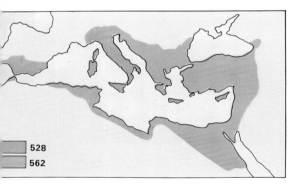

528
562

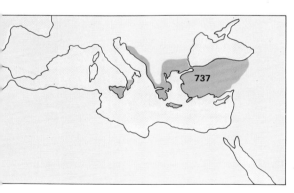

737

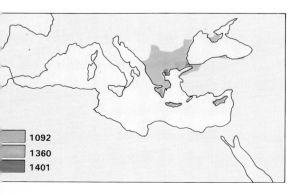

1092
1360
1401

TRADE

The Byzantine empire was rich in natural resources. Greece provided wine, olives, and olive oil which was used in cooking. Grain for export was produced in huge quantities along the coasts of North Africa, the Aegean, and the eastern Mediterranean. (Some of these areas are now far more barren than they were in those days because the land has been worked too hard.) Glass and cotton came from Egypt and Syria. Syria also produced silk, which was in great demand for luxurious clothes and costly coverings for furniture. Large quantities of gold came from Anatolia, while papyrus, used to write on, came from Egypt as it had in the time of the pharaohs. Other trade goods included timber and building stone, fish, meat and leather, salt, and dried fruits.

The goods produced inside the empire were traded for luxuries from far afield. China was the main source of silk. From India and the Far East came spices, sapphires and pearls. Africa provided ivory and gold, from Senegal and Ghana and possibly from as far south as Zimbabwe. The north traded Russian furs and Baltic amber. Great trading or "caravan" routes were established from Samarkand, the Indian Ocean, and the Caspian Sea. To the west, goods reached as far as Britain.

These maps show how the Byzantine empire shrank from its greatest under Justinian to a tiny remnant shortly before it was finally conquered by the Turks.

The Byzantine empire was at its greatest under the emperor Justinian (527–565). His general Belisarius conquered Sicily, Italy, and parts of North Africa. This portrait of Justinian comes from the Church of San Vitale in Ravenna, which was the capital of the Byzantine empire in Italy. Justinian organized existing Roman laws into a system known as the Code of Justinian.

An ivory carving possibly of the Byzantine empress Irene (752–803). Born in Athens, she reigned as regent for her young son from 780 to 790, and ruled again from 797 to 802.

The Near East

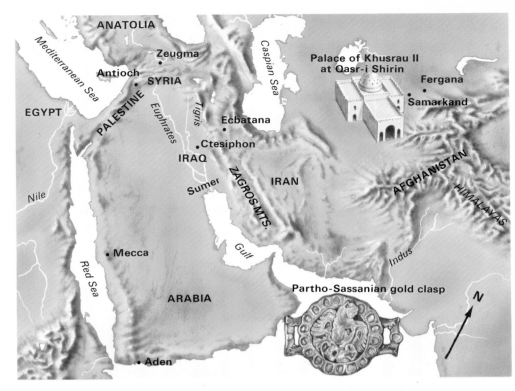

The Near East is a vast area, stretching from the Mediterranean in the west, eastward through Iraq and Iran to the Indian subcontinent. To the north lies Russia, and to the south the Indian Ocean and the Gulf. A great deal of the area is mountainous, and it includes the great deserts of Syria and Arabia. There are also many valleys with good farmland, and the flood plains of the rivers Tigris and Euphrates in Iraq are so fertile that one of the first great civilizations of the ancient world grew up there around Sumer.

In the 4th century B.C. Alexander the Great of Macedon brought all the Near East under his rule. After he died, his lands were divided among his generals. By the early centuries A.D. the lands along the Mediterranean were ruled by Rome, while those east of the Euphrates were controlled by an Iranian tribe, the Parthians.

In the 3rd century A.D. the Parthians were overthrown by another Iranian people, the Sassanians. They built up an empire which by the 7th century stretched from Afghanistan to the Mediterranean. Hardly had they conquered Egypt when the Muslims swept through the entire region, conquering it for the new faith of Islam.

CHRONOLOGY	
209	Sassanians under Ardashir build up an empire, defeating the Parthians overwhelmingly in 224
244	Shapur I defeats the Romans under Philip the Arab and later under Valerian
460	Hephthalite Huns control a large empire centered on Afghanistan (to 530)
531–579	Khusrau I re-establishes the Persian empire, gaining land from Byzantium, defeating Hephthalites, and making southern Arabia a dependency
571	Muhammad born in Mecca
612–620	Persians overrun Near East
622	Byzantines regain Anatolia and invade Mesopotamia (627). Khusrau II is murdered in a revolt
637	Muslim Arabs defeat Sassanians

Ruins of Khusrau I's palace at Ctesiphon, the most famous of all Sassanian buildings. The great arch is nearly 35 meters (115 feet) high and 50 meters (165 feet) long.

The Sassanians

The Sassanians came to power in the 3rd century A.D. They soon came into conflict with the Romans to the west. They defeated them on a number of occasions, and great reliefs carved in the rocks tell the stories of their triumphs. Roman prisoners were settled all through the empire and used for cheap and often highly skilled labor. The ruins of the bridges they built can still be seen today. Conflict in the west continued in the time of the Byzantine empire there.

During the late 4th and 5th centuries the Near East, like other areas, was devastated by the invasions of the Huns. Some of them, known as Hephthalites, settled in Bactria in the northeast and built up an empire there. Here too the Sassanians had to fight frequent wars.

The peninsula of Arabia was the home of Bedouin tribes, who then as now lived in tents and moved around with their flocks in search of grazing. Arabia also had trading, manufacturing, and fishing towns, and crops were grown in the big oases.

TRADE

Through the Near East ran the great overland trade routes which linked the Western world with India and China. The Parthians made trading contacts with Rome on the one hand, and China on the other. Silks and precious stones, spices and scent flooded through the area, in return for Roman gold, and the Parthians grew rich as middlemen. Caravans started at Antioch in Syria and crossed the Euphrates at Zeugma. Then they went over the Zagros Mountains to Ecbatana and east to Samarkand, Fergana, and onward to China. Other goods were carried by sea, sailing from India into the Gulf.

The sea routes for trade became important when the Huns were devastating Central Asia. The Sassanians extended their rule all along the north coast of the Indian Ocean, from the Gulf east to the delta of the Indus Valley. They prevented ships from other countries from buying direct from Indian merchants. When Arab traders tried to break the Sassanians' monopoly, Khusrau made southern Arabia a dependency, based ships in Aden and controlled the entrance to the Red Sea.

Part of a relief carving at Taq-i-Bustan. It shows Khusrau II standing in a boat and shooting at a great boar.

A 15th-century illustration to the story of Khusrau II and Queen Shirin, a favorite of Persian poets.

LUXURIOUS LIVING

The Sassanians loved luxury and good living. Cities like those at Bishapur and Ctesiphon had palaces decorated with sculptures, their walls painted or covered with glass mosaics. Floors too were decorated with mosaics or covered with silk carpets patterned like gardens. Vessels of gold and silver were skillfully decorated. The Sassanians loved jewelry, and Khusrau I wore clothes embroidered with gold thread. His enormous crown, made of gold and silver and decorated with precious stones, seems to have been so heavy that it had to be hung on a chain from the roof over the throne.

This Sassanian dish of gilded silver dates from the 7th or 8th century. Its decoration shows the mythical senmurw, part dog and part bird.

Khusrau

In 531 Khusrau I became ruler of the Sassanians. Their empire was impoverished by wars, famine, and a heavy tribute paid each year to the Hephthalite Huns to the northeast. Khusrau made peace with the Byzantines to the west and kept up the tribute payments. He set about bringing prosperity to his country. The land was surveyed in such detail that every fruit and olive tree was counted. Then an annual tax was set, to be paid in money and not in kind. Great irrigation works were carried out to bring more land into use, and when villagers had no seed to sow the state provided it. Khusrau was also remembered for his justice.

Some of the tax money was spent in building up a strong army and strengthening the borders. In 540 Khusrau was ready to strike. He invaded Syria and captured Antioch, where he found large amounts of gold and silver. He joined forces with nomad Turks to defeat the Hephthalites, and added much of Afghanistan to his empire.

Khusrau's grandson, Khusrau II, extended the empire in the west. His armies overran the Near East, capturing Syria, Palestine, and all Egypt. Meanwhile, however, a new threat was growing from an unexpected direction. The Arabs, converted to Islam (see page 73), were seeking to spread their faith by conquering and converting the countries nearest to them. In an amazingly short time all the Near East was under their control. But they took up many of the good things in Sassanian life, to become part of the civilization of Islam.

The Franks

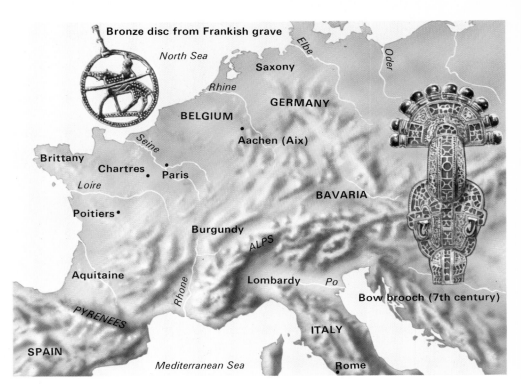

Bronze disc from Frankish grave

North Sea
Saxony
Elbe
Oder
Rhine
GERMANY
BELGIUM
Aachen (Aix)
Brittany
Seine
Chartres
Paris
Loire
BAVARIA
Poitiers
Burgundy
ALPS
Aquitaine
Rhone
Lombardy
Po
Bow brooch (7th century)
PYRENEES
ITALY
SPAIN
Mediterranean Sea
Rome

The kingdom of the West Franks was the greater part of modern France, a large country with a coastline which faces the Mediterranean in the south and the Atlantic in the north. High mountains separate the country from Spain and Italy, but the north is open to the Netherlands and Germany. Northern invaders can advance without much difficulty. In the Middle Ages, the north was rich in corn and dairy products, and olive oil and wine were the special produce of the south. Barley was a common crop, used to make porridge, beer, and bread. Beans, peas, and lentils were widely grown, providing the bulk of the peasant's diet, as meat was rarely eaten. Bees were kept for honey (the only sweetener) and this was sometimes used to make an alcoholic drink called mead, a kind of strong wine. Beer and wine were made according to the region. France has wide rivers and fish were plentiful. During the winter dried fish was an important food. The rivers were much used for transport and strings of barges were in use quite early on in the Frankish period.

The First Franks
Under the Romans, France had been known as Gaul. It was a settled and prosperous region. There were a number of large estates and thriving trading towns; many people had become Christian and bishoprics were set up. Toward the end of the Roman period, administration broke down (see page 60). Bands of robbers, often slaves in revolt, terrorized large areas. Tribes of "barbarians" from east of the Rhine moved into Gaul and settled there.

Early in the 5th century a small tribe from western Germany crossed the Rhine into Gaul. They were called the Franks. By the end of the 5th century two Frankish kings, Childeric and his son Clovis, had gained control over much of modern France and West Germany. King Clovis became a Christian, which gained him the support of the many Christians in Gaul. He was also recognized as king by the Byzantine emperor Anastasius. When he died in 511, Clovis's sons succeeded him. They are known as the Merovings. They brought still more of western Europe under their direct control.

Charlemagne was revered as the defender of Christianity, and many legends grew up about him. Some are illustrated in this 13th-century window at Chartres. He was canonized as a saint in the 12th century.

Right: A gold coin of Charlemagne's time.

The Emperor Charlemagne
The greatest of all the Frankish kings was Charlemagne, whose father, Pepin, seized the throne from the Merovings. Charlemagne was a large, strong man, who was tough and brave. His name means "Charles the Great." He was fond of swimming and hunting, but he encouraged learning, and built himself a palace at Aachen (Aix) in Germany where Byzantine art and architecture were copied.

Charlemagne came to the throne in 768, and spent almost all of his reign at war. At first he fought against his Christian neighbors, bringing the people of Aquitaine, Brittany, and Burgundy firmly under his control. At the pope's request, he subdued the Lombards of northern Italy and was crowned their king. To the east he fought savage wars against the heathen Saxons and the Avars who lived on the Hungarian plains. He defeated them with appalling cruelty and forcibly converted them to Christianity. To the southwest, he successfully stopped the Muslims from coming north of the Pyrennees. Charlemagne was looked on as the protector of Christian Europe, and in 800 the grateful pope crowned him Roman emperor.

THE EARLY MONASTERIES

In the middle of the 6th century St. Benedict of Nursia drew up a new rule, or scheme of organization, for monasteries. In time many monasteries followed it. They became better organized and the old jumble of churches and huts was replaced by well laid out cloisters, dormitories, *refectories* (where the monks ate), kitchens, and *scriptoria* (writing rooms). Nearby were the workshops and farm buildings, and the monks farmed the land around. The rule said that the monks should provide all they needed from the monastery and its lands.

Monasticism, or the coming together of men (and of women in a nunnery), was very important in the Middle Ages, Monasteries acted as inns and hospitals, they cared for the poor, they had almost the only libraries, and until the universities began to grow in the 12th century they and the cathedrals were the main centers of learning.

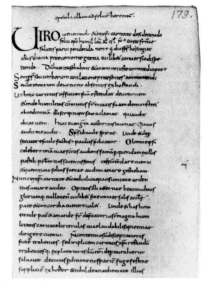

Part of a letter written by Alcuin of York. He was one of many scholars whom Charlemagne invited to his court. Alcuin helped to develop a new kind of small letter, known as the Carolingian minuscule.
Right: A 9th-century bronze statue of Charlemagne on his horse.
Below: The 11th-century monastery of St. Andrew at Chartres.

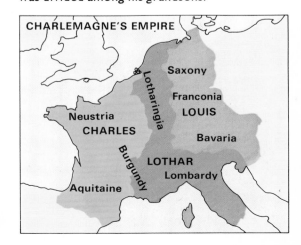

CHRONOLOGY

c.350	Romans allow Frankish tribes to cross the Rhine and settle in parts of Belgium
481	Death of Childeric the Frank, who has built up a kingdom in Belgium. He is succeeded by his son Clovis
481	Clovis extends the Frankish kingdom over much of modern France (to 511) and is converted to Christianity
561	Civil wars break out between branches of the Frankish royal family
629	Dagobert I reunites the Frankish kingdom (to 639)
732	Franks under Charles Martel defeat Moors at battle of Poitiers
751	Pepin the Short, son of Charles Martel, is crowned king of the Franks
756	Pepin leads an army to protect Pope Stephen III from the Lombards
768	Charlemagne, son of Pepin, king of the Franks (to 814); forces neighbors to accept his overlordship, annexes Lombardy, subdues and converts the heathen Saxons and Avars, and harries Muslims in northern Spain. In 800 he is crowned Roman emperor in the West
843	Charlemagne's empire is divided among his three grandsons

DIVIDING THE EMPIRE

By Frankish custom, a man's property was divided among his sons. When Charlemagne died his only living son, Louis the Pious, inherited all his lands. When Louis died, however, he had three living sons, Lothar, Louis, and Charles. They were already fighting over their shares of his land. In 843 they reached a settlement. Charles took West Francia, or France. Louis took Franconia, Saxony, Bavaria, and the rest of Charlemagne's empire east of the Rhine. Between their lands lay the rich Middle Kingdom. This, and the title of emperor, went to the eldest son, Lothar. It included Charlemagne's lands in Italy and his capital at Aachen (Aix).

When Lothar died, his lands were again divided. The Frankish lands in Italy and the title of emperor eventually went, with the pope's support, to a German king. The rest of the Middle Kingdom had no natural boundaries. Kings of France to the west and Germany to the east tried to take over these lands and towns by gaining the loyalty of the great nobles and churchmen who ruled them.

This map shows how Charlemagne's empire was divided among his grandsons.

CHARLEMAGNE'S EMPIRE

Saxony
Franconia
LOUIS
Neustria
CHARLES
Bavaria
Lotharingia
Burgundy
LOTHAR
Lombardy
Aquitaine

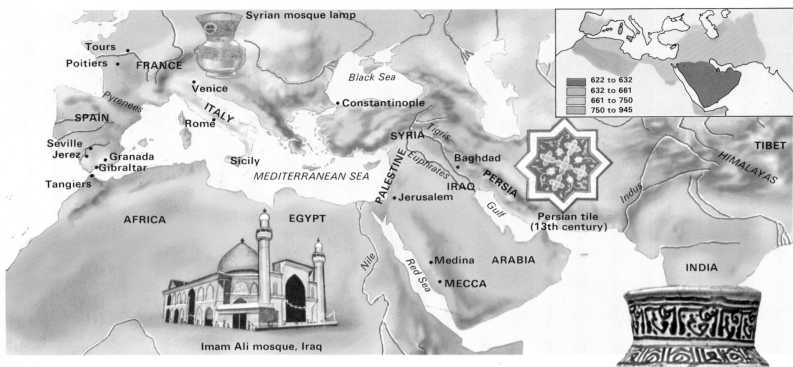

Syrian mosque lamp

Tours • • Poitiers • FRANCE

Venice •

Black Sea

• Constantinople

SPAIN
Seville • • Jerez
• Granada
• Gibraltar
Tangiers •

ITALY
Rome •

Sicily

MEDITERRANEAN SEA

SYRIA
PALESTINE
Euphrates
Tigris
Baghdad •
IRAQ
• Jerusalem
PERSIA
Gulf

Persian tile
(13th century)

TIBET

HIMALAYAS

Indus

AFRICA

EGYPT

Nile
Red Sea

• Medina   ARABIA
• MECCA

INDIA

Imam Ali mosque, Iraq

622 to 632
632 to 661
661 to 750
750 to 945

The Spread of Islam

In the 7th century A.D. a new religion was founded in Arabia. It was known as *Islam*, which meant "submission to the Will of Allah (God)." Its followers were called *Muslims*. They wanted to spread their faith as widely as possible and within less than a hundred years they ruled an empire which stretched from Spain east to the borders of India.

Over the centuries the Muslims gained more and more land from the Byzantine empire. They threatened Christian Europe a number of times. In France

Charles Martel defeated them near Poitiers in 732; his grandson Charlemagne fought them in the Pyrenees and, at sea, in the Mediterranean. For a time they controlled Sicily and even raided the suburbs of Rome in 846. From the 11th to the 13th centuries the Christians mounted Crusades to gain control of the Holy Land from them, but eventually they were unsuccessful. In the year 1453, the Muslim Ottoman Turks finally captured the last lands held by the Byzantine empire.

This drug jar, made in Spain in the 15th century, is decorated with Arabic writing. Muslims ruled much of Spain from the 8th to the 15th centuries.

A tribal battle among Arabs. They were skilled fighters, specializing in surprise attacks from the desert. Then they would retreat into it, knowing few enemies could follow them there.

THE PROPHET MUHAMMAD

Muhammad, the founder of Islam, came from Mecca in Arabia. It was then a trading town surrounded by desert, in which lived Bedouin tribes who moved from oasis to oasis with their flocks and herds.

Muhammad was born in A.D. 571. Muslims believe that when he was about 40 the angel Gabriel appeared to him as the messenger of Allah (God). Little by little he dictated to Muhammad Allah's commands, guidance for everyday life, warnings about hell and promises about paradise. Muhammad learned them by heart and repeated them to his followers. Later they were collected into a single book, the *Koran*. The language of the Koran is Arabic.

When Muhammad first preached Allah's message in Mecca, many people did not believe it. In 622 he went to Medina, another Arabian town. His journey is known as the Flight, or *Hijra*. Muslims saw it as the start of a new age and count their years from it. So 622 is the Muslim year 1. Muhammad gained many followers and his power grew. In 630 he went back to Mecca, this time as its ruler. In 632 (the Muslim year 11) he died, but his message lived and was spread by his followers.

Spreading the Faith

When Muhammad, the prophet, died in 632 a great period of conquest began. Muslim warriors on horses and camels moved north to attack the Byzantine empire. Within ten years of the prophet's death Syria, Palestine, and Egypt were in Arab hands. The Muslims moved westward through North Africa, and eastward to conquer Iraq, Persia, and Afghanistan. As they went, they spread their faith. Often the local people welcomed them, for the rule of the Byzantine Christians had been very unpopular. Millions of people became Muslims, until they far outnumbered the Arabs. Many Christians and Jews were not willing to be converted. Muslim rulers usually left them in peace.

The first *caliphs*, or rulers, were all Arabs. Later, power passed to the Turks. They were originally nomads who had moved into Islamic areas from Central Asia, been converted, and risen to immense power. Their story is told on page 108.

TRADE

The Islamic empire made trading in the Near East much easier and less dangerous than it had been in earlier times. Goods could be carried throughout the whole vast empire without ever crossing a single hostile border. A single kind of gold coin, the *dinar*, was used all through the empire.

Many goods were carried by sea. The Muslims imported wood from India and from Venice in exchange for gold which they got from West Africa, Arabia, eastern Europe, and even Tibet. Other goods were carried overland by camels, donkeys, mules, or horses roped together in small processions called *caravans*.

Products such as glass and cloth from Syria were spread through Islamic lands. So was sugar, grown first in Iraq and then in Egypt. Spices were a very profitable trade. Cloves, peppercorns, ginger, and other spices from the Far East were brought to Tibet by Chinese merchants. There they traded them with the Arabs.

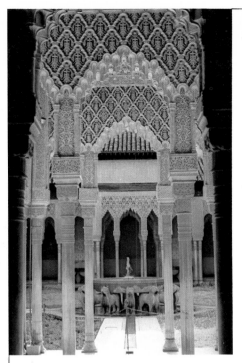

The Court of the Lions in the palace of the Alhambra at Granada in Spain. It was the last Muslim stronghold in Spain.

THE ARABS IN SPAIN

In 711 the second period of Islamic conquest began when Muslims crossed into Spain. They were led by the governor of Tangier. His name was Tarik and the huge rock at the southern tip of Spain was named Jebel al Tarik after him. We know it as Gibraltar. Soon much of Spain and Portugal was in Arab hands. They were prevented from conquering France by Charles Martel in 732.

Muslim farmers who knew about irrigation were able to cultivate vast new areas of Spain. For the first time, bananas, oranges, cotton, rice, and sugar cane could be grown there. Vines from Persia were planted at Jerez de la Frontera, which gave its name to the *sherry* made from their grapes. Enough food was grown to provide for a large population.

Bit by bit, Muslim Spain was conquered by Christians from the north. The last Muslims were driven from Granada in 1492.

This picture, painted in Baghdad in 1237, shows travelers arriving in a village.

CHRONOLOGY

571	Muhammad is born in Mecca
610	Muhammad has his first revelation
622	Muhammad moves to Medina (the Hijra)
630	Muhammad returns to Mecca
632	Death of Muhammad
633	Muslims conquer Syria, Iraq, Egypt, and Persia (to 640)
711	Muslims invade Spain and the Indus Valley
732	Muslims are defeated by the Franks at Poitiers
762	Baghdad becomes the Muslim capital
1055	Muslim Seljuk Turks seize Baghdad
1096	The First Crusade

The World in 800

Most of western Europe is now ruled by the Frankish king, Charlemagne, who is crowned emperor by the pope in 800. To the north, the Vikings raid and colonize. In the Near East the Muslims gain lands from the Byzantine empire, and spread their rule to the borders of India. Hindu civilization expands outside India, and China becomes increasingly rich through trade. In the Americas, the Toltecs build an empire in Mexico and farther south the Mayan civilization is at its height.

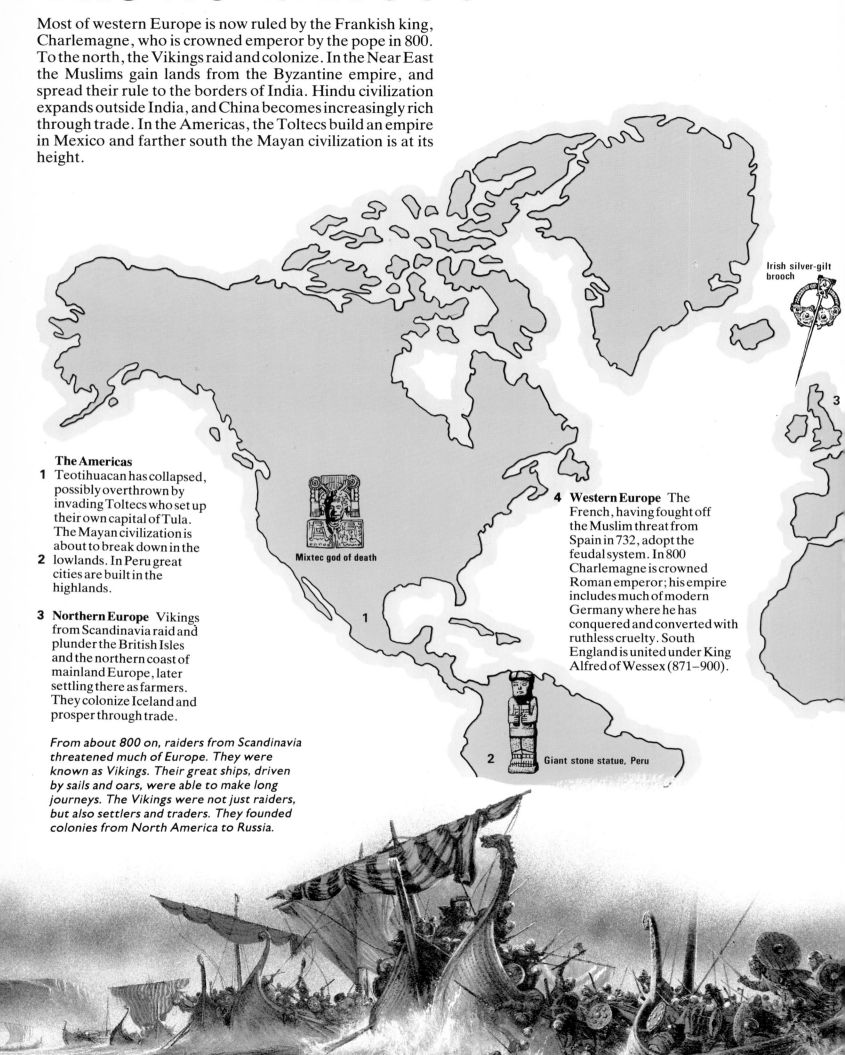

Irish silver-gilt brooch

The Americas

1 Teotihuacan has collapsed, possibly overthrown by invading Toltecs who set up their own capital of Tula. The Mayan civilization is about to break down in the

2 lowlands. In Peru great cities are built in the highlands.

3 **Northern Europe** Vikings from Scandinavia raid and plunder the British Isles and the northern coast of mainland Europe, later settling there as farmers. They colonize Iceland and prosper through trade.

From about 800 on, raiders from Scandinavia threatened much of Europe. They were known as Vikings. Their great ships, driven by sails and oars, were able to make long journeys. The Vikings were not just raiders, but also settlers and traders. They founded colonies from North America to Russia.

Mixtec god of death

4 **Western Europe** The French, having fought off the Muslim threat from Spain in 732, adopt the feudal system. In 800 Charlemagne is crowned Roman emperor; his empire includes much of modern Germany where he has conquered and converted with ruthless cruelty. South England is united under King Alfred of Wessex (871–900).

2 Giant stone statue, Peru

Pottery horse, China

This whalebone casket was made in Northumberland in the 8th century. It is carved with runes (the Scandinavian writing), and scenes including the Adoration of the Magi, shown here.

Bronze statue of Charlemagne

Buddhist statue, Japan

6 Eastern Europe In Russia the first states are founded at Kiev and Novgorod where the Vikings set up trading colonies. The Slav states of central Europe come under Charlemagne's control. At about this time Magyars from Russia move into the Hungarian plains.

Stone sculpture, Cambodia

Bronze cylinder. West Africa

11 The Far East China has broken up into small kingdoms, following rebellion against the T'ang ruler in 755. Woodblock printing develops in about **12** 858. Japanese society is modeled on that of China.

7 The Byzantine Empire is split by religious quarrels and has lost its lands in the Near East and North Africa.

8 Islam The Islamic empire now stretches from Spain and Portugal in the west, through North Africa and the Near East, to the borders of India. Its lands are given a common way of life and a common language (Arabic).

9 India In the north Islamic invaders are a constant threat. Under the Chola dynasty of the south **10** Hinduism is taken to Burma and Sumatra.

5 Africa The states just south of the Sahara grow rich through trade. On the east coast Muslims build trading ports.

A T'ang dynasty pottery figure of a Bactrian camel, laden with Chinese goods for trading abroad.

The Vikings

BAFFIN IS.

GREENLAND

Silver coin (9th century)

ICELAND

ATLANTIC OCEAN

NORWAY

SWEDEN

Baltic Sea

Novgorod

Oak carving for ceremonial wagon

Volga

North Sea

DENMARK

RUSSIA

BRITAIN

York

Dublin

London

Rouen

Paris

FRANCE

Alps

SPAIN

Rome

Seville

MEDITERRANEAN SEA

CARPATHIANS

Dnieper

Kiev

Black Sea

Constantinople

Prow of Viking longboat

From the late 8th to the 11th centuries the people of northern Europe were terrified by raiders from the sea. They called them by different names. To the Anglo-Saxons they were "Northmen" and Danes. The Germans called them *arcomanni*, the ship-men, and the Arabs of Spain called them the heathen, *el-Majus*. Now we call them the Vikings.

The Vikings came from Scandinavia – what is now Norway, Sweden, and Denmark. In those days they all spoke the same language and they moved freely from one region to another. Men from all over Scandinavia would join the warband of a chief who was known to be generous to his men. Scandinavians who went raiding were known as Vikings. We do not know just what this word means. It might have meant a man from a camp, or *wic*, or a man from a creek or *vik*. Perhaps it came from the word *vikja* which meant to go fast, or leave home.

The Vikings probably left their homes in search of farmland. Much of Scandinavia is mountainous or heavily forested, and only a tiny percentage of the land in Norway and Sweden could be farmed. Denmark provided better land where crops could be grown, as well as grazing land. Eventually there was not enough land to grow food for the increasing population, so many Scandinavians sailed away to set up colonies in Iceland, Greenland, and eastward in Russia.

Others raided and looted the coasts of France and the British Isles. Here too many of them settled, buying land, marrying local women, and turning from raiders to farmers.

In this Norwegian fjord, as in many others, the mountains drop sharply into the water. The only farmland lies at one end. The lack of land for growing food was one reason for the Vikings' raids and settlements.

CHRONOLOGY

789	First Viking attacks on England
830s	Vikings found Dublin
834	Vikings raid Netherlands
850	Swedes begin to settle in East Baltic and Russia
860	Discovery of Iceland; Norwegians settle in British Isles
886	Danes allowed to settle in eastern England
911	Vikings settle in Normandy
986	Eirik the Red founds colony in Greenland
1003	Leif Eiriksson lands in North America
1066	Duke William of Normandy kills King Harold of England and becomes King William I of England

Raiders and Farmers

The first Viking raids on England came at the very end of the 8th century. Their ships appeared without warning. A large raiding band might have 400 men though they usually came in small bands of 60 or so. They demanded money and valuable goods from monasteries and towns, and if they did not get them they looted and plundered. Most accounts of Viking raids come from Christian monks who were appalled by their actions, especially because monasteries were holy places and were usually left unharmed.

The Vikings were not just raiders. They used some of their plunder to buy land. Vikings from Norway settled in the Scottish islands, around York in northeast England, and in Ireland. The Danes were allowed to settle in eastern England and London, where their settlement had a Danish name, the Strand. King Alfred of Wessex stopped them spreading southwestward.

The Vikings first visited mainland Europe as traders. But from the mid-9th century on they rowed up the great rivers to attack towns including Rouen and Paris. They were given huge amounts of silver to leave the towns in peace. In 911 the Viking chief Rollo was allowed to settle with his followers in what is now Normandy.

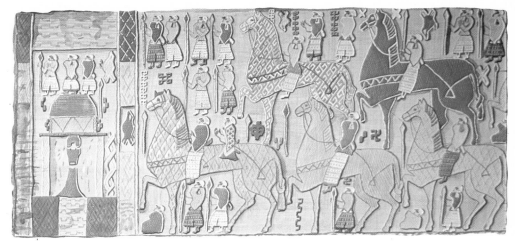

Part of a reconstruction of a tapestry found on the Oseberg ship, in which a Viking queen was buried in the 9th century.

TRADERS WITH THE EAST

While Danes and Norwegians explored western Europe, Swedes made their way along the great rivers to the east. They used small boats which could be carried overland from one river to another, which meant that they could travel eastward down the river Volga to Bulghar and down the Dnieper to the Black Sea and Constantinople. They met traders from the Near East and from distant China. The Swedes set up two large colonies at Novgorod and Kiev. They were known as the *Rus*, from which comes our word Russia. They collected furs, amber, tar, wax, and slaves which they exchanged for luxuries including amethysts from Arabia, glass from Persia and Syria, spices from India, and silk cloth from China.

NEW LANDS IN THE WEST

The search for new farmlands took the Vikings on long voyages. Iceland was discovered some time before 900 and farming settlements grew up there. Families from Norway set off with their possessions and animals, including horses, sheep, and goats. They traveled in open boats. The direct journey to Iceland took at least seven days with a good wind. It might take much longer if conditions were poor. Despite its name, Iceland is not terribly cold, and around the coasts the settlers found good grazing for their cattle. Sheep could graze on the poorer uplands. A little barley was grown. Fish and seabirds' eggs added to the food supply. The Iceland colonies did well. They set up their own national assembly, the *Althing*. Life there was less difficult than at home in Norway.

In 986 Eirik the Red founded a colony in Greenland. In spite of its name, much of this vast island is covered with ice, but the settlers could graze their cattle and there were many animals, among them foxes, seals, and caribou, which could be hunted for fur and meat. The settlers traded furs and hides, falcons and animal oil for the corn, iron, and timber they needed.

More timber came from North America. In 1001 Eirik the Red's son Leif set out to find some lands to the west of Greenland which had been seen by sailors lost in fog. He found a rocky coast, perhaps part of Baffin Island. He landed there and then sailed south to what sounds like Labrador, which he named *Markland* or Wood Land, after its forests. He and his crew spent the winter in what may have been Newfoundland, which he called *Vinland* or Pasture Land. Poems and stories called *sagas* tell how the Vikings explored the North American coast, sailing perhaps as far south as Florida.

The Vikings never successfully colonized North America, although traders from Greenland went there for furs and timber until the mid-14th century. For the Greenland settlement was itself a failure. It was too far from Norway, on which the settlers depended for supplies. As the climate got colder and pack ice started to close the harbors, Eskimos attacked the settlers. Those who did not die abandoned the island.

This carving shows the legendary hero Sigurd killing the dragon Fafnir. Stories and poems about gods and heroes were learned by heart and handed down from one generation of storytellers to the next.

The Feudal Age

In the mid-8th century rulers like the Frank Charles Martel gave huge grants of land he owned or conquered to armed horsemen. In return, they swore an oath to fight for him when he asked them to. From this developed a whole system of government and way of life, based on land given and received in return for service and protection. It is known as the feudal system, because land given in this way was called a fief, or *feudum* in Latin.

Under the feudal system, the king granted land to great lords or tenants-in-chief. They in turn gave much of this land to tenants called knights, who would fight for them in return. When he was given his land the tenant (or vassal as he was called) swore an oath of loyalty to his lord. Below the knights came minor lords, farmers, and peasants. All received land and a great lord's protection, which was important in the early days when local fights or wars between great lords were quite common. In return they all provided services for their lords, whether by working on the land or by fighting for him.

In France and England the feudal system dominated life in the Middle Ages. It was never so important in Germany, but it spread eastward to central and eastern Europe and there it lasted well into the 19th century.

In the Middle Ages great lords lived in castles. In times of war peasants from the surrounding countryside would come with their animals to shelter inside the castle's strong outer walls. Attackers would try many different ways to break into the castle. Great siege towers were wheeled up to the walls from which armed men could jump to the ramparts. Catapults hurled stones at the walls, and teams of men drove battering rams against them. The defenders shot arrows at the attackers, and dropped boiling oil and stones on to them. Often the attackers found they could not breach the walls, and then they camped around the castle, hoping the people inside would surrender for lack of food before help came.

CHRONOLOGY

1000s	Dikes and canals increase farmland in Flanders; forest is cleared in the Rhineland
1066	William of Normandy, king of England
1086	*Domesday Book* survey of England
1096	First Crusade
1154	Henry II, king of England; marries Eleanor of Aquitaine in France. He begins to give England a central government and a system of law
1180	Philip Augustus, king of France (to 1223); forces neighbors to acknowledge his overlordship
1205	King John of England has lost most of England's possessions in France
1215	Barons force John to seal Magna Carta limiting his rights over them
1226	Louis IX, king of France (to 1270); growth of French *parlement*
1265	Simon de Montfort summons English Parliament
1295	First truly representative English Parliament called by King Edward I
1316	Great famine in Europe, also in 1317
1337	Hundred Years' War (to 1453) between France and England
1346	English defeat French at Crécy
1348	The Black Death ravages Europe
1415	English defeat French at Agincourt
1429	Jeanne d'Arc raises English siege of Orléans; in 1431 she is burned as a relapsed heretic

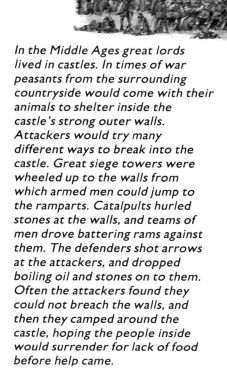

LIFE ON THE LAND

At the bottom of the feudal "pyramid" were the villeins, peasants who were tied to the place in which they were born. They were given strips of land in the village common fields, and in return they spent some time working on the lord's own fields. They might also have to pay the lord a sum of money each year, and give him some of their produce, such as corn, eggs, a lamb, and beeswax from their hives. They had to pay the lord a fee for having their corn ground in the lord's own mill.

The villagers' land was usually scattered in strips in the fields round the village, so that each villager had a share of good and bad land. Each field of many strips produced a crop such as wheat or barley, rye, oats, and some peas and beans, and every third year each field was left fallow (unplanted) so that the soil would recover its goodness. It was grazed by the villagers' sheep and pigs. Pigs could feed in the forest around, for in the Middle Ages there were far more forests than there are today.

FOOD

Ordinary peasants lived on coarse bread made from barley or rye flour, eggs, cheese, and milk, and on fruit and vegetables grown in their gardens. Sometimes they ate a chicken or a pig. Many trapped game, rabbits, and birds although this was against the law. Nobles ate much better food. Their bread was made from wheat flour, and they ate elaborate pastries with fruit soaked in honey. Meat was tough, and dishes were highly flavored with spices such as pepper, mustard, and garlic. Most of the cattle had to be killed in the autumn or they would starve in the winter, and the meat was salted or pickled. In Lent, no one was allowed to eat meat, and fish were an important part of the diet.

This picture comes from a 15th-century book called Les Très Riches Heures du duc de Berry. *The duke was a brother of King Charles V of France, and a great landowner. This picture shows work on the land in March.*

England and France

Under the feudal system large landowners could become more powerful than the king who was their overlord. When Duke William of Normandy conquered England in 1066 he claimed all its land as his own. He tried to stop his main tenants-in-chief from gaining too much power by giving each of them land in several different regions. Even so, almost every English king had to deal with rebellious barons, as these great lords were known. Edward I (1272–1307) managed to set up a firm central government. He ruled with the help of a Parliament in which were knights and townsmen called burgesses, as well as the barons. The towns were outside the feudal system, and their burgesses were often opposed to the power of the great lords.

For a long time the king of France was almost powerless. In theory he was the overlord of several great dukes, among them the dukes of Normandy, Burgundy, and Aquitaine. In practise the king only controlled his personal lands, a relatively small area between Paris and Orleans. If the dukes refused to take their oath of loyalty to him, he could not force them to do so. After 1100 the French kings began to build up a system of government. They employed paid officials from the *bourgeoisie*, the townspeople who as in England were outside the feudal system. King Philip Augustus (1180–1223) used the fortune built up by efficient government to hire soldiers. He gained control of Normandy, Anjou, and Maine from King John of England, and strengthened his power over other great vassals (tenants). From then on the French king was a true power in the land.

THE BLACK DEATH

The worst and most famous outbreak of disease in the Middle Ages is known as the Black Death. The disease was bubonic plague, and it was spread by fleas from the black rats which often lived on ships. Almost everyone who caught the plague died from it.

In 1348 rats on ships from the East brought the plague to Europe. All countries were affected by it and probably over a third of the people in Europe died. Whole communities were wiped out, houses lay empty and derelict, and fields were overgrown.

The weather in Europe seems to have got worse in the 14th century. Winters lasted longer and summers were cold and wet. There were great famines when crops failed and animals died. When the Black Death struck, many people were too weak to resist it.

The results of the Black Death were felt at once. Food became dearer because fewer people were working on the land. Peasants began to demand freedom from the feudal system and better wages. Revolts by peasants broke out all over Europe, helping to hasten the end of feudal society.

One of the greatest vassals of the French king was the king of England. When Duke William of Normandy conquered England in 1066 he kept his lands in France. Marriages brought more French land to the English kings until they controlled far more of France than the French kings. There were many wars between the two countries. They culminated in the Hundred Years' War which lasted (with lulls in the fighting) from 1337 to 1453. At first England gained great victories, but just when it looked as though France could never recover the peasant girl Jeanne d'Arc (Joan of Arc) brought new heart to the French. By 1453 the English had lost almost all their lands in France.

The World in 1000

By now most of northwestern Europe has developed the feudal system of land granted in return for service. The church plays a very important part in everyday life, and there are conflicts between popes and Holy Roman emperors who resent church power and interference. In 1095 Pope Urban calls for the First Crusade against the Muslim rulers of the Holy Land. In the Islamic world the Arabs are losing power to the Turks, and in Africa the empire of Ghana falls to the Muslims in 1075.

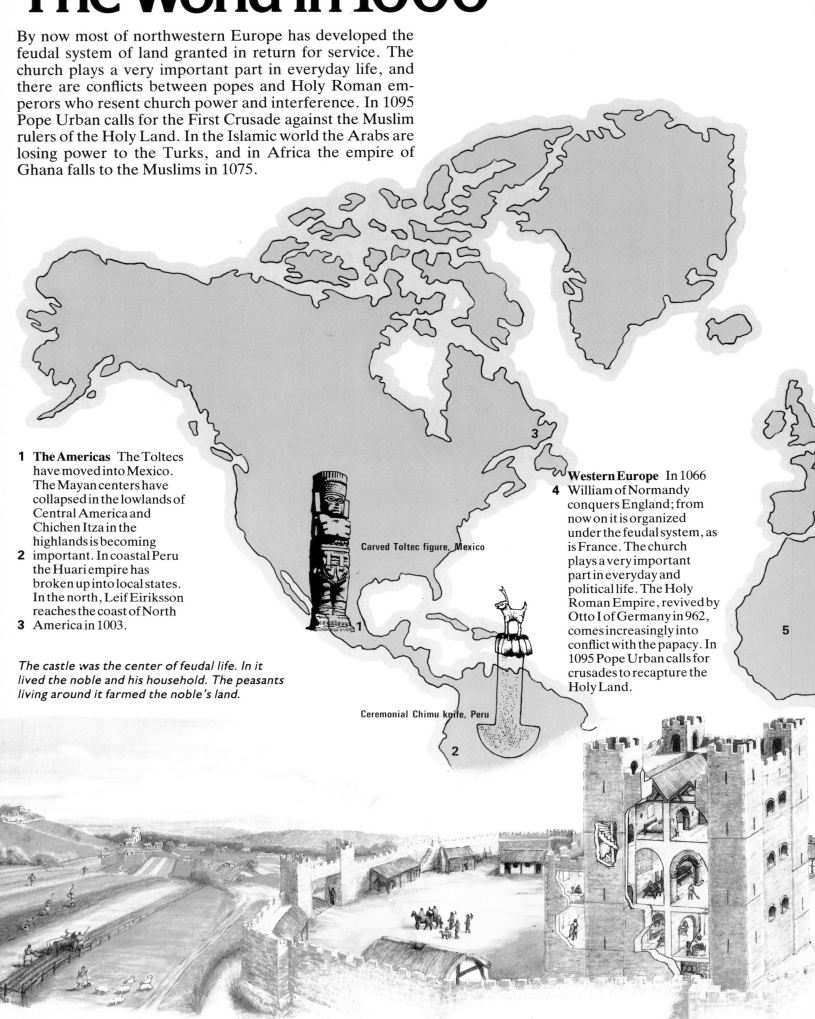

1 The Americas The Toltecs have moved into Mexico. The Mayan centers have collapsed in the lowlands of Central America and Chichen Itza in the highlands is becoming
2 important. In coastal Peru the Huari empire has broken up into local states. In the north, Leif Eiriksson reaches the coast of North
3 America in 1003.

The castle was the center of feudal life. In it lived the noble and his household. The peasants living around it farmed the noble's land.

Carved Toltec figure, Mexico

Ceremonial Chimu knife, Peru

Western Europe In 1066
4 William of Normandy conquers England; from now on it is organized under the feudal system, as is France. The church plays a very important part in everyday and political life. The Holy Roman Empire, revived by Otto I of Germany in 962, comes increasingly into conflict with the papacy. In 1095 Pope Urban calls for crusades to recapture the Holy Land.

The Abbey of Cluny in Burgundy, on the borders of France and Germany in the old Middle Kingdom. Founded in 910, the abbey followed the Benedictine rule. It was famous for the beauty of its services. A succession of strong abbots built up a great network of priories which obeyed the customs and example of Cluny.

6

Silver earring from Kiev, Russia

7

9

Near Eastern bronze mosque lamp

Bronze statue of Shiva, India

Ceramic bowl, China
10

Japanese pagoda

A carved ivory box from 10th-century Islamic Spain.

terracotta head, est Africa

12

11

6 Eastern Europe Vladimir of Kiev is converted to Byzantine Christianity in 988. Novgorod is now independent and Christian.
7 The Magyars have settled the Hungarian plains and St. Stephen centralizes government and introduces
8 Christianity. Slavs in the Vistula plain have founded the Polish nation and are converted to Christianity.

9 The Byzantine Empire In 1071 Anatolia (modern Turkey) falls to the Seljuk Turks, and the Byzantine lands in Italy and Sicily are taken by the Normans. Only Constantinople and lands in the Balkans remain in its possession.

10 Far East In 960 the Sung dynasty unifies China. Printing spreads and textiles and porcelain, iron, and steel are important
11 industries. In Cambodia Angkor Thom becomes the Khmer capital. Burma is united and Buddhism becomes its main religion.

5 Africa The kingdom of Ghana, south of the Sahara, is converted to Islam. In about 1100 building of Greater Zimbabwe begins.

12 India Northern India is attacked by Muslims from the west, who loot and destroy. In the south the Hindu Chola kingdom has grown and is also gaining power in Ceylon.

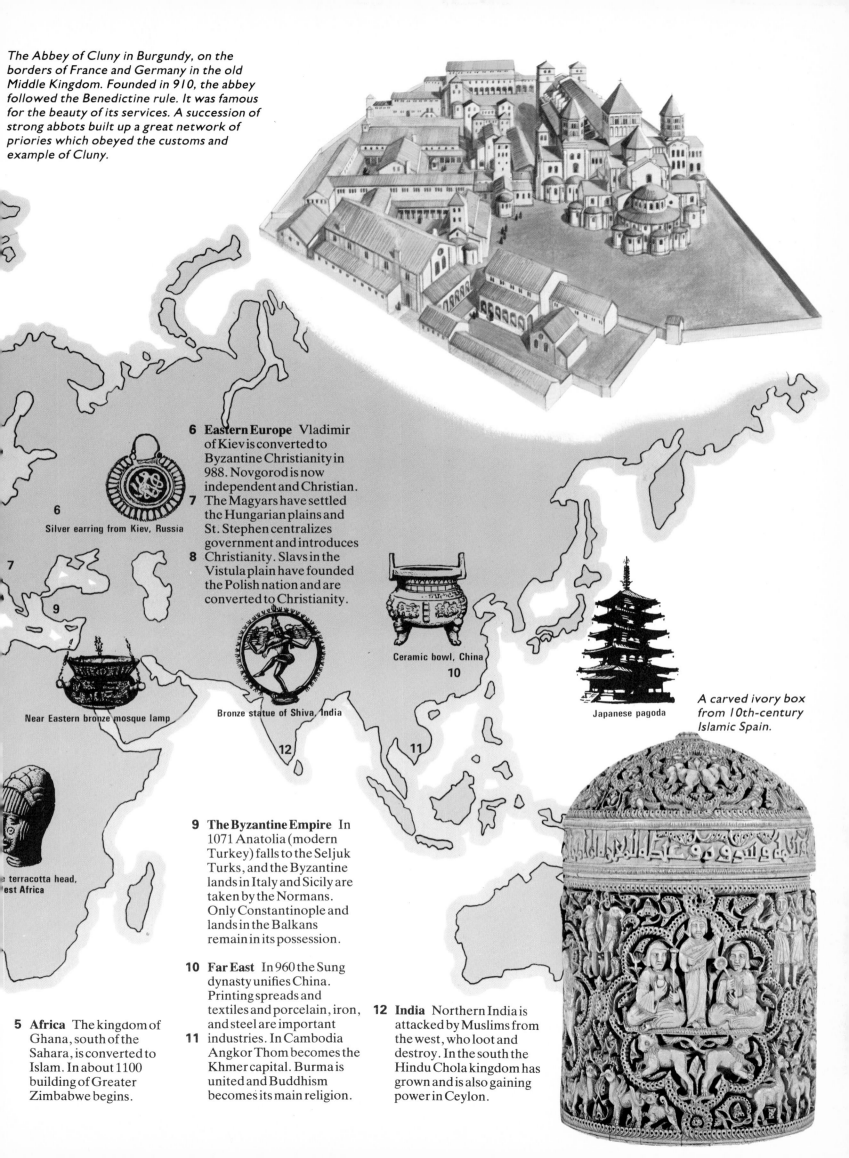

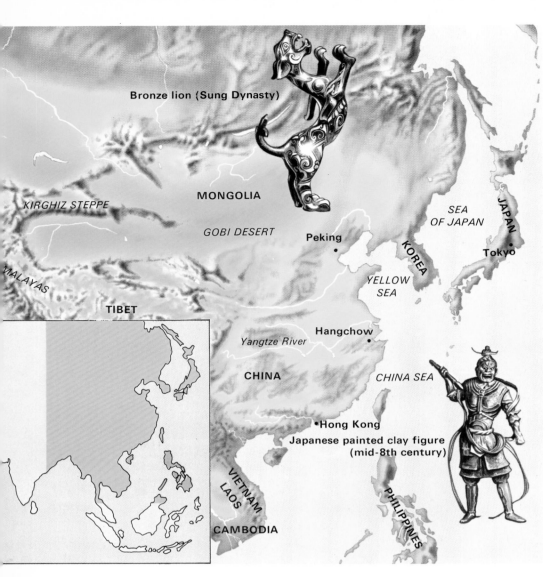

Bronze lion (Sung Dynasty)

KIRGHIZ STEPPE

MONGOLIA

GOBI DESERT

Peking

SEA OF JAPAN

JAPAN

Tokyo

KOREA

YELLOW SEA

TIBET

Hangchow

Yangtze River

CHINA

CHINA SEA

Hong Kong

Japanese painted clay figure (mid-8th century)

VIETNAM LAOS

PHILIPPINES

CAMBODIA

MALAYAS

This picture of the West Lake near the great city of Hangchow was painted in the 13th century. The lake was a famous beauty spot, and feasts and entertainments were held on the boats and in the island restaurants. At this time Hangchow was the largest and richest city in the world.

China and Japan

China is the third largest country in the world and takes up the major part of mainland East Asia. It includes every sort of country, from deserts in the west to lush tropical forests, and from high mountains to flat river plains. In the north wheat is generally the main crop, while in the wetter and warmer south rice is most important.

Off the coast of northern East Asia is the cluster of islands which forms Japan. These islands are very mountainous, and in some places winters are cold with plenty of snow. There are good harbors along the coasts and the Japanese are skilled fishermen. Inland, wheat and rice are grown on the plains of the larger islands and on terraces up the mountainsides.

Chinese civilization was well developed long before cities grew up in Japan. As a result of this, Chinese influence on Japanese ways of life has been very strong.

CHRONOLOGY	
552	Buddhism reaches Japan
618	T'ang dynasty in China (to 907)
624	Buddhism becomes established religion of Japan
645	All land in Japan comes under imperial control
751	Chinese armies in Central Asia are defeated by Arabs
907	End of T'ang dynasty is followed by civil war until 960. Mongols begin capture of parts of northern China
939	Civil wars begin in Japan
960	Sung dynasty in China (to 1279)
995	Japanese literary and artistic golden age (to 1028)
c.1000	Gunpowder perfected in China
1185	Kamakura period in Japan (to 1333)
1210	Mongols led by Genghis Khan invade China
1274	Mongols unsuccessfully attempt to invade Japan
1279	Sung dynasty falls to Mongols
1368	Yuan (Mongol) dynasty is overthrown; Ming dynasty (to 1644)
1421	Peking capital of China

The T'ang Dynasty

In A.D. 618 one of the greatest ages of Chinese history, art, and learning began. This was the start of the rule of the T'ang family, or dynasty, which lasted until about 900.

Everyday life in China at this time was still the same in many ways as it had been for centuries. Most of the people were farmers, living in small villages. During this period the population of China increased very much, and the taxes everyone paid brought large sums to the government. The cities grew rich and T'ang China became the greatest empire of its day. It was a splendid period for Chinese art. Porcelain making, painting, lacquer working, sculpting, and architecture all flourished. The old civil service entrance examinations were brought back at this time. All local officials were appointed by the central government, and were not simply the local aristocrats.

At this time the old religion of Taoism and the recently introduced Buddhism were both very important. Buddhist monasteries were centers of learning, and at the same time were used as public baths, inns, and even banks. Some of them had priceless collections of manuscripts, and the buildings themselves were decorated with wall paintings and sculptured figures.

The Sung Dynasty

The Sung dynasty was founded in 960 by a general called Chao K'uang-yin. He made China into a prosperous empire again. Habits, philosophies (ways of thought), and a general way of life became fixed in China during the Sung dynasty. They changed hardly at all from then until quite modern times. One great invention of the Sung period was the abacus, an ancient calculator that is still used today. At the same time the custom began of binding the feet of upper-class girls to stop them growing. These "lily feet," as they were called, crippled women for the rest of their lives.

Chao needed an enormous army of one and a quarter million men to protect his country against the barbarians in the north. This was a terrible drain on China's finances. In the end even this great army was no match for the invaders and in the 13th century all China was conquered by the Mongols.

A 6th-century Chinese pottery figure of an Armenian trader. He would have traveled along the Silk Road, the long caravan route that led from China, across Central Asia, to the Black Sea. From there Chinese goods were taken to Europe. Silk could be sold for a high price in the West because for a long time only the Chinese knew how to make it. It was the most valuable of all China's exports. Other important goods to come from China were porcelain, salt, tea, and spices. The Chinese usually employed middlemen to carry out their foreign trade.

The steep slopes of this Japanese island have been terraced so that food can be grown on them.

JAPAN

In the early centuries A.D. Japanese life was based on a clan system. Family groups called *uji* each had a chief, and a kind of totem god thought to be an ancestor. In the 5th century the Yamato uji became the most important clan in southern Japan. Its chiefs are thought to be the ancestors of the emperors of Japan. Government in Japan was modeled as closely as possible on that of the T'ang rulers in China. Styles of building and even court rituals came from China too.

In the Middle Ages at least half of Japan was public land. Wealthy land-owners owned the rest in large estates and a feudal system grew up. Warrior nobles called *bushi* and *samurai* became very powerful. They fought with bows and arrows and their magnificent curved swords were made of the finest steel in the world. The leader of one warrior family, who was given the title of *shogun*, became more important than the emperor. He and his successors paid great respect to the emperor but they held the power. They were able to fight off two great invasions by China and Korea in the 13th century.

The 15th century was a time of great luxury and extravagance at the Japanese court but it was also a time of terrible civil war. Great landowners and warrior clans devastated the countryside and peasants starved or became bandits. Bands of pirates raided along the coasts. Japan did not recover until the middle of the 16th century.

THE VOYAGES OF CHENG HO

Between 1405 and 1433 a Chinese explorer, Cheng Ho, made seven great voyages. Each expedition was very large; there were 62 ships on the first, carrying over 27,000 men. The largest ships were over 120 meters (400 feet) long, and 55 meters (180 feet) wide.

On each voyage the fleet called at Malacca on the Malay peninsula. Here traders from all over the East brought goods for exchange. Then the fleet split up. Some ships went to Java and Sumatra. Others went to Burma, India, Ceylon, and even westward to Hormuz on the Gulf. On his fifth voyage, which began in 1417, Cheng Ho reached Mogadisho on the east coast of Africa. Cheng Ho's ships carried Chinese porcelain, silks, gold and silver, iron, and copperware. These were traded for spices and ivory, precious stones, and dyes. But, unlike the Europeans later, the Chinese did not try to create colonies in India or Africa.

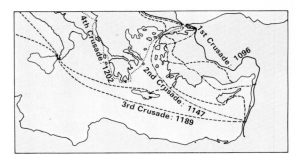

Above: The routes taken by crusaders on the first four Crusades.

The Crusades

During the Middle Ages many Christians went as pilgrims to Jerusalem and the other Bible lands (the Holy Land). They believed that by going on this dangerous journey they might be forgiven their sins. From the 7th century the Holy Land had been ruled by the Muslim Arabs, but they had generally not interfered with the pilgrims. Then, in 1071, the Turks conquered much of the area. They put many pilgrims to death, and robbed and tortured others. They moved north to threaten the Christian Byzantine empire.

In November 1095 Pope Urban II preached a sermon calling on faithful Christians to journey to the Holy Land on a holy war or *crusade* (from the Latin word for cross) against the Turks. He said:

> *... an accursed race, a race wholly alienated from God ... has violently invaded the lands of these Christians and has depopulated them by pillage and fire ... Accordingly undertake this journey for the remission [forgiveness] of your sins, with the assurance of the imperishable glory of the kingdom of heaven.*

Below: The siege of Jerusalem in 1099 lasted 40 days. When they finally captured the city, the crusaders massacred the Muslims who had defended it and the Jews who lived there.

The First Crusade

All over Europe men began to raise armies to march to Jerusalem. Before the great lords had organized themselves, thousands of peasants and vagabonds, led by a monk nicknamed Peter the Hermit, made their way to Constantinople. The Byzantine emperor, whose appeal for help had led to Urban's sermon, was nervous of their strength and quickly sent them on to the Holy Land. Almost all of them were killed by the Turks.

By November 1096 a large army was gathering at Constantinople, led by great lords including Robert of Flanders, Stephen of Blois, Raymond of Toulouse, and Robert of Normandy. They led their soldiers on what we call the First Crusade. It was a great success. Antioch in Syria was captured in 1098 and Jerusalem fell in 1099. The Turks were driven from much of the Holy Land and a new kingdom of Jerusalem known as Outremer, "the land beyond the sea," was set up.

CHRONOLOGY

1096	First Crusade begins
1099	Crusaders capture Jerusalem
1104	Crusaders capture Acre
1147	Second Crusade (ends 1149)
1174	Muslims under Saladin conquer Syria
1187	Saladin captures Jerusalem
1189	Third Crusade (ends 1192)
1191	Crusaders conquer Cyprus capture Acre
1192	Richard makes peace with Saladin
1202	Fourth Crusade (ends 1204)
1204	Crusaders sack Constantinople
1217	Fifth Crusade (ends 1222)
1228	Sixth Crusade (ends 1229)
1248	Seventh Crusade (ends 1270)

RICHES AND TRADE

Many of the crusaders were devout Christians, but some of them were more interested in gaining riches and even land for themselves. In the end, the Crusades did most good to the trading cities of Italy, above all to Venice and Genoa, which gained money from transporting the crusaders in their ships and from setting up trade networks with the East.

The Crusades brought knights from Europe into contact with the East. They returned with a taste for spices, such as ginger, pepper, and cinnamon; for new fruits such as dates and figs; and for comforts such as rugs for the floor and silk for clothes. Trade in all of these became very important.

Crusader States

Pope Urban II described Jerusalem as "the center of the earth." He said its land was "fruitful above others like a paradise of delights." This was an exaggeration, but there were fertile lands in and around the Holy Land. During the 11th and 12th centuries a number of states were set up there by European knights, most of whom had come to the area as crusaders.

In the 11th century the Normans set up a kingdom in south Italy, and in Sicily under Roger of Sicily and Robert Guiscard. In 1098 Robert's son Bohemond was among the crusaders who seized Antioch, and Bohemond made himself its prince. Jerusalem itself was taken in 1099 after a siege and Godfrey of Bouillon was chosen as ruler over the new Christian conquests.

Although Byzantium was a Christian empire, the Norman crusaders, in particular, soon became hostile to it. In 1147 Roger of Sicily raided Greece and sacked Corinth. During the Third Crusade King Richard conquered Cyprus from the Byzantines and made Guy de Lusignan its king.

By the 13th century Count Baldwin of Flanders ruled at Constantinople, and there were French kingdoms in Cyprus, Athens, Thessaly, and Achaea. Although this French power seemed to be very great, in many places control was poor. Rulers were not united. This disunity helped the Byzantines to reclaim some lands and drive the conquerors away.

The castle of Krak des Chevaliers in Syria was built by the Knights of St. John. It stood firm through 12 sieges before it fell in 1271. It was built on a cliff and within its strong outer walls were barracks, storerooms, and a windmill.

King Richard of England (above) and the Muslim leader Saladin (below), from a 13th-century tile. Richard defeated Saladin and marched within sight of Jerusalem. But he realized he could never capture the city and made peace.

The Later Crusades

The First Crusade had been a great success. But the Turks and Egyptians attacked the crusaders over and over again and began to win back the Holy Land. Several more crusades were called, and King Louis VII of France, Conrad III of Germany, and later Richard I of England, Philip Augustus of France, and Frederick Barbarossa of Germany all pledged to defend or, after its loss, to recapture Jerusalem.

Illness and disaster prevented several expeditions from even reaching the Holy Land, and quarrels often broke out among the crusaders. Richard I captured Acre and came within sight of Jerusalem, but he realized he could never retake it. In 1203 the Venetians and the crusaders captured the Christian city of Constantinople. Although many Christians dreamed of recapturing Jerusalem, and many set out on crusades, they never succeeded.

The crusaders land at Damietta in Egypt. They often traveled overland to the Near East, through the Balkans to Constantinople, and then south through Anatolia. Many went by sea, which was safer and healthier but took longer. In the 12th century two special orders of knights, the Knights Templar and Knights of St. John of Jerusalem, were formed to aid and protect pilgrims to the Holy Land.

Eastern Europe

Along the northern edge of Europe, stretching from Belgium far eastward to Russia, is a vast plain. Through it great rivers, the Rhine, the Weser, the Elbe, the Oder, and the Vistula, run north to the North Sea and the Baltic. In the Middle Ages this area was largely covered with forest which settlers cleared to get fertile farmland. South of the plain rise the mountains of Bohemia and the Carpathians, and south again is the great Hungarian plain around the river Danube. The Rhine and Danube formed the eastern border of the Roman empire for several centuries.

In the Age of Migrations from the 3rd to the 8th centuries A.D. "barbarian" tribes were moving through eastern Europe. Some moved south and west from the Baltic region, and others made their way westward from Central Asia. They included the nomad Huns and Avars, and also the Slavs who had settled in much of eastern Europe by A.D. 600.

Silver earring from Kiev (11th-12th century)

The 13th-century castle of Malbork, near Gdansk in Poland. It was the seat of the grand master of the Teutonic Knights from 1309 to 1457.

THE TEUTONIC KNIGHTS

In 1198 some German merchants joined together to help nurse the sick and look after pilgrims to the Holy Land. Ten years later they had become known as the Teutonic (German) Order of Knights. They worked under a monastic and military rule.

In 1226 the knights were invited to help a Polish duke defend his lands on the lower reaches of the river Vistula from the pagan Prussians. They colonized East Prussia and converted its people. The Order ruled East Prussia by setting up a series of military towns and using the local people ruthlessly to work on the land. They encouraged many German peasants to settle in the Prussian countryside. They farmed what had previously been wild land, from the lower Vistula and the Baltic coast to the southern borderland.

The knights grew more and more powerful until they controlled much of the Baltic coast. They quarreled with the merchants of the growing Hanseatic ports (see page 100) and became increasingly unpopular. In 1410 the Poles and Lithuanians defeated the knights at Tannenburg. In 1466 the Order came under Polish rule.

Poland

In the 10th century A.D. the Slav tribes on the plains around the Vistula joined together under their leader Mieszko to form Poland. At this time Germans were moving eastward, converting the Slavs and settling the land. To safeguard their country, Mieszko and his people became Christians and acknowledged the overlordship of the Holy Roman emperor. In the next century Polish rule was pushed eastward to Kiev, but in 1138 King Boleslaw died and his kingdom was divided among his sons. Split into small states, Poland could barely defend itself against the invasions of the Mongols from Central Asia, or from its pagan neighbors Lithuania and Prussia. The Poles called in the Teutonic Knights to help, and then found themselves faced by the powerful state of the knights in Prussia and Lithuania.

Gradually the Poles recovered their strength and unity. They were helped by many immigrants, who were peasants, traders, and craftsmen from Germany, and Jews who had been expelled from almost every other country at this time. From 1370 to 1382 Poland was united with Hungary under King Louis I. After he died the Poles chose his daughter Jadwiga to be their queen, and in 1386 she married Jagello, duke of Lithuania. The two countries were united. Jagello and the Lithuanians became Christians. In 1410 Jagello scored a great victory over the Teutonic Knights, and he built Poland-Lithuania into the largest state in eastern Europe.

Hungary

In the 9th century A.D. the Magyars, a tribe from Central Asia, settled in the Hungarian plains. Here, since Roman times, wheat and vines had been grown on the fertile soil around the Danube. The Magyars now raided deep into the rest of Europe. They were described as:

of a sickening ugliness. Their deepset eyes had an inhuman look; their heads seemed bald, but from their pates sprung thin pigtails. Their voices were frighteningly shrill, and their language was different from any human tongue. Like wild animals they devoured raw flesh and drank blood.

The Magyars were expert horsemen and raided as far west as central France and Italy. But in the mid-10th century they were defeated by the Germans in two great battles and then settled down in the Hungarian plains, with many Slav subjects. Not long after they became Christian.

The Magyars, or Hungarians as they became known, built up a large kingdom which was well organized on feudal lines. They were helped by wealth from rich gold and silver mines. But the position of their country meant that it was always in danger of attack from the east. In the mid-13th century it was ravaged by raids from the Mongols, who killed many people, and in the next century began a long series of struggles with the Turks.

Above: This Hungarian aquamanile (a vessel for carrying water for washing hands) dates from the 12th century. Below left: The crown of St. Stephen, part of the Hungarian royal regalia. According to tradition, it was given to Stephen by the pope in recognition of his work converting pagans to Christianity. Taken by the Nazis in World War II, it came into American hands, and was returned to Hungary only in 1978.

Russia

The first states in Russia were set up by trading colonies of Vikings at Novgorod in the north and farther south at Kiev. In 988 Prince Vladimir of Kiev was converted to the Orthodox Christianity of the Byzantine empire.

Within about 50 years Kiev is said to have had some 200 churches, built and decorated in the Byzantine style (see page 67). Trade in furs, wax, slaves, and honey brought the state wealth. Other states grew up to the north, loosely ruled by Kiev.

Nomads from Central Asia were a constant threat to these states. In the 13th century the Mongols conquered much of Russia, burning down towns and killing many of the people. The people of Novgorod paid tribute to the Mongols but were not conquered by them. They later set up a republic. Trade was becoming more and more important in the Baltic area and Novgorod allowed the Hanseatic merchants to build a settlement there (see page 100).

Meanwhile the trading town of Moscow to the southeast was growing bigger and more important, although it was captured twice by the Mongols. Under Ivan the Great, at the end of the 15th century, it gained control of the surrounding states including Novgorod, and Ivan claimed to be ruler of all Russia.

THE CENTRAL REGION

Modern Czechoslovakia is in the center of eastern Europe. Much of the country is mountainous and covered with forests. It was formed in 1918 out of Bohemia in the west, Slovakia in the east, and Moravia in the middle. These countries were surrounded by powerful neighbors: Germany in the west, Poland to the north, Austria and Hungary in the south, and on the east Russia. They struggled for independence all through the Middle Ages. In the 10th century Slovakia was conquered by the Magyars, and from then on it was subject to the ruler of Hungary. Bohemia and Moravia formed a Christian kingdom, dominated sometimes by the Poles and sometimes by the Germans. From the 16th century they were ruled by the Hapsburg family who also ruled the Holy Roman Empire.

A Mongol camp in the Kirghiz Mountains. Now, as in the Middle Ages, the Mongols live in felt tents called yurts, moving from winter pasture to summer pasture with their flocks and herds.

Mongol soldiers and their horses. The missionary John of Plano Carpini, who traveled through Mongol territory in the mid-13th century, wrote a description of the Mongol armies. Each soldier had three or four mounts, which he often changed. A soldier's weapons included two or three bows, three quivers of arrows, an ax, rope, and a sword.

The Mongols

Between northwest China and Siberia stretches a vast area of rolling grassland known as the steppes. This is the homeland of a nomadic people called the Mongols. The early Mongols migrated with the seasons, taking their sheep and horses from one good pasture to another. Then, as now, the Mongols were superb horsemen. This skill helped them to become unrivaled hunters and warriors. During the Middle Ages the Mongols built up an empire stretching from China to the borders of Hungary.

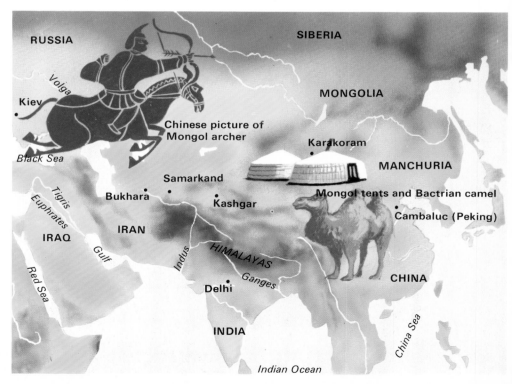

The First Empire

From ancient times Mongol tribes, greedy for the riches of the great Chinese cities to the south, would leave their bleak grasslands and attack them, destroying everything in their path. In the 3rd century B.C. the Chinese built the Great Wall to keep them out, but in the end even this was not to prove successful.

By the middle of the 10th century A.D. Mongol tribes had built up an empire covering much of Manchuria, Mongolia, and northeast China. The Mongols began to live in the cities they conquered, and used Chinese people to advise them in running the empire. They gradually adopted many Chinese customs. This group of Mongols was eventually overrun by another tribe from the west, but they mark the start of centuries of Mongol activity.

CHRONOLOGY	
1206	Temujin elected Genghis Khan (to 1227)
1215	Peking falls to Genghis Khan who also moves west to Gulf and builds up a vast empire
1227	Genghis Khan's empire is divided into four khanates
1238	Mongols annihilate Volga Bulgars and move on into Russia
1240	Kiev falls to Mongols
1241	Mongols ravage much of Hungary and Poland
1260	Kublai Khan makes Peking his capital
1274	Japanese fight off Mongol invasion
1279	Kublai Khan finally destroys Sung dynasty
1360	Timur the Lame, Great Emir (to 1405)
1368	Mongols driven from Peking
1388	Mongol capital Karakoram destroyed by Chinese
1393	Timur captures Baghdad
1398	Timur destroys Delhi

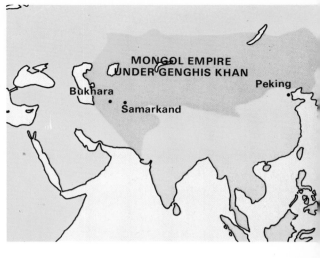

Trade

Trade went on busily during the Mongol empires, and contacts between China and the lands to the west increased very much. Travelers, merchants, and priests made journeys back and forth across Asia. To the West went trade goods of all kinds, including porcelain and silks, and technical knowledge such as the making of gunpowder. In return, Mongol converts took the religion of Islam back to parts of China.

The Italian Marco Polo visited the court of Kublai Khan at Cambaluc (Peking) in the late 13th century. He wrote a book describing his visit, which is the first accurate record of China by a European. For centuries his European readers could hardly believe the wonders he described.

"THE VERY MIGHTY LORD"

Genghis Khan, the great leader who brought all the Mongol tribes under his control, was born in 1167. His name was Temujin. Soon after he became chief of his tribe he managed to win the support of many other Mongol leaders by his bravery and daring. In 1206 he took the title Genghis Khan, which means "the very mighty lord."

Genghis Khan led his Mongol horde all across Central Asia, raiding and plundering and capturing cities such as Bukhara and Samarkand. His warriors encircled their enemies with flying columns of horsemen, and their most important weapon was a heavy bow. The Mongols controlled their horses with their feet, so that their hands were free for fighting. Messengers using relays of horses could ride 400 kilometers (250 miles) in a day.

Genghis Khan was wise enough to use the skills of foreign craftsmen and specialists to help rule his empire. He was interested in travelers and missionaries, and traders were allowed to journey through his lands. However, he admitted that he found his greatest joy in conquest, victory, and the glory of war.

The Four Khanates

When Genghis Khan died in 1227 his empire was divided, according to tribal custom, among his four sons. The grandsons of the Great Khan took the Mongol hordes to nearly every part of Asia, and deep into Europe. By the end of the 13th century four great Mongol kingdoms formed a "superstate" stretching from the China Sea to the borders of Poland and Hungary.

These four khanates, as they were called, were that of the Great Khan, including all of China and Mongolia; the Khanate of Chughtai centered around Kashgar, Samarkand, and Bukhara; the Khanate of Persia stretching from near the Indus River to the Black Sea; and the Khanate of Kipchak or the Golden Horde, which included Greater Russia as far east as Mongolia itself. However, the Mongols were better as conquerors than as rulers and settlers. After the devastating shock of conquest, local people were able to grow strong enough to drive them out.

Mongol soldiers, mounted on tough, stocky ponies, were almost unbeatable. They attacked with devastating speed and skill. At night they signaled their movements to one another with drums, horns, shouts, and even bird calls.

The Last Great Leader

In the late 14th century, Timur the Lame rose to power in Samarkand. He overran Persia, Mesopotamia, and the Golden Horde in south Russia, and devastated northern India. When he died in 1405 he was on his way to China to convert the Chinese to Islam. On his death, Mongol power in Central Asia was broken. With it went centuries-old links between East and West. The Mongols continued to be a great menace to the Chinese, but they never again controlled an empire. They went back to the old nomadic way of life they had known before.

The World in 1250

Mongols from Central Asia take control of northern China, invade India, gain control of part of the Near East, and raid deep into Russia and central Europe. The Crusades have brought western Europe in close touch with the Islamic world and trade between them grows. Towns are growing large and wealthy through trade, weakening the feudal system with its reliance on lord and land. In some of them universities are growing up. In 1271 Marco Polo sets out from Italy for China, where the Sung capital of Hangchow is the richest city of the world. The Turks become increasingly important.

Right: Part of the Catalan map, made for the king of France in about 1375. Much of it was based on seamen's charts which since the late 13th century had been drawn up using compass bearings. They were more accurate than any other kind of medieval maps. The Catalan map's information on Central Asia and China came largely from the writings of Marco Polo.

Muslims and Christians in battle. At the end of the 11th century Pope Urban called on Christians to journey to the Holy Land and capture it from the Muslim Turks so that pilgrims could safely visit Jerusalem and other holy places. From then on there were a number of Crusades, as such expeditions were called. At first the Christians were successful, but the states they set up were soon recaptured by the Muslims and in 1291 they were finally driven out of the Holy Land.

Toltec temple at Tula, Mexico

Chimu decorated gold beaker, Peru

1 The Americas In coastal Peru the Chimus control a well organized state. In
2 Mexico the Mixtecs are established in the Valley of Oaxaca.

3 Western Europe In England and France strong central governments are set up. More land is cultivated. Trade grows, and towns become larger and richer. The conflict between the empire and the papacy continues and in northern Italy towns gain independence. Universities are founded. The Crusades have failed to win back the Holy Land.

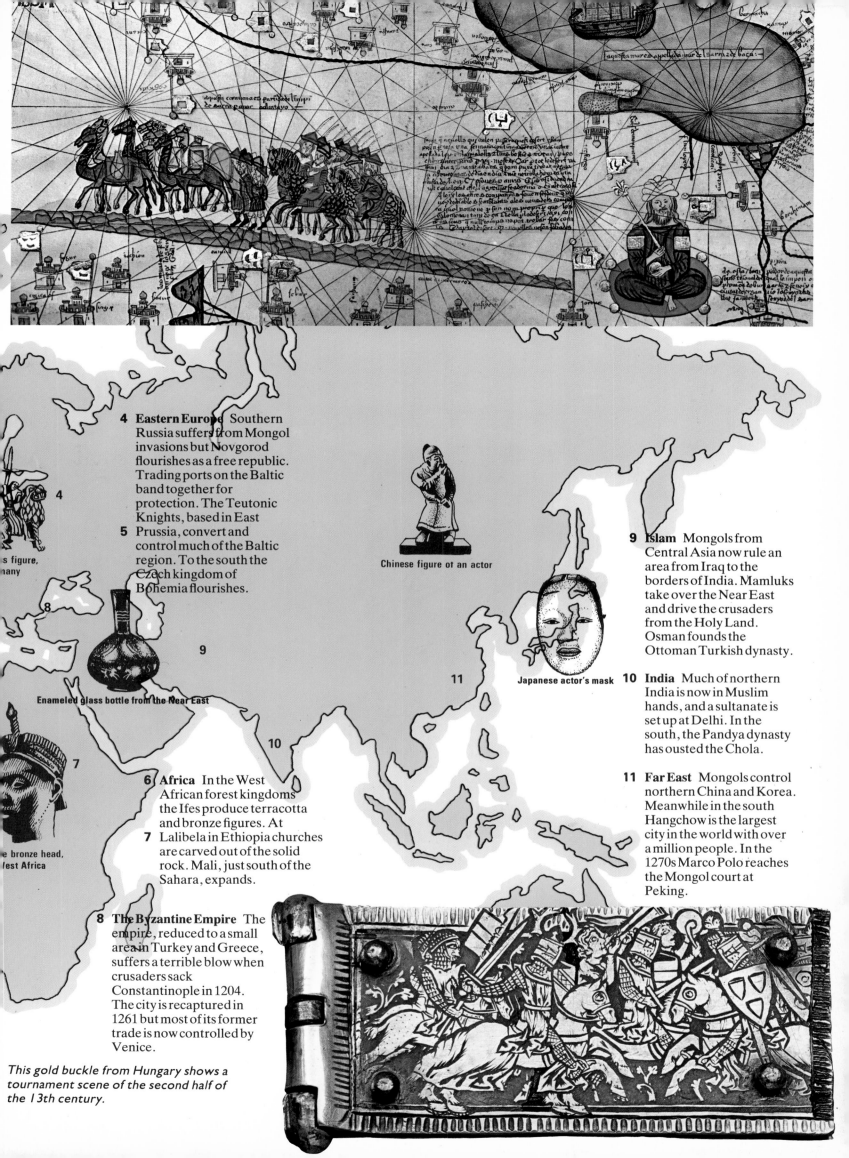

4 Eastern Europe Southern Russia suffers from Mongol invasions but Novgorod flourishes as a free republic. Trading ports on the Baltic band together for protection. The Teutonic Knights, based in East
5 Prussia, convert and control much of the Baltic region. To the south the Czech kingdom of Bohemia flourishes.

Chinese figure of an actor

9 Islam Mongols from Central Asia now rule an area from Iraq to the borders of India. Mamluks take over the Near East and drive the crusaders from the Holy Land. Osman founds the Ottoman Turkish dynasty.

Enameled glass bottle from the Near East

Japanese actor's mask

10 India Much of northern India is now in Muslim hands, and a sultanate is set up at Delhi. In the south, the Pandya dynasty has ousted the Chola.

6 Africa In the West African forest kingdoms the Ifes produce terracotta and bronze figures. At
7 Lalibela in Ethiopia churches are carved out of the solid rock. Mali, just south of the Sahara, expands.

11 Far East Mongols control northern China and Korea. Meanwhile in the south Hangchow is the largest city in the world with over a million people. In the 1270s Marco Polo reaches the Mongol court at Peking.

8 The Byzantine Empire The empire, reduced to a small area in Turkey and Greece, suffers a terrible blow when crusaders sack Constantinople in 1204. The city is recaptured in 1261 but most of its former trade is now controlled by Venice.

This gold buckle from Hungary shows a tournament scene of the second half of the 13th century.

bronze head, est Africa

s figure, nany

Towns and Traders

A market scene in a French town of the Middle Ages. Town life became increasingly important with the growth of wealth and trade, and the towns had a good deal of independence within the feudal system.

Most Roman towns survived the fall of the empire, although they became smaller. In the 10th century rulers and great lords and churchmen founded many new towns, some for defense and others as market and administrative centers. Roads were very bad, and in general trade was carried out by sea and river. Trading towns grew up on coasts and river banks, fortified against attacks from raiders.

In the 11th and 12th centuries new lands were cultivated. People became richer and trade became more important. A new class of people grew up. These were the merchants.

New Allegiances
Merchants were not closely tied to the feudal system. Their lives were based on trade and money, not on land. Towns of merchants grew up which often owed allegiance not to the local lord, but to the king. A serf who lived in a town for a year and a day gained his freedom from the land. The townspeople were known as burgesses, burghers, or bourgeoisie, from the words *burg* or *bourg* meaning a fortified place.

Many of the fortified places around which the towns grew up were church centers. Others began as trading settlements where roads crossed or a river could be forded. Some were founded by kings who realized that they would be useful as a balance to the power of the nobles. They promised good conditions to attract people and gain their allegiance. Nobles, too, founded towns in their own lands. This happened especially often on the eastern borders of Germany where new lands were being settled.

Some of the new towns grew very wealthy. They spent much of their money on defense, hiring soldiers and building strong walls to protect themselves against robbers and in times of war.

Great fairs grew up along the main trading thoroughfares. This 15th-century picture shows the fair at Lendit in France.

TOWN LIFE
The center of the town was the market-place, where people from the country around brought their produce to sell. Around it were streets of small shops, with symbols hanging outside to show their business – a shoe for a shoemaker, and a bush for an inn, for example. Often all the people working in one trade or selling one kind of thing would work in the same street. The streets were narrow and all kinds of rubbish was thrown down in them. Pigs and dogs ran about scavenging. Rich merchants built themselves fine houses but most people lived in cramped houses. They were often built of wood, which was a great fire risk.

Roads and Fairs

Trade routes overland generally followed the old Roman roads, although they were now usually just made of gravel and mud. Traffic on them was very heavy. Rich people traveled on horseback but most people walked everywhere. Merchants loaded their goods on trains of pack animals and often traveled in convoys for safety. No one dared travel at night for fear of robbers, and along the roads were many inns and hostels.

Many trade fairs grew up along the routes. The roads from Flanders, Germany, Italy, and southern France crossed in the region of Champagne, which became famous for the great fairs held there every year. The six most important fairs lasted for 49 days each, and merchants from many countries met there. The last two weeks were spent in settling accounts. Goods at such fairs were tested for weight and quality, and special courts were set up to sort out disputes.

The Guilds

The main organization of a medieval town was the guild. At first this was an association of all the merchants in a town, who joined together to give one another help and protection. Later craft guilds were formed by the masters of a certain trade in a town. There were guilds of goldsmiths, leather-workers, fishmongers, carpenters, and so on. The guilds made rules about the way in which people worked, and how long they worked for. They set prices and said what was the most a workman could be paid. They limited the number of people who could work in a particular trade or craft, and cheats and anyone giving the trade a bad name were punished. This strict system made sure that standards were kept high, but it stopped new ideas from developing.

In many cities the guilds became very rich and powerful. They built guild halls where they could meet. They gave stained glass windows to cathedrals and parts of town churches were often set aside for their members to worship in.

A boy who wanted to join a guild spent several years as an apprentice, working for little but his food and lodging. At the end of a set time he had to show the guild that he knew his job. Then he entered the guild as a craftsman. If he did very well he could become a master craftsman, one of the chief men in the guild.

An early bank in Italy, run from a stall set up in the market. Banks grew up in northern Italy in the 13th century, when merchant companies with agents in several important towns found it risky to transport money from one to another. People began to deposit money with a company in one place in return for a letter of credit, which meant that the same sum could be drawn from the company's agent in another place. Some bankers, for example the Medici of Florence, became rich.

Africa

Sankore Mosque, Timbuktu (15th century)

Bronze Ife head (14th century)

The Sahara, the world's largest desert, sprawls across North Africa, forming a dry, burning hot barrier between the Mediterranean lands of North Africa and the moist tropical lands to the south. But the Sahara was not a barrier to medieval traders who crossed it regularly, using the scattered oases as resting places. South of the desert lies a broad belt of savanna (tropical grassland). This region, called the Sudan, was the home of great medieval Sudanic states. South of the Sudan are the rain forests of West Africa and Zaire, where other kingdoms grew up.

On the east and southeast coasts of Africa, the Arabs found many good sites for ports. Their trade extended from East Africa as far as China. The flat coastal plains of south-central Africa are mostly narrow. Behind them, the land rises steeply to a series of high, flat plateaus. Inland travel was difficult and we know very little about this region in the Middle Ages. It was only fully explored in the 1800s.

Trade and the Sudanic States

The great Sudanic states of the Middle Ages included Ancient Ghana, Kanem-Bornu, Mali, and Songhai. Most of our knowledge about them comes from Arab writers. Some of them collected information from traders. Others traveled widely with the Arab trading caravans.

The Sudanic states gained power through trade. Arab traders brought such things as salt, textiles, and tools, which they traded for gold, ivory, slaves, and hides and skins. Gold was especially important. It probably came from mines which have long ceased to exist, and was not brought up from the south

where gold is mined today. There was so much gold around that, one Arab chronicle tells us, even the royal guard dogs in ancient Ghana had gold collars.

The peoples of the Saharan states were farmers, growing crops such as maize and groundnuts. They lived in villages, in huts built from mud baked hard in the sun. Arab reports tell us that they looked on their kings as gods. King-worship had probably spread south from Egypt down the Nile, and then westward. Contacts with the Muslim Arabs meant that many of the Sudanic peoples were converted to Islam, and cities such as Timbuktu became centers of learning.

CHRONOLOGY

c.325	Axum becomes Christian and conquers Kush
400	Iron-using peoples spread through south-central Africa
429–439	Vandals conquer Roman North Africa
641	Arabs conquer Egypt
683	Arabs enter Morocco
700–800	Arabs establish ports in East Africa. Ife grows up in Nigeria
800	Ancient Ghana is a major trading state in the western Sudan. Kanem-Bornu grows up to the northeast of Lake Chad
1054	Almoravid Berbers conquer Ghana
c.1100	First stage of the building of Greater Zimbabwe
1250	Mali expands
1335	Songhai dynasty begins
1400s	Ife declines and Benin starts to grow. Great Bantu kingdoms grow up in south-central Africa

A caravan of camels laden with salt prepares to leave Bilma, Niger. In the Middle Ages trade in northwest Africa depended entirely on the camel, with its ability to cross the desert from one oasis to another. Two of the most important goods traded were gold, which went northward, and salt which was taken south and which was literally worth its weight in gold. Ghana raised taxes on these goods as they passed through the kingdom, and it became immensely wealthy. Even the dogs wore collars of gold or silver.

FOREST CIVILIZATIONS

South of the savanna, in the hot, wet tropical forests, people led a very different sort of life. They cleared away patches of the forest to grow crops like cassava and plantains. From the forest itself they gathered palm nuts for food, and palm leaves for the roofs of their mud huts and for making cloth. Travel was difficult through the forests, and the kingdoms of this region were smaller than the great empires of the savanna.

As early as 250 B.C., realistic terracotta sculptures were being made around the present-day village of Nok, in northern Nigeria. Many scholars believe that Nok art influenced the Yoruba sculptors of the forest kingdom of Ife. Ife, in southwest Nigeria, flourished from the 700s to the 1400s. It produced some of Africa's finest terracotta and bronze sculptures. According to tradition, an Ife master craftsmen visited Benin City, capital of the Nigerian forest kingdom of Benin, in the late 1300s. There he passed on the secrets of his art. Portuguese explorers of the 15th century were amazed by the beauty and skilled craftsmanship of the Benin bronzes.

This Benin bronze relief shows a king (oba) and two kneeling subjects. The work of Benin craftsmen has changed very little over the centuries, and this is one reason why it is difficult to date African art with any certainty. Benin bronze-working probably began in the 15th century, with knowledge spread by Ife workers. The "lost wax" process was used. In this, an object is modeled in wax over a clay core. Then it is covered with clay and heated until the molten wax runs out through special channels. Molten metal is poured in through these channels, and replaces exactly the form of the wax.

WHO WERE THE BUILDERS?

Great Zimbabwe is a group of massive stone ruins, including a temple and a citadel, in Zimbabwe. Experts cannot agree about its origins. Some people argue that it was built by an Arab-influenced culture. Others claim that it comes from an early black civilization.

People were living on the site as early as the 4th century A.D., but the first stone buildings date only from about 1100. In the 1300s, another related people began to build larger stone buildings there and, soon afterward, Great Zimbabwe became the center of the Shona Karanga kingdom.

Great Zimbabwe is the only site of its kind in southern Africa. African nationalists look on it as a symbol of past glory, and so they have renamed Rhodesia, Zimbabwe. On its new flag is a design of a bird, taken from a carving on the walls of Great Zimbabwe.

Part of the ruins of the great fortified city of Zimbabwe. Stone buildings dating from this period are very rare indeed in most of Africa, and it is small wonder that the people of the region are so proud of the ancient city that they have renamed their country after it.

This Christian church, one of ten in Lalibela in Ethiopia, was carved out of solid rock. Christianity came to this region of northeast Africa when King Azana of Axum (a powerful kingdom in what is now northeast Ethiopia) was converted in the early 300s. From the 600s Axum was under pressure from Muslims to the north and east, and from pagans to the south. The Axumites finally withdrew into the mountains. There their civilization and "Coptic" form of Christianity has survived until modern times.

Empire and Papacy

In 751 Pepin the Short overthrew the Frankish king and took the throne for himself. The pope supported him, which was very important in helping him to keep his kingdom. Twenty years later, the pope's lands in central Italy were threatened by the rulers of Lombardy to the north. He called on Pepin's son Charlemagne to help him in return. Charlemagne defeated the Lombards, and northern Italy became part of his kingdom. In 800 the pope crowned Charlemagne Roman emperor.

All through the Middle Ages, relations between the popes and the emperors played a very important part. Sometimes they supported each other; at other times their disagreements flared into war. Sometimes a strong pope would have the final say in who would be emperor; sometimes a strong emperor would choose the pope. The countries most affected by their disputes were Germany, where the emperor was overlord of often unruly and resentful lesser rulers, and Italy, which became their battleground.

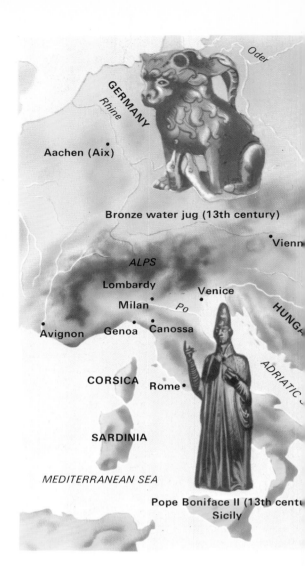

Bronze water jug (13th century)

Pope Boniface II (13th century)

Below left: Otto I "the Great" of Germany, who did much to strengthen the kingdom drawn together with difficulty by his father. In 955 he drove the Magyars from Germany, and this led to a period of security and prosperity in the lands under his control. He was crowned Holy Roman emperor in 962.

GERMANY

In the north, Germany is very flat with vast plains crossed by large rivers which flow north to the sea. In the center are rolling uplands, through which the rivers cut deep valleys. The south is much more mountainous. Even today more than a quarter of Germany is covered with forests, and in the Middle Ages trees covered much of the land.

The German king had the title "king of the Romans" with the right to be crowned emperor by the pope at Rome. He ruled over several Germanic tribes such as the Saxons, Franconians, Swabians, and Bavarians, who had their own customs and their own dialects. The kingship was sometimes passed from father to son and was sometimes given to the strongest duke.

The emperor's great problem in Germany was to curb the power of the other great dukes. Some of them tried to do this by granting great areas of land to bishops in return for their support. For a time this worked well. But in the 11th century churchmen felt that the emperor should not have any say in who was to be bishop. The clash came over the appointment of an archbishop for Milan in the 1070s. This was an important church post and it was politically important too, as Milan controlled the mountain passes from Germany to north Italy. Pope Gregory VII finally excommunicated the emperor Henry IV. This was a terrible punishment which cut him off from all the rites and services of the church. It also meant that Henry's subjects were no longer bound to be loyal to him. In order to prevent widespread revolt, Henry went to see Gregory in mid-winter at Canossa. "And there, laying aside all the trappings of royalty, he stood in wretchedness, barefooted and clad in wool, for three days before the gate of the castle," wrote a monk at the time. Then Gregory forgave him.

At last a compromise was reached in 1122. Churchmen met in the emperor's presence to choose a bishop. He first did homage to the emperor for his lands and then he was consecrated. This particular quarrel was settled, but the struggles for land and power between the empire and the papacy broke out again many times. In the long run neither won.

In the Middle Ages Italian towns were torn by civil strife. The fighting was often between the Guelphs, who supported the papacy, and the Ghibellines, who supported the empire. In the towns, important families built towers next to their houses so that they could take refuge in them. Such towers can be seen in this picture of the town of Siena in northern Italy. From the towers people threw stones and burning pitch at their enemies below. The opponents fought back with fire and heavy scaling engines.

ITALY

Much of Italy is mountainous and in the south it is very hot. The most fertile lands are in the Campagna around Naples and in the plains of Lombardy in the north. In the Middle Ages Italy had no single ruler. The lands in the center were controlled by the popes. The south changed hands from the Byzantine empire to the Normans of Sicily, and later to the Angevins of France and the Spanish house of Aragon. Lombardy, from the time of Charlemagne on, was subject to the Holy Roman emperor.

The balance between pope and emperor was always uneasy. When enemies such as the Muslims or Magyars threatened the Christians of Europe, the popes were quick to call for the emperors' support. But the popes did not want the emperors to become too powerful in Lombardy. There they might threaten church lands.

In the 11th and 12th centuries a new factor emerged. The cities of Lombardy grew rich and powerful through trade. Nobles living nearby moved into the cities, and brought control of the countryside around. These cities were anxious to be independent. When emperors tried to control and tax them they joined together to fight (sometimes with the support of the pope). At other times they would fight one another for a larger share of trade. For much of the Middle Ages, northern Italy was almost constantly at war.

THE VENETIAN EMPIRE

In the Middle Ages Venice was one of the most important cities in Italy. As early as the 10th century the Venetians were trading with a large part of the Byzantine empire and Venice was becoming a wealthy city. Later, during the 12th century, there was rivalry between Venice on the east coast and Genoa on the west coast. It lasted for 200 years, but Venice was to prove the stronger. Both wanted to have control of the new trading area that had been opened up in the East. Goods from there included silk, metalwork, cloth of gold, carpets, perfumes, grain, wine, drugs, and precious stones.

At this time also Venice was providing ships for the crusaders. This proved very profitable. They were made in the arsenal (dockyard) in Venice. During the Fourth Crusade the Venetians supplied an army for the crusaders, who agreed to pay 85,000 silver marks for it. The army was made up of 4,500 horses, 4,500 knights, 9,000 squires, and 20,000 foot soldiers. Venice also paid for the provisions of all these for a year. But, after a year, the crusaders found that they could not pay. Instead, they decided to capture Constantinople and the Byzantine empire and share them with Venice, which they did in 1204. This helped to destroy the Eastern empire.

The Venetian empire in the late Middle Ages was made up of many trading states in the eastern Mediterranean. The area from the Aegean to Crete and Rhodes was, in fact, dominated by the Venetians. By the 14th and 15th centuries Venice was the richest commercial city in Europe.

The castle of Kyrenia in Cyprus, including the 15th-century tower built by the Venetians when Cyprus formed part of their empire.

India

The Indian subcontinent lies in South Asia, between Iran and Afghanistan on the west and Burma, Thailand, and the rest of Southeast Asia on the east. To the north are the Himalayas, and beyond these mountains are Tibet and the great deserts of Chinese Central Asia. The geography of India varies from high mountains, always covered in snow, to jungles and flat river plains. It was on these plains that the great cities of the Indus and the Ganges river valleys grew up.

Kingdoms of the North

A great dynasty ruled in north India from about the early 4th century A.D. to the end of the 5th. They were called the Guptas, and like earlier rulers they made their capital at Pataliputra in the modern state of Bihar. Their power and influence were very great, and traces of their presence are found all over north India. Cities such as Pataliputra, Rajgir, and many others were large and full of well-built houses, usually of brick. There were palaces for the rulers and the rich, Buddhist and Hindu temples, markets, and public buildings of all sorts. Houses, sometimes with several stories, were usually built around courtyards. These cities were always walled and had large gates, closed at night against intruders.

Trade and commerce flourished at this time, and the influence of Buddhist India was spread far and wide, to China and to Southeast Asia.

The Guptas were eventually overthrown by the Hunds or Huns in the late 5th century. The Huns swept into India, destroying everything they found. A number of small kingdoms grew up in the wake of this confusion, ending in the 7th century with the empire of King Harsha, whose kingdom was centered at Kanarj on the Ganges. Harsha, a Buddhist, traveled far and wide in his empire seeing to its administration. This was a great age, of powerful armies, strong prosperous cities, flourishing monasteries, and busy trading.

In the later Middle Ages north India had a very complicated history, with changing dynasties and kingdoms. But these changes hardly altered the daily life of the ordinary people. Except when a fierce conqueror swept away everything of a previous rule, most people continued to live in large cities or in small villages, making a living from farming the fertile river plains.

This page of Buddhist Wisdom text, written on a palm leaf, dates from 1112. It is written in Sanskrit, a language used all over India by Buddhists and Hindus.

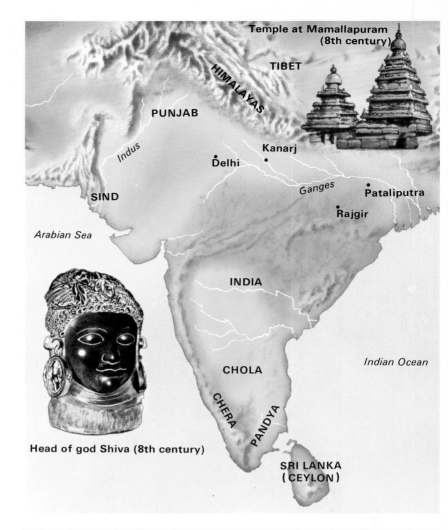

Temple at Mamallapuram (8th century)

Head of god Shiva (8th century)

HINDUISM AND BUDDHISM

The two great religions of the Indian subcontinent in the Middle Ages were Hinduism and Buddhism. Hinduism dates back to well before 1000 B.C., and teaches of a single world spirit, Brahman, of which all gods, people, and things are a part. The Hindu law of *Dharma* teaches that everyone must obey the divine order of the universe, working to fulfill the tasks laid down for them in the position in life into which they are born. Those who succeed in this are born again into a higher position. Many gods and beliefs are accepted in the framework of Hinduism.

Buddhism was developed in the 6th century B.C. by the Indian Gautama. He was known as the Enlightened One, or *Buddha*. He taught that men could free themselves from the suffering of life on earth only by obeying certain great rules. One rule, *Ahimsa*, was that no living thing should be harmed.

South India

The Tamil-speaking country in the south of India has always had a distinctive history and style. It was made up of three kingdoms: Chola, Pandya, and Chera (Kerala). In this period the Tamils wrote a great deal of poetry, much of which was on religious subjects. Hinduism was the main religion, and many stone shrines and temples were built, some of them in caves. A large number of temple-towns were built under Chola rule, and the region was famous for its beautiful bronze figures of Hindu gods. At one time the Cholas controlled all southern India, and parts of Ceylon, Burma, Malaya, and Sumatra, and traded with many other regions as well.

THE MUSLIMS IN INDIA

Muslim influence in India began in A.D. 711 when the Sind (now a state of modern Pakistan) was taken by the Arabs. The invasions of northern India by Mahmud of Ghazni in the 11th century established Muslim rule as far east as the Punjab. He slew, destroyed, and enslaved and, in 1022, took control of the Punjab. From that time onward a series of Muslim dynasties established themselves in north India, doing battle with the Hindu rulers of the day.

Buddhism had died out in India after Harsha and the Muslim empires savagely persecuted the followers of the Hindu faith. Temples were looted, shrines smashed, and libraries burned. The history of this part of the subcontinent up to the mid-15th century is again a series of invasions and power struggles. By the 1450s, however, Muslim rule was secure in north India and was to develop in the early 16th century into the great empire of the Mughals whose first ruler, Balim, came from Ferghana in central Asia.

Top: This huge sculpture was cut into the cliff face at Mahabalipuram, in southern India, in the 7th century A.D. Mahabalipuram was the capital of the Pallava king Mammala. This carving shows a scene from the Hindu legend of Arjuna. Above: These beautiful statues of Buddha at Polonnawura in Sri Lanka (Ceylon) date from the 11th century. The written history of Sri Lanka, the great island that lies southeast of India, begins in the 6th century A.D. and from that time on there is a continuous record. The people of the island were converted to Buddhism in the 3rd century B.C. and many temples, decorated with magnificent stone sculptures, were built there. The island was often attacked by the Hindu kingdoms of south India, and for a time part of the island came under Indian rule. Tamils from southern India settled much of the northeast.

The Hanseatic League

In the early Middle Ages trade in the Baltic and North Sea areas was dominated by the Vikings and Frisians. But in the late 12th and early 13th centuries, there was a change. German settlers around the Baltic gained control. Existing ports like Lübeck grew bigger, and new trading villages were founded on the Baltic coasts. Soon German merchants appeared in the Viking trading city of Novgorod in Russia. Meanwhile other German cities, among them Hamburg on the North Sea coast and Cologne on the river Rhine, were building up trade in northwest Europe.

These towns housed families of merchants who traveled far and wide. Often they were menaced by robbers and pirates. In 1241 the townspeople (burgesses) of Lübeck and Hamburg came together to make a treaty. They decided to pool their resources to safeguard the trading routes and protect each other's merchants. Soon many other towns banded together to help and protect their traders. They set up trading associations known as *hanse*, and together they are known as the Hanseatic League. Until the end of the 15th century, the League dominated the trade of northern Europe.

The Holstentor, one of the medieval gates of the north German city of Lübeck. Its position on the Baltic, between Scandinavia and the mainland of northern Europe, meant that Lübeck was an important trading center from early on. In the 13th century it was made a free imperial city by the emperor Frederick II. It became the leading town of the Hanseatic League.

The League was at its greatest in the 14th century. No official list of member towns was drawn up, but there may have been more than a hundred. Among the most important towns were Reval, Riga, Danzig, and Thorn on the Baltic; Cologne on the Rhine; Hamburg, Bremen, Amsterdam, and Antwerp on the North Sea coast. Most important of all was Lübeck. Grain, pitch, furs, timber, charcoal, flax, hemp, and wax from eastern Europe were shipped from the Baltic ports. From Sweden came copper and iron. Herrings from the sea around Sweden and cod and whale oil from Norway were also important.

Cologne Cathedral

CHRONOLOGY

1241 Formal alliance between Lübeck and Hamburg to secure common action against robbers and pirates

1265 Towns having "law of Lübeck" agree on common legislation to defend their merchants

1282 Lübeck and Hamburg join in "German Hanse"

1300 All north German trading associations, towns, and bases for foreign commerce are now bound together into a single league

1368 Danish War (to 1370); forces of the League defeat the Danes and safeguard their Baltic trade

1386 Union of Poland and Lithuania harms Hanseatic interests

1442 Frederick of Brandenburg gains control of Berlin

1462 Mainz loses privileges

1478 Ivan III expels Hanseatic merchants from Novgorod

1618 Thirty Years' War ruins the few remaining League members (to 1648)

Privileged Settlements

The Hanse towns had trading privileges in many non-member cities, where they built settlements of warehouses and living quarters. In London their settlement was known as the Steelyard, and the merchants were given better terms for customs duties than were other traders. The Hanseatic merchants in Britain were known as Easterlings, because they came from east of the British Isles. In time the word became sterling, and was used to mean a good reliable standard of coinage.

The merchants' position in Bruges was particularly important, for here they came into contact with traders from the Mediterranean area. It was also the main market for wool from England and for Flemish cloth. In 1358 the townspeople of Bruges took away the privileges of the Hanseatic merchants. The other League towns, led by Lübeck, banned all trade with Flanders. Two years later the merchants' privileges were given back.

The League Declines

In the 15th century the Hanseatic League began to lose its strength. The main cities had been independent, but now the German states were growing more powerful. Their princes were able to overrule the merchants. In 1442 Frederick of Brandenburg gained control of the city of Berlin and the citizens had to give up their independence. Twenty years later the same thing happened in Mainz on the Rhine. Merchants were forbidden to make trading agreements with towns outside their state. In 1478 Ivan of Moscow captured Novgorod and expelled the Hanseatic merchants.

In the meantime, English and especially Dutch traders were becoming more successful. As their countries' industries grew they became less dependent on Hanseatic imports. The Dutch herring fishery increased while the catches of the Hanseatic merchants became disastrously less as changes in the climate caused fish to move their feeding grounds. With the support of the Danes, the Dutch moved into the Baltic area and became the major traders with the West.

Above: The Furriers window in the French cathedral of Chartres. Fur from Russia and the Baltic region was an important part of the Hanseatic trade.

Left: The seal of Danzig (modern Gdansk) on the Baltic Sea, a leading Hanseatic town.

Below: Novgorod in the 15th century. It was an important center of trade in amber, furs, and wax and was the farthest into Russia that the Hanse merchants reached.

MEETINGS OF MERCHANTS

The Hanseatic League had a general assembly which met at irregular intervals. It had no absolute authority, but it could bring unruly members under control. Its members met not as politicians but as businessmen to deal with problems of trade. Very occasionally they did interfere in politics, as when they forced King Waldemar of Denmark to give them control of the Sound, the channel leading from the North Sea to the Baltic. They needed this because pirates in the area often threatened fishing and merchant fleets. When it was in the Hanse's interests, their great fleets of ships could be hired out to northern rulers.

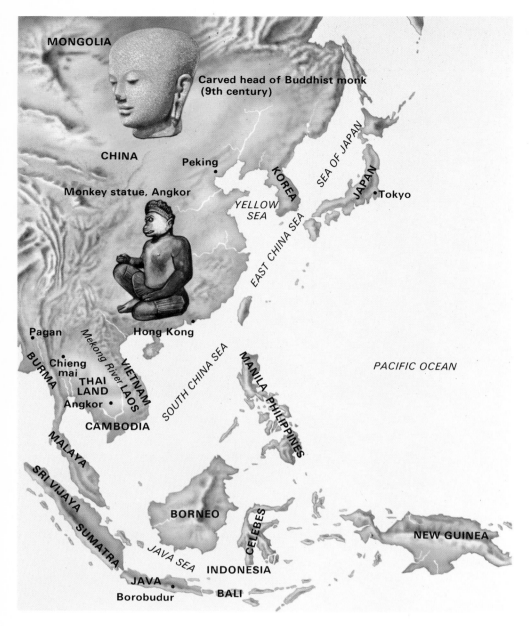

MONGOLIA

Carved head of Buddhist monk
(9th century)

CHINA

Peking

Monkey statue, Angkor

KOREA

SEA OF JAPAN

YELLOW
SEA

JAPAN

Tokyo

EAST CHINA SEA

Pagan

Mekong River valley

Hong Kong

BURMA

Chieng
mai

VIETNAM

THAI
LAND LAOS

Angkor

PACIFIC OCEAN

SOUTH CHINA SEA

MANILA
PHILIPPINES

CAMBODIA

MALAYA

SRI
VIJAYA

SUMATRA

BORNEO

CELEBES

NEW GUINEA

JAVA SEA

INDONESIA

JAVA

Borobudur

BALI

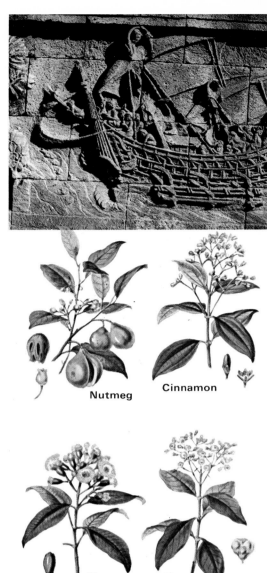

Nutmeg

Cinnamon

Clove

Allspice

Southeast Asia

Southeast Asia includes Burma, Thailand, Malaya, Cambodia, Laos, and Vietnam, on the mainland. It also includes the great islands of modern Indonesia: Java, Bali, and Sumatra, as well as Borneo, the Celebes and the Philippines. There are many rivers, mountains, and steaming jungles. Most people lived in cities and villages along the great rivers. Travel by river was easier than overland. Village people were mainly fishers and farmers, and rice, then as now, was their most important crop. In the jungles lived tribal people whose lives have changed very little since ancient times.

The building of the city of Pagan started in the 11th century A.D. Until the arrival of the Mongols in 1287, it was a center of Buddhism. Many temples, like this one, still stand as a reminder of this time.

Top: A relief carving from Borobudur, dating from about 800. It shows the sort of boat which traded among the islands of Southeast Asia. Above: Some of the many spices which grow in the area. They were taken to the West either by sea or by the long overland route through China, and fetched huge prices. Eventually spice traders from Europe sailed into the Indian Ocean.

Outside Influences

Southeast Asia developed no common culture or common language. The two great influences there in medieval times were India and China. Traders from India settled in colonies all through Southeast Asia. They brought with them the Buddhist and Hindu religions. These spread far and wide through the islands and the mainland. Chinese influence is most clearly seen in countries such as Vietnam, but evidence of trade with China is found all over the region. Chinese pottery and porcelain are excavated in nearly every part of Southeast Asia, and show that trading was carried on for centuries. Chinese influence was particularly strong in technology, culture, and ways of government but not in religion.

KINGDOM OF THE KHMERS

Several very important cultures grew up in Southeast Asia during the Middle Ages. Among them were those at Pagan in Burma and Chieng mai in Thailand, and the island kingdoms of Java and Bali. One of the greatest civilizations was that of the Khmers of Cambodia.

By the 5th century the Khmer people were living in a kingdom called Chenla, in the middle Mekong River region. They were Hindus, and although few of their cities have been excavated, some beautiful sculptures have been found there. In the 7th century their capital, Sambor Prei Kuk, had large public buildings and temples, built in a style rather like those in India. The Khmers had to fight off attacks by the Chams of southern Vietnam, who are often described as pirates. They caused havoc among the shipping along the coast and in the Mekong delta. The Khmers were also attacked by Indonesian kingdoms.

In the 9th century the Khmers made Angkor their capital and founded an empire that was to last for five centuries. They built a great network of irrigation canals which helped them to produce huge crops of rice from the fertile soil. Angkor has many ditches, canals, lakes, and reservoirs. Early buildings at Angkor were mostly wood. These have all disappeared, leaving behind only a few statues. From the beginning of the 11th century temples were built entirely of stone. These temples are Angkor's great glory. Each king built his own, and there he carried out ceremonies to make sure of good crops. Some of the most beautiful temples were built after the Khmers were converted to Buddhism from the the 12th century.

This relief carving of a battle scene comes from Angkor Wat, one of the great Hindu temples built at the Khmer capital of Angkor. It measures 1,550 by 1,420 meters (1,700 by 1,550 yards) and is enclosed by six kilometers (four miles) of moat.

The Buddhist shrine at Borobudur in Java was built in about 800. Five square terraces rise above its square base; they are topped by three round terraces crowned by a bell-shaped "stupa" (a building containing a relic of the Buddha or a Buddhist saint). Around it are 72 small stupas of openwork stone, each containing a figure of the Buddha.

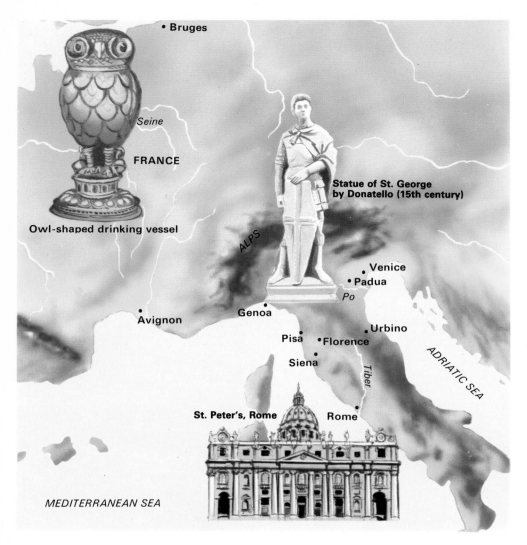

Owl-shaped drinking vessel

Statue of St. George by Donatello (15th century)

St. Peter's, Rome

The Renaissance

During the 13th century, the seafaring Italian cities of Venice and Genoa opened up new trade routes to the East through Constantinople. The cities of northern Italy, no longer dominated by the emperor or the pope, now found themselves at the crossroads of trade between East and West. In Florence, Genoa, Milan, Venice, and elsewhere, merchants began to make huge profits from the increase in trade. Contacts with the East gave them a wider outlook and a new interest in collecting rare and exotic things. Wealth and fashion led to astonishing advances in learning and the arts.

This period in Western civilization is called the Renaissance, a word meaning "rebirth." A new, adventurous spirit began to disturb the settled world of the Middle Ages, making way for an age of exploration, discovery, and scientific thought.

The poet Dante (1265–1321); behind him is his native city of Florence. He wrote in his native language, a north Italian speech called Tuscan. Before his time, Italians had preferred to write in French or Latin.

Trade and Travel

Italian merchants traveled far and wide. In the 1270s the Venetian Marco Polo took the route through Central Asia to China, then ruled by the Mongol emperor Kublai Khan. Italians traded in London and Flanders (Belgium), and along the shores of the Black Sea. They brought raw materials such as wool, hides, and precious metals back to Italy. There, skilled craftsmen turned them into finished goods, which were exported at a profit.

A system of banking grew up to support trade. A banker would lend a merchant the money to cover the period between buying, say, wool in northern Europe and selling it in Florence. The famous banks of Florence came to lend money to kings. One banking and trading family, the Medicis, came to rule Florence itself for more than 200 years. All over northern Italy, powerful families and groups of merchants beautified their cities with splendid new buildings. In Rome, too, several popes were patrons of artists and scholars.

The New Learning

In the late Middle Ages trade made northern Italy the wealthiest region in Europe. Italian merchant-princes competed to make their native cities brilliant centers of learning and the arts. There was a great fashion for collecting libraries. Agents were sent all over Europe to bring back rare manuscripts by famous Greek and Roman authors of the ancient world. Many were found in monastery libraries where they had long been forgotten. As few people could understand the ancient Greek and Latin in which they were written, scholars translated them into Italian. More and more people rediscovered the ideas and discoveries of Greek and Roman civilization, which the church had long condemned as "pagan."

This painting by Piero della Francesca (c. 1415–1492) is of the Duke of Urbino, Federigo da Montefeltro. A mercenary general, he spent much of his money on building churches, hospitals, and schools for his people and in caring for the poor. At his beautiful palace he collected a famous library.

The Arts

The Renaissance saw great changes in the arts. At the beginning of the period, most architects and painters were simply craftsmen. They were expected to work in old established styles and patterns. In architecture the style was Gothic, in which windows and arches were pointed, and the roofs were decorated with tall pinnacles. But in the 1420s the Florentine architect Brunelleschi began to build in the style he had learned from ancient Roman buildings. They were carefully balanced, with rounded arches and domes.

In painting, the medieval style was originally influenced by Byzantine art. Figures were flat and stylized against plain gold backgrounds. But around 1300 a painter called Giotto began to paint figures more realistically, making them appear more solid and setting them against backgrounds that looked like the real world. As time went on artists and architects developed these advances even farther.

By the end of the Renaissance, artists, sculptors, and architects were known far and wide by name. Men like Leonardo da Vinci, Michelangelo, and Raphael traveled from city to city where they were received as honored guests by powerful men.

THE RENAISSANCE AND THE CHURCH

Italy's great reputation as a center of science and the arts drew scientists, scholars, and painters from all over Europe. During the 15th century the development of the printing press in Germany helped to spread the latest advances in learning. One result of this was that people began to question the traditional teachings of the church, which had come to seem narrow and old-fashioned. The Dutch scholar Erasmus studied in Italy before returning to northern Europe. In his writings he criticized church attitudes, and produced an edition of the New Testament based on the original Greek text, instead of the Latin text used by the church. Such activities directly challenged the church's authority and encouraged people to read the scriptures for themselves, rather than simply accept what the church told them. This new questioning and criticism finally caused the church to split into two factions, Catholic and Protestant. The united Western church of the Middle Ages had gone forever.

A bronze panel by the sculptor Lorenzo Ghiberti of Florence (1378–1455). It is in the style of ancient sculpture, with natural-looking figures, unlike the stiffer and more formal sculpture of the Middle Ages. It shows Abraham about to sacrifice Isaac.

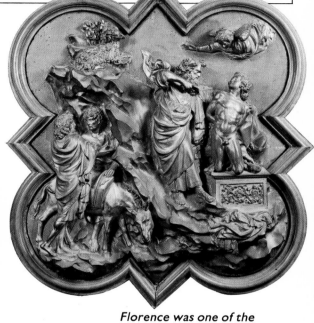

CHRONOLOGY

1250	Italy split into many separate city-states. Those in north and central Italy gain wealth and power. Southern Italy remains poor
1275	Marco Polo reaches Peking
1305	Papal See removed from Rome to Avignon
1306	Giotto completes series of frescoes in Padua
1307	Dante begins to write *Divine Comedy*
1341	Petrarch crowned Poet Laureate
1348	Black Death ravages Europe
1353	Boccaccio finishes writing the *Decameron*
1397	Medici bank founded in Florence
1402	Ghiberti wins competition for Baptistry doors, Florence
1434	Cosimo de' Medici rules Florence
1447	Pope Nicholas V founds the Vatican Library
1463	Venice begins 16-year war with Ottoman Turks
1465	First printing press in Italy

Florence was one of the richest cities in northern Italy and its wealthy merchants lived in great luxury. Some citizens disapproved very much of their way of life. In 1494 the friar Savonarola was made ruler of Florence. He built bonfires on which precious possessions were burned (below) and preached sermons telling people to give up their sinful way of life. Savonarola made many enemies, and he was sentenced to death.

Before Columbus

Perhaps the first European to reach the Americas was the Irish monk St. Brendan, in the 6th century A.D., who sailed west from Ireland in a boat made of leather. Early in the 11th century, Vikings from Greenland reached the coast of North America (see page 77). They never managed to set up successful colonies there, and the native people were unfriendly. Their last visits were early in the 14th century.

It was almost 200 years before the next Europeans reached the Americas. This time they were Spaniards, who landed first in Central America in 1519 and then in South America. There they found great civilizations which had grown up quite independently of the civilizations in the rest of the world. The most important were the empires of the Aztecs in Mexico and the Incas of Peru. Within a few years, the Spaniards had almost totally destroyed them as they conquered and converted the local peoples.

The lands ruled by the Aztecs and the Incas were mountainous but fertile. It was possible to grow good crops there, especially after people learned how to bring water to the fields through systems of irrigation channels. Maize was a very important crop, and beans, squashes, hot chili peppers, and avocados were grown. In the high Andes, where it was too cold for maize, potatoes were the most important food. The gold disc below was made by the Chimu people of north Peru in the 12th or 13th century A.D. In the center is the Earth Goddess. The various sections of the disc are a calendar for sowing the main crops.

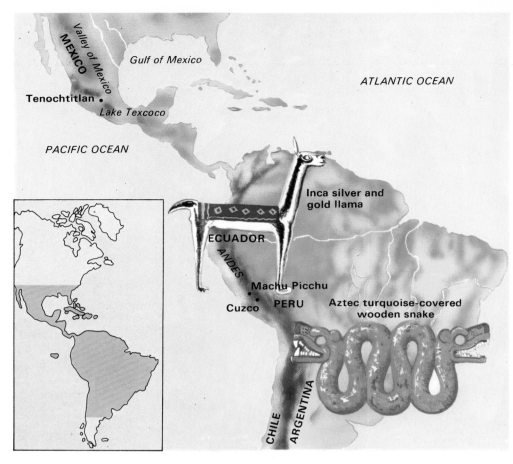

The Inca city of Machu Picchu was built high in the Peruvian mountains and surrounded by terraced fields where food could be grown. It was the last stronghold of the Incas who lingered on there after the Spanish conquest. Right: A gold figure of a llama, used by the peoples of the Andes as a pack animal and for wool. The Andes people were very skilled metalworkers, and it was rumors of the vast quantities of gold there that led parties of Spaniards to invade and conquer the area.

These illustrations come from a Mixtec document. The Mixtecs, whose name means "cloud people," lived in Mexico perhaps from the 7th century A.D. They were particularly skilled artists and craftsmen. Shortly before the Spaniards arrived, the Mixtecs were conquered by the Aztecs.

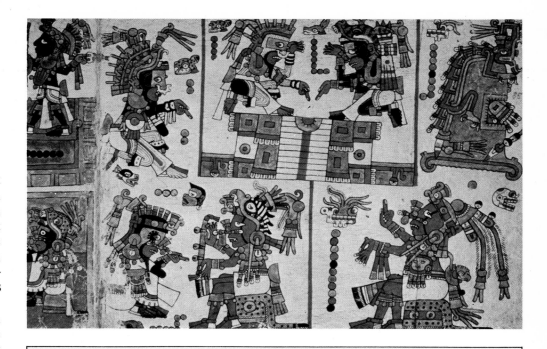

The Incas

In the 15th century the Incas built up a vast empire in South America. It stretched from modern Quito in Ecuador south through Peru into Chile and Argentina. Much of it was in the Andes Mountains, where there are grazing lands and fertile valleys between the high peaks. Along the coasts are flat deserts where only the land around the rivers can be farmed.

The ruling Incas came from a family which settled in the highland village of Cuzco in the 12th century. In the mid-15th century they conquered the highland area and then the Chimu empire along the coast. The Incas controlled 6 million people by strict and ruthless government. All land belonged to the state, and everyone had to spend much of their time working for the emperor. Armies and messengers could travel swiftly through the empire along a network of roads.

The peoples of the Inca empire were skilled craftsmen. They made beautifully decorated pots, and gold and silver ornaments and jewelry. Their weavers made brightly patterned cloth, sometimes working feathers into it. The Incas were also great builders, and ruins of their vast stone cities and temples still stand high in the mountains.

CHRONOLOGY

500	Tiahuanaco-Huari expansion in the Andes; Mochica and Nazca cultures in coastal Peru; Maya Classic Period in Central America (to 900); Teotihuacan important in Mexico
980	Toltecs establish their capital at Tula in Mexico
1000	Huari empire breaks up
1151	Toltec empire falls
1325	Aztecs found Tenochtitlan
1370	Chimu kingdom grows in coastal Peru
1428	Aztecs win independence
1438	Inca empire is built up in Peru and neighboring countries
1440	Aztecs begin to build up their empire
1450	Incas conquer Chimu kingdom
1521	Hernan Cortes conquers Tenochtitlan
1533	Francisco Pizarro conquers Incas

These pictures of North American Indians were drawn by the Englishman John White in about 1585. The lives of the North American Indians changed very little from the early centuries A.D. until the coming of the Europeans. In the south, they were influenced by the peoples of Mexico and built large settlements with ceremonial buildings. Farther north many lived by hunting and gathering food.

THE AZTECS

When the Spaniards arrived in Mexico in 1519 the Aztec empire stretched from the Atlantic Ocean to the Pacific Ocean. The Aztecs ruled it from their capital of Tenochtitlan, built on a swampy island in the middle of Lake Texcoco. It housed over half a million people.

The Aztecs had arrived in the Valley of Mexico at the end of the 12th century. At first they were slaves but before long they became independent. They built up their empire during the 15th century, forcing the tribes around them to pay a heavy tribute. This included food such as maize and beans, luxuries, and raw materials for craftsmen in gold, silver, and jade to work with. Traders brought turquoise from the Pueblo Indians to the north, and from the south came brightly colored parrot feathers which were made into capes, fans, and headdresses.

The Aztecs were ruled by their emperor. Next in importance were officials including judges, army commanders, and the governors of conquered provinces. They were given their own land and were allowed to wear ornaments of gold and precious stones. Then came free commoners, grouped into clans, and below them landless peasants and slaves. Every Aztec boy served in the army from 17 to 22. Some stayed on, for a peasant could rise to be a commander.

The priests were a special class. There were several thousand of them in Tenochtitlan alone. The Aztec religion was very cruel, and prisoners of war were sacrificed in a bloodthirsty manner to gods such as the war god Huitzilopochtli and the rain god Tlaloc.

The Turks

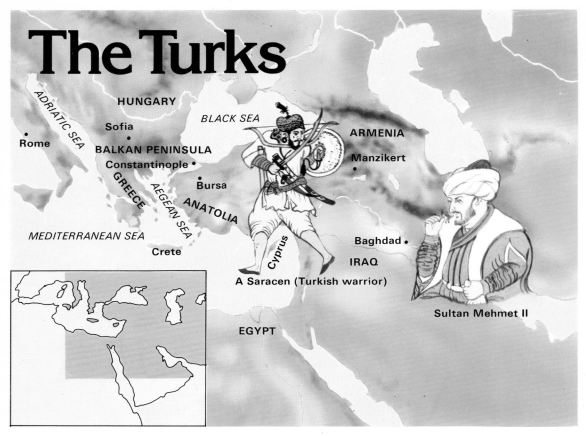

A Saracen (Turkish warrior)

Sultan Mehmet II

Above: A decorative panel from the Seljuk period.

Below: Bursa was the capital of the early Ottoman sultans before the fall of Constantinople in 1453. Today the ruined walls of the citadel mark the site of the old fortified city. By the road leading west from the town is the Muradiye Mosque. It was built by Murad II in the 15th century. Many other tombs and monuments have been built around it and in the cemetery shown here are buried 11 Ottoman princes and princesses. Elsewhere in Bursa are the tombs of Osman and Orhan, founders of the Ottoman dynasty.

All through the Middle Ages, invaders from Central Asia menaced the civilized areas of the world. In many cases, these nomads settled down in the countries they conquered and adopted at least some of their ways. This is what happened to the Turks, a nomadic people who came to the Near East as invaders and who ended up in control of the great Islamic empire.

CHRONOLOGY	
970	Seljuk Turks become Muslim
1055	Seljuks seize Baghdad
1064	Seljuks take Armenian capital
1071	Seljuks defeat Byzantines at Manzikert
1288	Osman becomes leader of "Ottoman" Turks, who from now on gain land from empire
1326	Bursa becomes Ottoman capital
1385	Sofia falls to Ottomans
1389	Ottomans defeat Serbs
1402	Ottomans temporarily defeated by Mongols
1453	Ottomans under Mehmet capture Constantinople

The Seljuks

The Turks were warlike nomads whose homeland was east-central Asia. They are first heard of under the Chinese name of T'u Kue in the 6th century A.D. In the 10th century Muslim missionaries converted many of them to Islam, and soon afterward a large group of Turks moved westward under their leader Seljuk. They came right into the heart of the Islamic empire, and in 1055 they reached Baghdad.

At this time the caliph of Baghdad was the ruler of all Islam. Under him were sultans who ruled over different regions. The caliph hoped that the Seljuks would support him. They used the title of sultan, and soon became excellent administrators of Islamic lands and ways of life. They gained control of much of the Near East.

Next the Seljuks moved northward to the Byzantine empire. They defeated a large Byzantine army and moved into Anatolia, where they established a large sultanate. Although fighting broke out many times, they managed to build up a prosperous state. Agriculture and mining production improved, and trade with Europe increased with the help of Italian merchants.

The Ottomans

In the mid-13th century Mongols from Central Asia devastated Anatolia and the Near East. After a time of great confusion, a new powerful state grew up in Anatolia. It was ruled by the Ottoman Turks, whose first great leader was called Osman. The Ottomans gained control of the Balkan peninsula from the Byzantines. Many people there had suffered under Byzantine rule, and welcomed the Ottomans. With the help of soldiers from the Balkan countries the Ottomans soon controlled almost all of Anatolia. Constantinople and the land around it remained a tiny outpost of Christianity in this Muslim empire. Another wave of Mongol raiders halted the Ottomans only briefly. In 1453 they captured Constantinople. The great Byzantine church of Holy Wisdom (Hagia Sophia) was proclaimed a mosque, but much of the city was left alone. As in the other Ottoman lands, many people remained Christian.

Soon the Ottomans ruled over an enormous empire which stretched from Algeria along the south Mediterranean coast, south to the Sudan, and east into Iraq. They kept control of the Balkans and pushed northward far into Hungary. The Ottomans were able to rule such an enormous area because they were efficient governors. They had a network of central and local officials which spread down into tiny villages. Trade with Europe and the East brought wealth. Above all, the Muslim way of life, with religion giving guidance on every aspect of daily living, helped to keep the Ottoman empire together.

By 1453 the Turks had conquered all the Byzantine territory except the capital, Constantinople. The Turkish leader Sultan Mehmet II (right) was determined to capture Constantinople. For more than a year he made plans and then his troops laid siege to the city (below). It was six weeks before Constantinople fell. This painting shows the Turks camped outside the city. They are bombarding the walls with cannon. The Ottoman empire now became the greatest of all the Muslim states. Ottoman domination, under the sultan, lasted until the 20th century.

THE JANISSARIES

The Ottoman sultan needed many soldiers to protect and control his empire. The most famous of his troops were the *Janissaries.* They were first recruited in the late 14th century and their name comes from the Turkish words for "new forces." The early Janissaries were battle captives. Later they came from the many slaves who were collected from Christian villages in the empire as children, and then converted to Islam.

The Janissaries were very fierce and brave and in the 15th and 16th centuries they were thought to be unbeatable. In peacetime they staffed border towns and policed Istanbul (Constantinople). When the Janissaries were unhappy with their conditions they kicked over the great copper cauldrons in which their food was cooked. Everyone dreaded this, for the Janissaries were very powerful and even helped to overthrow several sultans.

THE
AGE OF
DISCOVERY

The queen's bedroom with its elaborate decoration is typical of many huge rooms throughout the Château de Versailles.

Widening Horizons

In 1450 Europe was only one of many great civilizations, including those of China, Japan, Hindu India, the Aztecs and Incas in America, and Islam, which was beginning a great movement of expansion under the Ottoman Turks. Europe was by no means the most important, civilized, or wealthy of these. Yet by 1750 the situation had changed. European states had gained control of the ocean routes, organized worldwide trade, and conquered vast territories in America, India, and Siberia. The period from 1450 to 1750 stands halfway between the isolation of earlier centuries, and the "one world" of the 19th and 20th centuries, when what happened in one part of the world could have important results elsewhere.

This Flemish picture was painted in the early 1600s and shows the interior of an art gallery. On the table are a globe, maps, and navigational instruments including an astrolabe and a compass. These show the immense interest in exploration and discovery which people had at that time.

Isolated Peoples

In 1450 the different parts of the world had little contact with one another. Some people, like the Australian Aborigines, had had no contact with others for 50,000 years. The people of North and South America were almost as cut off from the rest of the world, since the existence of the continent was not known to people outside it. Africa south of the Sahara had been largely isolated for 6,000 years, since the Sahara became so dry that it was difficult to cross.

Only in Europe and Asia was there much contact between different areas and even this was confined to trade in a few articles. Textiles, pearls, gems, and spices had for centuries been imported into Europe from the Far East but little was known about the lands they came from. Not till the 13th century, when missionaries and merchants such as John of Plano Carpini and Marco Polo visited Central Asia and China, did Europeans know much about Asia.

The geographical knowledge of Europeans had not changed much since the time of the Roman empire. Then the most important geographer was the Egyptian Ptolemy, who lived in Alexandria in the 2nd century A.D. His *Geography* was lost for much of the Middle Ages, but was rediscovered and published in 1406. It was widely read after that, though it contained several important errors, such as indicating that there was no way around Africa, which were to hinder exploration.

All this was changed by the voyages of discovery. By 1780 the shape of all the continents was accurately known. Only the in-

PRINTING

Knowledge of these discoveries was spread by one of the most important advances since the invention of writing: printing. Until then books were slowly copied out by hand. They were scarce and expensive and most people, even the wealthiest, could not read. The first person in Europe to use movable metal type and an oil-based ink was Johannes Gutenberg, a diamond polisher in Mainz in Germany. The Gutenberg Bible, which he produced in 1455, was the first European printed book. By 1500 other printers all over Europe had followed his lead and about 35,000 editions of printed books had been published – between 15 and 20 million copies, which is probably more than the total number of manuscripts copied by hand in the previous thousand years. Books were now much cheaper and easily available. More people learned to read and write than ever before and information spread quickly.

teriors of areas such as Africa south of the Sahara and Australia were unexplored.

Europeans Grow Rich

Until Columbus found America in 1492 European society had been changing very slowly. Apart from the farmland gained by clearing forest and draining marshes, the amount of land available to European farmers had remained almost unaltered.

All this changed with the discovery of the New World. American bullion, and the profitable trade carried on by the Portuguese, Dutch, English, and French with India, the Spice Islands (now Indonesia), and the Far East, brought unheard of riches to Europe. The gold and silver which Drake brought back in the *Golden Hind* after his plundering expedition to Spanish America provided the money for two English trading companies, the East India Company and the Levant Company. The profits of these companies were invested, at the end of the 17th and in the 18th century, in English industries: cotton in Lancashire, iron in Birmingham, and the potteries of Staffordshire. Here are the origins of the Industrial Revolution, which put Europe ahead of the world in the 19th century.

If such wealth had been spent on luxuries, jewels, vast houses, and a great number of servants, in the way that Indian princes used their enormous wealth, there would have been no Industrial Revolution. What was needed to enable Europe to move from an agricultural to an industrial society was a group of people ready to seize the new opportunities and invest in industry. It was formed by merchants, bankers, and businessmen. Why did such a group rise in Europe and not elsewhere? Trade was as great in India and China as it was in Europe. However, merchants in these countries were not highly regarded.

China and Japan Withdraw

Just as these pushing and confident Europeans were expanding overseas, they received an unexpected benefit. The Chinese and the Japanese withdrew of their own will from the seas. The voyages of Cheng Ho between 1405 and 1433 had shown what the Chinese were capable of doing. He had sailed round Malaya to India and then on to the Gulf in seven voyages. His first fleet consisted of 62 large ships and 28,000 men. However, a decree from the Chinese emperor ended these voyages. The Tokugawa ruler of Japan also cut his country off from the outside world in 1635, when Japanese were forbidden to travel abroad. If the Chinese and the Japanese had resisted the Europeans, instead of ignoring them, the history of the world might well have been different.

Europe's Impact on the World

In spite of the vast empire they conquered, the impact of Europeans on most parts of the

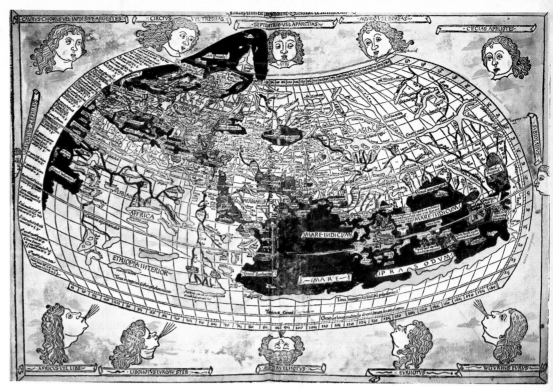

world between 1450 and 1750 was not very great. China and Japan continued in their own way, unaffected by what Europeans were doing. In Africa and India European influence was limited generally to scattered areas on or near the coast. Only in America and some of the Spice Islands did Europeans overthrow an existing way of life and deeply affect the inhabitants. Not until the new scientific discoveries and their application in the Industrial Revolution in the 19th century did Europe profoundly affect the rest of the world.

In Europe too the number of people directly affected by the voyages of discovery was small. Life went on as it had been going on for centuries. Most people lived their lives in the village in which they were born and rarely, if ever, moved beyond the nearest market town. The slow rhythm of the seasons and the need to get in the harvest decided their pattern of work and leisure.

The map above dates from 1486 and is based on the world of Ptolemy, who lived in the 2nd century A.D. America had not yet been discovered, and no one knew how far south Africa stretched. Below is a map of the world printed in 1570, less than 100 years later. By then Dias had sailed round Africa, da Gama had gone on to India, and Columbus, Vespucci, and Magellan had explored the coasts of America. In the south is shown the huge block of Terra Australis nondum Cognita, the unknown land to the south; not until Cook's voyages of the 1770s was this shown not to exist.

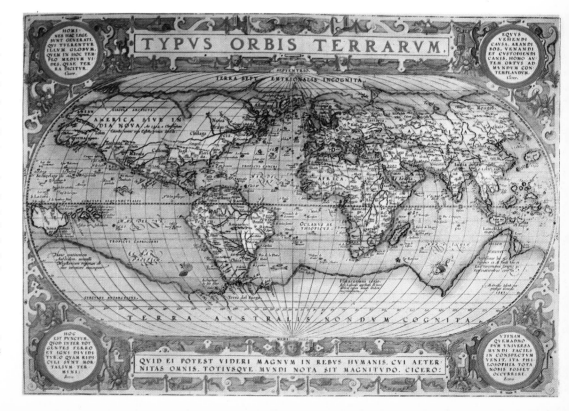

Ships, Navigation and Guns

Before explorers could find an all-sea route to the Spice Islands (Indonesia), they needed ships which were strong enough to brave the stormy seas of the Atlantic and to battle against the wind down the coast of Africa. The first ships capable of doing this were developed by the Portuguese and the Spaniards, and so it was they, rather than the Arabs or Chinese, who discovered America and sailed around the world.

In 1450 there were no ships which were capable of long journeys in open seas. The Arabs were masters of the Indian Ocean but their ships, called *dhows*, were difficult to hold on course, particularly as they were steered by an oar. The planks were held together by wooden pegs and coconut fiber rope, which were weaker on the open sea than the nailed planks of the European ships. Chinese junks sailed long distances, but they had to have the wind behind them and were often driven helplessly off course by storms. The long, narrow oared galleys of the Mediterranean could not stand up to the Atlantic breakers, while the cargo-carrying cog of northern Europe was heavy and slow. It had a square sail, which prevented it sailing near the wind.

In the middle of the 15th century the Portuguese developed a new type of ship, the *caravel*. It was small and light, with a triangular lateen sail, so that it could sail close to the wind. By the end of the century another and larger ship, the *nao*, had been designed. It had high castles (built-up ends), large holds, and both square and lateen sails. By 1500 all European ships had this combination of sails, making them more maneuverable than any other type of ship in the world.

After this ships became bigger but their design was basically unchanged until the steam ship. The captain of a 19th-century clipper would have felt at home in Columbus's ships, though he would have found them small and cramped.

Navigation

When they were out of sight of land, sailors needed to work out their position at sea. The compass, which had been used at sea since about 1250, told them in which direction they were going, as the needle always pointed north. It was much more difficult to work out how far they had traveled in any direction.

Latitude (movement north or south) could be measured by finding the angle of the sun above the horizon at noon. To do this instruments such as the astrolabe or cross staff were used. With the help of tables, which gave the position of the sun at different latitudes for each day of the year, a sea captain could work out how far north or south of the equator he was, to within about 48 kilometers (30 miles). Accurate tables were needed for this. These were provided by Prince Henry "the

Top: A caravel of the late 1400s, the sort of ship in which the Portuguese sailed southward to explore the coasts of Africa.

Above: A reconstruction of the Santa Maria, the ship in which Christopher Columbus made his first Atlantic crossing in 1492. With him were two smaller caravels, the Nina and the Pinta. He sailed first to the Canary Islands, as he knew winds there blew to the west. When he left the Canaries he was very fortunate, as the winds blew steadily. Even so, after 30 days at sea the crew of the Santa Maria demanded that he turn back. He agreed to do so within a few days if land had not been sighted, but two days later a lookout on the Pinta saw land. They had reached the Bahamas.

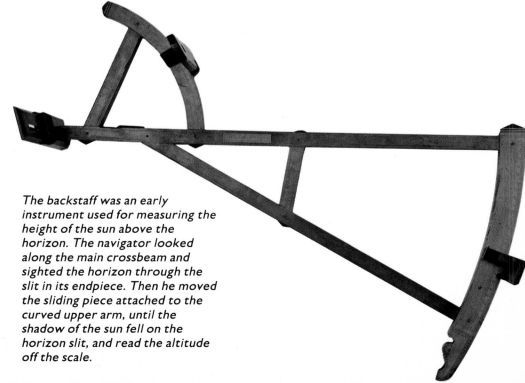

The backstaff was an early instrument used for measuring the height of the sun above the horizon. The navigator looked along the main crossbeam and sighted the horizon through the slit in its endpiece. Then he moved the sliding piece attached to the curved upper arm, until the shadow of the sun fell on the horizon slit, and read the altitude off the scale.

Navigator" of Portugal (1394–1460), whose astronomers and mathematicians worked out the necessary information for Portuguese seamen.

There was no accurate way of deciding longitude (movement east or west) until the marine chronometer was invented in 1762. In spite of this, knowledge of latitude enabled seamen to travel long distances across the open sea and yet steer a ship to a particular place. In 1497 Vasco da Gama spent 97 days out of sight of land and still steered accurately for the Cape of Good Hope.

Guns

Europeans sailing into unknown waters did not only need stout ships and aids to navigation. They also had to be able to defend themselves. In the Middle Ages warships carried soldiers, who boarded an enemy ship after it had been rammed. So naval battles then took the form of hand-to-hand fighting on deck. This continued in the Mediterranean as late as the battle of Lepanto in 1571.

In the 15th century guns were fitted to European ships, but they were only small. They could kill men but not damage ships. Between 1500 and 1520 new methods for casting guns were developed in the Netherlands and Germany which gave greater firepower. These guns could fire round stones, and later cast-iron balls, that weighed from about 2 to 27 kilograms (5 to 60 pounds) and could damage ships 275 meters (300 yards) away. The aim now was not to ram and board the enemy ship but to sink it by gunfire. This new type of warfare meant that ships had to be built more strongly with a large keel, heavy ribs, and double oak planking. Soon they could carry 40 guns and could take the recoil of cannon without being damaged. Europeans had learned to build stout ships to sail the Atlantic. Ships built for less stormy seas fell apart after a few shots had been fired. No Asian country learned to redesign its ships to carry heavy guns, so the Europeans had a great advantage that enabled them to seize and keep control of the oceans of the world. From 1500 their supremacy was not successfully challenged until 1905, when the Japanese (who had learned to build western-style ships) defeated the Russian fleet at Tsushima.

The traverse board helped sailors know how far they had sailed. The helmsman inserted pegs to show how many half-hour periods the ship had sailed on any particular course. Estimated speed was shown in the four rows of holes at the foot of the board. Below: The defeat of the Spanish Armada. The English ships were faster and more maneuverable than the great Spanish galleons, and their guns had a longer range.

The World in 1450

In Europe, this is a time of change. The feudal system is breaking down. In the independent cities of northern Italy a new interest in learning and art is growing up; it spreads through Europe, helped by the invention of the printing press in the 1450s. Soon the western church will be split when Protestants break away in the Reformation. In 1453 the Ottoman Turks capture Constantinople, the last stronghold of the Byzantine empire. In Portugal Prince Henry the Navigator gathers sailors, mapmakers, and ship designers; the great age of exploration is about to begin.

Western Europe The devastation caused by the Black Death of the 1340s has helped break down the feudal system; central governments are being formed. The Hundred
5 Years' War between England and France ends in 1453 with the loss of almost all England's lan[...]
6 in France. The Italian Renaissance – an increas[...] interest in learning and t[...] arts – soon spreads
7 northward. In Germany Gutenberg invents his printing process.

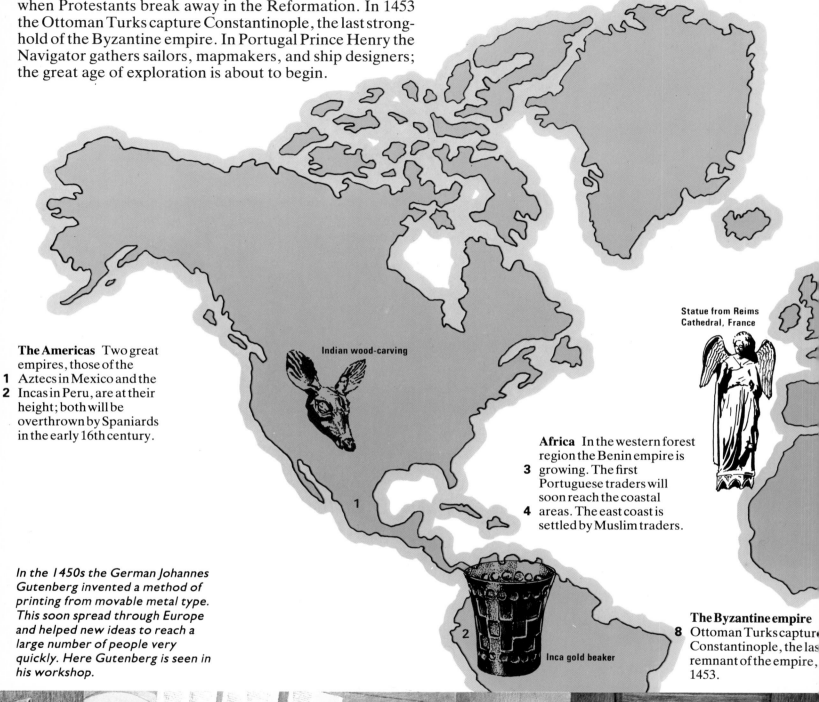

Indian wood-carving

Statue from Reims Cathedral, France

The Americas Two great empires, those of the
1 Aztecs in Mexico and the
2 Incas in Peru, are at their height; both will be overthrown by Spaniards in the early 16th century.

Africa In the western forest region the Benin empire is
3 growing. The first Portuguese traders will soon reach the coastal
4 areas. The east coast is settled by Muslim traders.

In the 1450s the German Johannes Gutenberg invented a method of printing from movable metal type. This soon spread through Europe and helped new ideas to reach a large number of people very quickly. Here Gutenberg is seen in his workshop.

Inca gold beaker

The Byzantine empire
8 Ottoman Turks captur[...] Constantinople, the las[...] remnant of the empire, 1453.

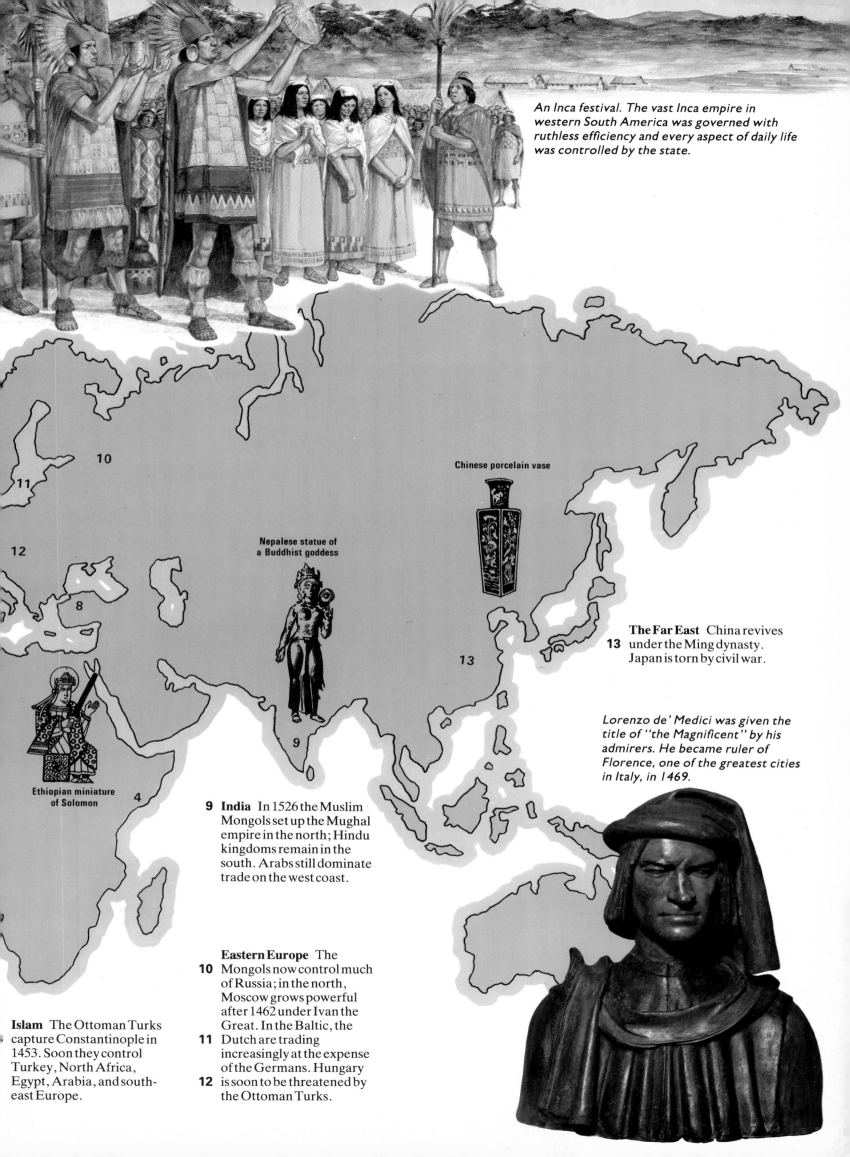

An Inca festival. The vast Inca empire in western South America was governed with ruthless efficiency and every aspect of daily life was controlled by the state.

Chinese porcelain vase

Nepalese statue of a Buddhist goddess

The Far East China revives
13 under the Ming dynasty. Japan is torn by civil war.

Lorenzo de' Medici was given the title of "the Magnificent" by his admirers. He became ruler of Florence, one of the greatest cities in Italy, in 1469.

Ethiopian miniature of Solomon

9 India In 1526 the Muslim Mongols set up the Mughal empire in the north; Hindu kingdoms remain in the south. Arabs still dominate trade on the west coast.

Eastern Europe The
10 Mongols now control much of Russia; in the north, Moscow grows powerful after 1462 under Ivan the Great. In the Baltic, the
11 Dutch are trading increasingly at the expense of the Germans. Hungary
12 is soon to be threatened by the Ottoman Turks.

Islam The Ottoman Turks capture Constantinople in 1453. Soon they control Turkey, North Africa, Egypt, Arabia, and south-east Europe.

Voyages of Discovery

In the 15th century Portugal was a poor country. Two-thirds of the land was too rocky or steep to be cultivated. Yet Portugal was well placed to begin the explorations of the coast of Africa. Its sailors were used to the rough waters of the Atlantic. Prince Henry "the Navigator," son of the Portuguese king, provided the leadership.

Henry the Navigator

Henry wanted to make contact by sea with the gold-producing areas of West Africa. He was a very sincere Christian and hoped not only to seize the gold trade from the Muslims but also to convert the native people of Africa to Christianity.

Cape Bojador was the southernmost limit of the Atlantic then known. Here there were violent waves and strong currents and it was difficult to turn around and sail back north because of the strong southerly winds. In 1434 one of Henry's ships rounded Cape Bojador and did return. It was his greatest achievement. After this the Portuguese lost their fear of unknown seas and were soon moving farther south. By the time Prince Henry died in 1460, the Portuguese had reached Sierra Leone. Madeira, the Azores, and the Cape Verde Islands had been colonized. As the Portuguese sailed down the coast of Africa their aims changed. Instead of gold from Africa, they sought an all-sea route to the Spice Islands around southern Africa.

In 1487 Bartolomeu Dias set off to find this route. He battled down the coast in the teeth of the southeast trade winds and was blown out to sea by violent storms. When they eased off and he reached land he found that he had come around the tip of Africa.

Vasco da Gama

Vasco da Gama left Lisbon with three ships in 1497. At the Cape Verde Islands he swung far west into the Atlantic. By doing this he avoided the opposing winds along the coast and was able to pick up the Westerlies, which would bring him to the Cape. This route has been followed ever since by sailing ships. After passing the Cape he sailed up the east coast of Africa. When he reached Mozambique he found himself in a busy trading area, which had already been accurately mapped by the Arabs. He picked up an Arab pilot, Ibn Majib, who guided his ships across the Indian Ocean to Calicut. Da Gama was the first European to reach India by sea. Here he collected a cargo of pepper, cinnamon, ginger, and precious stones and set sail for Portugal. He reached Lisbon in 1499. Two-thirds of his crew had died on the way, but the sale of his cargo was worth 60 times the cost of the expedition.

Christopher Columbus

Christopher Columbus, a Genoese sailor, believed that the shortest and easiest route to the Spice Islands lay in sailing west. No one in Europe then knew that there was a vast continent in the way, though the Vikings had landed in North America in the 11th century.

With the backing of Queen Isabella of Spain, Columbus set sail in 1492. He first went to the Canary Islands, as he knew that the winds there blew to the west. He sailed for over a month before reaching the Bahamas and later Cuba.

On three more voyages Columbus discovered Jamaica, Trinidad, the northern coast of South America, and Central America. Until his death in 1506, he was convinced that he had reached Asia.

Vasco da Gama left Lisbon on July 8, 1497, with three small ships to sail to the East. An Arab pilot took him to Calicut on the west coast of India; he took presents for the Hindu ruler including striped cloth, strings of coral beads, six hats, and six wash basins. The Indians laughed at these and demanded gold. The journey back across the Indian Ocean took nearly three months and 30 members of the crew died of scurvy.

As a result of Henry the Navigator's expeditions, many Portuguese trading stations grew up along the west coast of Africa. By the time this map was drawn in 1558 much of the coast had been charted and named.

CHRONOLOGY	
1434	Cape Bojador rounded by the Portuguese
1487	Dias leaves Lisbon to sail around the Cape and enters the Indian Ocean (1488)
1492	Columbus discovers the Bahamas Islands, and explores the north coast of Cuba and Hispaniola (to 1493)
1493	Columbus explores the south coast of Cuba, thinking it is part of mainland China
1497	Da Gama sails to India (to 1499)
1498	Columbus discovers Trinidad and the coast of South America
1500	The Portuguese Pedro Cabral sees the coast of Brazil
1502	Columbus's last voyage (to 1504). He explores the coast of Central America
1519	First voyage around the world by Magellan's expedition (to 1522)

Ferdinand Magellan

Any hope of reaching the Spice Islands by sailing west now depended on finding a passage through the new continent or on sailing around it. Explorers continued to move down the coast of South America. One of these was Amerigo Vespucci, after whom America is named. The most famous of all was Ferdinand Magellan, a Portuguese in Spanish pay, who set sail from Spain in 1519. He crossed the Atlantic to Brazil and then turned south. Eventually he reached the strait at the tip of South America that was to be named after him. It was 560 kilometers (350 miles) long and full of reefs. Ice-covered mountains rose sheer on both sides and acted as a funnel for the wind, creating violent squalls. It took Magellan 38 days to sail through the strait into an ocean that was so calm and smooth that he called it "the peaceful [Pacific] ocean."

Magellan sailed up the coast of Chile before turning west. It was over three months before he next reached land in the Philippines. There he was killed in a local war. But one of his ships under Sebastian del Cano managed to reach Spain in 1522 and so completed the first voyage around the world.

The difficulties Magellan had found while sailing around South America meant that the Strait of Magellan would never be used as a trade route to the East. The main trade route would long continue to be the Portuguese one around Africa and across the Indian Ocean. Yet the importance of the voyages of Spain and Portugal was immense. They had found a continent previously unknown in Europe, and they had shown that all the oceans in the world were connected and that the world was much bigger than expected.

This early map of South America shows the Strait of Magellan and fanciful pictures of the local people and animals.

HARDSHIP AT SEA

Pigafetta described the terrible conditions on board Magellan's ship when sailing across the Pacific:

We were three months and twenty days without getting any kind of fresh food. We ate biscuit, which was no longer biscuit, but powder of biscuits swarming with worms, for they had eaten the good. It stank strongly of the urine of rats. We drank yellow water that had been putrid for many days. We were even forced, so that we might not die of hunger, to eat pieces of leather with which the mainyard was covered to prevent it from wearing the ropes. These pieces of leather, constantly exposed to the water, sun, and wind, were so hard that they required being soaked four or five days in the sea in order to make them supple; after this we boiled them to eat. Frequently indeed we were obliged to live on sawdust, and even rats . . . were sought after with such greed that they sold for half a ducat apiece.

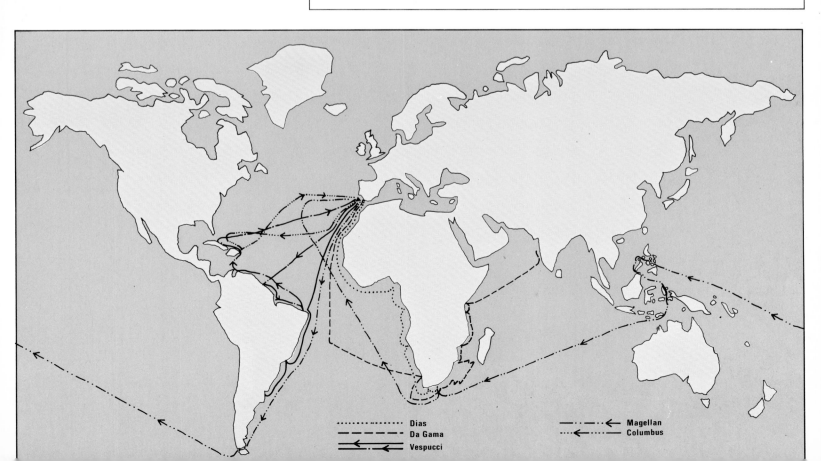

·······	Dias	———	Magellan
– – –	Da Gama	-·-·-	Columbus
⇒⇒⇒	Vespucci		

Overseas Empires

In 1519, the same year in which Magellan left Seville on his voyage around the world (see page 110), Hernan Cortes left Cuba in the West Indies and landed on the American coast near present-day Veracruz. In the 30 years that followed, a few thousand Spanish adventurers (*conquistadors*) conquered the first great European overseas empire.

The Conquistadors

Although Cortes had only a small number of Spanish soldiers, he had the great advantage of having horses, gunpowder, and steel weapons. The Aztecs, rulers of a great empire in Central America, had seen none of these before and were terrified by them. Cortes learned that other tribes hated the Aztecs and persuaded them to join him. In 1521 Cortes finally defeated the Aztecs and captured their capital city, Tenochtitlan.

Even more remarkable than the defeat of the Aztecs was the conquest of the vast Inca empire. Soon after the conquest of Mexico rumors of the fabulous riches of the Incas in Peru reached the conquistadors. Francisco Pizarro decided to find out if they were true. He set off in 1531 from Panama in three ships with 180 men, 27 horses, and 2 cannon. When he reached the port of Tumbes he heard that the Inca leader, Atahualpa, was only 565 kilometers (350 miles) away at Cajamarca. Pizarro and his men marched up the steep gorges of the Andes, breathless from lack of oxygen. At Cajamarca he captured, and later killed, Atahualpa and seized huge quantities of gold. Within 20 years the Spaniards ruled the whole Inca empire.

The success of Cortes and Piazrro inspired other conquistadors to march through large areas of both North and South America, searching for booty. They found nothing like the Aztec and Inca treasures but they conquered Central America and what is now Colombia and Venezuela. By 1550 they had followed the Amazon from Peru to its mouth. By 1600 they were familiar with the entire coast of South America, from the Gulf of California south to Tierra del Fuego and north from there to the West Indies.

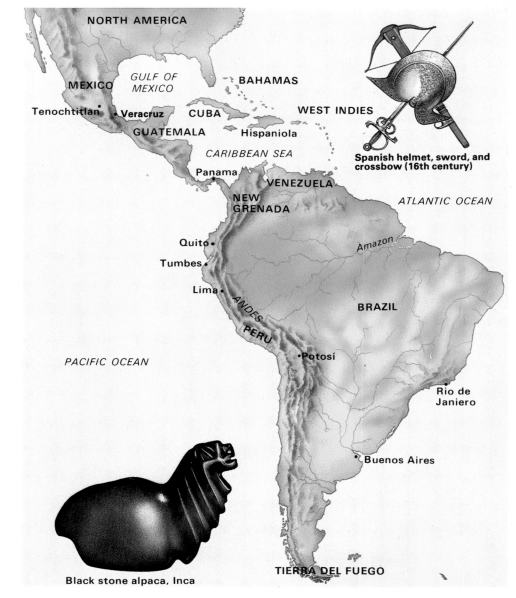

Spanish helmet, sword, and crossbow (16th century)

Black stone alpaca, Inca

The Royal Road of the Incas wound through the high Andes, and was used by the Inca emperor and his officials and soldiers. Ravines were crossed by rope bridges.

NEW SPAIN

Many people from Spain went to live in the new Spanish empire. These colonies were ruled by the Council of the Indies in Spain. It appointed all officials to run the new territories, especially the viceroys. One viceroy lived in Mexico City (formerly Tenochtitlan) and governed New Spain, which consisted of all Spanish lands in North America, the West Indies, Venezuela, and the Philippines. The viceroy of Peru at Lima ruled the rest of Spain's possessions in South America.

Many of the laws made for the colonies show that the Spanish government tried to make sure that Indians were well-treated, but it was impossible to prevent the conquistadors from treating the Indians badly. Soon many were made slaves or were killed, while thousands died as they had no resistance to European diseases such as measles and smallpox. The population of Peru at the time of the conquest was 7 million; by 1600 it was 1,800,000.

The value of the new empire to Spain became clear in the 1540s, when silver mines were discovered in both Mexico and Peru. Potosí in Peru was the biggest source of silver in the world and was to provide Europe with most of its precious metals for the next 300 years.

The 17th-century cathedral at Quito, capital of Ecuador. The city was planned on typical Spanish lines by de Belalcazar, one of Pizarro's lieutenants, in the 1530s.

Spanish and Portuguese lands in Central and South America. In 1494 the Tordesillas demarcation line was agreed; Portugal had the right to land east of this line, while that to the west could be claimed by Spain.

□ Spanish control
■ Portuguese control

Brazil

In 1500 the Portuguese Pedro Alvares Cabral, sailing to the Indian Ocean, moved too far out into the Atlantic and reached Brazil. It was the only part of South America which became Portuguese rather than Spanish. Sugar plantations were set up near the coast. Few of the other early settlements were successful, and in the mid-16th century King John took Brazil under royal control and appointed a governor general. By 1600 Brazil had become the most important sugar-producing area in the world. When Brazil began to lose its lead in sugar production because the soil was exhausted, gold was discovered there. Much of this went to England, which supplied most of the manufactures Brazil needed.

Brazil was only one part of the Portuguese empire. More important to Portugal were its colonies in Africa and in the Spice Islands (see page 132).

A picture of Brazil in 1600. Rowing up the river, and in the stockade, are Portuguese soldiers. By this time Brazil was under the direct rule of the Portuguese king, and settlers were arriving in great numbers.

CHRONOLOGY

1492	Columbus reaches the Bahamas
1493	Spaniards begin to settle Hispaniola
1494	Treaty of Tordesillas signed between Spain and Portugal, giving Spain rights to all land west of line of demarcation; Portuguese retain rights to east
1500	Pedro Cabral claims Brazil for Portugal
1509	First Spanish settlement of American mainland
1519	Cortes begins conquest of Aztec empire
1523	Spanish begin to settle Guatemala
1532	Pizarro begins conquest of Inca empire
1535	Spanish establish viceroy in Mexico
1536	Spanish begin to settle New Granada
1545	Silver mines discovered at Potosí, Peru
1549	First governor general of Brazil brings the country under royal control
1564	Spanish start to send convoys of ships carrying silver back to Europe, accompanied by warships

Reformation and Counter-Reformation

In 1500 nearly everyone in western Europe was a member of the Catholic church but many people were discontented with it. Some rulers wanted its wealth and lands for themselves. Other people criticized the immorality and ignorance of many of the clergy, and the sale of indulgences, by which the pope's representatives forgave people their sins in return for money.

Martin Luther

One man who showed this discontent forcefully was Martin Luther in Germany. He said that only God, not the pope or priests, could forgive sins. He denied that salvation from the everlasting fires of hell depended on good deeds. Only faith in God, he said, could bring salvation. He also said that priests should be allowed to marry, as he did himself. In 1517 he publicly attacked the sale of indulgences by pinning his 95 "theses" (arguments) to the church door at Wittenberg.

In doing this Luther began a movement known as the Reformation (as it was an attempt to reform the Catholic church), which was to lead to a split in the church. Thanks to the invention of printing his ideas were known throughout Germany in only a few weeks. Luther's supporters set up a "reformed" church which became known as Protestant, a name later given to other reformed churches as well.

In Germany many princes backed Luther in order to seize church lands. This led to a war between the Catholic emperor Charles V and the Protestants. Neither side won a clear victory, so in 1555 the emperor had to allow each German prince to decide whether his state should be Catholic or Protestant. By this time Lutheranism had spread over nearly all northern Germany and Scandinavia.

John Calvin

In Switzerland appeared another great religious reformer, John Calvin. He was more severe than Luther and believed that from the moment we are born, we are destined to go to heaven or hell. Nothing we can do in our lives can change this. By the time Calvin died his ideas had spread to much of Switzerland, France, and The Netherlands. In Scotland Calvinists led by John Knox overthrew the Catholic Mary Queen of Scots, and Calvinism became the main religion. It also spread to parts of Germany, Poland, Bohemia, and Hungary.

Martin Luther, the monk who led the Protestant split from the Roman Catholic church.

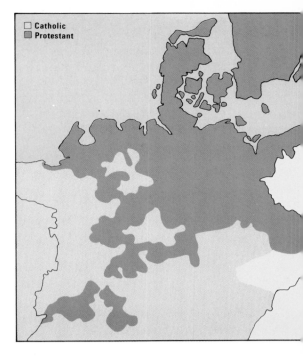

The main Protestant and Catholic areas in northern Europe in the mid-16th century. The cream-colored region on the right was mixed. In southern Europe the Reformation had little success; Portugal, Spain, Italy, and Austria remained firmly Catholic.

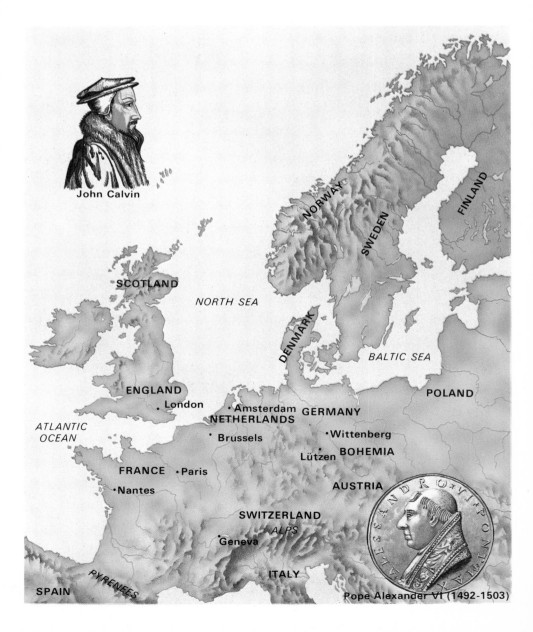

The Counter-Reformation

The Catholic church tried to stop the spread of Protestantism and to put right some of the things that had been wrong with the church. This movement was called the Counter-Reformation. One of its leaders was Ignatius Loyola who, in 1540, founded the Society of Jesus. The Jesuits, as its members were called, were organized strictly to obey their leader and the pope without question. In Europe they worked tirelessly to convert Protestants to Catholicism, and their missionaries went to many parts of the world, including China and Japan. Catholicism was also strengthened by the Council of Trent (1545–1563), a church assembly which made clear what Catholic doctrine was, and reorganized the church to keep up high standards among the clergy.

As a result of the Counter-Reformation Catholics began to regain lost ground. By 1570, 40 percent of the people in Europe had become Protestants; by 1650 this was down to 20 percent. Poland became largely Catholic again, as did France.

Religious Wars

In France, the Netherlands, and Germany, Catholic rulers tried to get rid of Protestantism in a series of wars which lasted until 1648. Though the wars were fought in the name of religion, many rulers took part in order to increase their power and territory. In France Queen Catherine de' Medici tried to have all the Huguenots (French Calvinists) killed in a great massacre on St. Bartholomew's Day in 1572. Many were killed but Protestantism survived. In the Netherlands, Philip II tried to intensify Spanish rule and impose Catholicism, but he was resisted by William of Orange. The Dutch War of Independence against Spain went on for 80 years.

In central Europe the Habsburg emperor Ferdinand II began the Thirty Years' War (1618–1648), when he brutally crushed Protestants in Bohemia. He seemed likely to defeat all the Protestant princes in Germany, but then King Gustavus Adolphus of Sweden joined in on the side of the Protestants. Gustavus Adolphus saved Protestantism in Germany and won many victories before his death at the battle of Lützen in 1632. Support for German Protestants now came unexpectedly from Catholic France, which wanted to prevent its great rivals, the Habsburgs, from increasing their territories. When the war ended Germany was split into a mainly Protestant north, with Catholic states in the south and west. The divisions in the Christian church begun by the Reformation remain today.

The Council of Trent met between 1545 and 1563. It consisted of leading members of the Roman Catholic church. It had two purposes: to get rid of the slack practices of the church which Luther had criticized, and to set down clearly the teachings of the church.

CHRONOLOGY

1517	Luther pins his theses to the church door at Wittenberg
1534	The Act of Supremacy makes Henry VIII head of the church in England
1540	Loyola founds the Society of Jesus
1541	Geneva becomes a Calvinist city
1545	The Council of Trent first meets
1572	The Massacre of St. Bartholomew's Day in France
1598	The Edict of Nantes gives French Protestants freedom of worship
1609	The United Provinces become independent
1632	Death of Gustavus Adolphus at Lützen
1648	Peace of Westphalia ends the Thirty Years' War

THE CHURCH OF ENGLAND

England developed its own kind of Protestantism. Henry VIII wanted a male heir, and his wife had given him only one living child, a daughter. Because the pope would not give him a divorce, he broke away from the Catholic church and in 1534 declared himself head of the church in England. The Anglican church became established under Queen Elizabeth I and is still the state religion in England.

A scene during the Massacre of St. Bartholomew's Day in 1572, when some 29,000 French Protestants were murdered.

Plate from Iznik, Turkey

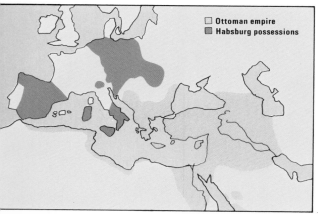

Ottoman empire
Habsburg possessions

The emperor Charles V.

The Mediterranean Area

The Mediterranean was the cradle of European civilization from the time of the Ancient Greeks. The Roman empire was created there and the area kept its importance right up to the Renaissance, when the trade of the Italian city-states such as Venice and Genoa made it the richest area of Europe. In the 16th century Venice and Genoa became less important. Two great powers, the Spanish Habsburgs and the Ottoman Turks, at each end of the Mediterranean, struggled to control it.

The Habsburgs

In 1516 Charles V of the Habsburg family inherited Spain and its Italian lands. Three years later he received the Habsburg lands in central Europe – Austria and the nearby regions of Germany. In addition his father left him Franche Comté, Luxembourg, and the wealthy Netherlands. To crown it all Charles was elected Holy Roman emperor in 1519. When the new Spanish empire in America was conquered, he ruled a greater empire than had any European since Charlemagne 700 years before. Habsburg power was increased still more when Charles's brother Ferdinand inherited Bohemia and Hungary.

The Valois kings of France were determined to prevent the Habsburgs from dominating Europe. The result was a long series of Valois-Habsburg wars, which began in Italy in 1494. Italy was divided into many states, which made it an easy prey for large, united countries like France and Spain. The wars ended in 1559 with the defeat of France, which left Spain supreme in Italy: it controlled Milan in the north, Naples and Sicily in the south, and the island of Sardinia.

Charles gave up his throne in 1556 and divided his territories. The Habsburg lands in central Europe, together with the title of Holy Roman emperor, went to his brother Ferdinand, the Spanish lands and the Netherlands to his son Philip II. With its control of southern Italy, Spain was in the front line of defense against the other great Mediterranean power, the Ottoman Turks.

The Ottomans

The Ottomans were originally a band of Turks who moved into Anatolia (Asia Minor) in the 13th century. They took their name from their leader, Osman. They soon ruled over Anatolia, and in the 14th century they gained control of most of the Balkan peninsula. In 1453 Mehmet "the Conqueror" added to his empire the richest prize of all, the city which had for over a thousand years been the capital of the Byzantine empire – Constantinople.

While Spain gained control of much of Italy on the northern shore of the Mediterranean, the Ottoman Turks were moving along the south. Sultan Selim I (the Grim) defeated the Mamluk rulers of Egypt in 1517. This victory decided the fate of the Near East for the next 400 years, as it gave the Ottomans control not only of Syria, Egypt, and Iraq but also of the Muslim holy cities of Mecca and Medina.

SULEYMAN THE MAGNIFICENT

With their Muslim enemies defeated, the Ottoman Turks could now attack Christian Europe again. This was done by Suleyman, who became sultan in 1520 and ruled till 1566, a long reign which saw the Ottoman empire at the height of its power. In 1522 Suleyman captured the island of Rhodes and then led an expedition across the Danube into Hungary, where he won a great victory at Mohacs in 1526. The fall of Hungary opened the way to the Austrian and German lands, so in 1529 Suleyman advanced toward the imperial capital of Vienna and besieged it. If Vienna had fallen, all central Europe might have passed under Ottoman control. As it was, the Turks were driven back. This marked the limit of their advance in Europe.

Suleyman besieges Bucharest, in modern Romania.

OTTOMAN DECLINE

In the 17th century the Ottoman threat to Europe grew less. From 1606 to 1639 the Ottomans were fighting the Persians and did not mount a major offensive in Europe, in the grand style, until 1683. Again Vienna was the target and again the Ottomans failed. This failure was final. The Austrians and their allies advanced rapidly into Ottoman territory in Hungary and defeated the Turks at Zenta in 1697. The Turks made peace at Karlowitz and gave up much territory, including most of Hungary, to the Habsburgs. It was the first time the Ottomans had signed a peace as a defeated power and had given up territory. After this the Ottoman empire was always on the defensive.

Muslim pirates from North Africa raided shipping in the Mediterranean and the Turks captured southern Greece and Cyprus. In 1571 a Christian fleet defeated a much larger Turkish force at Lepanto (below) but the Turks soon rebuilt their navy.

The World in 1550

Europeans have developed ships, navigational aids, and guns which enable them to sail around the world. In doing so they have discovered a new continent, America, where the Spaniards have set up an empire. The Portuguese have sailed to Southeast Asia and ended Muslim control of the spice trade. There have been further Muslim setbacks in Russia, where Muscovy has broken away from Mongol control. Elsewhere the Muslims are advancing; the Ottoman threat to Europe is severe, while in India and Persia great Islamic empires are firmly established. In western Europe the Reformation has seen Protestants break away from the Catholic church. China remains powerful but has little contact with the rest of the world.

Western Europe In
4 Germany Luther has begun the Reformation by setting up a "reformed" Protestant church. The wars which follow between Catholics and Protestants are still going on but Lutheranism has spread over most of northern Germany and
5 Scandinavia. The ideas of John Calvin, another Protestant reformer, have spread from his native
6 Geneva to Scotland, France and the Netherlands. In
7 Italy the Valois-Habsburg wars (begun in 1494) are still going on, as is the Council of Trent (1545–1563), which strengthens the Catholic church in its struggle against Protestantism.

Russian dignitary

Tobacco plants

Spanish ivory and gold amulet

The Americas The Aztec
1 civilization has been destroyed by Cortes (1521) and the Incas by Pizarro (1533). Much of North and South America has been explored by Spaniards, who by 1550 have followed the
2 Amazon from Peru to its mouth. The French are
3 established in Canada after Jacques Cartier's journey up the St. Lawrence river (1535).

At the battle of Panipat in 1526 Babur the Mongol, ruler of Kabul, fought Sultan Ibrahim, the ruler of northern India. Babur was victorious, and Ibrahim and 20,000 of his men were killed. Babur moved on to Delhi where he declared himself emperor. He founded the Mughal empire. Babur himself did not like India much but longed for the hills and streams of Kabul.

Benin plaque of Portuguese trader, West Africa

Spanish conquistador

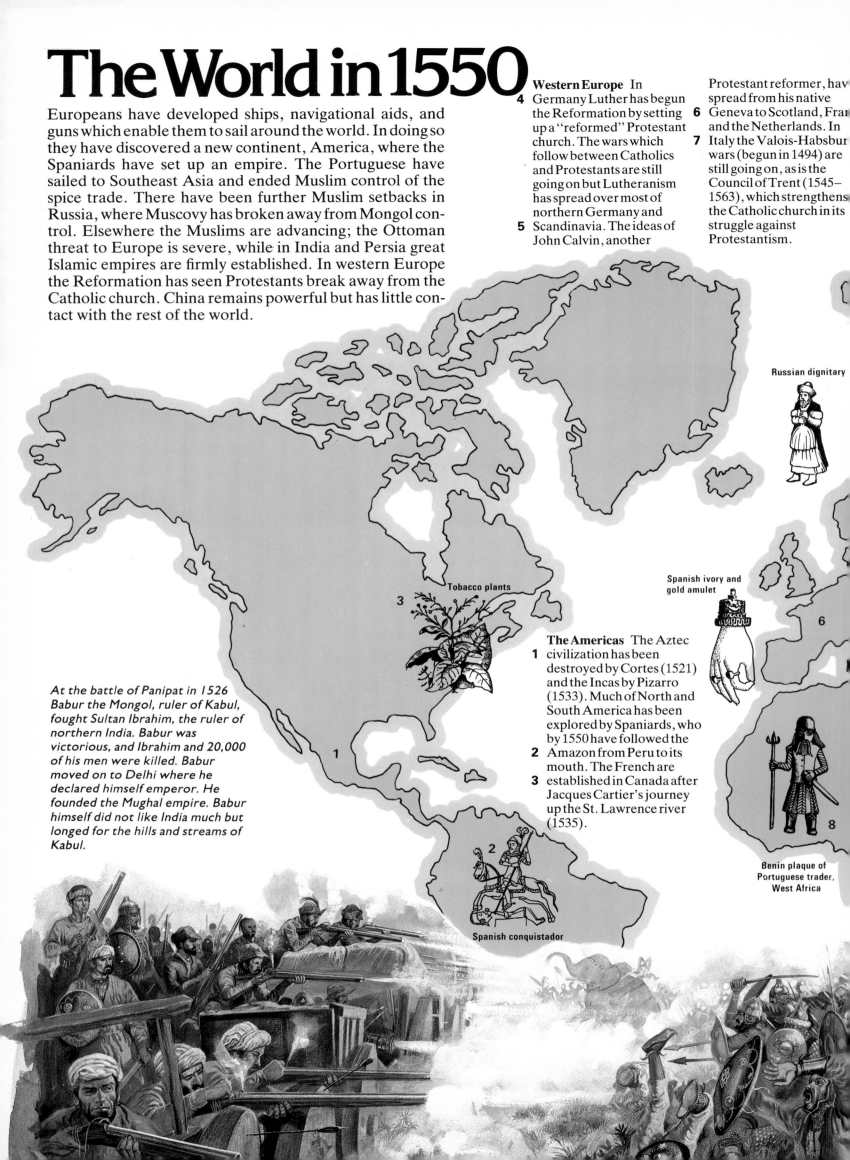

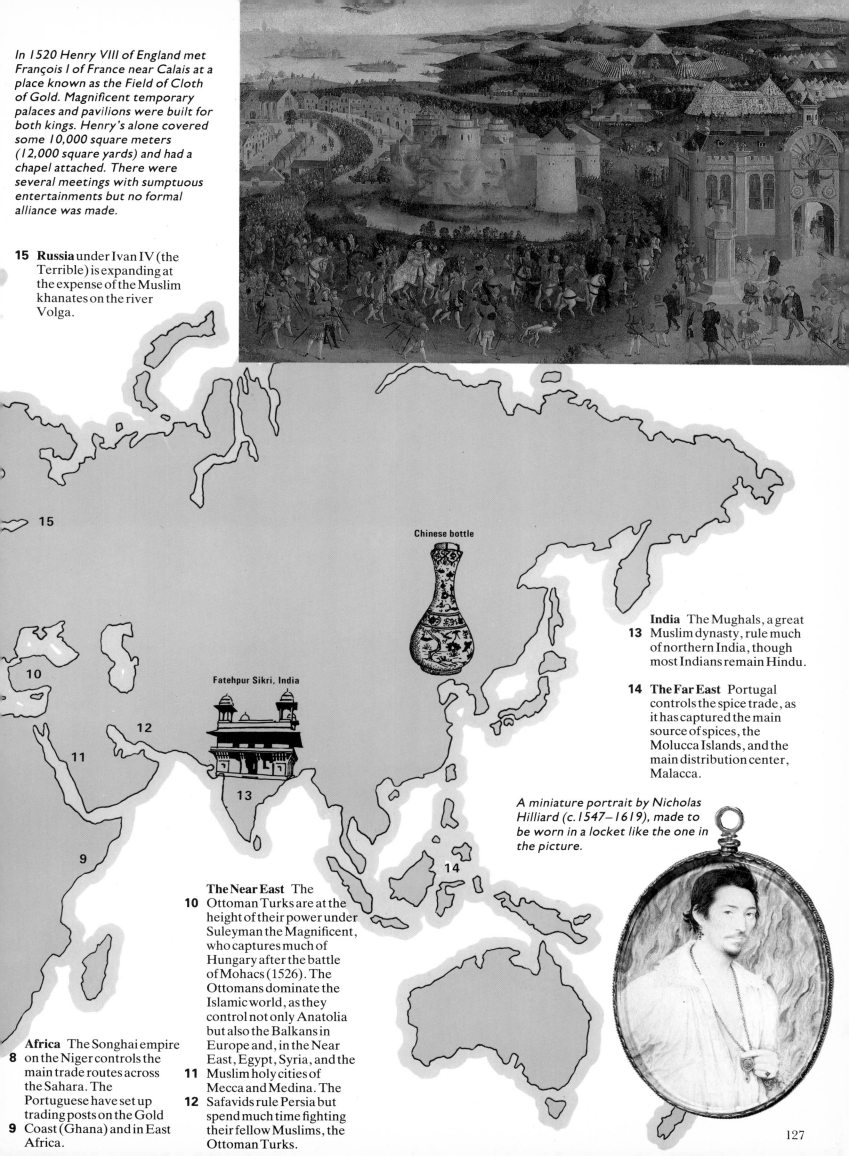

In 1520 Henry VIII of England met François I of France near Calais at a place known as the Field of Cloth of Gold. Magnificent temporary palaces and pavilions were built for both kings. Henry's alone covered some 10,000 square meters (12,000 square yards) and had a chapel attached. There were several meetings with sumptuous entertainments but no formal alliance was made.

15 Russia under Ivan IV (the Terrible) is expanding at the expense of the Muslim khanates on the river Volga.

15

Chinese bottle

Fatehpur Sikri, India

India The Mughals, a great
13 Muslim dynasty, rule much of northern India, though most Indians remain Hindu.

14 The Far East Portugal controls the spice trade, as it has captured the main source of spices, the Molucca Islands, and the main distribution center, Malacca.

A miniature portrait by Nicholas Hilliard (c.1547–1619), made to be worn in a locket like the one in the picture.

The Near East The
10 Ottoman Turks are at the height of their power under Suleyman the Magnificent, who captures much of Hungary after the battle of Mohacs (1526). The Ottomans dominate the Islamic world, as they control not only Anatolia but also the Balkans in Europe and, in the Near East, Egypt, Syria, and the
11 Muslim holy cities of Mecca and Medina. The
12 Safavids rule Persia but spend much time fighting their fellow Muslims, the Ottoman Turks.

Africa The Songhai empire
8 on the Niger controls the main trade routes across the Sahara. The Portuguese have set up trading posts on the Gold
9 Coast (Ghana) and in East Africa.

127

The Spread of Islam

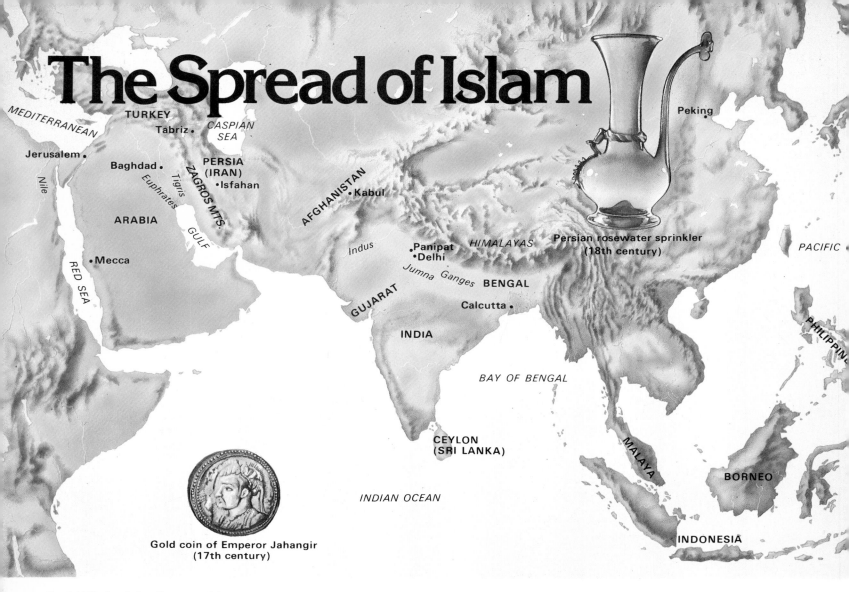

Persian rosewater sprinkler
(18th century)

Gold coin of Emperor Jahangir
(17th century)

In 1450 the Muslim world was far larger than the Christian, and Islam went on spreading vigorously after that date. As the Spaniards were conquering an empire in the New World and Portugal was gaining a foothold in India and the East Indies, the Muslim Ottomans were pushing into central Europe, overrunning Hungary. In India the Mughal emperors were steadily moving south until they controlled almost the whole peninsula. In Persia a third great Islamic empire, the Safavid, arose in 1500. Elsewhere the faith of Islam continued to spread in Africa, Central Asia and, with remarkable speed, in Malaya and Indonesia.

The Mughal Empire

In 1504 a group of Turks led by Babur seized Kabul in Afghanistan. Babur claimed descent from Genghis Khan and so was called Mongol, which became Mughal. He invaded the rich plains of India to the south, and at Panipat in 1526 his matchlock muskets and artillery, serviced by Ottoman Turks, enabled his small force of 12,000 men to defeat an Indian army of 100,000. After this victory he occupied Delhi, his new capital, and four years later he died.

Babur's empire survived because of the genius of his grandson, Akbar. A great military leader, he defeated the Hindu Rajputs, conquered the fertile cotton-growing region of Gujarat, and went on to take Bengal. This was the richest province in the north, producing rice and silk, and was Akbar's main source of income. By the time he died his empire stretched from the Bay of Bengal in the east to Afghanistan in the west and included Sind and most of central India. But though the rulers of much of India were now Muslim, less than a fifth of the ordinary people were converted to Islam.

How Islam spread through Asia (left) and Africa.

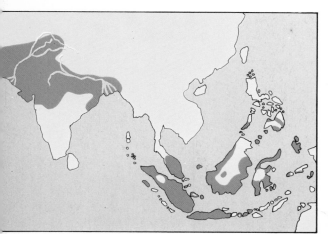

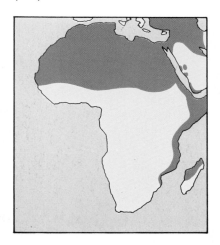

AFRICA AND SOUTHEAST ASIA
Islam expanded in West Africa and Southeast Asia through the missionary work of Muslim traders and holy men. Muslim merchants crossed the Sahara with their camel caravans and converted the people, so that Muslim states grew up in Timbuktu, Kano, and Bornu. Muslim Arab traders settled on the east coast. The islands of Indonesia, much of Malaya, and parts of Borneo and the Philippines also became Muslim because of the influence of Muslim traders.

Safavid Persia

At the same time as Babur was laying the foundations of the Mughal empire, a new dynasty, the Safavid, came to power in Persia (Iran). Its leader was Ismail, who captured Tabriz in 1500 and crowned himself shah. By 1508 all of Persia and most of Iraq were under his control. The Safavid dynasty was to rule Persia for the next 200 years.

The Safavids were Shi'ites, who said that the leaders of Islam should be descended from the family of the Prophet Muhammad. Most Muslims were Sunnis, who believed that the caliph (leader) should be chosen by the Muslim community and need not be descended from Muhammad. This dispute between Sunnis and Shi'ites tore the Muslim world apart, just as the Reformation in Europe led to religious wars between Catholics and Protestants. The Ottomans were Sunnis and fought a long series of wars with the Safavids. These were due both to religious differences and to the desire to possess the same territory.

In 1514 the Ottoman Sultan Selim I (the Grim) advanced into Persia and was victorious, largely because of his use of artillery. He was unable to follow up his victory and conquer the whole of Persia, as he feared attack from Egypt. The division of the Islamic world therefore became permanent. For the rest of the century, except for brief periods, the Ottomans were at war with the Safavids, a war which did not end until 1639.

The emperor Babur gives instructions to his gardeners. Babur, a fearless warrior, was also a poet and lover of nature. He complained that India had no horses, no grapes or musk melons, no good fruits, no ice or cold water.

DECLINE OF THE MUSLIM EMPIRES

By 1750 Islam was on the defensive. The Ottomans had lost Hungary to the Christian Habsburgs and were no longer powerful enough to threaten Europe. The Safavid dynasty came to an end in Persia in 1736 and the country was ravaged by civil war. In India Aurangzeb (1659–1707) had weakened the Mughal empire by fighting to conquer territory in the south. He left India so low in resources that in the 18th century Muslim fought Hindu, Persians and Afghans invaded from the northwest (the Persians sacked Delhi in 1739), and Europeans seized areas on the coast.

The Safavid dynasty was at its greatest under Shah Abbas the Great (1587–1629) who built a magnificent mosque and palace at Isfahan.

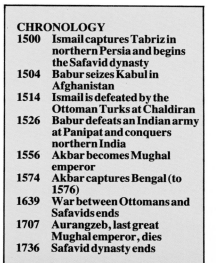

CHRONOLOGY

1500	Ismail captures Tabriz in northern Persia and begins the Safavid dynasty
1504	Babur seizes Kabul in Afghanistan
1514	Ismail is defeated by the Ottoman Turks at Chaldiran
1526	Babur defeats an Indian army at Panipat and conquers northern India
1556	Akbar becomes Mughal emperor
1574	Akbar captures Bengal (to 1576)
1639	War between Ottomans and Safavids ends
1707	Aurangzeb, last great Mughal emperor, dies
1736	Safavid dynasty ends

Northwest Europe

Dutch man-of-war, 161

The Armada Medal of Elizabeth I

The remarkable rise to power and prosperity of the Netherlands and England was partly due to their geographical position. England was an island protected by the sea from outside attack: it had never been invaded since 1066. The Netherlands (what are now Belgium and the Kingdom of the Netherlands) stretched across the estuaries of great rivers, the Rhine, Maas, and Scheldt. It had excellent harbors and was therefore well placed to be a great trading nation.

Dutch Trade

Dutch prosperity began in the 15th century, when herrings migrated from the Baltic to the North Sea and were caught in great numbers by their fishermen. The Dutch found new methods of preserving and smoking the herrings and exported them to the Baltic, in return for wheat and timber. They also picked up cargoes in Lisbon and Seville from the Spanish and Portuguese empires and took them to Antwerp, where merchants from all over Europe bought them. Antwerp became one of the richest cities and the banking center of Europe, where kings borrowed money to pay for their wars.

The Dutch invented and built the ideal carrying vessel, the *fluit* or "flyship." This was really a sea-going barge, designed to carry bulky goods like grain. It was cheap to build, which was a help in keeping the Dutch freight rates lower than those of other nations.

CHRONOLOGY	
1562	Hawkins takes slaves from Sierra Leone to Hispaniola
1567	Duke of Alva becomes Spanish governor of the Netherlands
1577	Drake's voyage around the world (to 1580)
1581	The seven northern provinces of the Spanish Netherlands declare their independence as the United Provinces
1584	William of Orange, leader of the Dutch revolt, is murdered
1588	Spanish Armada defeated
1609	United Provinces (Holland) become independent
1651	First English Navigation Act
1652	First Anglo-Dutch naval war begins
1688	William of Orange becomes King William III of England
1707	Act of Union joins England and Scotland as Great Britain
1713	End of Dutch wars against Louis XIV of France

These merchants' houses in Amsterdam date from the 17th century. It was a time of great prosperity due to the Dutch trading empire.

THE REVOLT OF THE NETHERLANDS

The 17 provinces of the Netherlands were ruled by Spain from 1516. There was no trouble until Philip became king in 1556 (see page 124). Philip was a devout Catholic and was determined to stamp out Calvinism, which since 1563 had spread to The Netherlands. In 1567 he made the duke of Alva governor so that he could crush opposition by terror. He began by executing two leaders, Count Egmont and Count Hoorn. A revolt followed which spread more widely as Alva became more ruthless. Public executions became daily events. Whole towns were pillaged and their populations massacred. In 1576 Antwerp was sacked by Spanish troops and never recovered its former prosperity. This benefited the north, as many merchants and bankers transferred their business to Amsterdam. After a long struggle, in 1609 Spain had to accept the independence of the seven Protestant northern provinces, known as the United Provinces or Holland. Though war began again, they finally gained their independence in 1648.

By 1680 the Dutch had captured the Portuguese trade to the Spice Islands and built up an empire of their own. Though weakened by a series of naval wars against England (1652–1674) and land wars against France (1672–1713), which a small country with a population of only 2 million could not afford, the United Provinces in 1760 still had a larger share of the carrying trade than any other nation.

England

The English, like the Dutch, became prosperous as a great trading nation. Their sailors gained experience in sailing the oceans by catching cod off Newfoundland, where the seas were teeming with fish. By 1500 sailors from Cornwall and Devon were making regular visits to the fishing grounds there.

The first English to trade with Spanish America took what was most needed there, slaves. In 1562 John Hawkins carried slaves from Sierra Leone to Hispaniola and exchanged them for hides and sugar. These were then sold. The profits were so great that Queen Elizabeth invested in a second voyage. It returned with so much silver that Hawkins became the richest man in England. Hawkins's third expedition in 1567 was attacked by the Spaniards. After that many Englishmen turned from trade to piracy. One of the most successful was Francis Drake.

THE SPANISH ARMADA

England relied on its navy to protect it from foreign attack. The most serious threat came in 1588 when Philip II of Spain prepared to invade England with his Armada. The 130 Spanish ships included many splendid galleons but they were not very maneuverable against the wind, as they were tall-sided. The English ships were lower, faster, and more maneuverable. They fired at short range and avoided the Spanish grappling and boarding tactics. The English broke up the Armada with fire ships at Calais and forced the Spaniards to return home by sailing around Scotland and Ireland, where many were wrecked by storms. After this there was no attempt to invade England until that of Napoleon.

The Growth of Industry

In 1500 woolen cloth was England's main export. Nearly all of it went to Europe. Other industries expanded in the next 200 years, including the manufacture of cannon and gunpowder which were in great demand in Europe during the Thirty Years' War (1618–1648). The output of coal greatly increased too from 200,000 tons in 1550 to 3 million in 1700, as it became more widely used as a fuel. But the increase in trade and industry was mostly due to the English colonies.

From 1651 Navigation Acts made sure that goods carried to or from an English colony must be carried in English ships. As a result England built up a great re-export trade. Goods such as sugar, rum, tobacco, and Indian cottons were sent to England and from there were exported to the rest of Europe. The trade increased rapidly. In 1619 Virginia sent only about 9,000 kilograms (20,000 pounds) of tobacco to England. By 1700 this had become 10 million kilograms (22 million pounds). The English colonies imported nearly all the manufactures they needed. By 1770 England was exporting more to the colonies than to Europe and the foundations of the Industrial Revolution had been laid.

Francis Drake (1543–1596) is the most famous Elizabethan seaman. He began raiding Spanish colonies in South America in 1572. In 1577 he set off to raid the coast of South America. He captured the treasure ship Cacafuego in the Pacific and made a profit of £1,500,000 on his voyage around the world, the first by an Englishman. On his return Queen Elizabeth knighted him on the deck of his ship The Golden Hind. When the Spaniards prepared to invade England he attacked Cadiz and "singed the King of Spain's beard" by destroying 33 ships and delaying the Armada for a year. He took part in the battles against the Armada in 1588 and died in 1596 on another search for plunder in the West Indies. He was known to the Spaniards as "El Draque," the Dragon.

The English fleet chased the Spanish Armada into Calais harbor and anchored to windward of them. Then they sent in fire ships, small craft filled with gunpowder and set alight. The Spaniards cut their anchor cables in panic and drifted hopelessly out of formation. They were defeated by the English at Gravelines.

Colonies in the East

Two countries dominated trade in the Spice Islands of Southeast Asia. They were Portugal and the Netherlands. From these islands, known today as Indonesia, they carried astonishingly valuable cargoes back to Europe.

Albuquerque

The Portuguese did not set out to found a great empire. They wanted to control the trade along the spice route, which meant seizing the ports through which the trade passed, as well as the Spice Islands themselves. The man who did this was Afonso de Albuquerque. Although he failed to capture Calicut in India, he took Goa instead in 1510. He made it his main naval base and headquarters. A year later he captured Malacca and in 1515 he took the island of Ormuz at the entrance to the Gulf. Now Portugal controlled the main centers for the collection and distribution of spices. In the Spice Islands the Portuguese captured the Moluccas but never conquered the large islands of Java, Sumatra, and Borneo. Most spices now came to Europe around the Cape of Good Hope but Portugal was not able to close the spice route which went through the Red Sea to the Near East and then to Mediterranean countries. Albuquerque tried to capture Aden, the key to the Red Sea, in 1513 but failed.

Once they were established in Southeast Asia, the Portuguese made great profits by trading between Asian ports. With the money from this they were able to buy spices to send to Europe. They acted as carriers for much of the trade between China, Japan, and the Philippines. In 1513 they reached Canton. They set up a trading settlement at nearby Macao in 1557. In the 1540s the Portuguese became the first Europeans to land in Japan. Soon they were taking Chinese silk and gold to Japan and bringing back Japanese silver to China. The Portuguese carried on trading with Japan for almost a century, but in the 1630s Japan deliberately cut itself off from contact with other countries. Merchants were forbidden to trade there, except for the Chinese and one Dutch ship a year.

Albuquerque's ship, Frol de la Mar.

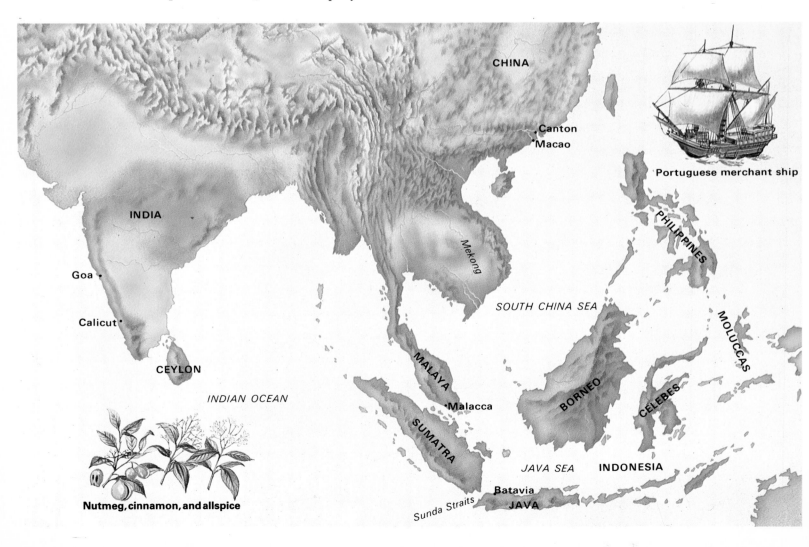

Portuguese merchant ship

Nutmeg, cinnamon, and allspice

The Dutch Take Over

During the 16th century the English and Dutch were becoming important naval powers. In the late 1590s both reached the Spice Islands and soon formed East India companies to start a regular trade. The Dutch wanted to drive the Portuguese from the islands and control the spice trade themselves.

The man who did this was Jan Coen. Between 1618 and 1629 he drove the Portuguese from the Spice Islands and captured Batavia (modern Djakarta, the capital of Indonesia) on the island of Java, which he made his headquarters. Coen also forced the English out of the Spice Islands. His successors captured Malacca (after a six-year blockade, in 1641), Ceylon (1658), and finally the Portuguese forts on the west coast of India but they were not able to capture Goa.

A New Route

The Dutch found a more direct route to the Spice Islands, which meant they did not have to call at Malacca or India. After passing the Cape of Good Hope they sailed due east with the help of westerly winds in the "roaring forties." When they reached the area of the southeast trade winds they turned north to the Sunda Straits. After this Malacca became less important and fewer spices went to the Red Sea and the Gulf.

The kind of goods carried by the Dutch also changed. At first spices were the most valuable cargoes brought to Holland, but by 1700 Indian cotton goods were more important. After 1700 tea and coffee were most valuable. The Dutch introduced coffee bushes into Java and forced the farmers there to grow coffee, tea, sugar, and tobacco. In 1711 they produced 45 kilograms (100 pounds) of coffee; by 1723 this had risen to over 5 million kilograms (12 million pounds). Coffee became a popular drink in Europe and the Dutch were the main suppliers.

This ivory cabinet, mounted with silver, was made in Ceylon in about 1700. The scenes, showing Adam and Eve, were copies from a Dutch engraving.

Like the Portuguese before them, the Dutch carried goods between different parts of Asia, a trade which was much larger and more valuable than the trade with Europe. After the Japanese expelled the Portuguese from Japan in 1639, the Dutch were the only Europeans allowed to trade there, a position they held for over 200 years.

The Dutch were never able to control all the trade in the Indian Ocean, as they had no strong base on the coast of India. In the wars against Louis XIV of France, which did not end until 1713, they had to spend most of their wealth on their army. The navy was neglected. As a result England, Holland's great rival at sea, was able to take control of India.

This drawing of Batavia (modern Djakarta) in Java was made in Amsterdam in 1682. It was an important port of call for European traders.

CHRONOLOGY

1510	Albuquerque captures Goa and Malacca (1511)
1513	Portuguese reach Canton
1515	The Portuguese capture Ormuz at the entrance to the Gulf
1557	Portuguese set up trading settlement at Macao
1564	Spain establishes a colony in the Philippines
1602	Dutch East India Company formed
1605	Dutch drive Portuguese from the Molucca Islands
1619	Coen captures Batavia
1629	Dutch drive the Portuguese from the Spice Islands (Indonesia)
1638	Dutch begin conquest of Ceylon (Sri Lanka)
1639	Portuguese expelled from Japan
1641	Dutch seize Malacca
1713	End of Dutch wars against Louis XIV of France

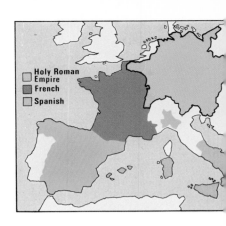

A Struggle for Power

In the early 17th century Europe was torn by religious conflicts. After these came to an end a new issue arose: the struggle for dominance between France and the Holy Roman Empire, the two most powerful states. When the king of Spain died without children, the ruling families of both states had a claim to the vacant throne, and in the resulting war many lesser states were involved.

Louis XIV's magnificent palace at Versailles.

The Sun King

Louis XIV became king of France in 1643 at the age of five. For many years the real ruler of France was Cardinal Mazarin. On the day after Mazarin's death in 1661 the 22-year-old king called his ministers together and told them that he intended to rule personally. "From now on you will not make any decisions, or sign any papers, except on my orders." In his *Mémoires* he later wrote: "The one emotion which overpowers all others in the minds of kings is the sense of their own greatness and glory."

Louis XIV is known in France as *le grand monarque* (the great king) and the time in which he lived as *le grand siècle* (the great century). He would not have disagreed, as he took for his symbol the sun, *le soleil*, which casts its light on all the world. He was also known as *le roi soleil*, the Sun King.

In 1661 France needed strong leadership, as the country was exhausted by the recent rebellion of the nobility, known as the *Fronde*. Louis worked hard at governing France but for this he needed large sums of money. Fortunately, France was a large and fertile kingdom with a population of 20 million. His minister of finance, Colbert, did much to build up France's strength. He created new industries, promoted commerce, increased the navy, and improved roads and canals. The Languedoc Canal, completed in 1681, was the first great canal in Europe since Roman times and carried goods from the Atlantic to the Mediterranean. France also had its trading companies and colonies in the West Indies and Canada.

Some of Colbert's work was undone in 1685, when Louis ended the freedom of worship which Protestants (called Huguenots) had enjoyed since the Edict of Nantes in 1598. Many, including skilled craftsmen and merchants, fled abroad.

DEFENDING THE FRONTIERS

Under Louis XIV France became so powerful that other countries feared it would dominate Europe. Louis's aims were more limited and were concerned with the security of France's northern and eastern borders. He felt that the Habsburgs pressed like a ring around France, which could be invaded from the Spanish Netherlands (modern Belgium) in the north, Lorraine and the Belfort gap in the east, and the Barcelonette valley from Italy. Spain still held Franche Comté on France's east. To protect his borders, Louis waged a series of wars from 1667 to 1697.

THE PALACE OF VERSAILLES

Versailles was designed to provide a suitable setting for *le roi soleil*, the Sun King. An enormous amount of money was spent on the finest materials, architects, craftsmen, painters, and sculptors. It was vast in size – the front was 415 meters (1,361 feet) and the Hall of Mirrors 73 meters (240 feet) long. Behind the palace were extensive gardens and a park.

Louis made Versailles the center of European culture; there the comedies of Molière could be seen or the operas of Lully heard. The main attraction was Louis himself and the elaborate ceremonial of the court.

There was little comfort in the palace. Both courtiers and servants were crowded into tiny, dark, airless rooms. The plumbing was poor and baths almost unheard of. Instead, men and women splashed themselves freely with perfume.

Louis XIV, who ruled France for over 70 years.

The Spanish Succession

France's main enemies were the Habsburg rulers of the Holy Roman Empire. The empire itself had been threatened from the east by the Ottoman Turks. In 1683 Vienna was besieged by the Turks and was saved only by the timely appearance of John Sobieski, King of Poland. From then on the Habsburgs took the offensive and won a crushing victory over the Turks at Zenta in Serbia in 1697. When peace was made two years later the emperor was free to turn his attention to the west – to France.

It was certain that Charles II of Spain would die without children. This meant that the Spanish and Austrian Habsburg lands might be united again, as they had been under the Emperor Charles V (see page 124). As the Spanish lands included Spanish America, the Netherlands, and parts of Italy, this would have made the Habsburgs the dominant power in Europe. Louis XIV could not accept this. He had a claim to the Spanish throne himself, through his wife and mother. The War of the Spanish Succession was a struggle between France and Austria over who was to rule Spain.

England, as usual, fought against its old enemy France, as one of Austria's allies. When the French boldly tried to march on Vienna they were thwarted by the duke of Marlborough, who joined the army of Prince Eugene of Savoy at Blenheim in Bavaria. Here the French suffered their first great military defeat, in 1704. The war dragged on until 1711, when the Austrian emperor died. The Archduke Charles, the Habsburg candidate for the Spanish throne, now became emperor. If he became king of Spain too there would be the same situation the Allies had tried to avoid – the union of Spain with one of the great powers of Europe. It was agreed, therefore, at the Peace of Utrecht in 1713 that the Spanish empire should be divided. Philip of Anjou, a Bourbon prince, would become Philip V of Spain but the thrones of France and Spain would never be united. Austria received the Spanish lands in Italy and the Netherlands.

The result of all these wars was that the balance of power was preserved – no one state dominated Europe.

The battle of Blenheim, in which the Duke of Marlborough and Prince Eugene of Savoy led the English and Austrian forces to victory over the French. Above: The English attack the village of Blenheim. Below: Prince Eugene's troops attack the French. This battle was a terrible blow to French pride. It saved Vienna and ended Louis's hopes of defeating Austria.

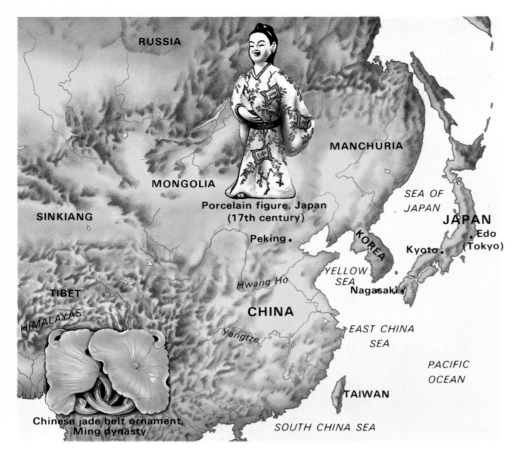

Porcelain figure, Japan
(17th century)

Chinese jade belt ornament,
Ming dynasty

China and Japan

In much of Asia Europeans easily defeated local rulers, but in the Far East they faced two powerful empires, China and Japan. In 1450 China was a greater military force than the whole of Europe. Until new weapons and the Industrial Revolution brought greater strength to the Europeans, they could not hope to conquer either empire.

In the 12th century Mongols invaded China from the north and took control of the whole country. In 1368 they were overthrown by the native Chinese Ming dynasty (ruling family), whose name means "clear" or "brilliant." Under the Ming, China became powerful. The population grew rapidly from 100 to 150 million, as new crops including maize, peanuts, and the sweet potato were brought in from America. The sweet potato could be grown in poor soils and on hillsides where rice would not grow. Cotton spinning and weaving brought fresh wealth to the rich cities of the Yangtze Valley. A splendid new capital, Peking, grew up, and a canal was cut to link it with the Yangtze.

A 17th-century drawing of ambassadors at the Meridian Gate, Peking. There were four walled cities at Peking, each surrounded by great walls. Most people lived in the Outer City. To its north was the Inner City, within which was the Imperial City where the most important members of the government lived. Within the Imperial City was the Forbidden City, which few could enter. Here lived the imperial family.

The Manchus

The Ming emperors became unpopular because of heavy and unjust taxation. Rebellions all over China allowed a nomadic tribe from the north, the Manchus, to seize Peking in 1644. They set up a new dynasty, the Ch'ing (meaning "pure"). The Manchus were to rule until the empire collapsed in 1911. They soon restored peace and order and accepted Chinese ways. They relied on Chinese civil servants to run the empire but kept the leadership of the army in their own hands.

Trade boomed, and Chinese silk, tea, cotton goods, and porcelain (known as "china" in Europe) went overland to Russia and by sea to other parts of the world. Chinese styles and designs were very popular in Europe in the 17th and 18th centuries. The growing taste for tea-drinking in Europe in the 18th century led to a big new export trade.

A great task facing all Chinese dynasties was to control the barbarian tribes on the northern border. Here the mounted archers of the steppe were difficult to defeat until firearms were introduced. The Manchus began a long series of campaigns which, between 1688 and 1757, added Mongolia and the vast region of Sinkiang to the empire. Tibet was made a protectorate, and remained so until it became independent, briefly, in 1912. The Chinese also drove the Russians out of the Amur Valley. On its other borders most states, including Korea, Annam, Burma, and Siam (Thailand), paid a yearly tribute to China, but were left to govern themselves. The Chinese empire had never been as extensive and apparently secure as it was in 1757.

Tokugawa Japan

For over a century from 1467 there was confusion in Japan. There was no effective government and the great lords fought among themselves. The fighting ended in 1603 when Ieyasu, a member of the Tokugawa family, was made *shogun* (military leader) by the emperor.

As the emperor was supposed to be descended from the sun goddess (the sun is still Japan's national symbol) he was sacred. As a result there has been only one ruling family in Japan: the present emperor is descended from the earliest emperors. In theory he was all-powerful but real control belonged to the shogun.

The Tokugawas set up their capital at Edo, later called Tokyo. This was a small fishing village, which they made into an enormous fortress-city. By 1721 Tokyo had a population of 800,000, the largest of any city in the world. There the Tokugawas established a strong, efficient dictatorship. The shogun compelled the great lords to spend a lot of time at his court, where he could keep an eye on them. When they returned to their own estates, they had to leave their wives and children at court as hostages. No revolution threatened the peace and order of Tokugawa rule for 250 years.

A well-known figure in 16th-century Japan was the "samurai" or mounted warrior. Samurai prided themselves on their toughness and self-discipline and preferred death to dishonor or capture. But in 1542 muzzle-loading muskets were introduced into Japan and in battles such as this infantry with firearms were able to defeat the samurai, still armed with their traditional weapons.

This flask of cloisonné enamel was made in China in the early 17th century.

THE "CHRISTIAN CENTURY"

For a time Japan's contact with Europe was much greater than that of China, and the period from the 1540s to the 1630s has been called the "Christian Century."

The first Portuguese ship reached Japan in 1542. Merchants were followed by missionaries, who were able to make many converts to Christianity (150,000 by 1580). The shogun regarded this as a dangerous threat to Japanese beliefs, so there was a brief, violent, and successful persecution of Christians, all of whom were put to death. By 1650 Christianity was almost completely wiped out in Japan.

Not only missionaries were kept out of Japan. In the 1630s foreign merchants were forbidden to trade there, except for the Dutch, who were allowed to send one ship a year to Nagasaki, and the Chinese. The Japanese were forbidden to trade abroad or to build large, ocean-going ships. This cut off Japan from contact with other countries until 1854.

Christian missionaries are tortured by the Japanese; they were looked on as a serious threat to Japanese religious beliefs.

Gustavus Adolphus of Sweden was known as the Lion of the North. An inspiring leader and a splendid horseman, he loved danger and was always first in the attack. He modernized the Swedish army and made Sweden the greatest military power in the north.

The Baltic Region

The Baltic is a large, almost land-locked sea, parts of which are covered with ice in the winter. In the 15th and 16th centuries the area around it provided most of the timber, tar, and hemp which seagoing nations like Spain, Portugal, the Netherlands, England, and France needed to build their ships. From the Baltic also came most of the grain which was eaten in western Europe, and the copper which was used for its money. Ships carrying these goods had to pass through the narrow Sound between Denmark and Sweden to reach the North Sea, and paid tolls there. This made Denmark, which usually controlled the Sound, very wealthy but it made its neighbors jealous and led to a series of wars.

The Rise of Sweden

From 1397 until 1523 Denmark, Norway, and Sweden were united. Then Sweden became independent. The Swedes wanted to be a strong naval and military power but they had enemies on all sides: Denmark, Poland, and Russia (which wanted Finland, under Swedish control).

In 1611 the 17-year-old Gustavus Adolphus became king of Sweden and during his reign he was to do a great deal to control the Baltic like a Swedish lake. His army was the best equipped, trained, and disciplined since the Romans. In 1617 he took Ingermanland and Karelia and so cut off Russia from the Baltic. Next he extended Sweden's territories on the southern shore of the Baltic to include Livonia. He was killed at Lützen in 1632, but this Swedish victory confirmed that Sweden was the greatest military power in the north. It gained even more territory in north Germany at the Peace of Westphalia, which ended the Thirty Years' War in 1648. Ten years later Sweden had pushed its territory to the northern shore of the Sound, so that Denmark no longer controlled both sides of the seaway. Fear of Sweden led its enemies to unite against it. Foremost among these was Russia, under Peter the Great.

Peter the Great

For over 200 years following the Mongol conquest of 1237, Russia had been cut off from all contact with the rest of Europe. Its rulers realized how much it lagged behind other countries in technical skills. Tsars like Ivan III and Ivan the Terrible wanted firearms and artillery from the West, and foreign officers to train their army. Peter the Great speeded up this process by forcing his people to copy Western customs. He ordered Russians to shave off their beards and forbade them to wear the big Russian cloak. He himself traveled in disguise to England and Holland, where he worked as a laborer in the shipyards to learn about shipbuilding. He wanted to make Russia strong and above all, he wanted a "window on the West."

The Great Northern War

Russia's coastline in the Arctic made trade with Europe difficult, as the White Sea was frozen for a large part of the year. In the south the Ottomans and Crimean Tartars kept Russians from the Black Sea. Peter was determined to gain a foothold on the Baltic and recklessly attacked Sweden, with Denmark and Poland, before he had time to build a western-style army. In 1700 a large Russian army was defeated at Narva by a much smaller Swedish force. Fortunately for Peter, Charles XII of Sweden turned aside from Russia and spent the next six years fighting in Poland and Saxony. While Charles was occupied there Peter reorganized his army. He introduced conscription (one person in every 20 households had to serve for 25 years, a system that lasted until 1874) and based his training and tactics on German, French, and Swedish models.

When Charles XII had completed his conquest of Poland and Saxony he turned to Russia. His aim was to strike at Moscow. The Russians avoided a pitched battle and used a "scorched-earth" policy, retreating before the invaders and destroying everything they could not take with them, so that the Swedish army could not live off the land. Charles, therefore, turned to the rich country of the Ukraine, but there many of his men died in the bitter winter of 1708–1709. Finally, in 1709, Peter totally defeated Charles's diminished army at Poltava. The whole position in northern Europe was changed. Peter went on to capture the Swedish provinces, including southeast Finland, Estonia, and Livonia, on the Baltic coast and his influence replaced that of Sweden in Poland. Sweden also lost most of its territories in north Germany.

This marked the end of one major power in the north, Sweden, and the rise of another, Russia. For the first time Russia was feared by her neighbors. "It is commonly said," wrote the contemporary German philosopher Leibniz, "that the Tsar will be formidable to all Europe, that he will be a kind of Northern Turk."

The port of Archangel on the White Sea, northeast of Karelia, was the only Russian seaport before the building of St. Petersburg. The town began when the English Muscovy Company built a trading station there in the late 16th century. In the winter the harbor froze over.

ST. PETERSBURG
In 1703 Peter began to build a new city on land taken from Sweden at the mouth of the river Neva (a Finnish word for "swamp"). It was a damp, unhealthy site, with dark, long, and very cold winters. While building St. Petersburg, as it was called after him, 200,000 laborers died from cold and fever. It was to be Peter's "window on the west," a city built by French, Dutch, German, and Italian architects. It was a great symbol of the new Russia, just as Moscow, with its onion domes, was of the old. "We have lifted the curtain of our country's curiosity," he said, "which deprived it of communication with the whole world." He made it his new capital in 1712, and it remained the capital of the Russian empire for over 200 years. It is now renamed Leningrad.

The World in 1650

The century-long religious wars between Catholics and Protestants end with the Thirty Years' War (1618–1648), which has brought ruin and famine to Germany. The 1640s have been a period of turmoil in Europe, with civil war in England and France; the Dutch and Portuguese have gained independence from Spain. In the north, Sweden controls the Baltic; unnoticed in the west, Russia is expanding across Siberia and has already reached the Pacific. In the East, too, there have been upheavals. In China a new dynasty, the Ch'ing, has replaced the Ming; Japan has been united, after a century of civil war, by the Tokugawa family. The Portuguese have lost most of their eastern empire to the Dutch.

The Americas In the north, the English, French, and
1 Dutch have begun to colonize the Atlantic coast of North America. Spanish
5 colonies in Central and
2 South America send vast quantities of silver and gold to Europe; Brazil, under
3 the Portuguese, is important as a sugar producer.

Northern Europe Civil war in England has ended in the execution of Charles I (1649) and the setting up of a Commonwealth (Republic). The seven northern provinces of the Netherlands are finally independent of Spain.
6 Germany is divided into a mainly Protestant north and a Catholic south and west. In the Baltic region
7 Sweden is the leading power.

Western Europe France is
4 suffering from civil war (the *Fronde*) in which nobles try to prevent an increase in the power of the king. Spain has declined, following years of war with France, and Portugal has regained independence in 1640 after 60 years of Spanish rule.

Louis XIV of France looks at plans for his palace at Versailles.

Puritan settlers, Massachusetts

Isaac Newton's telescope of 1672

Benin head, West Africa

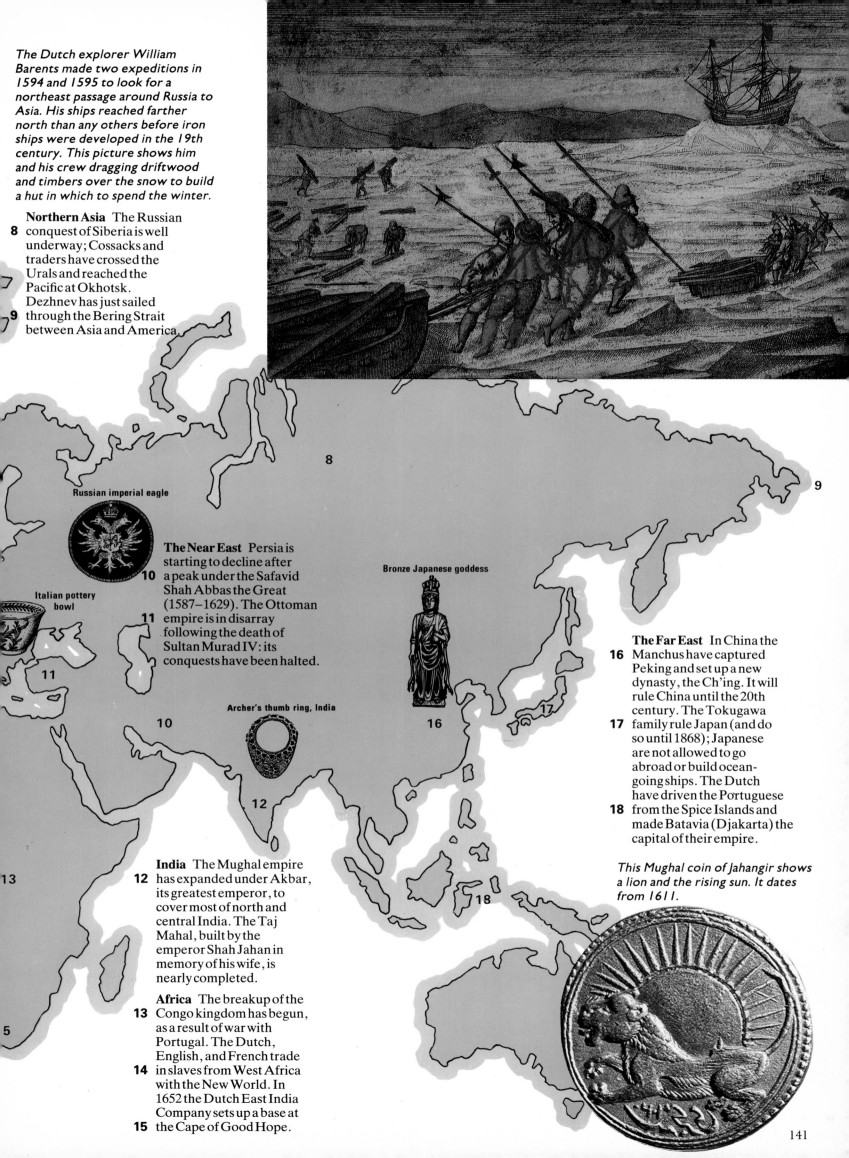

The Dutch explorer William Barents made two expeditions in 1594 and 1595 to look for a northeast passage around Russia to Asia. His ships reached farther north than any others before iron ships were developed in the 19th century. This picture shows him and his crew dragging driftwood and timbers over the snow to build a hut in which to spend the winter.

Northern Asia The Russian
8 conquest of Siberia is well underway; Cossacks and traders have crossed the Urals and reached the Pacific at Okhotsk. Dezhnev has just sailed
9 through the Bering Strait between Asia and America.

Russian imperial eagle

Italian pottery bowl

The Near East Persia is starting to decline after
10 a peak under the Safavid Shah Abbas the Great (1587–1629). The Ottoman empire is in disarray
11 following the death of Sultan Murad IV: its conquests have been halted.

Bronze Japanese goddess

Archer's thumb ring, India

The Far East In China the
16 Manchus have captured Peking and set up a new dynasty, the Ch'ing. It will rule China until the 20th century. The Tokugawa
17 family rule Japan (and do so until 1868); Japanese are not allowed to go abroad or build ocean-going ships. The Dutch have driven the Portuguese
18 from the Spice Islands and made Batavia (Djakarta) the capital of their empire.

This Mughal coin of Jahangir shows a lion and the rising sun. It dates from 1611.

India The Mughal empire
12 has expanded under Akbar, its greatest emperor, to cover most of north and central India. The Taj Mahal, built by the emperor Shah Jahan in memory of his wife, is nearly completed.

Africa The breakup of the
13 Congo kingdom has begun, as a result of war with Portugal. The Dutch, English, and French trade
14 in slaves from West Africa with the New World. In 1652 the Dutch East India Company sets up a base at
15 the Cape of Good Hope.

North America

At one time there were four colonial powers in North America. The Spaniards gradually moved from Mexico into Texas and up the west coast to California. By 1767 Spain claimed territory as far east as the Mississippi River and as far north as San Francisco. They stopped only when they met the Russians, moving down the Pacific coast from Alaska. The Dutch founded New Amsterdam (later New York) in 1612. It was a thriving base for exporting furs which came down the Hudson River. It was also a center for Dutch trade with the Spanish, English, and French colonies in America. Because of this the English captured it in 1664. The main struggle for control of North America was between England and France.

Carved wooden thunderbird, Canada

Hudson's ship Half Moon

Anglo-French Rivalry

French explorers like Jacques Cartier had sailed up the St. Lawrence River by 1535. They built ports in Nova Scotia, Quebec, and Montreal. From the St. Lawrence they pushed west by water to Lake Superior and south to the Ohio River. In 1682 La Salle paddled down the Mississippi to the Gulf of Mexico and claimed the whole river basin for France. He called it Louisiana, after King Louis XIV. The French had reached the heart of North America and circled the English colonies on the seaboard by building forts from the St. Lawrence to Louisiana.

English colonization first began successfully with the founding of Jamestown, Virginia, in 1607, and with the Pilgrim fathers in the *Mayflower* who landed in Massachusetts Bay in 1620. By 1700 there were 12 English colonies on or near the Atlantic coast of America (Georgia was added in 1733). It was clear that when the English crossed the Appalachian Mountains they would clash with the French.

In both the French and English colonies there were few Indians, so the colonists could not use Indian labor, as the Spaniards had done in South America. Unlike the Spaniards, the English and French found no gold or silver, so they had to make a living by agriculture, fishing, and the fur trade. Virginia was an exception; here the colonists grew tobacco and exported it in large quantities to Europe.

More Englishmen than Frenchmen emigrated to America. By 1688 there were 250,000 Englishmen on the Atlantic coast, compared with only 20,000 Frenchmen in the vast area of Canada and the Mississippi Valley. By 1760 there were over 2 million Englishmen; Massachusetts alone had as many settlers as New France. This largely explains the victory of the English over the French in their American wars.

The city of Quebec in 1754, seen from a ferry house across the St. Lawrence River. At this time the city was French, but five years later it was captured by the British, during the Seven Years' War. Under General Wolfe a British force scaled the cliffs to the Plains of Abraham (on the left) and took the French by surprise. Both Wolfe and the French commander Montcalm were killed.

An Indian chief, probably in ceremonial attire, drawn in about 1585. As French and English settlers moved westward into the interior of North America and took over the most fertile lands they came increasingly into conflict with the Indian tribes.

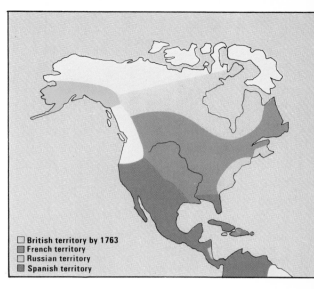

☐ British territory by 1763
■ French territory
☐ Russian territory
■ Spanish territory

Anglo-French Wars

The struggle between England and France in America began early. Quebec was first attacked by the English in 1629 and Nova Scotia changed hands many times. Each war between England and France in Europe was fought in America too. The Peace of Utrecht in 1713 gave Britain Nova Scotia, Newfoundland, and a large area around Hudson Bay. The main war which decided the fate of North America was the French and Indian War of 1754 to 1760, which became part of the Seven Years' War in Europe.

The war began as a struggle for control of the Ohio Valley. British settlers were moving across the mountains into the valley and built a fort in 1754 where the Monongahela and Allegheny rivers meet. The French immediately captured it and named it Fort Duquesne. A young Virginian, George Washington, hurried to reinforce the English garrison but arrived too late. In 1755 General Braddock with a British army tried to recapture Fort Duquesne but was defeated and killed. The French continued to do well through the brilliant leadership of the Marquis de Montcalm, probably the finest general on either side, until William Pitt (later earl of Chatham) became the English prime minister. He left his ally, Frederick the Great of Prussia, to fight the French in Europe and concentrated on the navy and the war in the colonies. His policy succeeded. The British navy controlled the seas, while a large force of 50,000 British soldiers and American colonists was formed. They captured one French fort after another, including Fort Duquesne, which they renamed Fort Pitt (now Pittsburgh). The climax came with the capture of Quebec in 1759. This was the end of the French empire in America.

In the Peace of Paris, which ended the war, France lost Canada and most of its American possessions. It kept only French Guiana in South America, the islands of St. Pierre and Miquelon off the Newfoundland coast and the West Indian sugar islands of Guadeloupe and Martinique. Britain gained the St. Lawrence Valley and all territory east of the Mississippi. Spain had entered the war late on the side of France and gave up Florida to Britain. As compensation, France gave Spain western Louisiana, territory west of the Mississippi. North America was now to develop as part of the English, rather than the French, world.

Below: Bacons Castle, Virginia, was built in 1655. The Virginia Company was given a charter by King James I in 1606 and sent colonists to establish the first permanent English settlement there in 1607. Soon the colonists were growing and exporting tobacco and in 1624 Virginia was made a royal colony.

THE FALL OF QUEBEC

Quebec was a great natural stronghold defended by Montcalm. It seemed impossible to capture, as cliffs rose straight up from the banks of the St. Lawrence. The British commander, 33-year-old General Wolfe, tried a daring plan. At night on September 13, 1759, he silently ferried his troops upstream, where they climbed the steep paths up the cliffs and reached the Plains of Abraham above the town. At dawn Montcalm was surprised to see a red-coated British army on the plains. He attacked immediately. In less than an hour the French were defeated; both Wolfe and Montcalm were killed. Quebec fell five days later.

Ivan the Terrible

WHITE SEA

Archangel

MUSCOVY

St. Petersburg
(Leningrad)

Neva

Moscow

Kazan

RUSSIA

Volga

Astrakhan

CASPIAN SEA

URAL MTS.

Ob

Sibir

Yenisei

Irtysh

SIBERIA

ARCTIC TUNDRA

Lena

Tungus tribesmen

Yakutsk

STANOVOI MTS.

Amur

Okhotsk

PACIFIC
OCEAN

MONGOLIA

CHINA

TIBET

Russia in Asia

At the same time as western Europeans were moving overseas to all corners of the world, the Russians were advancing overland across the whole length of Asia. Russia today is a vast country, which covers one-sixth of the earth's land surface. When night falls in Leningrad (St. Petersburg) on the Baltic, day is breaking in Vladivostok on the Pacific 8,000 kilometers (5,000 miles) away. Most of Russia is a flat plain. The Ural Mountains run across it from north to south and are usually taken as the dividing line between European and Asiatic Russia, but they are a narrow, worn-down chain of mountains with an average height of only 600 meters (2,000 feet). This explains why the Russians were able to move eastward so easily into the area called Siberia.

The Land of Russia

The main divisions of Russia do not stretch from north to south but from east to west. In the north along the Arctic is the barren tundra, frozen for most of the year. Below this is the forest belt. Farther south is the fertile soil of the open steppe or grasslands. The southern boundary is a chain of mountains, deserts, and inland seas. These mountains keep out the moisture-laden winds from the Pacific and the Indian Ocean and are the cause of the deserts of Central Asia and the cold, dry climate of Siberia. The

whole of Siberia has the same climate; short, hot summers and long, cold winters. Russian settlers therefore felt equally at home anywhere in the plains.

Because the land is flat, Russian rivers are generally long and wide, and have few rapids. East of the Urals, there are four great rivers: the Ob, Yenisei, Lena, and Amur. As Siberia slopes down from the huge mountains of Tibet, all these rivers flow north except for the Amur, which flows into the Pacific. Using these rivers and their tributaries, Russian explorers and settlers could move almost all the way across Siberia by water. This made trade and conquest easier.

A view of Moscow in the time of Ivan the Terrible.

The Defeat of the Mongols

When the Mongols conquered Russia the Russians retreated from the steppe deep into the forest belt, where the state of Muscovy, based on the city of Moscow, grew up. Ivan III declared his independence from the Mongols in 1480, overcame rival Russian princes and took the title of *tsar* (the Russian form of "caesar"). There was still much fighting to do before Ivan IV "the Terrible" defeated the Mongols. Ivan was able to capture Kazan in 1552, because he had better artillery and the help of a Dane who mined and blew up the walls of the fortress. When the Russians captured Astrakhan at the mouth of the Volga, they controlled the whole Volga basin to the Caspian Sea. The way was now open for expansion across the Urals.

The conquest of Siberia was largely the work of rough frontiersmen, called Cossacks. Siberia was thinly populated, so there was little effective resistance to the Russians with their firearms. They were lured on by the search for furs – sable, squirrel, and ermine. As they advanced the Cossacks built fortified posts or *ostrogs*. They built one at Yakutsk on the river Lena in 1632 and moved out from there in all directions. Some Russians reached the Arctic in 1645 and the Pacific two years later, at Okhotsk. In 1648 Semion Dezhnev set out from Yakutsk down the Lena, which was so broad in places that he could not see either bank. He reached the Arctic and sailed east to the tip of Asia. Then he sailed through the Bering Strait, which separates America from Asia, 77 years before Vitus Bering after whom the straits are named.

China and the Amur

The Russians met their first serious opposition when they moved south into the Amur Valley. This territory was claimed by China. When the Cossacks pillaged the area the Chinese sent an expedition which forced the Russians to withdraw. The Chinese and the Russians settled their border problems by the Treaty of Nerchinsk in 1689. This was the first treaty signed by China with a European country. The border was fixed along the Stanovoi Mountains north of the Amur, so the Russians had to pull out of the whole valley. In return the Russians were given permission to trade with China. Caravans took gold and furs to China and brought back tea, which soon became the national drink in Russia.

With the Treaty of Nerchinsk the first stage of Russian expansion in Asia ended. Russia did not continue its advance south until the middle of the 19th century.

Top: The valley of the river In'a in Siberia. Above: These Tungus tribespeople, from central Siberia, were drawn on a map of 1729 showing the explorations of Vitas Bering.

YERMAK

Yermak was the red-bearded son of a Don Cossack and a Danish slave woman. Condemned to death at the age of 21 for stealing horses, he fled to the Volga and became a river pirate. He was then hired by a wealthy merchant to stop raids by Siberian Tartars (Mongols) from across the Urals, led by the blind Khan Kuchum. In 1581 Yermak set off with 840 men to attack the khan. He had firearms and cannon, which terrified the natives. Kuchum had far more men and fought desperately but in vain to save his capital, Sibir. When Yermak occupied Sibir the Russians gave its name to the entire area across the Urals–Siberia. Ivan the Terrible was so pleased with Yermak that he pardoned him for his earlier crimes. In 1584 one of Kuchum's raiding parties surprised Yermak, who tried to escape by swimming across a river. He drowned, according to legend, under the weight of armor given to him by the tsar.

CHRONOLOGY

1237	The Mongols begin the conquest of Russia
1480	Ivan III declares his independence from the Mongols
1552	Ivan the Terrible captures Kazan
1556	Astrakhan seized; Ivan now controls the whole of the Volga, Russia's longest river
1581	Yermak crosses the Urals; captures Sibir
1584	Port of Archangel founded on the White Sea
1632	Ostrog (fort) built at Yakutsk
1645	Russians sail down the Lena to reach the Arctic
1647	The Pacific reached at Okhotsk
1648	Dezhnev begins journey which leads to discovery of the Bering Strait
1689	Treaty of Nerchinsk; Russians withdraw from the Amur Valley

Africa

The Mediterranean connects the peoples of North Africa with others around its shores. But the Sahara with its trackless, burning dunes cuts off people to the south. The Sahara is not the only obstacle to contact with the outside world. Africa's coastline is unbroken by bays, gulfs, or inland seas. The result is that its coastline is shorter than Europe's, though Africa is three times the size of Europe. As it lacked anything like the Baltic, Mediterranean, or Black Sea, which open up the interior of Europe, Africa remained closed to most people from outside.

Africa is like an upside-down saucer. It is a vast plateau that falls away to the narrow coastal plain which surrounds the continent. Except for the Niger and the Zambezi, the great rivers of Africa plunge in falls and rapids from the plateau to the lowlands. This means that few rivers are navigable far inland.

The Songhai Empire

In the Middle Ages huge African empires had grown up as a result of trade across the Sahara. The greatest were Ghana and Mali. By 1500 these had declined and been replaced by Songhai. The Songhai people lived on the river Niger around the city of Gao. By the time of Askia the Great, who ruled from 1493 to 1528, the Songhai empire included great trading cities like Jenne and Timbuktu, which were also centers of Muslim learning. The empire controlled the main trade routes from West Africa to Tunis, Tripoli, and Egypt. It remained important until the Moroccans sacked Timbuktu in 1593; their firearms were too much for the bowmen and cavalry of Songhai. This broke the power of Songhai. The mainstream of West African trade now moved east to the Hausa states and Kano. By 1750 Islam was important here too.

THE CONGO KINGDOM

Powerful kingdoms were rising in other parts of Africa too, among them the Luba and Lunda kingdoms in Central Africa and the Monomatapa in the Zambezi Valley. When the Portuguese landed near the Congo River in 1484 they found a Congo kingdom there. In 1506 a Congolese Christian prince seized the throne with the help of the Portuguese, but there were never enough missionaries to convert his people. The Portuguese were more concerned with the slave trade than religion and by 1650 were openly at war with the Congolese. After the Portuguese victory the Congo state began to decline.

This carving from West Africa shows Portuguese soldiers and a miniature ship's crow's nest or lookout point.

Since the 12th century Europeans had been wondering about Prester John, a Christian king and priest who, they believed, ruled in Africa beyond the lands controlled by Arabs. The Portuguese hoped that they would be able to reach Prester John's successor. In 1493 a Portuguese disguised as an Arab reached the court of the Christian emperor of Ethiopia – perhaps the king they were looking for – but alliance with him did not give them power in the African interior. This detail from a 16th-century Portuguese map (right) shows the legendary Prester John surveying his kingdom.

Europeans in Africa

The first Europeans in Africa were the Portuguese. They explored the coast when looking for a route to the Spice Islands and in 1482 they built the first of their forts on the Gold Coast. As they sailed up the coast of East Africa they reached Muslim ports which had been trade centers for 150 years. Through Sofala, for example, passed the gold trade of Mozambique and Zimbabwe. There were other thriving ports such as Kilwa and Mombasa, many of which the Portuguese captured or destroyed.

The Dutch followed the Portuguese and pushed them out of the Gold Coast by 1642, though the Portuguese continued to trade from their base at Luanda in Angola. It was a Dutchman, Jan van Riebeeck, who was sent by the Dutch East India Company to found a supply station at the Cape of Good Hope. Here Dutch ships on their way to India could stock up with fresh food and vegetables. Some Dutch settlers went inland, and started to farm. But most Europeans in Africa stayed on or near the coast. This was partly because it was difficult to travel inland, and partly because of deadly diseases such as malaria and yellow fever which thrived there. The main reason the Europeans stayed on the coast was that they had no need to go inland. Their chief interest was in slaves and these were brought to the coast by powerful African kingdoms such as Ashanti and Dahomey.

In 1750 Europeans controlled only small areas of Africa. The sources and courses of the great African rivers were unknown to them but in 1778 Sir Joseph Banks founded the Africa Association. This began to organize explorations and led to the opening up of Africa in the 19th century.

TIMBUKTU

A description by Leo Africanus, a Moor from Spain, who visited Songhai early in the 16th century:

The rich king of Timbuktu has many plates and scepters of gold . . . and he keeps a magnificent court . . . He has always three thousand horsemen and a great many footmen, who shoot poisoned arrows, waiting upon him. They often have skirmishes with those who refuse to pay tribute and those they capture they sell [as slaves] to the merchants of Timbuktu . . . Here are many doctors, judges, priests, and other learned men, who are well kept at the king's expense. And here are brought different manuscripts or written books out of Barbarie [North Africa], which are sold for more money than any other merchandise.

CHRONOLOGY

1482	First Portuguese fort on Gold Coast
1493	Askia the Great rules the Songhai empire
1498	Vasco da Gama sails around Africa to India
1505	Portuguese capture Kilwa
1506	Nzinga Mvemba becomes Christian king of the Congo
1513	Start of the slave trade across the Atlantic
1571	Portuguese begin conquest of Angola
1591	Moroccan invasion of Songhai empire
1593	Moroccans sack Timbuktu
1652	Jan van Riebeeck lands at the Cape of Good Hope
1665	Portuguese defeat Congolese army at the battle of Ambuila. Decline of Congo kingdom
1750	Ashanti empire conquers African states on Gold Coast

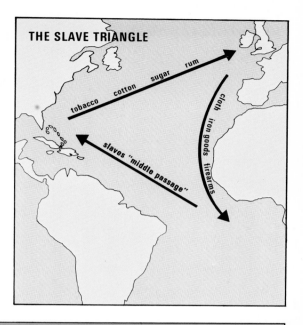

THE SLAVE TRIANGLE

THE SLAVE TRADE

Arabs had been trading in slaves on the East African coast before Europeans sailed around Africa, but it was Europeans who began this brutal trade on a huge scale. The Portuguese were the first to deal in slaves, but the British, Dutch, and French soon joined in, so that over 10 million Africans were transported to America and the West Indies. There they produced cotton, sugar, rum, and rice, which were exported to Europe. Guns, cloth, and tools were sent to Africa to pay for the slaves and complete this triangular trade. The normal passage across the Atlantic lasted seven to eight weeks, during which many slaves died because of the overcrowded and filthy conditions on board. The description below is by Olaudah Equiano, a Nigerian who was captured by African slave dealers at the age of 11:

The stench of the hold was intolerably loathsome. The closeness of the place and the heat of the climate, added to the number in the ship, which was so crowded that each had scarcely room to turn himself, almost suffocated us. The air became unfit to breathe and many of the slaves fell sick and died. Our wretched situation was aggravated by the heavy chains on our legs, the filth of the necessary tubs, and the shrieks of women and the groans of the dying.

Willem Adriaan van der Stel, governor of Cape Colony from 1699 to 1707, on his farm. He is said to have made the first South African wine.

Warfare

In the Middle Ages, wars were fought by mounted knights in heavy suits of armor, armed with lances and swords. Foot soldiers were chiefly archers and pikemen. The siege was an important part of warfare, and the siege machines used to attack heavily fortified castles were little different from those of ancient times. Towards the end of the period, however, the first firearms came into use. As they developed, so methods of warfare changed.

The First Handguns

Throughout the 16th century the Spaniards were the military leaders of Europe, as they were the first to make wide use of firearms. The arquebus, an early portable gun, revolutionized warfare. Gonzalo de Cordoba of Spain used arquebuses instead of crossbows. His victory over the French at Cerignola in 1503 made infantry carrying firearms the most important soldiers on the battlefield.

Handguns were cheaper to make and easier to use than the crossbow. Later in the 16th century the matchlock musket gradually took over from the arquebus. It was heavy and needed a forked rest to support the barrel, and it could fire only one shot every two minutes, compared with the arquebus's one shot every minute. Its advantages were its greater range and reliability. It could crash through the heaviest armor at 275 meters (300 yards), so it was most valuable against cavalry. Once they had fired, musketeers moved back into the protection of squares of pikemen, who did the real fighting. They checked the cavalry charge with their 5-meter (16-foot) long pikes, pulled riders off their horses with the hooks of their halberds and finished them off with their swords. By 1600 there was one musketeer in the Spanish armies for every pikeman and half of them had matchlocks.

Artillery and Siege Warfare

Improvements in artillery were just as important as changes in firearms. Great guns could knock down the walls of the strongest medieval castles, as Mehmet the Conqueror showed when he destroyed the walls of Constantinople in 1453.

As a result a new type of fortification had to be developed and warfare became more defensive. Fortifications were sunk deep into the ground, and instead of high walls there were low and very thick earth banks, sometimes faced with stone. Circular towers were replaced by four-sided angular works called bastions, which overlooked all possible approaches. Sieges were great set-pieces and replaced the open battle for a hundred years. There was no major battle in Europe between Mühlberg in 1534 and Breitenfeld in 1631.

Heavy artillery was useful only in sieges, as it was difficult to move and very expensive. In 1600 one gun needed 20 to 30 horses to pull it, and another 40 horses for the ammunition carts. One of the most successful people at siege warfare was Marshal Vauban in the reign of Louis XIV. He built 33 fortresses and improved 300 others on the borders of France, and carried out 55 successful sieges.

"The Lion of the North"

In the 17th century a new military power, Sweden, arose, led by Gustavus Adolphus. His reforms affected every part of 17th-century armies and were copied all over Europe. He supplied his infantry with a

lighter musket, the wheel lock, and introduced paper cartridges containing powder and shot, which made reloading quicker. His army still used pikes in attack (each squadron had 192 musketeers, but 216 pikemen) although he cut them down to a length of 2.5 meters (8 feet). His reform of artillery was even more important. He reduced the types of gun to three: 24-pounders for sieges, 12-pounders, and 3-pounders. The last were light enough to be moved by one horse or three men. For the first time cannon could keep up with infantry on the battlefield. The 3-pounder had prepacked rounds and a rate of fire slightly better than that of a musket.

Other countries sent their young officers to serve with and learn from the Swedes. The French copied them so successfully that from the 1640s to the 1690s they were the main military power in Europe. Oliver Cromwell's New Model Army also followed the Swedish example.

Flintlock Musket and Ring Bayonet

Two developments at the end of the 17th century were the flintlock musket and the ring bayonet. The matchlock, with its exposed gunpowder and lighted matches, was unsafe to load. The flint made a spark only when it was needed and was much safer. The plug bayonet had fitted into the muzzle of the musket and made firing impossible when it was fixed. The use of the ring bayonet, fastened to the outside of the barrel, meant that an infantryman could defend himself immediately after firing. The British Duke of Marlborough was one of the first generals to use both the flintlock musket (his "Brown Bess") and the ring bayonet.

The pike was no longer needed and had almost disappeared by 1700. Infantry now formed in lines of three to six men deep and would stand in a hollow square when facing a cavalry charge. Cavalry remained important. The French used it mainly for its firepower, as the riders used pistols. Marlborough and the Austrian general Prince Eugene, like Gustavus Adolphus, used a

Suleyman the Magnificent was ruler of the Ottoman empire from 1520 to 1566. He greatly extended Ottoman power in eastern Europe and the Mediterranean. Here he is seen during his campaign to capture the island of Rhodes from the Knights Hospitalers. Under Suleyman the Ottomans had 30,000 soldiers; most of them were cavalry, carrying bows, lances, and swords, but they also used artillery and muskets.

cavalry charge with drawn swords as a shock tactic to decide a battle. All Marlborough's victories were completed in this way.

Frederick the Great

The last great general in this period was Frederick the Great of Prussia. He showed his brilliance in the Seven Years' War (1756–1763) when Swedish, French, Russian, Austrian, and some German armies were fighting against him. He managed to survive, a remarkable feat, by defeating each of his enemies in turn in a rapid war of movement. He believed in going on to the offensive rather than waiting to be attacked. His drill and discipline were severe – "The men must fear their officers more than the enemy," he said – but, like Gustavus Adolphus, he was widely copied.

A British grenadier, from a tapestry showing the battle of Blenheim. Grenadiers, first used in about 1670, carried hand grenades as well as muskets. At first companies of grenadiers were attached to infantry regiments; from the 1750s on, they formed their own regiments.

Frederick the Great was nicknamed the "Soldier King." His army was a very efficient fighting machine. He introduced light, horsedrawn guns which could be moved from place to place during the course of a battle.

Great Voyages

In the 15th and 16th centuries Europeans attempting to reach Asia by sea find a new continent and the shape of those already known. The Portuguese become the first to sail around Africa to Asia when Vasco da Gama reaches India in 1498. The Spaniards try a western route but Columbus finds a new continent, America, in the way. Efforts are made to find a way around or through this continent; Magellan succeeds, and the English and Dutch, sailing northward, fail but learn much about Canada and the Arctic. The Pacific remains largely unexplored until the 17th century. With Cook's explorations in the 18th century the voyages of discovery come to an end: the size and shape of all the continents are now accurately known.

John Cabot, born like Columbus in Genoa, looks for a northwest passage to Asia on behalf of England. He reaches North America in 1497. Further attempts to find this passage, led by **Frobisher**, **Baffin**, and **Hudson**, fail as ice blocks the way, but they learn much about the North American coast.

Jacques Cartier for France tries to find a strait through North America and discovers the St. Lawrence River (1535).

Henry Hudson, in Dutch service, sails up the Hudson River in 1609.

Magellan, looking for a way around South America, discovers the strait named after him, crosses the Pacific, and is killed in the Philippines (1521). **Del Cano** continues, reaches Spain, and becomes the first to sail around the world.

Christopher Columbus discovers the West Indies, which he thinks are part of Asia, and the coast of Central America and Venezuela (1492–1504).

Amerigo Vespucci explores the coast of South America, which he is the first to call *Mundus Novus* (New World), from 1497. Martin Waldseemüller, a map-maker, in 1507 calls this New World "America" after Vespucci, who used the Latin name Americus Vespucius.

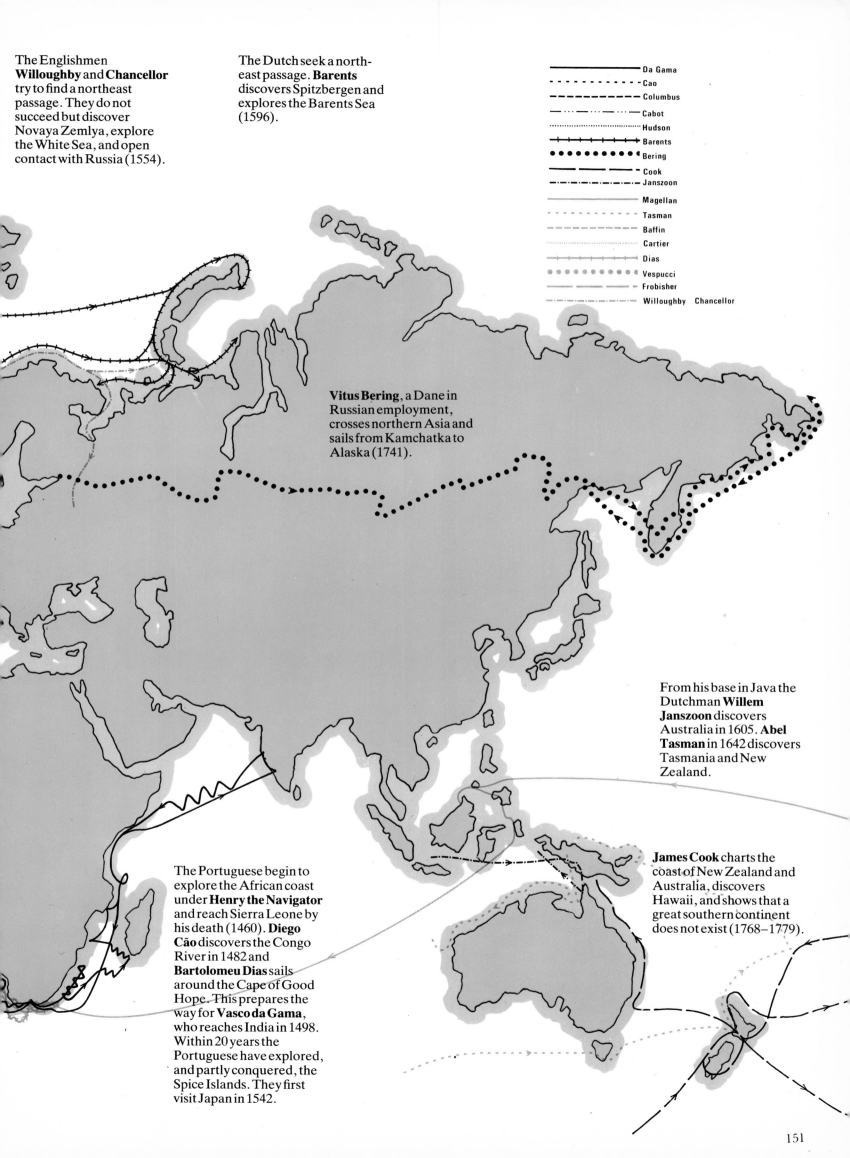

The Englishmen **Willoughby** and **Chancellor** try to find a northeast passage. They do not succeed but discover Novaya Zemlya, explore the White Sea, and open contact with Russia (1554).

The Dutch seek a northeast passage. **Barents** discovers Spitzbergen and explores the Barents Sea (1596).

————————————	Da Gama
– · – · – · – · –	Cao
– – – – – – – – –	Columbus
— · · — · · —	Cabot
· · · · · · · · · ·	Hudson
+++++++++++	Barents
● ● ● ● ● ● ● ●	Bering
— — — — —	Cook
– · · – · · – · · –	Janszoon
————————————	Magellan
· · · · · · · · · ·	Tasman
– – – – – – – – –	Baffin
· · · · · · · · · ·	Cartier
+++++++++++	Dias
● ● ● ● ● ● ● ●	Vespucci
— — — — —	Frobisher
– · – · – · – · –	Willoughby Chancellor

Vitus Bering, a Dane in Russian employment, crosses northern Asia and sails from Kamchatka to Alaska (1741).

From his base in Java the Dutchman **Willem Janszoon** discovers Australia in 1605. **Abel Tasman** in 1642 discovers Tasmania and New Zealand.

The Portuguese begin to explore the African coast under **Henry the Navigator** and reach Sierra Leone by his death (1460). **Diego Cão** discovers the Congo River in 1482 and **Bartolomeu Dias** sails around the Cape of Good Hope. This prepares the way for **Vasco da Gama**, who reaches India in 1498. Within 20 years the Portuguese have explored, and partly conquered, the Spice Islands. They first visit Japan in 1542.

James Cook charts the coast of New Zealand and Australia, discovers Hawaii, and shows that a great southern continent does not exist (1768–1779).

151

India

The Portuguese were the first Europeans to set up bases on the coast of India. When Vasco da Gama reached India he said that he had come to look for "Christians and Spices" and he made no attempt to seize territory. It was Albuquerque who captured Goa in 1510. This was followed by the capture of other ports. But the Portuguese never tried any large-scale conquest in India.

When the Dutch were at war with Spain and Portugal in 1580, they could no longer pick up spices in Lisbon or Cadiz, so they decided to take them directly from the East Indies. They first sent a fleet to the East in 1595, and in 1602 they formed their East India Company. They built trading stations on the coast of India and captured Ceylon (Sri Lanka), where they could buy pepper and cinnamon, from the Portuguese. But India was less important to them than the Spice Islands. The two countries to which India was really important were England and France.

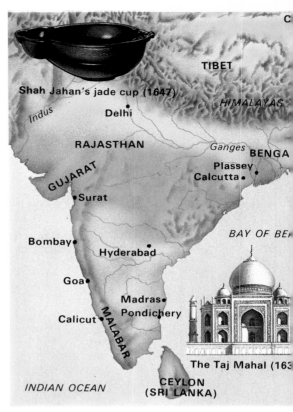

The port of Calicut, on the Malabar coast of southern India, was a busy Arab trading center when Vasco da Gama reached it in 1498. It was a Portuguese trading post for a short time, and then the English East India Company set up a base there. It was famous for its cotton cloth and gave its name to the Indian cotton cloth known as calico.

The English East India Company

The English founded an East India Company shortly before the Dutch. They began to trade with the Spice Islands, but were driven out by the Dutch. This led the English to concentrate on India. They gained control of the sea by defeating a Portuguese fleet off Surat, and the Mughal emperor gave them permission to trade in return for their fleet's protection of Muslim pilgrims on their way to the holy city of Mecca.

By 1700 the English had set up more trading stations in India: at Madras in the south, Bombay in the west (this became English when a Portuguese princess married Charles II in 1662), and Calcutta in the east. Trade was mainly in cotton goods, indigo from Gujarat, pepper from the Malabar coast, silks and saltpeter (used for making gunpowder) from Bengal. In return the Indians bought lead and tin but many Indian goods had to be paid for in silver. The English, like the Portuguese and the Dutch, also carried goods between one part of Asia and another. Some ships were sent from India to China for tea, which by 1700 had become the national drink in England.

Right: A painting of a Frenchman from Rajasthan in northwest India, around 1700. Below: The Mughal emperor Aurangzeb is given the head of his brother, whom he had killed as a rival for the throne. Aurangzeb's ruthless rule hastened the breakup of the Mughal empire.

The French in India

The French too began to trade in India after the formation of their East India Company in 1664. They established two major trading posts, at Chandernagore near Calcutta and Pondichéry near Madras. In the 17th century Europeans could trade in India because the Mughal emperors allowed them to do so. The emperors could have driven the English or the French out, if they had wanted to. The situation changed with the collapse of the Mughal empire after the death of Aurangzeb in 1707. After that Indian governors in the provinces paid little attention to the emperor in Delhi and behaved like independent rulers. They had to be wooed by the Europeans.

The directors of the English and French East India companies were concerned only with profit and not with conquest but it took a year to send messages to India, so many company officials acted without waiting for instructions from London or Paris. The first European to interfere in Indian affairs on a large scale was the French governor Dupleix. As he had few French troops he trained Indian soldiers (*sepoys*) in the same way as he trained the French. These enabled him to back up various Indian princes.

When Britain and France were at war in Europe, they also fought in India. In 1746 the French captured Madras but they had to give it up when peace was made in 1748, in exchange for Cape Breton Island, which the British had captured in North America.

Dupleix was recalled to France in 1754 but he left the French in a stronger position in India than the British, and with more Indian allies when war broke out again two years later. This, the Seven Years' War (see page 143), was to be a turning-point in the history of India, just as it was in North America. Control of the sea and the leadership of Robert Clive turned the tide in favor of the British, who could take troops and supplies out from England while preventing the French from receiving reinforcements. After the defeat of the Indian army of Siraj-ud daula at Plassey, Clive took control of the rich area of Bengal. The end came in 1760 with the defeat of the French at Wandiwash and the fall of their base at Pondichéry.

When peace was made in 1763 the French kept their trading stations in India but they were not to be fortified. The French were allowed to stay only as traders. Clive's victory meant that the British in India were to take the place of the Mughals. India was the base which, in the 19th century, enabled Britain to expand into the rest of South Asia and into the Far East as well.

(see page 143)

THE BATTLE OF PLASSEY

Siraj-ud daula, the nawab (governor) of Bengal, attacked and captured the British settlement at Calcutta in 1756. He put 146 British prisoners in a small cell ("The Black Hole of Calcutta") on a hot night; only 23 came out alive. Robert Clive was sent from Madras to recapture Calcutta. He then plotted to overthrow Siraj-ud daula and put one of his nobles, Mir Jafar, in his place. The armies of Clive and the nawab met at Plassey in June 1757. Clive had 900 European soldiers, 2,100 sepoys and 10 field guns. The nawab had 34,000 infantry, 15,000 cavalry armed with pikes and bows and arrows, 53 heavy guns, and war elephants covered with scarlet cloth. When the nawab bombarded Clive's troops he withdrew them to a mango grove for safety. At noon the rain began to fall. The nawab's powder became wet, so he could not fire his guns. The British had kept their powder covered during the rain and now took the offensive. Their artillery and musket shot maddened Siraj-ud daula's elephants, which stampeded through the Indian ranks. When the time was ripe Mir Jafar with his troops deserted the nawab and joined the British. Siraj-ud daula fled on a camel. Clive had won at a cost of 18 dead and 45 wounded.

CHRONOLOGY

1510	Albuquerque captures Goa for Portugal
1600	English East India Company formed
1618	Mughal emperor gives English the right to trade at Surat
1623	The Amboina "massacre": the Dutch finally push the English out of Spice Islands
1658	Dutch take Ceylon from the Portuguese
1662	England gets Bombay when Charles II marries Catherine of Braganza
1664	French East India Company formed
1707	Death of the last great Mughal emperor
1742	Dupleix becomes governor of the French settlements in India
1746	The French capture Madras
1748	Madras restored to Britain in exchange for Cape Breton Island
1754	Dupleix recalled to France
1757	Battle of Plassey – Clive defeats Siraj-ud daula and takes control of Bengal
1760	French defeat at Wandiwash
1763	Peace of Paris leaves Britain dominant in India

The Mughal emperor Shah Alam hands Robert Clive of the East India Company documents which grant him the right to collect revenues.

The Scientific Revolution

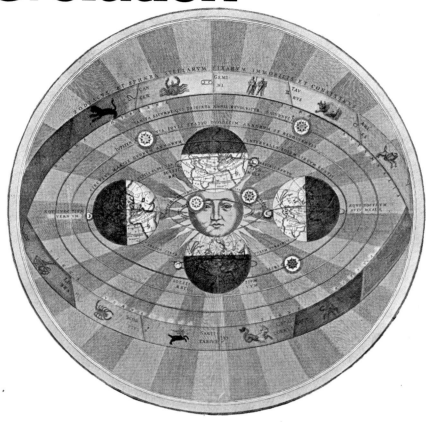

The solar system, as described by the Polish scientist Nicolaus Copernicus in 1543, showing the sun and not the earth at the center of the universe. Copernicus was educated first at Cracow in Poland and later went to the great Italian universities at Padua, Bologna, and Ferrara.

MATHEMATICS
The Scientific Revolution would have been impossible without new achievements in mathematics. In the study of motion on earth or in the sky, the peak of 17th-century science, experiment could not play a large part. The problem of gravity would never have been solved without the analytical geometry (which changes geometrical figures into numerical or algebraic equations) of Descartes, or the calculus of Newton and Leibniz. There was development in almost every branch of mathematics. The decimal system was introduced, signs were made simpler ($\times$, $>$, $<$), and logarithms and the slide rule were used to make calculations easier.

Other means of measuring were also needed. Galileo invented the thermometer and the surveyor's theodolite. The microscope, barometer, pendulum clock, and air pump were all invented between 1590 and 1657.

In the Middle Ages people in western Europe considered life on earth of little importance compared with eternal life in heaven. The most important knowledge was what the church taught. This was that the universe had been created to serve people's needs and that the earth was at the center of the universe. The sun and planets moved in circles around the earth. In the 16th century these ideas were challenged, and a Scientific Revolution began which was to lead to new understanding of the way in which things work.

The Revolution in Astronomy

The first person to challenge the established ideas seriously was Nicolaus Copernicus. In 1543 he put forward the theory that the earth and planets moved around the sun and that the earth rotates daily on its axis. To most people this seemed against common sense: if the earth revolved, would not its movement create a mighty wind? Copernicus did not bring about a scientific revolution, as not for another 150 years was there a satisfactory way of explaining why the earth and the planets behaved as Copernicus said they did.

Some evidence to support Copernicus was provided by Galileo Galilei. He built his

own telescope and discovered the moons of Jupiter, which revolved around the planet. This showed that the earth was not the only center of movement in the sky. Galileo became an enthusiastic supporter of Copernicus's ideas and for this he was brought before the Inquisition (the church's council to inquire into possible heresy) in 1663. In 1600 the Inquisition had burned Giordano Bruno at the stake for saying the earth moved around the sun, as this was against the teaching of the church. Galileo had to withdraw his views.

Vesalius with one of his anatomical models. He was born in Brussels in 1514 and published the first complete description of human anatomy in 1543. His works, which were beautifully and clearly illustrated, were based on the anatomy he learned by dissecting dead bodies. This led him into serious trouble with the church authorities.

A microscope used by the English physicist Robert Hooke in the late 17th century. In his work Micrographia *he described the plant and animal cells he had seen through the microscope. This led to its wider use. He also studied the movement of light and of stars and planets, assisted Newton, invented the wheel barometer, and began to use spiral springs in watch balances. From 1677 to 1683 he was secretary of the Royal Society in London.*

There was no satisfactory explanation of Copernicus's view until the work of Isaac Newton, who was born in 1642, the year of Galileo's death. Galileo had already put forward the idea that a body continues in motion in a straight line until something stops or deflects it. Newton accepted this; but if it was true why did the earth not move in a straight line away from the sun? One of Newton's friends told how the great scientist thought of an answer to this question when he saw an apple falling from a tree: the same gravity which pulled the apple toward the earth prevented the earth from leaving the sun and the moon from leaving the earth. In his *Mathematical Principles* of 1687 Newton showed mathematically how the force of gravity worked.

Medicine

The Scientific Revolution was not limited to astronomy, physics, and mathematics. In 1543, the same year in which Copernicus published his book, Vesalius's *The Fabric of the Human Body* appeared. It had detailed illustrations and was the result of Vesalius's dissections of human bodies. Vesalius showed the structure of the human body and so prepared the way for others, who would show how it worked.

One of these was William Harvey, who studied at Padua in Italy where Vesalius and Galileo had been professors. Harvey found by careful experiment that the amount of blood the heart would throw out in an hour was greater than the weight of a person. It was impossible to say where it went unless it circulated around the body. He also showed that valves in the veins would allow blood to flow only toward the heart, while valves in the arteries permitted blood to flow away from the heart. His book, published in 1628, did not give a complete account of the circulation of the blood, as he did not know how the blood got from the arteries to the veins. The final proof of Harvey's teaching came in 1661, when capillaries (tubes connecting the arteries and veins) were discovered by using a microscope. All modern physiology has been based on Harvey's work.

The Spread of Scientific Knowledge

In the Middle Ages books had to be copied out by hand, a very slow and expensive process. Ideas therefore did not spread quickly. With the invention of the printing press books became cheaper and more available. Learned men could now get their works into the hands of colleagues in a few months.

The rise of scientific societies also helped the spread of ideas. Academies were first formed in Italy; in England the Royal Society (so called because Charles II was a member) was established in 1662, and in 1666 the Academy of Sciences was founded in Paris by Louis XIV. These societies collected facts, carried out experiments, and published journals, so that others could learn about the latest ideas and discoveries.

The Scientific Revolution was important because it taught people that they must not rely on what the Greeks or Arabs had written in the past, but they must make their own observations. They must question everything and test their theories by experiment to see if they were true. It was the critical attitude which made possible the great scientific and industrial advances of the 19th and 20th centuries, which were to affect the whole world so deeply.

In 1752 the American Benjamin Franklin showed the electrical nature of lightning by flying a kite in a thunderstorm and drawing sparks from a key tied to the lower end of its string.

Discovering the Pacific

In the Middle Ages people believed that there was a great southern continent, which they called Terra Australis or South Land. By the 16th century geographers had decided that it must lie in the South Pacific, somewhere between Africa and Cape Horn, the southernmost tip of South America.

The Dutch Discover Australia

The Spaniards seemed well placed to explore the Pacific, as they had bases in Mexico and Peru and traded between Acapulco in Mexico and the Philippines. Unfortunately the southeast trade winds pushed ships north toward the equator and made it almost impossible for ships from Mexico to enter the South Pacific. Exploration of this area would have to start from the west, around the Cape of Good Hope, from where ships could sail with the westerly winds. The first to do this were the Dutch, who sailed from the Cape to Java. In 1605 Willem Janszoon left Java to survey the southern coast of New Guinea. He became the first European to discover Australia, which the Dutch called New Holland. By 1642 the Dutch had explored the whole of the west coast and part of the north and south coasts of Australia.

In that year Abel Tasman sailed from Batavia, heading first south and then east. He discovered the island later named Tasmania after him, and journeyed on till he reached New Zealand, which he thought was part of Terra Australis. He then returned to the Dutch East Indies by sailing north and west, and so proved that Australia was an island.

James Cook

After Tasman's voyage there was little interest in a southern continent until the British Admiralty sent Samuel Wallis and Philip Carteret to discover it in 1766. Instead Wallis rediscovered Tahiti, though he was certain "we saw the long wished for Southern Continent."

Another expedition was sent in 1768. It was led by Captain James Cook who had joined the British navy as a seamen in 1755. He was a skillful navigator and surveyor and helped to chart the St. Lawrence River before the British attack on Quebec in 1759. Cook was very popular with his crew and much concerned about their health. He was horrified that so many men on a long voyage died from scurvy. To prevent this he insisted that his men eat sauerkraut (a kind of pickled cabbage), fruit, and carrots.

A drawing by Abel Tasman showing native boats, Dutch ships, and Fiji Islanders.

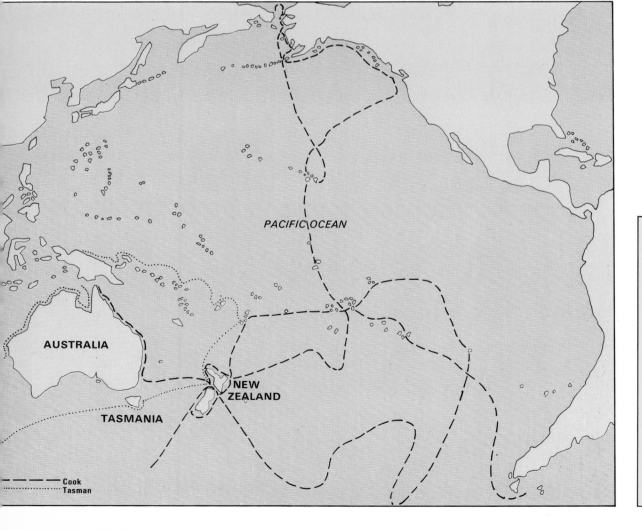

PACIFIC OCEAN

AUSTRALIA

NEW ZEALAND

TASMANIA

------ Cook
········· Tasman

CHRONOLOGY

1605   Willem Janszoon surveys southern coast of New Guinea and discovers Australia

1642   Abel Tasman discovers Tasmania and New Zealand

1766   Samuel Wallis rediscovers Tahiti

1768   James Cook's first voyage to the Pacific (to 1771); he charts the coast of New Zealand and the east coast of Australia

1772   Cook's second voyage (to 1775) shows there is no southern continent

1776   Cook's last voyage (to 1779); he fails to find a northwest or northeast passage from the Pacific to the Atlantic. He returns to Hawaii, where he is killed

Cook's First and Second Voyages

Astronomers forecast that in 1769 the planet Venus would move across the face of the sun, something that would not happen again for another hundred years. Cook was sent to the Pacific to observe this and reached Tahiti by sailing around Cape Horn. He next sailed to New Zealand, found the strait between North and South islands and charted nearly 4,000 kilometers (2,400 miles) of coast. He claimed New Zealand for Britain before sailing on to the unknown east coast of Australia. He kept close to the shore so that he could chart the coast, only to find that the Great Barrier Reef lay between his ship *The Endeavor* and the sea. His ship was holed and only managed to reach the open sea with great difficulty. Cook charted 3,200 kilometers (2,000 miles) of the Australian coast, claimed it for Britain, and returned home in 1771.

Cook was soon off on his second voyage to the Pacific, this time by sailing around the Cape of Good Hope. He was instructed to sail around the earth in as southerly a latitude as possible. This he did. Keeping close to 60° he crossed the Antarctic Circle three times, the first man to do so. This too was full of dangers. There was dense fog and towering icebergs threatened to destroy his two small ships, but he proved without any doubt that the fabled southern continent stretching right across the world did not exist.

Death in Hawaii

Cook set sail on his last voyage to the Pacific in 1776. He was looking for a northwest passage linking the Atlantic and Pacific oceans. He charted the North American Pacific coastline, and sailed through the Bering Strait separating America from Asia, before ice blocked his progress. Cook then turned back for Hawaii, which he had discovered earlier. The natives tired of the Englishmen demanding food from them. There was a quarrel, in which Cook was stabbed to death and cut into pieces.

THE DEATH OF COOK

James King, one of Cook's lieutenants, describes his death:

An accident happened which gave a fatal turn. The boats, having fired at some canoes, killed a chief. The [islanders] armed themselves and a general attack followed. Our unfortunate Commander was stabbed in the back, and fell with his face in the water. His body was immediately dragged ashore and surrounded by the enemy, who . . . showed a savage eagerness to share in his destruction. Thus fell our great and excellent Commander!

This drawing of red honeysuckle was made by Sydney Parkinson on one of Cook's voyages. Before the days of photography, drawings were an important record of explorers' finds.

This picture of Cook's ships Resolution and Adventure at Tahiti was painted by William Hodges, who traveled with him.

FROM CAPTAIN COOK'S JOURNALS

Australia, June 11–12, 1770:

A few Minutes before 11 the Ship Struck. We found that we had got upon a reef of Coral. The ship being quite fast we throw'd over board our guns, Iron and stone ballast, Casks, Hoops, staves, oyle Jars, decay'd stores etc. About 20 past 10 o'Clock the Ship floated, we having at this time 3 feet 9 inches water in the hold . . . At 8 hauld her bow close a shore which gave us an opportunity to examine the leak. The whole was cut away as if by a blunt edge tool. A large piece of Coral rock was sticking in one hole and several pieces of fothering [caulking], small stones, sand etc. had stoped the water.

Tahiti, September 1, 1777:

A man was to be sacrificed. The unhappy victim seemed to be a middle-aged man; and one of the lowest class of the people. They generally make choice of guilty persons or else of common, low, fellows, who stroll about without any fixed abode. We were told that he had been knocked on the head with a stone. Those who are [selected] to suffer are never apprized of their fate, till the blow is given.

Captain Cook. His detailed surveys and observations set new standards for the explorers who followed him.

THE MODERN WORLD

The World Trade Center towers in New York rise above the city's financial district along the Hudson River.

A Changing World

By 1760 European states had conquered vast empires in India, America, and Siberia; they controlled the ocean routes and organized worldwide trade. Yet the effect of Europe on the rest of the world was not very great. China and Japan were not concerned with what Europeans were doing: in Africa and India European influence was limited to areas on or near the coast. Large parts of South America and Africa were unknown to Europeans. Scientific discoveries and inventions altered all this in the Industrial Revolution. In the next 200 years European science and technology changed the lives of people all over the world.

The Scientific Age

The Industrial Revolution, which began in Britain, had spread to other parts of Europe by 1870. The manufacture of goods like cloth and iron had been speeded up by the invention of new machines, but there was nothing new in the sort of things produced. After 1870 came new inventions, which were completely different from anything in the past – electricity, the telephone, and the automobile. They changed people's lives dramatically. In the last 20 years automation and the computer have brought even more rapid change. In addition to new machines

In 1850 Britain was the "workshop of the world" and wanted to show off its achievements. The idea was born of a great international exhibition, that would show progress in science and technology. It was held in 1851, in a huge three-storied palace of glass on a strong framework of iron pillars and girders. This "Crystal Palace," built in London's Hyde Park, was itself a great technical achievement. The 100,000 exhibits inside included British machinery and inventions, power looms from America, fabrics from France, and steel cannon from Germany, as well as goods from countries all over the world. This picture shows the opening by Queen Victoria.

The late 19th century saw the westward expansion of America as thousands of pioneers packed all their belongings into wagons and journeyed across the continent in search of land. At the same time, immigrants from Europe were arriving in great numbers. Agriculture, industry, and trade all grew rapidly and within a hundred years the United States had become a world "superpower."

came progress in hygiene and in medicine, which allowed people to live longer and in better health than ever before. All this has been the result of science, which has reduced the physical effort needed to work and live.

For the first time home life was deeply affected. The washing machine, refrigerator, radio, TV, and electric or gas stove became common features in every household in the West. People were better off not only at home but at work too. The dirty and dangerous conditions, long hours of work, and low wages in the factories at the beginning of the Industrial Revolution had largely disappeared by 1980.

A Wider World

The interior of Africa was unknown to Europeans until the explorations of Mungo Park, Burton, Speke, Stanley, and Livingstone. Most Africans did not come into contact with Europeans before the last quarter of the 19th century when almost all of Africa became part of the colonial empires of Britain, France, Germany, Portugal, and Italy. In Asia, China and Japan avoided contact with the world outside until they were forced to trade with the West – China in the Opium War of 1839 to 1842, Japan when American ships sailed into Tokyo Bay in 1853. Europeans were able to dominate other nations because of their superior weapons, products of the Industrial Revolution. Most of the world was under European control by 1914. It was a process that had begun 500 years earlier, when Portuguese seamen hesitantly began to explore the coast of Africa.

The End of Empire

The domination of the world by one small part of it had never happened before and it was not to last long. The people in the new colonies resented the way Europeans treated them as inferior, and rebelled. These rebellions had no chance of success if they only had old weapons with which to fight modern armies. The only way to defeat the West was to imitate it, as the Japanese did by having their army and navy trained by European officers and by using the latest weapons.

Other countries were helped, unintentionally, by the European powers themselves, who needed educated Africans and

A soldier in a United Nations peace-keeping force. Such forces patrol strife-torn areas, observing and acting much like police but not fighting for either side. The United Nations was set up in 1945, with 51 countries signing its charter; today it has nearly 150 members. Although it has not succeeded in its aim of preventing all wars, it has helped to stop several. It provides a meeting place where nations can talk about their differences, and it has a number of special agencies to deal with problems such as health, food, and money. Its International Court of Justice settles cases of international law.

Indians to run their empires for them. Men like Nehru of India, educated at an English public school, Harrow, and at Cambridge University, and Nkrumah of Ghana, educated in America and at the London School of Economics, learned how to organize their own political parties which led their countries to independence. They were helped in this when the European nations weakened one another in two world wars. European empires collapsed in the 1950s and 1960s and new, independent states arose in India, Africa, the West Indies, and Southeast Asia.

The Poor Get Poorer

Once these colonies gained their independence their difficulties remained. Many were backward and needed to provide education and skills on a large scale, something which could not be done quickly. Some states, especially in Africa, had borders which cut across tribal boundaries. They tended to split up, as Nigeria did for a time when the eastern region declared its independence as Biafra in 1967. Many of these countries were very poor and found that the gap between them and the rich, industrial nations grew bigger rather than smaller. In 1800, at the beginning of the Industrial Revolution, the rich (white) countries had an income per head double that of the poor (nonwhite) nations. By 1945 the rich nations were 20 times, and by 1965, 40 times, better off.

The "Superpowers"

By the end of the 19th century the United States was rapidly overtaking its European rivals in Industrial production. In World War I, America's involvement largely caused the defeat of Germany. After the war America refused to join the League of Nations and cut itself off from affairs in the rest of the world. In World War II it came out of its isolation, and again played an important part in the defeat of Germany and Japan.

This war saw the rise of a second "superpower," Soviet Russia. At the end of the war Europe was dependent on these "superpowers." Eastern Europe became in effect part of a greatly expanded Russian empire, while western Europe had to rely on American money to rebuild its industries and on American nuclear weapons to defend it from the communist threat.

A third, economic "superpower" has arisen since the war in Japan. It is now ahead of all the countries of Europe in production of manufactured goods.

The Future

The scientific and industrial age has seen a continuous growth in production and this means that the earth's natural resources are being used up at an increasingly fast rate. How long can this go on before we run out of the minerals we need? A further question mark hangs over the future. There are today about 4.8 billion people in the world. It is impossible for them all to have a high standard of living. In the year 2000 it is expected that there will be 6 billion people. Will it be possible to feed them, let alone give them a happy and prosperous life? Another problem arises with automation. Machines are taking over many of the dull, routine jobs on the factory floor but, as fewer people are needed, there is greater unemployment. Are we facing a future in which many people will be permanently unemployed? The greatest danger of all is that, with nuclear weapons, people can wipe out a large part of the human race. Yet we cannot put the clock back. We cannot do without science. We will have to learn to use it to advantage so that, instead of destroying us and our way of life, it gives us all a better future.

The mid-20th century saw the first exploration of space. In 1957 the Russians launched the first artificial satellite, Sputnik I, and in 1961 the Russian Yuri Gagarin became the first man in space. In 1969 the Americans landed the first men on the moon. This picture shows an astronaut from the 1972 Apollo 17 landing (the last carried out by the Americans) collecting samples from the moon's surface.

Left: Ironworks at Coalbrookdale, in the north of England, in 1805. Here Abraham Darby first used coke for smelting iron in 1709. Coalbrookdale was also the site of the world's first iron bridge, built in 1782 by Darby's grandson. Above: Conditions in the early coal mines were very bad. Workers were lowered to the pit face by basket and chain, and when the men had hacked coal out of the seams women dragged it or carried it on their backs through the narrow tunnels. During the 19th century many laws were passed to limit working hours and make conditions better.

The Industrial Revolution

People's ways of life have changed more in the past 200 years than in the previous 5,000. In the 18th century they were living in almost the same way as the Ancient Egyptians. They used the same materials, wood and stone, for building; the same animals for transport; sails and oars for ships; wool and cotton for clothes; candles for light. Today metals are used in building, the railway, car and airplane have replaced the ox and horse for transport, oil and atom power provide energy instead of wind and water, artificial fibers compete with wool and cotton for clothes, while electricity has replaced the candle for light.

These changes are a result of the Industrial Revolution. This was given its name because of the dramatic changes that occurred in the production of textiles, iron, and steel; in the use of coal as fuel; in the introduction of new sources of power, such as the steam engine; and in the mass-production of goods in the factory system. At the same time came new methods of transport, a rapid rise in population, and the gathering together of people in towns and cities.

Why Britain?

The Industrial Revolution began in Britain for many reasons. Britain had valuable minerals like coal, iron, tin, and copper. Its farms were able to supply food for its growing population and wool for its clothing industry. Many rivers, such as the Severn and Trent, were suitable for boats, and heavy, bulky goods could often be sent by sea. The damp climate of Lancashire was good for the manufacture of cotton materials.

Many European countries in the 18th century suffered from wars which ravaged their land. Britain fought its wars abroad. By conquering the French empires in North America and India it gained large overseas markets. The American colonies became independent but Britain still sent large quantities of manufactured goods there, and during the Napoleonic wars it captured new trading areas in South America. While customs barriers within and between states curbed trade in much of Europe, goods could move freely all over Britain.

Coal and Iron

One of the most important changes of the Industrial Revolution was the use of coal instead of charcoal as a fuel. This was to lead to a rapid increase in the production of iron. Charcoal had previously been used to smelt iron ore, but as the English forests were cut down it became scarce and expensive. Coal was used instead but at first there were difficulties. It contained impurities, mainly sulfur, which caused the iron to break easily. In 1709 Abraham Darby solved the problem by "coking" the coal, releasing the gas and

tar fumes in it and leaving mainly carbon. But it was not till 1760 that large, efficient blast furnaces were built. Unlike the old forges they could mass-produce iron. By 1800 Britain produced more coal and iron than the rest of the world put together. British coal output increased from 6 million tons in 1770 to 12 million in 1800 and 57 million in 1861. Iron production increased from 50,000 tons in 1770 to 130,000 in 1800 and 3,800,000 in 1861. Iron was now so cheap that it could be used for constructing bridges and buildings as well as machines.

Textiles

The first industry to be mechanized was cotton manufacture, because light and washable cotton goods became increasingly popular. Spinning machines were too slow to provide enough yarn for weavers, so a series of inventions, such as the spinning jenny of 1767, provided machines which could spin over 100 threads at the same time. These machines now produced more thread than could be handled by weavers, so a power loom was invented to speed up weaving and after 1789 it was driven by steam. By 1820 it had largely replaced the handloom weaver in the cotton industry. The result of these inventions was a great boom. Raw cotton imports rose from 2.5 million kilograms (5 million pounds) in 1778 to 360 million kilograms (800 million pounds) by 1880.

Steam Power

The new cotton machines needed a more plentiful and reliable source of power than windmills and waterwheels. James Watt provided this with his invention of the steam engine. By 1800, 500 of his engines were in use – some for pumping water, the rest pro-viding power to run textile mills and iron furnaces. The steam engine used heat to drive the machines and ended reliance on animal, wind, or water power as a source of energy.

Transport

Heavy goods like coal and iron were very difficult and expensive to move by road, so canals were built. The first important step was the building of an 11-kilometer (7-mile) canal by the duke of Bridgwater from his coal mines at Worsley to Manchester. This cut the price of coal in Manchester by half. Canal building on a large scale followed, so that by 1830 there were 4,000 kilometers (2,500 miles) of canals in England. In that year Stephenson's engine *Rocket* pulled a train 50 kilometers (31 miles) at 22.5 kilometers (14 miles) an hour from Manchester to Liverpool. Within a few years railways were the best way to travel long distances, as they could move passengers and goods faster and more cheaply than roads or canals. By 1838 Britain had 800 kilometers (500 miles) of railways; by 1850, 10,600 kilometers (6,600 miles) and by 1870, 25,000 kilometers (15,500 miles).

By 1850 a quarter of the world's trade passed through British ports, and over a third of the world's industrial output of goods for trade came from British mines and mills. Two thirds of the value of British exports were textiles, coming mainly from Lancashire. Britain dominated the world economy to an extent not seen before or since, but other countries, particularly the United States and Germany, were catching up. Meanwhile a new wave of inventions was to bring about a second Industrial Revolution (see page 178).

(see page 178)

The first steam engines were used in the early 1700s to pump water from mines. They were very inefficient. In 1768 a Scottish engineer, James Watt, developed a much better steam engine which produced enough power to drive machines. By 1789 cloth mills were using steam power, and in the early 1800s steam was harnessed to pull trains. This picture of 1830 shows second-class carriages on the Liverpool–Manchester line in northwest England.

During the Industrial Revolution many works and factories were built, and people flocked from villages to the new factory towns. There they lived in tiny houses crowded together, and worked long hours in dangerous conditions. The air and countryside around were badly polluted by the smoke and waste.

The World in 1763

In Europe the Seven Years' War ends with Prussia, in the north, as the new military power. Britain has taken over former French colonies in America and India and the Industrial Revolution is beginning which, combined with Britain's domination of the seas, brings the country to a leading position. The Ottoman Turks have begun the slow decline that will make them the "sick men of Europe" in the next century. In the East, the Chinese empire, unaffected by Europe, is greater than ever before, and the settlement of Australia will soon begin. In the Americas, many colonies are growing increasingly unhappy with their rulers.

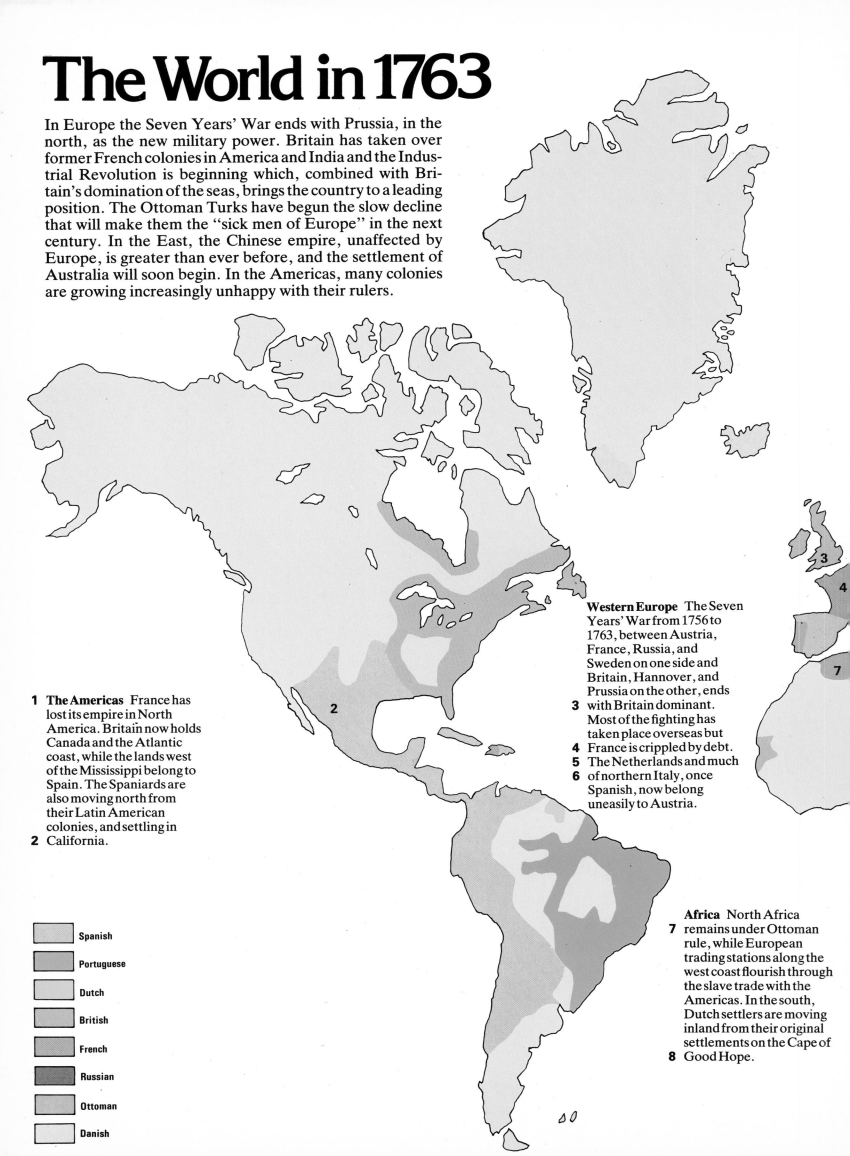

1 **The Americas** France has lost its empire in North America. Britain now holds Canada and the Atlantic coast, while the lands west of the Mississippi belong to Spain. The Spaniards are also moving north from their Latin American colonies, and settling in 2 California.

Western Europe The Seven Years' War from 1756 to 1763, between Austria, France, Russia, and Sweden on one side and Britain, Hannover, and Prussia on the other, ends
3 with Britain dominant. Most of the fighting has taken place overseas but
4 France is crippled by debt.
5 The Netherlands and much
6 of northern Italy, once Spanish, now belong uneasily to Austria.

Africa North Africa
7 remains under Ottoman rule, while European trading stations along the west coast flourish through the slave trade with the Americas. In the south, Dutch settlers are moving inland from their original settlements on the Cape of
8 Good Hope.

Spanish

Portuguese

Dutch

British

French

Russian

Ottoman

Danish

9 Northern Europe Prussia has become the leading military power in Germany and gains rich land by the **10** Seven Years' War. Russia has gained land on the Baltic Sea.

13 The Far East With the annexation of Turkestan in 1759 the Chinese empire reaches its greatest extent. Soon Captain Cook will **14** explore Australasia and the last great continent will be linked with world history.

11 The Near East The Ottomans still rule the area but their days of expansion are ended. Many of the countries become increasingly independent under powerful governors.

12 India The British East India Company under Robert Clive has driven the French from India. Now it will increase its control over the rest of the subcontinent.

North America

In 1783 the newly formed United States was a small, weak country with just over 3 million inhabitants. By 1914 its population was larger than that of any European country except for Russia, and it was the leading industrial nation in the world.

Independence

The 13 British colonies, stretching along 2,400 kilometers (1,500 miles) of the Atlantic coast of America, were prepared to put up with British rule as long as they needed British help against their French neighbors. When the French were defeated and driven out of North America in 1763, the British colonists became more independent. The British government was tactless. It tried to tax the colonies to pay for the recent war against the French. The colonies objected to taxes laid down by a Parliament in which they had no members. Relations between Britain and its colonies got worse and worse until war began in 1775. A year later the American leaders signed the Declaration of Independence, claiming complete freedom from British rule.

At first the British did well, but in 1778 France entered the war on the side of the colonists. The French defeated the British at sea and, with an American army under George Washington, forced the British to surrender at Yorktown. The colonies became independent; the border on the north was the Great Lakes, and in the west the river Mississippi.

The different colonies had acted together to win the war. Afterward, it seemed that the new Union would fall apart. To save it, George Washington presided over an assembly at Philadelphia which produced the Constitution of the United States of America. Each state could decide many questions

1840s engine

Revolutionary War Liberty medal

for itself, but there was to be a strong federal government, made up of an elected president to govern, an elected Congress to pass laws, and an independent Supreme Court to settle disputes over the powers of the government. When all the states accepted the Constitution in 1789, Washington became the first president of the United States of America.

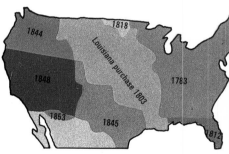

The growth of the United States.

THE AMERICAN FRONTIER

The British colonies stretched along the coast east of the Appalachian Mountains. Independence opened the way to the Mississippi and in 1803, through the Louisiana Purchase, America bought from France a vast area stretching from the Mississippi to the Rockies. Pioneers who entered this area had to be self-reliant, tough, and ready to fight Indians. They fought Spaniards, too, when they moved south into what was then part of Mexico, and seized Texas. By 1853 the American frontier ran along the Rio Grande all the way to the Pacific.

In the north the United States clashed with Canada in the American-British War of 1812. Peace in 1814 fixed the boundary between the United States and Canada along the 49th parallel of latitude, from the Great Lakes to the Rockies. In 1846 this was extended to the Pacific.

A wagon train of pioneers makes its way westward through the Rocky Mountains. These formed a fearsome barrier across the routes to the rich farmlands of the west coast. Among the dangers the pioneers had to face were drought and snow, dangerous animals, and attacks by Indians.

The Civil War

In the northern United States textile and iron industries developed. The south had little industry. There plantations, worked by black slaves, produced tobacco, rice, sugar, and, most important of all, cotton. The north was strongly against slavery and trouble arose over allowing slavery in the new states being formed. By 1861, when Abraham Lincoln was elected president, the hatred of the north and the south for each other had made civil war likely. Lincoln opposed slavery, but said that he did not mean to interfere with it in the south. Even so his election was taken as a threat by the southern states. Led by South Carolina, they *seceded* (withdrew) from the Union to form the Confederate States. Civil war began.

After five years, the Confederate armies were destroyed. The Union was preserved, and 4 million slaves were freed, but the war exhausted the south and left much bitterness there. More Americans were killed in the Civil War than in all the other wars in America's history.

The battle of Williamsburg, during the Civil War. Here the advancing Union forces (in blue) clashed with the Confederate rear guard on May 5, 1862. The Confederates withdrew after heavy fighting.

CANADA

In 1763 the British took over the French lands in Canada. During the American Revolution the Canadian colonies stayed loyal to Britain, and after the war some 40,000 people moved from the new United States to settle there. Explorers traveled west across the continent and new settlements, based on timber and fisheries, grew up. The Canadian colonies were afraid that the United States might try to expand northward. In 1867 English- and French-speaking Canadians joined to become a self-governing Dominion of the British empire. Soon two western provinces, Manitoba and British Columbia, joined Canada, whose new lands were opened up by the Canadian Pacific Railway.

The Indian Problem

As the settlers moved westward, they came increasingly into conflict with the Indians whose land they were taking. In 1830 it was decided to move the Indians in the south to land west of the Mississippi, to a vast area known as the Indian Country. Treaties guaranteed them this land "as long as the rivers shall run and the grass shall grow." In the 1850s gold was found on Indian land. The government began to buy back Indian land and to settle the Indians in reservations. The Indians fought for their lands with great but hopeless ferocity. The Indians' way of life was destroyed as the white men ruthlessly slaughtered the great buffalo herds which had provided them with food and clothing. By 1890 both Indians and buffalo existed only in reservations.

The settlement of the Pacific coast began with the gold rush to California in 1848 and the discovery of lush pastureland in Oregon. The Great Plains were empty except for Indians, who lived off the huge herds of buffalo roaming there. Railways changed this and made settlement of the plains possible. The first transcontinental railway was completed in 1869 and by 1890 there were more railways in America than in all Europe. New harvesting machines and fertilizers helped to treble the cultivated land between 1860 and 1890, and during this period wheat exports became 12 times greater. Beef also became an important export after refrigeration was invented.

The money earned from beef and wheat was invested in industry. By 1900 the United States was the largest steel producer in the world. Rich deposits of iron ore were found in Minnesota and around Lake Superior. Oil was found, too, and some Americans made enormous fortunes. When he retired in 1897, John D. Rockefeller of Standard Oil was the richest man on earth.

CHRONOLOGY

1775	War of Independence begins
1776	Declaration of Independence
1781	Surrender of British at Yorktown
1783	Independence of United States recognized by Britain
1787	Constitution of the United States
1789	George Washington becomes first president
1803	Louisiana Purchase from France
1812	War between the United States and Britain (to 1814)
1845	Texas annexed
1846	War with Mexico (to 1848)
1848	California gold rush
1861	Civil War (to 1865)
1862	Battle of Gettysburg, the decisive battle of the war; the South under Lee defeated
1865	Abraham Lincoln assassinated
1867	British North America Act unites Ontario, Quebec, New Brunswick, and Nova Scotia in the Dominion of Canada
1869	Canada buys the Northwest Territories from the Hudson's Bay Company. First transcontinental railway in America completed when Union Pacific and Central Pacific lines meet in Utah
1885	Canadian Pacific Railway completed
1898	Spanish-American War

THE IMMIGRANTS

While Americans were moving westward across the continent, Europeans were traveling west to America. In the early 19th century they came largely from northern Europe – from Britain (especially Ireland), Germany, and Scandinavia. They were spurred on by poor harvests and economic difficulties in their home countries. In the late 1880s there was a great new wave of immigration. The new arrivals came from southern and eastern Europe, in particular from Italy, Hungary, Czechoslovakia, Poland, and Russia. Many of them had left their countries because they had been persecuted for political reasons or because they were Jewish. The earlier immigrants had often become farmers; the new immigrants, many of whom were illiterate, mostly worked in the rapidly growing industries. In the west, large numbers of Chinese came to work on the railways.

NORTH SEA
NORWAY
SWEDEN
FINLAND
•St. Petersburg
DENMARK
BALTIC SEA
Dvina
BRITAIN
Elbe
Oder
Vistula
•Warsaw
RUSSIA
Waterloo
•Leipzig
NETHERLANDS
Jena
Seine
•Paris
Rhine
Austerlitz
•Vienna
Dnieper
Loire
BAVARIA
AUSTRIA
Danube
BLACK SEA
Sèvres vase
1785
FRANCE
Switzerland
Garonne
SAVOY
NICE •
ITALY
Elba
Corsica
•Rome
Ludwig van Beethoven
1770–1827
TURKEY
PORTUGAL
Tagus
SPAIN
Sardinia
• NAPLES
MEDITERRANEAN SEA

Napoleon's Europe

In the 18th century France fought a series of costly foreign wars which used up its resources. At last the peasants, who were more and more heavily taxed, revolted. King Louis XVI was overthrown and executed, and the countries around France began to move in on a state torn by civil war. Almost miraculously, France fought them off, and under Napoleon built up a great European empire. Napoleon's defeat caused many of the borders to be restored to their 1790 position; but Europe had been significantly and lastingly changed.

The French Revolution

The burden of taxes to pay for France's wars fell almost entirely on the peasants. Attempts to tax the nobility and the church, who paid little taxes and lived in great luxury, were not successful. The nobility would not give up their rights and King Louis XVI supported them. When the king tried to bring in troops to end the movement for reform, revolt broke out. On July 14, 1789, the Bastille, a fortress prison in Paris, was stormed by a furious mob. A National Assembly was formed to govern. It freed peasants from labor services on their lords' lands and from paying the tithe, a tenth of their produce which was given to the church. There was no attempt to get rid of the monarchy, but control of France was taken from the king and given to the assembly.

The king and the nobility did not accept their loss of power. In 1791 Louix XVI tried to flee from France but was recognized and brought back to Paris. France went to war with Austria and Prussia the next year, and the king was blamed when the war went badly. The monarchy was overthrown and in 1793 the king was executed. Civil war broke out; enemy armies began to invade. A Committee of Public Safety was formed and saved France by a series of harsh measures. Anyone found guilty of opposing the Republic was sent to the guillotine, and fear and hatred grew under this "Reign of Terror." Eventually its leader, Maximilien Robespierre, was himself executed, and in 1795 a new assembly was elected. Gradually, order was restored.

Below: Napoleon Bonaparte. Toward the end of his life he wrote: "I have fought 60 battles and I have learned nothing which I did not know at the beginning." His genius was not in introducing new ways of fighting but in taking the right decision at the right time.

A EUROPEAN EMPIRE

In 1792 France, weakened by revolution, looked an easy prey. Austria and Prussia, followed by Britain, the Netherlands, and Spain, joined forces against it, but the French revolutionary armies threw out the foreign invaders and attacked in their turn. They took over the Netherlands, Nice, and Savoy to secure France's "natural frontiers," and all the countries except Britain made peace. One of the army's outstanding officers was Napoleon Bonaparte, and in 1799 he took power in France.

Napoleon proved a brilliant administrator. He restored order and gave France a code of law which is still used today. He paid great attention to education and road systems. In 1804 he crowned himself emperor. In a series of campaigns he gained control of much of Europe, and by 1811 the French empire stretched from the Baltic to south of Rome. He reorganized Germany, which had been a patchwork of over 300 states, into 39 states. He took land from Prussia and Austria to set up the Grandy Duchy of Warsaw. Napoleon made his brothers and generals the kings and princes of lands not ruled directly by France, and insisted that the newly conquered territories should accept French reforms and codes of law. He also introduced conscription (compulsory service in the army) and taxed the people heavily to pay for his wars. They had to buy French goods and were not allowed to trade with Britain. All these measures were unpopular.

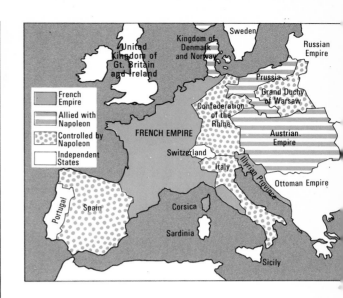

Napoleon's Downfall

Napoleon's fall began with his invasion of Spain in 1808. He put his brother Joseph on the throne, and this caused the Spanish people to revolt. Fighting went on for four years. He had to keep large numbers of troops in Spain (300,000 at one time) when he badly needed them elsewhere.

Another blunder was his invasion of Russia in 1812, with his Grand Army of 600,000 men. The Russians retreated in front of him, burning everything they could not take with them. Napoleon took Moscow but the Russians, retreating to St. Petersburg, still did not ask for peace. As winter was approaching Napoleon decided to retreat. On the way back to Poland he lost many thousands of troops through frostbite, starvation, disease, and Russian attacks. Only 30,000 men returned in fighting condition.

In 1813 Austria and Prussia joined Russia in attacking Napoleon and defeated him at Leipzig. Six months later Paris was occupied, and Napoleon was exiled to Elba. He escaped from there and fought his last great battle at Waterloo, when he was defeated by the British and the Prussians.

Above: The duke of Wellington, Napoleon's most formidable opponent. He led the British at the battle of Waterloo, where Napoleon was finally defeated.

The Congress of Vienna

In 1814 the allies who had defeated Napoleon met at Vienna to settle the boundaries of Europe. In many cases, as in France, Spain, and Portugal, the old monarchies were restored. Russia, the major military power, gained land on its western boundaries, including Finland and part of Poland. Prussia gained control of a large Rhineland province and part of Saxony. It was now the major power in northern Germany. Austria gained land and power in northern Italy, but showed no interest in taking back control of the Austrian Netherlands (Belgium). Instead, it was joined with the Dutch republic to form a Kingdom of the Netherlands.

The Congress of Vienna wanted a balance of power in Europe, with no country strong enough to dominate the others. On the whole, its settlement worked well, until the rise of nationalism brought first a spate of revolutions and then the unification of Germany and of Italy, and the balance was destroyed.

Napoleon's greatest victory was at the battle of Austerlitz in 1805, in what is now Czechoslovakia. Here his 73,000 French troops defeated 90,000 Austrians and Russians. He lured the enemy troops to attack his right wing, then cut their forces in two. He drove the Russians onto frozen lakes where the ice broke under the weight of their guns and horses. By mid-afternoon the battle was over. The Russians returned home and the Austrians sued for peace. Their alliance against France had crumbled.

Latin America

Latin America is the area south of the Rio Grande, the river which separates Mexico from the United States. It includes, besides Mexico, all of Central and South America and some West Indian islands like Cuba. Most of this area became part of the Spanish empire, apart from Brazil which was Portuguese; its conquerors spoke languages related to Latin, which gaves the area its name. The descendants of the Spaniards and Portuguese, born in Latin America, were known as Creoles. Some Spaniards married Indians, so a *mestizo* (mixed) race grew up. In many parts of Latin America mestizos outnumbered both Europeans and Indians. There were also blacks, brought over from Africa as slaves.

Simón Bolívar's revolutionary troops defeat the Spanish at Ayacucho in 1824, winning Peru from Spain. Bolívar, the son of a wealthy Venezuelan landowner, helped Venezuela, Colombia, Ecuador, Peru, and Bolivia to gain independence from rule by Spain.

José de San Martin

Independence

For centuries Latin America was governed by officials sent from Spain and Portugal. Creoles were kept out of power. When the American colonies gained independence from Britain, the Creoles wanted their own independence too. In 1810 most of the people in Spanish America rose in revolt. Simón Bolívar, a brilliant general, freed the north from Spanish rule. The outstanding leader in the south was José de San Martin. After freeing Argentina in 1826 he crossed the Andes and helped to free Chile and Peru. A Creole rising freed Mexico by 1822. Brazil gained independence peacefully under the king of Portugal's son, and eventually became a republic in 1889.

For the Indians and mestizos independence brought no benefits. Creoles replaced Spaniards as rulers. Governments were overthrown by military *coups* but these simply replaced one military dictator by another and did not improve the lot of the peasants. Power remained in the hands of the wealthy landowners.

Boundary Wars

Boundary disputes between the new states sometimes led to war. In the 1840s Mexico lost Texas, southern California and 40 percent of its original territory to the United States; in the Paraguayan War of 1865 to 1870 Brazil, Argentina, and Uruguay defeated Paraguay and took much of its territory. In the War of the Pacific Peru, Chile, and Bolivia fought for control of the valuable nitrate deposits in the Atacama Desert. Chile's victory made it the most powerful state on the Pacific coast of South America.

The great opera house at Manaus, in Brazil, was completed in 1896. Manaus lies on the river Amazon in the heart of the rain forest, and during the rubber boom from 1890 to 1920 it became very rich. Magnificent buildings were erected and some of the streets were paved with marble. But when the rubber boom came to an end the wealth drained away. The city is still the trading center for the Amazon basin.

Economic Growth

Between 1870 and 1914 Latin America attracted foreign settlers and investors, which caused the growth of railways, ports, and cities. Argentina, for example, had only 2 million inhabitants in 1861, but between then and 1930, 6 million immigrants from Spain, Italy, and Germany settled there. British-owned railways opened up its vast, level plains (the *pampas*), and Argentina became one of the world's largest producers of grain and of beef which, with refrigeration, could be carried anywhere in the world.

The Problems Today

Latin America has vast natural resources. Venezuela produces oil; Brazil, Venezuela, Peru, and Chile have a third of the world's deposits of iron ore; Chile has the largest copper reserves in the world; Mexico and Peru have lead, zinc, and silver. In addition Latin America has for long been a major producer of coffee, sugar, bananas, cereals, meat, and wool. Yet there are great problems. Great modern cities like Rio de Janeiro and Buenos Aires have a wealthy middle class, but in the countryside, poverty-stricken peasants cultivate the large estates. The condition of the Indians has hardly changed since independence, and a prosperous life for them seems as far away as ever.

Below: Bogota is the capital and largest city of Colombia. It is built high in the Andes Mountains.

AMERICAN INTERFERENCE

The plantations of Guatemala, which grew nine tenths of the main exports of coffee and bananas, were owned mainly by Americans. Poor wages and living conditions led to a revolution in 1944. When the president began to take over the large estates and give land to the Indian peasants, the United States became alarmed. It supported an invasion by Guatemalan exiles in 1954 which overthrew the president and slowed down reforms. A similar thing happened when Salvador Allende, a Marxist, was elected president of Chile. His attempt to carry out far-reaching reforms ended with his death in an American-influenced military coup in 1973.

American interference in Cuba was less successful. In 1958 a rising against the American-supported dictator brought Fidel Castro to power. He soon declared that he was a Marxist. He took land away from the large landowners, and foreign industries, many of them American, from their owners. The United States replied by refusing to buy Cuban sugar, which made Castro more dependent on the Soviet Union. It also half-heartedly supported an invasion of Cuba by Castro's enemies at the Bay of Pigs. This was a disastrous failure and made the United States unpopular throughout Latin America.

The World in 1830

The Industrial Revolution has made Britain the richest nation in Europe. The defeat of Napoleon has left Russia as the largest military power in Europe, and Britain with the strongest navy. At the Congress of Vienna they protect their interests and try to establish a balance of power in Europe. The Ottoman empire, though weak, survives. Apart from a few places on the coast, Africa is little affected by the world outside and the same is true of China and Japan. The United States of America has gained independence but expansion westward has hardly begun. Many of the Spanish colonies in Latin America, cut off from their home country during the Napoleonic Wars, have become independent.

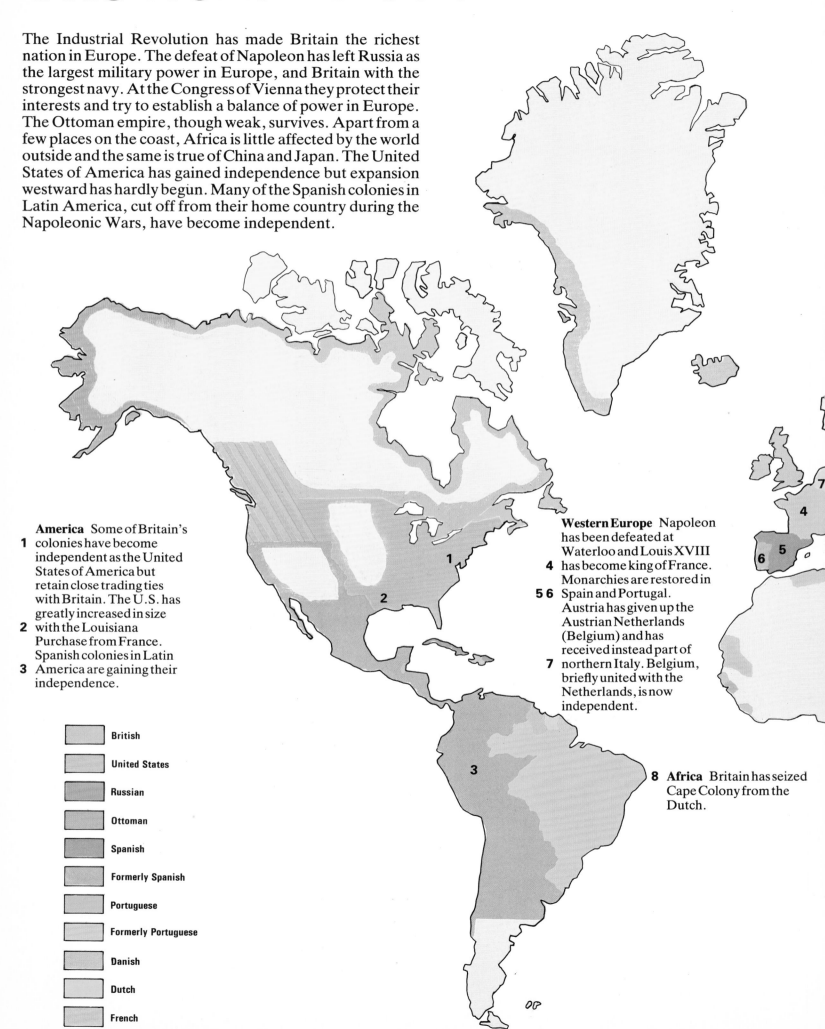

America Some of Britain's
1 colonies have become independent as the United States of America but retain close trading ties with Britain. The U.S. has greatly increased in size
2 with the Louisiana Purchase from France. Spanish colonies in Latin
3 America are gaining their independence.

Western Europe Napoleon has been defeated at Waterloo and Louis XVIII
4 has become king of France. Monarchies are restored in
56 Spain and Portugal. Austria has given up the Austrian Netherlands (Belgium) and has received instead part of
7 northern Italy. Belgium, briefly united with the Netherlands, is now independent.

8 **Africa** Britain has seized Cape Colony from the Dutch.

British

United States

Russian

Ottoman

Spanish

Formerly Spanish

Portuguese

Formerly Portuguese

Danish

Dutch

French

9 Northern Europe Prussia has added the Rhineland and part of Saxony to its territories and is the most powerful state in north Germany. Russia has gained territory from Finland, Poland, and Bessarabia. Greece has gained independence from the Ottoman empire.

11
12
13

10

1

12

14

15

17

17 The Far East China and Japan still go their own ways, cut off from the rest of the world.

15 India The British East India Company's control of India is almost complete. Britain has taken Ceylon from the Dutch.

16

14 The Near East The Ottoman empire, though weak, still controls the Near East at least in name, though many areas are virtually independent under their own governors.

16 Australia The first British settlements have been established, with the help of convict labor. (Britain soon claims all Australia.)

Prussian helmet

NORWAY
FINLAND
SWEDEN
ESTONIA
NORTH SEA
BALTIC SEA
LATVIA
LITHUANIA
SCHLESWIG
GREAT BRITAIN
HOLSTEIN PRUSSIA
RUSSIA
London
NETHERLANDS
Berlin
POLAND
ENGLISH CHANNEL
BELGIUM
Rhine
Frankfurt
Elbe
Oder
Vistula
LORRAINE
GERMANY
ATLANTIC OCEAN
Seine Paris
ALSACE
CZECHOSLOVAKIA
Versailles
Loire
BAVARIA
Munich
Budapest
FRANCE
ALPS
LOMBARDY
AUSTRIA
Count Cavour
PIEDMONT
VENETIA
ROMANIA
Garonne
Milan
Venice
BALKANS
Danube
BLACK SEA
SAVOY
Parma Modena
YUGOSLAVIA
PYRENEES
Marseilles
Nice
TUSCANY
BOSNIA Sarajevo
BULGARIA
ITALY
HERZEGOVINA SERBIA
CORSICA
Rome
MONTENEGRO
PORTUGAL
Madrid
PAPAL STATES
MACEDONIA
SPAIN
Naples
SARDINIA
TURKEY
MEDITERRANEAN SEA
GREECE
ATLAS MTS.
NORTH AFRICA
SICILY

Nationalism Takes Root

Napoleon's conquests produced national risings against him in Spain and Russia, as they wanted to be free from foreign domination, but in the first part of the 19th century nationalism was not strong. Up to 1860 most Italians and Germans were attached to their different rulers and states (such as Bavaria or Tuscany) and did not think of uniting with others speaking the same language. Only where foreigners ruled were there national movements or risings to get rid of the oppressors. These movements were usually supported by the middle classes (lawyers, teachers, businessmen) and had little appeal for the peasants.

The great Ottoman, Habsburg, and Russian empires included many different peoples. Their rulers strongly opposed nationalism, as it could lead to the breakup of their empires. The only successes of nationalism up to 1848 were in Greece, which revolted against Turkey in 1821 and became independent in 1830, and Belgium, which broke away from the Kingdom of the Netherlands also in 1830. Greece was considerably smaller than it is today; the northern area of the mainland and many of the islands were added much later. Rhodes and neighboring islands became Greek only in 1948.

Revolutions and Nationalism

The French Revolution brought new ideas to Europe, including nationalism, the idea that people who speak the same language and have the same traditions should be united in one state and not be ruled by foreigners. Before the French Revolution the state was regarded as belonging to the king. The French Revolution changed all that. "Sovereignty resides in the nation," said the Declaration of the Rights of Man in 1791 and by this it meant that the people living in a country should control it. At the same time, people were rebelling against the harsh control of many rulers. The French revolutionary ideals of liberty, equality, and fraternity (brotherhood) made them hope for a new kind of society.

THE YEAR OF REVOLUTIONS

In February 1848 revolution broke out in France. King Louis Philippe was forced to abdicate and a republic was set up under Napoleon's nephew Louis Napoleon. Later he became a second emperor of France. Then came a spate of revolutions. In Italy there were unsuccessful risings in Venice and Milan aimed at breaking Austrian control, while Tuscany, and in the south Naples, gained short-lived liberal constitutions. In March Austrian students demonstrated against the harsh rule of the chancellor, Prince Metternich. He fled the country; liberal reforms were promised and the emperor abdicated in favor of his son. Hungary managed to break away briefly from the Habsburg empire after a revolution in Budapest, but the rising was put down with Russian help.

Meanwhile a group of liberals formed the Frankfurt Parliament, which aimed to unite Germany. They had no hope of success unless Austria or Prussia supported the movement. Neither did so. When they offered the crown of Germany to the king of Prussia he refused it, saying he would not pick a crown up from the gutter.

The revolutions of 1848 largely failed; but they showed that ideals of freedom and nationalism were growing stronger.

Italy Is United

In the mid-19th century much of Italy was under Austrian rule or control. In the center were the Papal States, while the Kingdom of the Two Sicilies in the south was ruled by the repressive King Ferdinand. The strongest and most liberal state was Piedmont in the north.

Count Cavour, the prime minister of Piedmont in the 1850s, was an anti-Austrian liberal. He wanted to extend Piedmont's borders but realized that he could not take on Austria on his own. He found a powerful ally in France. Together they defeated the Austrians at Magenta and Solferino. France quickly made peace, for fear other powers would join against it, but Piedmont gained Lombardy from Austria. Meanwhile, revolutions broke out in the central duchies of Parma, Modena, and Tuscany. Their people voted to join Piedmont, and France supported them and in return was given Savoy and Nice. Piedmont had now doubled in size.

Cavour aimed at unifying Italy in the north. But at this point the patriot Garibaldi led an expedition to help the people of the Two Sicilies rise against their ruler. Soon Garibaldi held all southern Italy and threatened Rome itself. The Papal States voted to join Piedmont and Garibaldi handed over his conquests to its King Victor Emmanuel, who was elected king of Italy. Venice was added to Italy after Austria's defeat by Prussia in 1866, and Rome joined after its French protectors were defeated (again by Prussia) in 1871.

This picture of Garibaldi appeared on the cover of a popular song. He was the son of a fisherman, and spent some years in South America. When he returned to Italy and took up the fight for Italian unity and independence he became immensely popular. In 1860 he raised a volunteer force – his "Thousand Redshirts" – and led a brilliant campaign.

A Greater Germany

The patchwork of little independent states which for centuries had made up Germany began to be simplified in the late 18th and 19th centuries. In the north Prussia grew larger and more powerful, while Napoleon joined states together in the Confederation of the Rhine. In 1815 Prussia was given part of the Rhineland in the west and part of Saxony in the east, both lands rich in coal and iron. To link them, Prussia formed customs unions with other German states.

In 1862 Prince Otto von Bismarck became chief minister of Prussia. He aimed first to make Prussia the leading state, and then to unite all Germany. His great rival would be Austria. Bismarck went to war with Austria over the government of Schleswig and Holstein (which they jointly controlled) and won in only seven weeks. Some of the little German states had fought with Austria. Those in the north joined the North German Confederation under Prussian leadership, while the southern states agreed to come under Prussian command if war broke out. Bismarck provoked France into declaring war and this time all the German states joined Prussia in victory. The French provinces of Alsace and Lorraine were handed to Germany, and the southern German states joined with those of the north to form a German empire. King Wilhelm of Prussia was its first emperor, and Bismarck its chancellor.

The battle of Navarino, in October 1827, was a key point in the war for Greek independence from Turkey. An allied fleet of British, Russian, and French ships defeated a Turkish-Egyptian fleet in Navarino Bay, in the southwest of Greece, destroying 60 vessels and killing about 8,000 men. Allied losses were 176 officers and men, with no ships lost.

BALKAN NATIONALISM

From 1870 nationalism spread rapidly in the Balkans. Russia fought a war against Turkey, after which Serbia, Montenegro, and Romania were recognized as independent states at the Congress of Berlin in 1878. Their success spurred on other peoples in the Balkans. Bulgaria gained independence in 1908 and after the Balkan Wars of 1912–1913 Macedonia was divided between Greece and Serbia. Turkey had lost nearly all its territory in Europe.

The Habsburg empire still existed as a multinational state and even expanded, when Austria annexed Bosnia and Herzegovina in 1908. There were many Serbs in Bosnia who had wanted to join Serbia rather than Austria. One of these, Gavrilo Princip, assassinated the Austrian Archduke Franz Ferdinand at Sarajevo in 1914 and so helped to bring about World War I. This war saw the victory of nationalism in Europe. The Ottoman, Habsburg, and Prussian empires were demolished, to make way for new, independent states like Czechoslovakia, Poland, and Yugoslavia. Nationalism had become one of the most powerful forces in world history. It had changed the map of the world and the lives of millions of people.

Empire Builders

Imperialism, the rule of one people by another, is as old as history. Ancient Egyptians, Romans, Mongols, Arabs, Turks, Incas, Europeans have all at one time or another conquered other peoples and ruled over them. By 1800 France had already lost an empire in North America and India, and Britain had lost many of its American colonies. All the Portuguese and Spanish colonies in Central and South America were independent by 1830 (see page 170). Yet France was soon to build up a new empire, beginning with the conquest of Algeria in 1830; and the British empire, which already included Canada, part of India, and some West Indian islands, was to increase dramatically. At the end of the Napoleonic Wars in 1815 Britain took the Cape of Good Hope and Ceylon from the Dutch, some West Indian islands from France and Spain, and Malta. In the 1830s it claimed the whole of Australia and in 1840 New Zealand. Britain and France were joined by nations which had not had colonies before – the United States, Germany, and Japan.

India and Southeast Asia

India was looked on as the "jewel in the British crown." It took a large number of British exports, especially cotton goods, and played an important part in the trade of the Far East through its exports of opium, much of which went to China. The British East India Company gained France's Indian possessions at the end of the Seven Years' War in 1763, and during the next hundred years it conquered more large areas. It controlled much of the rest of India through treaties made with the ruling princes. In 1857 the Indian Mutiny broke out. It began as a rebellion of Indian soldiers against their British officers and turned into a movement to restore power to the Mughal emperor. In 1858 peace was made and the British government took over rule from the East India Company.

On India's eastern border there was trouble with the Burmese, until 1886 when the whole of Burma became a British colony. The independent states of Malaya were also taken over by the British, in order to guard their shipping routes.

The French built a new empire in Southeast Asia. Between 1858 and 1860 they occupied the Saigon delta, and from there they moved out to conquer Annam, Tongking, Cambodia, and Laos.

(see page 170)

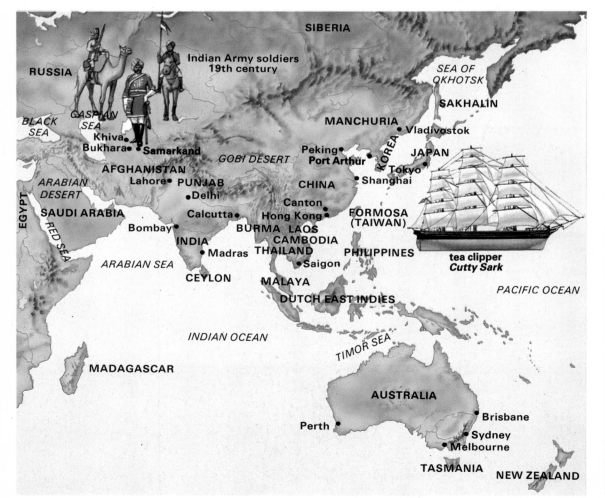

A Dutch colonial building in Batavia (modern Djakarta) in Java.

JAPAN'S GROWING EMPIRE

In the Far East, Japan and Russia were rivals for power. Russia granted Japan control of the Kurile Islands in return for Sakhalin Island. China, Japan, and Russia all wanted control of Korea; the westernized armies of Japan easily defeated the Chinese in 1895 and in the war of 1904 to 1905, to everyone's surprise, Japan defeated Russia. Russia then had to give up half of Sakhalin, and its lease on Port Arthur, and the Liaotung Peninsula on the Chinese mainland was handed over to Japan. Korea came under Japanese influence, and in 1910 Japan formally took it over.

In the 1930s the Japanese seized Manchuria and much of China, including the main ports. In World War II Japan conquered French Indochina, British Hong Kong and Malaya, the Dutch East Indies, and the Philippines. This vast empire disappeared after Japan's defeat in 1945.

China

For a long time China resisted all dealings with Europeans, who (except for the Portuguese at Macao) were allowed to trade only at Canton. During the 19th century a series of wars gave Britain Hong Kong and allowed European traders to live in several ports, although they were hedged around with many restrictions. At the end of the 19th century the British prime minister, Lord Salisbury, suggested that China should be divided into areas of influence by the great powers; the Yangtze Valley and Shanghai should go to Britain, north China and Peking (Beijing) to Russia, and Yunnan in the south to France. It seemed that China would be divided like Africa. However, the great powers could not agree which territory each should have, and the Boxer rebellion of 1900 against foreigners, although put down by European troops, showed the difficulty imperialists would have if they tried to rule China.

THE UNITED STATES

The United States extended its frontiers by taking New Mexico and California from Mexico in 1846–1848. Expansion was brought to a halt for a time by the Civil War, except for the purchase of Alaska from Russia in 1867. It was bought for 7 million dollars, less than 2 cents an acre. In 1898 the United States went to war against Spain and gained 3,141 Pacific islands, including Hawaii and the Philippines. Puerto Rico was taken over while Cuba became a protectorate. In a short time the United States had become an imperial power.

The pomp and splendor of empire: a British party is lavishly entertained by an Indian prince. Under the British, the princes still had a large measure of control over their kingdoms, though this grew less when rule passed from the East India Company to the British crown.

The settlement at Port Jackson, Australia, in 1792. It had been started four years before as the first of a number of British convict settlements in Australia. Before long many free settlers came to farm the continent's fine agricultural land. In 1851 the discovery of gold was announced, and in the next ten years Australia's population doubled. Many of those looking for gold were unsuccessful but they stayed on as farmers. In 1901 the different colonies of Australia united as the Commonwealth of Australia.

Central Asia

In the 1860s Russia began the conquest of the Muslim khanates (states) of Central Asia. A serious problem for Russia was how to control these border areas, inhabited by nomadic tribes which raided Russia. After the conquest of the Kazakh steppe the Russians moved on to the settled communities of Khiva, Bukhara, and Samarkand. All had fallen by 1873 and Russia then turned to Transcaspia, where the Turcoman nomads lived. The Russians captured their capital, Geok Tepe, and then Merv, which brought them down to the Afghan border. In all this there was little plan or direction from St. Petersburg; most of the decisions were taken by generals on the spot.

East and south of Russia lay China, a great market for goods and a major exporter of tea, silk, and porcelain. In 1689 Russia had signed a treaty with China by which it promised to keep out of the Amur Valley, but in 1847 the governor of Eastern Siberia, without telling the Russian government, set up forts on the banks of the river Amur. He took over territory between the Amur and Ussuri rivers and the Pacific, down to the Korean border. There Russia built the port of Vladivostok.

In the 1890s Russia began to build up industries on a large scale. It hoped to trade in the East, and so the Trans-Siberian Railway was begun in 1891.

An oil refinery. Here crude oil is separated into different substances, the most valuable of which is gasoline. Many petrochemicals are also produced, from which nylon, plastics, polyethylene, insecticides, and even animal foods are made. While the first Industrial Revolution saw old industries being mechanized, the second Industrial Revolution saw the growth of quite new industries based on new scientific discoveries and techniques.

The Second Industrial Revolution

The second Industrial Revolution, which began about 1870, was very different from the first. It was based much more on the work of scientists (scarcely any of the early inventors had any scientific training) and it introduced new goods and sources of power. It was also far quicker in its results and had a greater effect on people's lives. Coal and iron, the foundation of the first Industrial Revolution, were still important but were rapidly overtaken by steel, electricity, oil, and chemicals.

Steel
Up to the 1850s steel was a semiprecious metal, costing between £50 and £60 a ton, compared with £3 to £4 a ton for cast iron. Then Bessemer and Siemens developed new ways of making steel, but these could not be used for ores with a high phosphorous content. Twenty years later a process invented by Gilchrist-Thomas allowed Germany to make use of its rich phosphoric ores, so that by 1914 Germany was producing almost twice as much steel as Britain. The United States became the largest producer. Steel was now used for all purposes for which iron had previously been used and for many others. The first steel steam loco-

motive and the first steel ship were built in 1863. By 1900 steel was used in building railways, ships, machine tools, and skyscrapers, and in canning, and world production had risen from 80,000 tons in 1850 to 28 million tons a year.

Chemicals
Chemical industries also developed rapidly after 1870. For centuries chemicals had been taken from natural substances, such as the roots of plants. Now more and more chemicals were produced from the by-products of coal. Textiles were colored by aniline dyes made from coal tar; other by-products were used for explosives and fertilizers. The chemical industry also produced drugs, insecticides, and perfumes. Plastics were made from coal tar, and synthetic fibers, including artificial silk, and later nylon and rayon, were used in clothing. Germany was the leader in this new industry.

The Spread of Industry
In 1850 Britain was the leading manufacturing country in the world and had changed from a mainly agricultural nation into an industrial one. Britain was still an important industrial country during the second Industrial Revolution but it was Germany, united in 1871, and the United States which now set the pace. By 1914 Germany was ahead of all other European countries in the iron, steel, chemical, and electrical industries and was next to Britain in coal and textile production.

NEW SOURCES OF POWER
The development of electricity provided a new source of light, heat, and power. Efficient dynamos were built in the 1860s and from then on electricity was used to drive machinery and trains and to provide lighting for streets, factories, and homes. It brought power into the home for the many small appliances, from refrigerators to television sets, we take for granted today. Water was used in hydro-electric power stations to produce electricity, especially in countries like Italy, which had no coal.

A new form of energy was produced by the internal combustion engine, using gas as fuel. A huge new oil industry grew up, first in the United States and Russia and later in the Near East. Cars, ships, and machines were driven by gas or diesel oil. Oil largely replaced coal as the fuel producing power for industry, as it was much easier to move and use. Without electricity and the internal combustion engine the rapid industrial development of Europe and the United States would not have been possible.

The latest form of power to be produced is nuclear energy, which is used by some power stations. As the world's oil resources are used up it may be used on an increasingly large scale.

MEDICINE

Advances in chemistry led to a dramatic improvement in medicine. Pasteur and Koch used the new aniline dyes to help them identify a vast range of disease-carrying bacteria. Drugs to kill bacteria were discovered by Paul Ehrlich in Germany (Salvarsan, 1909) and by Fleming, Florey, and Chain in Britain (penicillin, 1938). Insulin, discovered in the 1920s, saved the lives of many people with diabetes. New ideas about the causes of illness came with the discovery of viruses. From their study, vaccines to prevent yellow fever, polio, and influenza have been developed.

Great advances in surgery were made in the 19th century with the discovery of antiseptics and anesthetics. Many people still died after operations until blood transfusions were made possible by identifying blood groups in 1901 and citrate was found to stop clotting. Today surgeons, using many complicated machines and with a great knowledge of the body's working and response to drugs, can transplant an organ from one person to another. International campaigns have removed the threat of tuberculosis, wiped out smallpox, and got rid of malaria in many parts of the world, while medicine is now available free in many countries. All this progress has helped to keep many people alive, but this itself has created problems, such as how to feed the increased populations, which will be very difficult to solve.

Pills are automatically packed into bottles under fast and hygienic conditions. The development of new medicines in the 20th century has saved countless lives, but many people are alarmed by the enormous quantities of pills which are now being taken.

CHRONOLOGY

1856 Henry Bessemer converts pig iron into steel by blasting air through the molten metal

1861 After Louis Pasteur's work on microorganisms pasteurization is introduced to preserve milk and wine

1963 Open-hearth process of making steel by Martin brothers in France, using a furnace designed by Frederick Siemens

1869 Union Pacific and Central Pacific railways meet to complete the first transcontinental line in America

1876 Alexander Graham Bell invents the telephone

1878 First successful electric lamp

1879 Gilchrist-Thomas process for making steel from phosphoric ores

1893 Henry Ford makes his first automobile

1895 First public motion picture show in Paris. Guglielmo Marconi invents the wireless telegraph

1897 Rudolf Diesel produces a heavy oil engine

1903 First flight in an airplane by Wright brothers

1909 Paul Ehrlich produces the first antibiotic, Salvarsan

1914 Conveyor-belt mass production by Henry Ford for his "Model T" Ford car

1926 Television first successfully demonstrated in England

1929 Alexander Fleming discovers penicillin mold, though the drug is not produced on a large scale until 1943

1930 Gas turbine for jet aircraft
1937 developed by Frank Whittle

1942 Enrico Fermi produces a nuclear chain reaction in Chicago

1944 First automatic general-purpose digital computer

1956 Nuclear fuel used to produce electricity at Calder Hall, England

1957 Russia launches first artificial satellite, *Sputnik I*

The United States was the leading industrial nation in the world by 1900. It led the way in the production and use of new goods, among them the typewriter (1874), telephone (1876), electric light and power (1882), and the automobile (1893). The first transcontinental railway was completed in America in 1869. Everywhere railways lowered costs, opened up new trading areas, and allowed new resources to be tapped. As the great prairies were developed the United States became a major food producer, especially of wheat and beef. Russia too began to industrialize rapidly from the 1890s. It had oil at Baku and coal and iron deposits in the Donets basin.

The rapid industrial development of both Russia and the United States was made possible by their vast natural resources. Japan's rise was more remarkable because it had few natural resources. By copying European and American methods it became the only Asian country to have a sound industrial base by 1914. Its great industrial expansion came after World War II and has been so rapid that Japan has become the major producer of ships, hi-fi equipment, televisions, and motorcycles. Soon it may be the major producer of automobiles and microprocessors. Japan is the pacesetter in the automation of industry and in the use of robots in car production, so now it is European manufacturers who are copying Japanese methods.

The second Industrial Revolution has changed the lives of most people in the world, and particularly of those in industrial countries. We now live longer, have more leisure, and a higher standard of living than at any other time. The speed of change is such that the computer and the microchip will probably affect our lives even more in the next few years than the vast changes brought about by the Industrial Revolution so far.

HENRY FORD

In 1893 Henry Ford made his first gas-driven car in his backyard toolshed, mainly from bicycle parts. Eleven years later he formed the Ford Motor Company and in 1908 designed the Model T, the famous "Tin Lizzie." He mass-produced cars by making standardized, interchangeable parts and assembling these on a conveyor belt or assembly line, which carried the parts to the place where they were needed by the workers. This method was widely copied. By 1928 Ford had sold over 15 million Model Ts. He introduced the eight-hour working day for his employees in 1914, and profit-sharing schemes for his workers.

Dropping car bodies onto the chassis on an early Model T Ford Assembly line.

Japan

In the 1630s the Tokugawa shoguns (military leaders) of Japan cut their country off from the rest of the world. The Japanese people were not allowed to go abroad nor foreigners to visit Japan. This prevented change in Japan at a time when life in Europe was changing rapidly. Japan fell far behind. By the 1980s, however, Japan has become a highly industrialized nation with one of the highest living standards in the world.

Modernization of Japan

The isolation of Japan was brought to an end in 1853 by Commodore Perry of the United States Navy, who demanded that Japan allow foreign trade. The arrival of his four "Black Ships," two driven by steam, created a sensation. The Japanese had never seen such ships before and they realized that they could not hope to defeat them in battle. The shogun had to accept the demands made by the Americans.

In 1868 the shogun was overthrown. Power passed to the young emperor, who chose as the title of his reign *Mei-ji*, meaning "enlightened rule." He was determined that Japan should become rich, with strong armed forces so that no foreign power could dictate to it again. This meant copying the West in all the ways that had made it powerful. Foreigners were brought to Japan to train the Japanese in western technology, from electroplating to the use of anesthetics, and Japanese people were also sent abroad to learn these skills. Most important was the building up of a strong army and navy. German and British instructors trained the armed forces so well that in 1894 Japan was able to defeat China and ten years later to take on Russia, Japan's rival in Manchuria and Korea.

The Russo-Japanese War

The Japanese began the war by making a sudden attack on the Russian fleet at Port Arthur. To the surprise and shock of most people in Europe the Japanese were victorious. On land they captured Port Arthur and pushed the Russians out of Southern Manchuria, but the most important battle took place at sea. The Russians sent their Baltic fleet on the long voyage round Europe and Africa to the Pacific. But when the fleet reached Japan it was torn to pieces at Tsushima. In two days 38 out of 40 Russian ships were sunk or captured. The Japanese lost only three torpedo-boats. It was the most decisive and dramatic sea battle since Trafalgar in 1804. People all over Asia rejoiced as this was the first defeat of a major European country by Asians since the Mongols 700 years earlier.

Japan was now a military power of the first rank. In less than 40 years it had modernized so effectively that it could defeat one of the greatest European powers. As a result of the war Japan gained influence in South Manchuria, which was part of China. Korea was annexed by Japan in 1910. During World War I it took over the parts of China occupied by Germany (see page 185). This was the beginning of the Japanese empire.

The opening of the first railway station in Japan. During the late 19th century the Japanese copied everything Western: men wore top hats and tails at court functions, while women dressed in bustles and corsets. Knives and forks were used instead of chopsticks, and horseracing, waltzing, and billiards were popular.

Japanese soldiers
late 19th century

Expansion

World War I gave a great boost to Japanese industry. While the major industrial powers were fighting one another it took over trade with China and India. But in the Great Depression Japanese exports, particularly silk, fell drastically. Many people now argued that Japan should enlarge its empire, so that it could get the raw materials it needed and also find markets for its exports. In 1931 the Japanese army (without orders from the home government) overran Manchuria, which was rich in coal and iron ore. In 1937, the Japanese invaded China itself. Soon they held much of the coastline and the most important cities.

When World War II began Japan decided to set up a "Great East Asian Co-Prosperity Sphere." This meant Japanese control of Southeast Asia, especially Malaya and the Dutch East Indies (Indonesia), rich in the oil, tin, and rubber which the Japanese needed. This alarmed the Americans. When the Japanese moved into French Indochina (Vietnam) the Americans, who supplied four fifths of Japan's oil, cut off supplies. The Japanese replied with a surprise attack on the American naval base at Pearl Harbor. The attack on December 7, 1941, marked the entry of Japan into World War II – a war that was to lead to its defeat and the loss of all its empire.

A crowded street in modern Tokyo. The buildings are like those of any great European city. Since World War II Japan has become a leading industrial power in the world.

THE JAPANESE ECONOMIC MIRACLE

In 1945 Japanese industry was in ruins and Japan was occupied by the Americans, who were determined to make it into a democracy and prevent its waging war again. The new constitution said Japan was to have no armed forces. All men and women were given the vote and political parties and trade unions were encouraged. Land was given to the peasants. When the communists in China defeated the American-backed Chiang Kai-shek and the communists in North Korea attacked the south in 1950, America needed Japan as a friend and ally. The Americans placed large orders for war supplies in Japan and this began the rapid revival of Japanese industry. In 1952 the Americans withdrew and Japan became independent again.

From 1953 Japanese production grew each year by 10 percent, so that by 1968 Japan produced more goods than any country except the Soviet Union and the United States. Before World War II most Japanese exports were textiles. After the war the main industrial advances were in chemicals, steel, shipbuilding, automobiles, and hi-fi and electronic equipment. Japan is now the world's largest shipbuilder, producing half the tonnage built in the world. It is also the largest producer in the world of radios and television sets. Production of automobiles, many of which are being sold in Europe, increased 15-fold in the 1960s. There are many reasons for this "miracle." Savings are high, so there is plenty of money to invest in new factories and techniques; Japan spends little on defense, as it does not have a proper army; many workers are paid a bonus if the firm is successful, so they work hard and there are few strikes. Today national pride in Japan centers on scientific and industrial achievements and not on building up an empire overseas.

CHRONOLOGY

1853	Commodore Perry of the United States demands that Japan open up its ports to foreign trade
1868	The Tokugawa lose power after controlling Japan for over 250 years. The emperor takes control. He chooses *Mei-ji* (enlightened peace) as the title of his reign
1889	New constitution sets up an elected assembly
1894	War against China (to 1895), in which Japan gains Formosa (Taiwan)
1902	Alliance with Britain
1904	Russo-Japanese War (to 1905). Japan, victorious, gains control of southern Manchuria and Korea (annexed 1910)
1914	World War I: Japan takes over German-controlled areas of China
1931	Japanese army seizes control of Manchuria, called Manchukuo (1932)
1936	Young army officers try unsuccessfully to set up a military dictatorship. The leaders are executed
1937	Japan invades China
1941	Japanese aircraft attack Pearl Harbor. Japan enters World War II
1945	Japan surrenders after the atom bomb is dropped on Hiroshima and Nagasaki. American occupation of Japan (to 1952)
1946	New constitution makes Japan a democracy

Scramble for Africa

The European impact on Africa came much later than that on America and Asia. Africa had no known riches like the gold and silver of Peru and Mexico, or the spices of the East Indies, to appeal to Europeans, and they were put off by the poor climate, the threat of disease, and the difficulty of moving far inland. Along the coast flourishing ports grew up based on the export of such goods as timber, ivory, and slaves, but by the mid-19th century much of the interior of the continent was still unexplored. Then in the 1860s and 1870s explorers journeyed far into the continent, and soon the Europeans were scrambling to set up colonies there. By 1914 only Liberia (founded in 1847 for freed American slaves) and Ethiopia were independent.

Zulu women

Ashanti gold-weight

West Africa

In 1876 and 1877 H. M. Stanley explored the Congo basin in West Africa. King Leopold of the Belgians saw the possibility of developing this area. Stanley entered Leopold's service and signed treaties with African chiefs by which 1,440,000 square kilometers (900,000 square miles) were handed over to the International Association of the Congo, an organization set up by Leopold. The chiefs did not know that in signing pieces of paper they were giving up their tribal lands.

Soon other European powers joined in. The Italian de Brazza, on behalf of France,

claimed land north of the river Congo, while Germany claimed Southwest Africa, Togoland, and the Cameroons. A clash between Europeans seemed likely in the Congo region and around the river Niger, where the British and French were moving in. The German statesman Bismarck called a conference at Berlin in 1884–1885 to settle these issues. It was decided that much of the Congo basin should be a free state under Leopold, that the upper Niger should be French and the lower Niger British. An agreement with France in 1898 gave Britain northern Nigeria and increased the size of the Gold Coast.

France decided to extend its borders inland from its old trading posts on the Ivory Coast, in Dahomey and in Gabon, to link with Senegal and Algeria and form a French West African empire. This they hoped would stretch right across to the Nile. Marchand led an expedition from Gabon to Fashoda on the Nile, which he reached in 1898 after a journey of two years. A few weeks later Kitchener, at the head of a stronger British force, reached Fashoda too. War looked possible, but the French withdrew and it was avoided.

A French mission station on the shores of Lake Chad, in western Africa. Most of this vast area was under French rule, as the map shows. Some of the settlers were missionaries, but many Europeans came to Africa simply to exploit its mineral and agricultural resources.

CHRONOLOGY

1830	France begins the conquest of Algeria
1835	The Great Trek begins (to 1837)
1843	Natal becomes a British colony
1847	Independent republic of Liberia founded
1854	Faidherbe, French governor of Senegal, extends the colony far inland (to 1864)
1868	Britain annexes Basutoland
1869	Suez Canal opened
1876	Anglo-French control of Egypt
1880	De Brazza claims north bank of the Congo for France
1881	Rising of Egyptian army, led by Arabi Pasha, against foreign control. France occupies Tunisia
1882	British defeat Arabi at Tel el-Kebir
1884	German protectorate over Togoland and the Cameroons. Berlin Conference (to 1885)
1885	German protectorate over East Africa
1886	Gold discovered on the Witwatersrand in the Transvaal
1896	Emperor Menelek of Ethiopia defeats Italy at Adowa
1898	Kitchener defeats the Mahdi at Omdurman. Marchand reaches the Nile at Fashoda. Boer War (to 1902)
1910	Union of South Africa formed from Cape, Natal, Transvaal, and Orange Free State
1912	Morocco becomes a French protectorate
1913	Italy conquers Libya

North Africa

For centuries North Africa had been part of the Ottoman empire, but in the 19th century control there shifted to Europeans. France began to conquer Algeria in 1830, which involved it in 50 years of war with the Muslims. France also took Tunis in 1881 and gained a shared control of Egypt with Britain, when the khedive (ruler) could not pay his debts to European bankers. A revolt in Egypt was put down by the British as the French would not intervene. Britain looked on Egypt as vital to its interests after the Suez Canal opened in 1869. It cut 5,600 kilometers (3,500 miles) off the journey between England and India. The British stayed in Egypt until after World War II. The remaining areas in North Africa were seized early in the 20th century, Morocco by France and Libya by Italy.

South Africa

The southern tip of Africa had been settled by Europeans since the Dutch arrived at the Cape in 1652. Their descendants, the Boers or Afrikaaners, resented the British who took over during the Napoleonic Wars. To escape from the British and to look for new land, the Boers began a Great Trek inland in 1835. Families, their possessions piled into ox-wagons, traveled inland across the Orange and Vaal rivers to set up the republics of the Transvaal and Orange Free State.

In 1886 gold was discovered on the Rand in the Transvaal, which became the richest state in Africa. By 1900 it was producing a quarter of the world's gold. Cecil Rhodes, prime minister of the Cape, hoped that he would be equally successful in finding gold in Mashonaland to the north, and dreamed of a British empire stretching from the Cape to Cairo. He formed the British South Africa Company which gained control of the lands to the north; they were named Rhodesia after him. Relations between Britain and the Boer republics grew worse and ended in the Boer War (1898–1902). With the defeat of the Boers and the foundation of the Union of South Africa, the "scramble" in the south was over.

East Africa

The chief rivals in East Africa were Britain and Germany. Karl Peters had persuaded African chiefs in 1884 to sign away 96,000 square kilometers (60,000 square miles) of land. Germany claimed a protectorate over this territory, German East Africa (known later as Tanganyika and today as Tanzania). The British replied by taking control of what are now Kenya and Uganda, and won control of the whole length of the Nile when General Kitchener defeated the Mahdi, a Muslim religious leader, and conquered the Sudan.

Bitter fighting broke out between the British and the Boers in 1898. The Boers, using guerrilla tactics, only surrendered in 1902. In 1910 four South African colonies, including the former Boer republics, united to form the Union of South Africa.

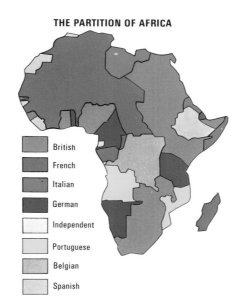

THE PARTITION OF AFRICA

- British
- French
- Italian
- German
- Independent
- Portuguese
- Belgian
- Spanish

Tripoli in Libya, where Italian buildings are a reminder of the colonial period. Italy was the last European nation to join in the "scramble" for Africa. It gained two barren colonies, Eritrea and Somaliland, on the coast of the Red Sea, and in 1896 tried unsuccessfully to conquer Ethiopia. By 1913 it had gained Libya, which had been part of the Turkish empire. Many Italians settled and farmed there until it became independent after World War II.

SUPERIOR WEAPONS

All over Africa Europeans met resistance to their conquests, but they overcame it easily because their weapons were better than those of their opponents. When Lord Lugard hoisted the Union Jack over the town of Lokoja on the Niger in 1900, the Sultan of Sokoto organized resistance. His main fighting force, the infantry, was dressed in blue skirts and carried bows and arrows and iron spears. His cavalry, wielding swords and axes, were protected by padded cotton armor as were their horses. They were mown down by the machine guns and rifles of the European-led troops. A British official reported: "They came at us . . . I thought we were all going to be killed. Someone gave an order. Everyone fired, then a whistle blew, everyone stopped and there was no horseman left alive in front."

China

Ever since European countries began to trade with China, they had to pay for Chinese goods such as tea, silk, and porcelain in gold or silver, as there was nothing Europeans produced which the Chinese wanted. But in the late 18th century the British did find something the Chinese would accept instead of silver. It was opium, a drug produced in India. War broke out over this trade and the defeated Chinese had to let foreigners into their country. In little more than a century the Manchu dynasty had been overthrown and China had become a communist republic.

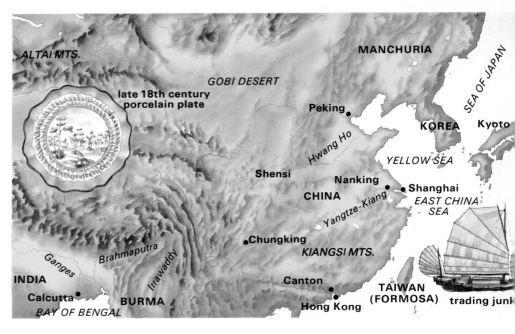

late 18th century porcelain plate

trading junk

The Opium War

In 1839 the emperor appointed Commissioner Lin to wipe out the opium trade. He went to the port of Canton and seized 20,000 chests of opium, which he then destroyed in a public ceremony. As much of this belonged to British merchants the British government demanded compensation. War followed in which the British, with a squadron of ships and a few thousand men, were able to seize port after port. The Chinese fought valiantly but their war junks were no match for British steamships. In 1842 the emperor had to accept peace at the Treaty of Nanking. Hong Kong island was given to Great Britain and five ports were opened to foreign trade.

Western countries, particularly Britain, gained more and more control over China. In doing so they were helped by the Taiping Rebellion, a great peasant revolt from 1851 to 1864 in which 10 million people died. European powers came to control all the coastal cities of China, in particular Shanghai, and also the great inland waterways. Their gunboats patrolled the Yangtze River between Shanghai and Chungking, a distance of 2,400 kilometers (1,500 miles) across the heart of China.

CHRONOLOGY	
1840	Opium War (to 1842)
1851	Taiping rebellion (to 1864)
1860	Occupation of Peking (Beijing) by British and French troops
1894	Sino-Japanese War (to 1895). Japan wins and gains Formosa (Taiwan)
1898	Hundred Days of Reform
1900	The Boxer Rising: siege of foreign legations in Peking, ended with arrival of European troops
1908	Death of empress dowager
1911	China becomes a republic
1921	Chinese Communist party founded
1925	Death of Sun Yat-sen. Chiang Kai-shek becomes leader of the Kuomintang party
1927	Chiang attacks communists in Shanghai
1931	Japan occupies Manchuria
1934	The Long March (to 1935) takes the communists from Kiangsi in the south to Shensi in the north
1937	Japan invades China
1946	Civil war between communists and Kuomintang resumed
1949	Communists are victorious. People's Republic of China proclaimed under Mao Zedong

CHINESE SPELLINGS IN ENGLISH	
The way Chinese names are transliterated into English has recently changed. The old spellings and the new spellings of some Chinese names are given below.	
Old	*New*
Chou En-lai	Zhou En Lai
Canton	Guangzhou
Chunking	Chongqing
Hangchow	Hangzhou
Khomintang	Guomindang
Kiangsi	Jiangxi
Nanking	Nanjing
Mao Tse-tung	Mao Zedong
Peking	Beijing
Shansi	Shaanxi
Yangtze	Changjiang

Western sailing ships, of the kind known as East Indiamen, on the Canton River in southern China in 1835. Foreigners were discouraged from trading with China, but by this time the British were bringing in large quantities of opium. Shortly after this picture was painted, Chinese efforts to check the opium trade led to war with Britain.

184

A Japanese painting of a battle during the war with China in 1894. The Chinese, fighting in their traditional manner, were easily defeated by the Japanese (in black uniforms), trained by German and British instructors and armed with Western weapons.

Attempts at Reform

In the 1860s a Western-trained Chinese army (the Peking Field Force), equipped with Russian guns, was set up and Chinese students were sent abroad for training. But many people in China were against these measures and the effects were small. This was seen in 1894–1895 when China was easily defeated in war by Japan. This demonstration of China's weakness led to the "Battle of the Concessions" when Russia, Germany, Britain, and France tried to increase their trading privileges and territory in China. Britain obtained more land around Hong Kong (the so-called "New Territories") on a 99-year lease.

In 1898 there was a desperate attempt at reform. The young emperor issued a series of decrees modernizing the army and ending the old out-of-date examination system for entry to the government service. At this stage the empress dowager T'su-Hsi, one of the opponents of change, seized and imprisoned the emperor and took over control. Nearly all the reforms were abolished. It was clear to many Chinese that the Manchu dynasty would have to be overthrown before the drastic changes necessary for China's survival could take place. In 1908 the empress dowager died and in 1911 the dynasty collapsed, to be replaced by a republic.

Revolution

The new republic, far from bringing strength and unity to China, brought worse conditions. The local army commanders and warlords divided China among themselves, pillaged the countryside, and paid little attention to the republican government which tried to rule from Peking.

To defeat the warlords and unite China Dr. Sun Yat-sen formed the Kuomintang (Nationalist) party. He realized that he would need outside help. He tried to get support from the Western countries but was rejected, and so he turned to Russia (communist since 1917), which sent advisers to Canton. These Russians soon held important positions in Sun's Kuomintang and worked closely with the Chinese Communist party, which was founded in 1921. A new army was organized with Russian help. When Sun died in 1925, General Chiang Kai-shek became the leader of the Kuomintang and began a drive to the north against the warlords. He was unhappy with Sun's alliance with the communists and in 1927 he

decided to break with them. With the backing of some Shanghai businessmen he carried out a purge of communists in that city in April, 1927. He executed all the communists he could lay his hands on. After this Chiang completed his destruction of the power of the northern warlords.

China was now more united than at any time since the republic began in 1911, but Chiang did not take the opportunity to carry out much-needed reforms. This was not entirely his fault. In 1931 Japan conquered Manchuria and to took away from China one of its richest industrial areas. The Japanese extended their invasion to the south in 1937 and quickly occupied the chief ports and industrial centers of China. Chiang had to flee with his government to Chungking. Even so, Chiang had ten years before Japan launched its main attack, in which he might have begun such reforms as giving more land to the peasants; but nothing was done.

Mao Zedong, the communist leader, in a mountain hideout. He led the Communist forces on the "Long March" north, and during the war with Japan he made a truce with the Kuomintang. After Japan surrendered civil war broke out again and under Mao's leadership the communists soon defeated the Kuomintang. They proclaimed a People's Republic, with Mao as its chairman.

THE COMMUNISTS TAKE OVER

The communists had lost many of their leaders in the purge of 1927, but those who escaped joined their comrades from other parts of the country in the mountains of Kiangsi in the south. There, under the leadership of Mao Zedong, they built up a separate army and government. "Whoever wins the support of the peasants," Mao declared, "will win China; whoever solves the land question will win the peasants." Mao did win the support of the peasants by giving them land taken from the big landowners. Chiang attacked Mao and the peasants and forced them to flee to Shensi. Their flight is known as the Long March. It lasted 368 days.

The Communist party survived in the safety of the north and, with peasant support, built up its strength until it was able to defeat Chiang Kai-shek in 1949.

Russia

The 18th century saw Russia grow from a backward nation into a major European power. Peter the Great (1682–1725) reformed and reorganized his country and made it a military power. His work was carried on by Catherine the Great (1762–1796). Under her Russia gained much new territory, including the Crimean peninsula in the south, and more land north of the Black Sea which it took from the Ottoman empire (Turkey). She pushed Russia's borders far to the west in the Ukraine, and gained a large part of Poland. Much of this new territory was very fertile and became the main grain-growing area of Russia.

The Crimean War

The defeat of Napoleon left Russia the greatest military power in Europe. It had already annexed Finland and Bessarabia (Turkey's European possessions) and at the Congress of Vienna in 1815, which ended the Napoleonic Wars, Russian gains included the greater part of Poland. In 1914 Russia's borders in Europe were still those of 1815, but to the south and east it had expanded in the Caucasus and in Central Asia, and had taken some territory from China.

Russia wanted to extend its influence in the Balkans, ruled by the weakening Ottoman empire. People in the Balkans were, like the Russians, mainly Slavs and members of the Orthodox church. Russia also disliked the Ottomans' control over the Bosporus and the Dardanelles, the straits which linked the Black Sea with the Mediterranean. Britain and France resented Russia's attempt to gain land from the Ottomans, and when Russia invaded Turkish territory in 1853 they went to the Ottomans' aid, at-

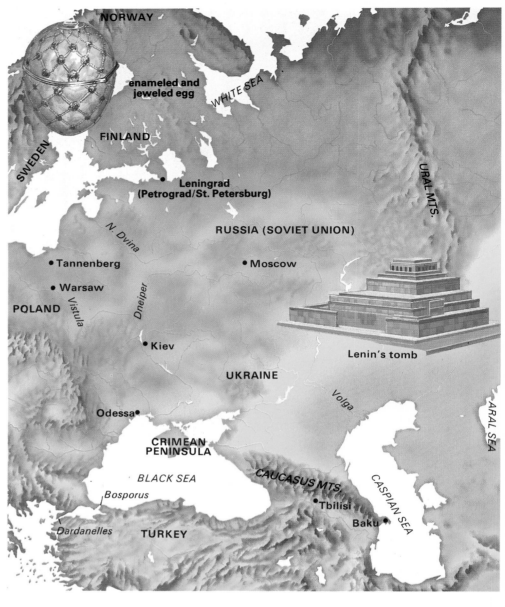

enameled and jeweled egg

Lenin's tomb

tacking the Russians in the Crimean peninsula. Surprisingly, Britain and France, fighting far from their home bases, defeated the Russians on their own soil. Russia had to give up some land to the Ottomans, and its warships were banned from the Black Sea.

In 1905 the Russian fleet was surprisingly and humiliatingly defeated by the Japanese at Tsushima. This was a cause of the revolution in that year.

Peasants on a collective farm clear the soil between rows of trees in a giant orchard. Stalin thought that collectivization would bring greater production and prosperity to farming, but many peasants hated it. Despite this, there are still a large number of these huge farms in Russia, many of which have a great deal of modern machinery and processing equipment which individual farmers would never be able to afford to own.

Reform and Revolution

Defeat in the Crimea was a great shock to the Russians and showed that reform was long overdue. The serfs, poor, backward, and ignorant peasants, were freed from the control of their landlords. They were given some land but had to make yearly payments for it for the next 49 years. Russia also began to develop industries. A huge new industrial area grew up in the Ukraine, near sources of coal and iron ore. Railways were built to link the main cities with the ports and with industry. In the 1890s industrial production was growing faster than anwhere else, but to pay for it the peasants were heavily taxed and their position grew worse. Violent peasant risings reached a peak in 1905.

In 1904 the government had gone to war with Japan (see page 180). It expected a quick victory, and the uniting of the country behind the tsar. However, Japan defeated Russia. By October 1905 the whole nation was on strike. The tsar had to promise that a national assembly, the *Duma*, would be elected to represent the people. This satisfied many Russians and the army remained loyal, so the revolution was put down.

Little changed. The tsar, Nicholas II, was not prepared to give the Duma power to make laws and control the government. Discontent was rising again when war broke out in 1914.

In World War I the Russians lost much land and millions of soldiers were killed or wounded. By 1917 the strains of war were affecting people of all classes, and they turned against the tsar. Bread shortages in Petrograd (St. Petersburg) led to riots. In March, when soldiers were ordered to fire on the crowds, they mutinied. The tsar, Nicholas, had to abdicate. This was the end of the Romanov dynasty which had ruled Russia for 300 years.

The new government was moderate in its views. But in November the *Bolsheviks*, members of a communist party, seized power. They made peace with Germany but three years of brutal civil war followed, in which the White Russians (their opponents) were given money and weapons by the Allies. The Bolsheviks were successful in the end but 13 million people had died through war and famine and much of Russia was in ruins. The Bolsheviks set up a dictatorship under Lenin and opposition parties were banned.

Bolsheviks in Petrograd (formerly St. Petersburg and now Leningrad) during the revolution of 1917.

THE FIVE-YEAR PLANS

In 1920 Russia produced only one seventh of the goods it produced in 1913, but it revived rapidly. In 1927 Joseph Stalin became leader. He determined to make Russia (now the Soviet Union) a strong military power, and in 1928 he introduced the first of his Five-Year Plans. It included *collectivization*, which meant forcing peasants to give up their own land and merge it into large collective farms run by the state. Stalin hoped that this would be more efficient than small peasant holdings, which could not afford fertilizers or tractors. The peasants hated collectivization and many *kulaks* (rich peasants) were killed in resisting it. This left great bitterness in the countryside, and many peasants were hostile to the Communist government.

The plans dealt mainly with heavy industry – coal, steel, railways, and armaments. This was very successful. Huge new industrial towns grew up, such as Magnitogorsk near the iron ore of the southern Urals. Much of this industrialization took place in the east. This meant that Russia could survive the German onslaught from the West in World War II, as these industries were beyond the reach of the German armies.

The dark side of Stalin's rule was shown in a reign of terror, in which he imprisoned or executed his rivals. He also turned on the army, and in 1937 14 of the 16 Soviet generals were arrested. They were accused of spying for Germany and Japan and shot. Less important people were sent to labor camps, which by 1941 contained millions of prisoners.

187

The Near East

The Near (or Middle) East stretches westward from India to North Africa. It includes Iran, Turkey, Iraq, Syria, Lebanon, Israel, Jordan, the Arabian peninsula and in Africa, Egypt and the Sudan. Libya, Tunisia, Algeria, and Morocco can be included.

These countries (with the exception of Israel) are Muslim in religion and all are arid. There are few forests and little rainfall, and agriculture depends on irrigation. Most of Arabia is desert, and so is Egypt, except for the Nile Valley. The only fertile areas in North Africa are the coastal belt and a few oases. In Turkey and Iran much of the land consists of steppe and desert. Some of these deserts support nomadic herdsmen, with flocks of sheep and goats, but others are completely barren. All these areas were very poor until the discovery of oil in the 20th century.

The Ottoman Empire

In the late 18th century the whole of the Near East, except for Iran and Morocco, was part of the Ottoman empire, though some parts like Egypt were largely independent. During the 19th century the Ottoman empire collapsed. The French invaded Algeria in 1830 and took control of Tunis in 1881. Egypt came under British and French control (see page 183). France took Morocco in 1912 and Italy overran Libya a year later.

The Turks kept control of the remaining Muslim parts of their empire until World War I. After Turkey's defeat its empire was split up. The Turks were confined to Anatolia (Asia Minor) and a small part of Europe, including Constantinople (Istanbul). Mustapha Kemal, a successful general, led a revolt which declared the sultanate abolished and set up a republic in 1923. Syria and Lebanon became French "mandates," which meant they were to be ruled by France, on behalf of the League of Nations, until they were ready for independence. Iraq, Palestine, and Transjordan became British "mandates."

A monument to Mustapha Kemal, the Turkish general who became president of the new republic in 1923. He worked unceasingly to modernize his country, whose ways of life had changed little for hundreds of years under the rule of the Ottomans. His reforms included the introduction of the Latin alphabet, rather than the Arabic one; a campaign against illiteracy; and measures to increase women's rights.

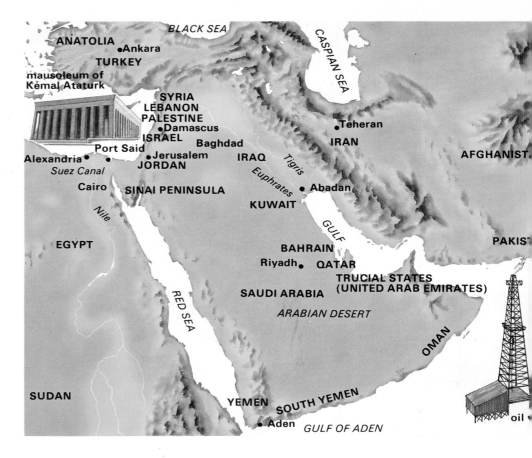

Independence

In the 1920s two independent states were formed in Arabia: Yemen in the southwest, Saudi Arabia in the rest. Egypt and Iraq also became independent between the wars, though Britain still controlled their military affairs.

British and French rule in the Near East came to an end in the ten years after World War II. Syria, Lebanon, and Transjordan soon became independent. In North Africa the first to gain freedom was Libya, as Italy had been defeated in the war. It was followed in 1956 by the Sudan, Tunisia, and Morocco. The last to become independent was Algeria, after a bitter and lengthy struggle in which the *colons* (French settlers) fought against the Muslims. Britain withdrew from the area around the Gulf, beginning with Kuwait and ending with the Trucial States (United Arab Emirates) in 1971.

CHRONOLOGY	
1830	French begin conquest of Algeria
1869	Suez Canal opened
1881	French take over Tunisia
1882	British occupation of Egypt
1912	France controls Morocco
1913	Italy conquers Libya
1920	Mandates for Palestine and Transjordan given to Britain, for Syria and Lebanon to France
1922	Egypt becomes independent
1923	Turkey becomes a republic, with Mustapha Kemal (Ataturk) as its first president
1945	Syria, Lebanon, Transjordan become independent
1948	Ben Gurion announces the state of Israel. War between Israel and the Arab League (to 1949)
1952	King Farouk deposed in Egypt, which becomes a republic
1955	Baghdad Pact
1956	Suez Crisis. Sudan, Tunisia, and Morocco become independent
1962	Algerians gain independence
1967	Six-Day War between Israel and Arabs
1973	Arab-Israeli "October War"
1974	OPEC (Organization of Petroleum Exporting Countries) increases oil prices fourfold
1979	Muslim revolution in Iran under Ayatollah Khomeni
1980	War between Iran and Iraq

ARAB-ISRAELI CONFLICTS

For centuries most of the people in Palestine were Arab-speaking Muslims, though some Christians and Jews also lived there. In the late 19th century more Jews, escaping from persecution in Russia and eastern Europe, came to Palestine. During World War I the British government said that it looked with favor on the setting up of a Jewish "National Home" in Palestine. After the war Britain ruled Palestine as a mandate of the League of Nations, and when Hitler persecuted the Jews many of them emigrated to Palestine. After World War II thousands more Jewish refugees flocked to the country. Britain withdrew from Palestine in 1948 and Ben-Gurion, the nationalist leader, proclaimed the state of Israel.

War followed between Jews and Arabs. The Israelis were successful and took most of Palestine, the rest joining Transjordan (now Jordan). Two thirds of the Arabs in Palestine left home and became refugees in neighboring Arab countries, where most of them still remain. The Palestinian Arabs demanded their own state, something Israel always opposed. Three further wars followed. Negotiations between Egypt and Israel are now going on; Egypt wants Israel to give up territory occupied since 1948 and accept an independent Palestinian state. In return, the Arab states would recognize the state of Israel.

Israel's great military leader Moshe Dayan (with a black eye patch) holds a conference during the October War of 1973.

OIL

The discovery of oil changed the situation in the Near East. The industrial countries of western Europe, Japan, and the United States depended more and more on Near Eastern oil to run their factories, cars, and power stations. The oil companies, mainly British and American, obtained concessions to extract and sell the oil. As governments of the oil-producing states became stronger they gained more of the oil revenues.

Oil has meant that countries like Saudi Arabia, Libya, and Kuwait, which were some of the poorest in the world, have become rich. They can provide their people with free education, medical and social services, import vast quantities of consumer goods and military equipment, and invest in property and industry in western Europe and the United States. They also give aid to poorer (especially Muslim) countries. Oil has given the Arabs a new strength. It has also given the Near East a new importance in the world, as industrial countries cannot afford to have their main source of energy cut off. Any attempt to do this, by Russia or the Arab states themselves, could lead to a Third World War.

Superpower Rivalry

In 1956 Gamal Abdel Nasser, the president of Egypt and the most popular and powerful Arab leader, took control of the Suez Canal Company, owned by British and French shareholders. Britain and France made a secret agreement with Israel that it should invade the Sinai peninsula, which was Egyptian territory. This was followed by Anglo-French attacks on Egyptian airfields and paratroop landings at Port Said. All were successful but the United States condemned the invasion. The Soviet Union even hinted at a nuclear attack in support of Egypt. In such a crisis there was only one course of action and British, French, and Israeli forces were withdrawn.

As Britain and France pulled out of the Near East, Russia and America became great rivals for influence there. Each tried to find allies who depended on them. Israel needed American help against Arab states, so Egypt and Syria turned to Russia for help against Israel. Britain, with American support, joined Turkey, Pakistan, and Iran (and for a time Iraq) in the Baghdad Pact, as part of western defenses against the Soviet Union. Most independent countries preferred to remain neutral, so they could receive aid from both sides, or formed local organizations such as the Arab League.

The oil of the Near East has led to extraordinary contrasts between great wealth and luxury, and the traditional ways of life which still exist unchanged in many places. Here a shepherd moves his flock against a background of flaring oil wells in the Ahwaz region of Iran. In 1980 this region became the scene of war between Iraq and Iran.

The opening of the Suez Canal in 1869. A fleet of 20 ships sailed down it, led by the French emperor's yacht Aigle, with the Empress Eugenie on board. The canal was the work of a French engineer, Ferdinand de Lesseps. It took ten years to build and throughout this time it was bitterly opposed by the British, who looked on it as a French attempt to threaten the route to India. After the canal was opened the British attitude changed, and de Lesseps was made a member of the Order of the Star of India by Queen Victoria. In 1875 the British prime minister bought up most of the shares in the company that owned and ran the canal. It now came under British control.

A World Economy

The effects of the Industrial Revolution are rapidly creating a world civilization. Different ways of life, customs, and dress are becoming fewer. A steelworks or a cotton mill is the same in Korea as it is in Germany. Cities throughout the world are more and more alike; high office and apartment blocks built of concrete are much the same in New York, Hong Kong, or Moscow. People even dress alike. Japanese businessmen wear shirts, ties, and suits like businessmen in Europe. Japanese teenagers wear jeans, watch American films and listen to pop (or classical) music just like their counterparts in the United States. All this has come about this century, and particularly since 1945.

The Rise of a World Economy
In the Middle Ages there was some trade between different parts of the world. Chinese silks and porcelain, precious stones from India, and spices from Southeast Asia reached Europe but trade was in luxury goods only and on a small scale. After the discovery of North and South America, and the setting up of colonies there, gold and silver came to Europe from Mexico and Peru and was used to pay for the spices brought from Southeast Asia. The new gold and silver helped the growth of international trade, linking Asia, America, Europe, and Africa. A world economy was beginning to take shape.

The Industrial Revolutions gave another boost to world trade. Industrial countries in western Europe could not get enough local raw materials and so went looking for them throughout the world. Britain imported raw cotton for the mills of Lancashire from the United States and Egypt. Tin for the plating and canning industries and rubber for the transport and chemical industries were found in Malaya, which increased its trade one hundredfold between 1874 and 1914. Many other materials were also brought across the world to Europe.

Transport
New forms of transport made this increase in international trade possible. Until the development of railways, world trade had been kept mainly to coasts or river valleys which could be reached by ships. By linking the interiors of countries with the coast, railways opened up vast new trading areas. The first transcontinental railway in the United States, linking the Atlantic and Pacific, was opened in 1869; the first line across Canada followed in 1886. These railways opened up the prairies, which soon became one of the main beef, and grain-producing areas in the world. The Trans-Siberian Railway in Russia reached the Pacific at Vladivostok in 1904. Outside Europe and North America there were only 14,500 kilometers (9,100 miles) of railways in 1870. By 1911 this had increased to 281,600 kilometers (175,000 miles).

The amount of shipping also increased rapidly. In 1870 most ships were sailing ships; by 1914 most were steamers. They were larger, faster, and able to carry bulk cargoes cheaply over long distances. Refrigeration allowed food to be moved around the world without going bad. Refrigerated wagons, in use by 1876, brought meat from Kansas City to New York and soon made Argentine beef available in Europe. The first shipload of frozen New Zealand lamb arrived in England in 1882. The Suez Canal, opened in 1869, cut the journey from India to Europe by thousands of kilometers; the opening of the Panama Canal, finished in 1914, meant that ships could sail from the east to the west coast of the United States without going around South America. The effect of all these changes was that foreign trade trebled in value between 1870 and 1914.

This increase in world trade did not always benefit the poorer countries. Some local industries were destroyed by the mass-produced goods of the more efficient industrial countries, so the gap between the living standards in the rich and poor countries widened. In 1800, at the beginning of the Industrial Revolution, income per head in rich countries was about twice as much as that in the poor countries. By 1945 the richer countries were 20 times better off, and by 1965 40 times better off.

American Importance

During World War I industry in Britain and other European countries had to produce armaments, and their exports fell. The United States had large resources of raw materials and food, and at the end of the war was the richest country in the world. In 1914 it owed money to European investors. By

1918 most European countries were in debt to America.

The United States' domination of the world economy increased during World War II, when it owned half of the world's shipping and produced half of the world's manufactured goods and 30 percent of world exports. Like Britain before 1914, it spent or loaned much of its money abroad and so kept the world economy developing. The American Marshall Plan helped Germany to set up industries after the devastation of the war, and the United States also helped Japan to get on its feet again.

This postwar system began to break up in the 1970s. The war in Vietnam cost Americans so much that they cut back on their overseas spending. There was also a great rise in oil prices in 1974. Oil countries like Saudi Arabia, Kuwait, and Iran earned large sums of money. The smooth running of the world economy depended on their lending money or buying goods abroad. But most of the oil-producing states have small populations and do not need to spend so much.

The last spike is driven into the Transcanada Railway in November 1885. This helped to open up the center of North America, allowing grain and meat to be shipped to heavily populated areas and people to travel quickly and easily across the continent.

A diagram of the electric telegraph, first used in 1838. An electric current was sent along a wire to a receiver, which clicked each time the current was switched on or off. Letters of the alphabet were represented by a code of dots and dashes, or short and longer sounds, invented by Samuel Morse. Soon telegraph wires were laid from one continent to another. Telephones were developed in 1879, allowing people to speak to one another at a distance. In 1901 dependence on wires ended when Marconi sent the first wireless telegraphy (radio) message across the Atlantic.

THE SPREAD OF KNOWLEDGE

The spread of communications has helped to make the whole world one. In the early 19th century it often took two years to send a message from India to London and to receive a reply. With the telegraph, and later the telephone and radio, messages could be sent anywhere in under a minute. Today our television screens can show us events in different parts of the world on the day they happen.

In the past scientific discoveries in China, like iron casting, were unknown in Europe for centuries. Today the knowledge of discoveries and inventions spreads very quickly. The Americans tried to keep the secret of the atom bomb but it was known to scientists all over the world within a few years. The isolation of different countries or continents from one another has ended.

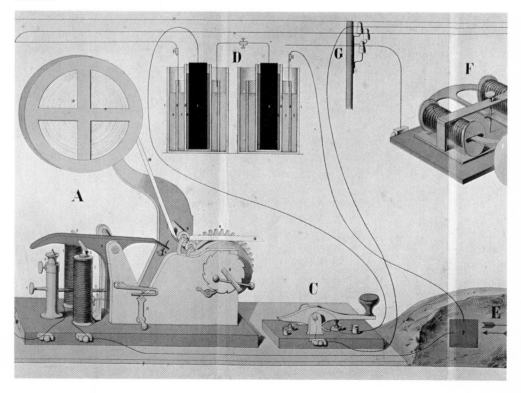

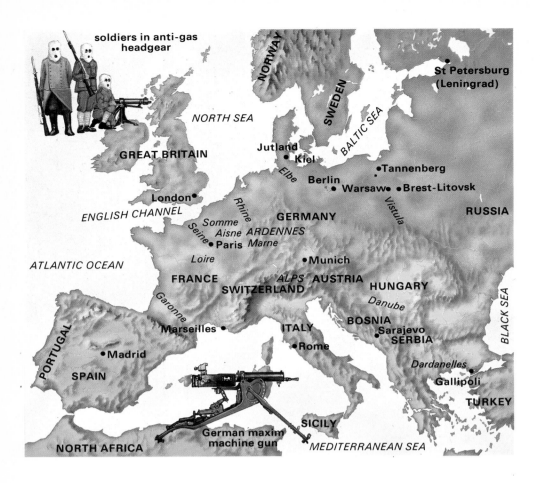

soldiers in anti-gas headgear

NORWAY

SWEDEN

NORTH SEA

BALTIC SEA

St Petersburg
(Leningrad)

GREAT BRITAIN

Jutland
Kiel

Tannenberg

Elbe

Berlin
Warsaw
Brest-Litovsk

London

Rhine

Vistula

RUSSIA

ENGLISH CHANNEL

Somme
Aisne ARDENNES
Paris Marne

GERMANY

Seine

ATLANTIC OCEAN

Loire

Munich

FRANCE

ALPS AUSTRIA

SWITZERLAND

HUNGARY

Danube

BLACK SEA

Garonne

Marseilles

ITALY

Rome

BOSNIA
Sarajevo
SERBIA

PORTUGAL

Madrid

SPAIN

German maxim
machine gun

SICILY

Dardanelles
Gallipoli

TURKEY

NORTH AFRICA

MEDITERRANEAN SEA

The First World War

Wars in the later 19th century were mainly local affairs, fought by two or three states, and scarcely affected other countries. The "Great War" of 1914 to 1918 was fought by many countries and its effects were felt around the world. Troops from the British empire (Australia, New Zealand, Canada, South Africa, and India) took part, as did Japan, which joined the Allies and seized German colonies in the Pacific and China. There was fighting too in Africa, as the German colonies there were conquered. This was truly the first World War.

The Origins of the War
The Franco-Prussian War (see page 175) had ended with the defeat of France and the unification of Germany, which proved to be a new military power in Europe. For 20 years after the German chancellor Bismarck was "a fanatic for peace" and kept Germany out of more wars. In the 1890s France made an alliance with Russia and this alarmed Germany, which feared an attack from both east and west in any future war.

When the Germans began to build up their navy the British, who regarded this as a challenge to their command at sea, settled their differences with France and Russia to form the Triple *Entente*. Germany now regarded itself as "encircled" by hostile powers. It was also concerned about the weakness of its ally, Austria-Hungary. Austria knew that the many Serbs in the south of its empire wanted to join Serbia and felt threatened when Serbia greatly increased its territory in the Balkan Wars of 1912–1913. Austria wanted to fight and defeat Serbia and found an excuse when the archduke Franz Ferdinand of Austria was assassinated at Sarajevo in Bosnia by a Serb nationalist.

Germany encouraged Austria to attack Serbia, and Russia rallied to its support. France was allied to Russia, and Britain entered the war when Germany invaded Belgium on its way to France. World War I had begun.

The Western Front
Everyone expected the war to be over by Christmas. General von Schlieffen of Germany had devised a plan to knock out France in six weeks, before the Russians could mobilize their vast army. In this way the Germans would avoid a war on two fronts. The plan was to advance in strength through Belgium, bypassing the French defenses along the German border, sweep down west of Paris, and then move east to attack the main French armies in the rear. But the British and French halted the German advance at the battle of the Marne, and Germany was condemned to fight the war on the two fronts it dreaded.

Soon the western front stretched from Belgium to Switzerland as both sides dug in. Trench warfare had begun. In the next four years the western front did not move more than 32 kilometers (20 miles), though there were repeated attempts by both sides to break through the line of trenches. All the battles on the western front followed the same pattern: an intensive bombardment of enemy trenches and barbed wire defenses, followed by infantry going "over the top" to be mown down by enemy machine guns. The attack would stop after shattering losses with, at most, a few kilometers gained.

The Eastern Front
In the east the Russians attacked the Germans in East Prussia. They were defeated at Tannenberg and the Germans went on to occupy much of western Russia. The war here was not as static as it was in the west, because the front was much longer. In 1916 the Russian general Brusilov mounted a brilliant offensive, but he could not win a decisive victory.

Heavy losses and war weariness helped to bring about a revolution in Russia in 1917. The tsar abdicated and after the Bolsheviks seized power in November they made peace with Germany.

CHRONOLOGY
1914   **June 15 Assassination of archduke Franz Ferdinand at Sarajevo**
Aug. 1 Germany declares war on Russia
Aug. 4 Britain declares war on Germany
Aug. 30 Germans defeat Russians at Tannenberg
Sept. 12 French and British halt German advance at battle of the Marne
1915   **Dec. British withdraw from Gallipoli**
1916   **Feb.–July German attack on Verdun**
May 31–June 1 Naval battle of Jutland: indecisive
June–Sept. Brusilov offensive
July 1–Nov. 18 Battle of the Somme
1917   **Mar. 3 Russia makes peace with Germany at Brest-Litovsk**
Mar. 11 British occupy Baghdad
Apr. 6 U.S. enters war against Germany
1918   **Mar. Great German offensive begins**
Oct. 28 Mutiny in German navy at Kiel
Nov. 9 German Emperor (Kaiser) Wilhelm II abdicates
Nov. 11 Ceasefire on western front

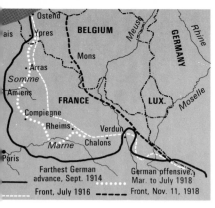

The western front.

THE TANK
The tank was first introduced by the British in 1916 to try to break the stalemate of trench warfare. Its heavy caterpillar tracks could go over the roughest ground, crushing barbed wire in its path. Its crew, protected by steel armor, could use its guns against enemy soldiers in the trenches. The few times that the tank was used in large numbers it was devastating. On November 20, 1917, British tanks lumbered out of the mist and smashed through the Hindenburg line near Cambrai. "The immediate onset of the tanks inevitably was overwhelming," wrote D. G. Brown of the Tank Corps. "The German outposts, dazed or annihilated by the sudden deluge of shells, were overrun in an instant. The triple belts of wire were crossed as if they had been beds of nettles and 350 pathways were sheared through them for the infantry."

The Near East
In the Near East, Turkey entered the war on the side of Germany. The British wanted to break through the Dardanelles Strait to the Black Sea, so they could send supplies to Russia, but their attack at Gallipoli in 1915 was a complete failure. They had more success in protecting their oil supplies from Iran and Iraq. Turkish resistance was fierce and the British had to commit 600,000 troops to fighting them, but by the end of the war they had captured the three main cities, Basra, Baghdad, and Mosul. The British tried to weaken Turkey by stirring up the Arabs in the Turkish empire to rebel, promising to create independent Arab states (a promise they broke after the war).

German troops in the trenches. Conditions were appalling; soldiers fought and lived in seas of mud among the corpses of their comrades and enemies.

The End of the War
In April 1917 German submarine attacks on American ships carrying food and supplies to Britain and France brought the United States into the war. Germany then knew it had to mount a successful offensive before large numbers of American troops arrived in France. When the Russians made peace in late 1917, the Germans could concentrate their armies in the west, and they launched a series of attacks. These failed. American arms and men were now pouring into Europe. The Allies counter-attacked, and when they broke through the Hindenburg line of defenses, the German general Ludendorff asked his government to seek an armistice. In October the German navy mutinied, the kaiser abdicated and fighting stopped on November 11.

Left: Canadian troops fight off an attack at the second battle of Ypres in 1915. Hundreds of thousands of men were killed in such battles, but the front line hardly shifted. Below: Europe as it was settled after the war.

The World in 1919

The United States has emerged as the leading industrial power in the world. World War I has seen the end of the ruling dynasties in Russia, Germany, and Austria and the carving up of the Ottoman empire. Germany, following the Peace of Versailles, must accept responsibility for the war, lose some territory, pay reparations (compensation), and limit its armed forces. In China the Manchu empire has been overthrown by a republic and power is in the hands of local warlords. Japan is the strongest power in the Far East. In Russia the communists are fighting a savage civil war to keep control. Africa has been almost wholly taken over by European powers.

1 **America** leads the world in industry and exports beef and wheat. President Wilson successfully urges the foundation of the League of Nations but Congress prevents the U.S. from joining it. A policy of isolationism is taken up.

2 **Africa** Morocco has been taken by France and Libya by Italy. Britain occupies
4 Egypt, controlling its main sea route to the East, the Suez Canal. In West Africa the French have built up a
5 vast empire from Senegal to Lake Chad. The Union of South Africa has been formed from the Boer
6 republics and British colonies. East Africa is largely British.

British
British Mandates

French
French Mandates

Belgium

Italian

Japanese

Dutch

Spanish

Portuguese

United States

Turkey

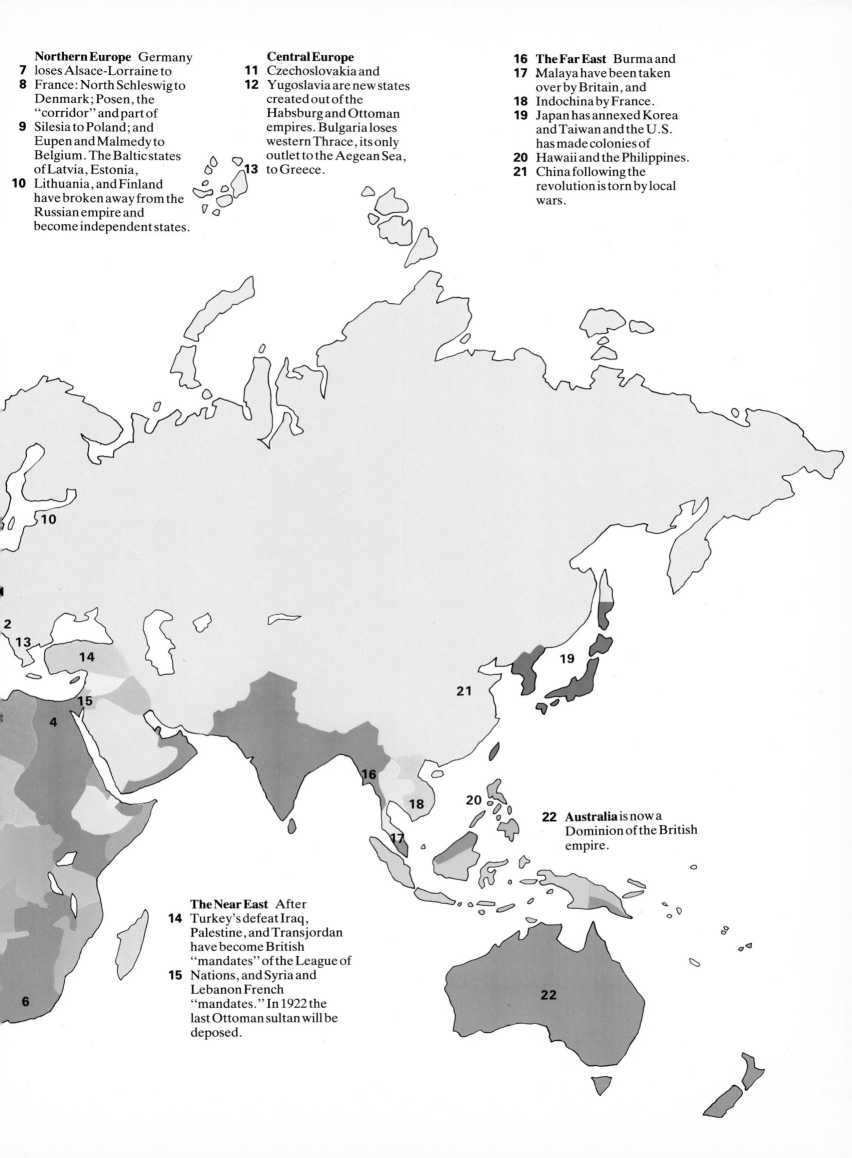

Northern Europe Germany
7 loses Alsace-Lorraine to
8 France; North Schleswig to
   Denmark; Posen, the
   "corridor" and part of
9 Silesia to Poland; and
   Eupen and Malmedy to
   Belgium. The Baltic states
   of Latvia, Estonia,
10 Lithuania, and Finland
   have broken away from the
   Russian empire and
   become independent states.

Central Europe
11 Czechoslovakia and
12 Yugoslavia are new states
   created out of the
   Habsburg and Ottoman
   empires. Bulgaria loses
   western Thrace, its only
   outlet to the Aegean Sea,
   to Greece.

16 **The Far East** Burma and
17 Malaya have been taken
   over by Britain, and
18 Indochina by France.
19 Japan has annexed Korea
   and Taiwan and the U.S.
   has made colonies of
20 Hawaii and the Philippines.
21 China following the
   revolution is torn by local
   wars.

The Near East After
14 Turkey's defeat Iraq,
   Palestine, and Transjordan
   have become British
   "mandates" of the League of
15 Nations, and Syria and
   Lebanon French
   "mandates." In 1922 the
   last Ottoman sultan will be
   deposed.

22 **Australia** is now a
   Dominion of the British
   empire.

In 1933 the U.S. government set up the Tennessee Valley Authority, an agency to control floods, improve irrigation, and produce electricity in the region of the Tennessee River and its tributaries. At this time the country was in the depths of depression, and President Roosevelt was all in favor of a scheme which would give work to thousands of people and help the region's economy. The Norris Dam, shown here, was the first to be built; it is named after Senator George W. Norris, who introduced the bill to set up the Authority.

Years of Depression

In October 1929 the booming American stock market suddenly collapsed. The "Wall Street Crash," as it was known, ruined many thousands of investors and ushered in a time of unemployment and economic difficulties in many parts of the world. It is known as the Great Depression. Some countries were led out of depression by the rise of new political parties such as the Fascists.

Boom and Slump
In the 1920s the United States was the most prosperous nation in the world. It was owed 12 billion dollars by other countries. Americans developed a craze for consumer goods, such as cars, refrigerators, and vacuum cleaners, paid for in installments. Mass production meant there were enough goods for everybody: Henry Ford produced 5 million of his Model T cars by 1921, and 10 million by 1924.

Then in 1929 the bubble burst. The main reason was overproduction. Factories flooded the market with more goods than people could afford to buy, so factories worked part time and this reduced people's wages and meant they could afford still less. The slump was made worse by the stock-buying fever of the 1920s, when everyone wanted to buy shares and competition increased their value. Then, in the autumn of 1929, some investors realized that while stock prices were going up, production was going down, and they sold their shares on the Wall Street stock exchange. This started others selling in panic, and share values plummeted. People who had borrowed money could not repay their loans and 5,000 banks closed. By 1932 output had fallen 40 percent and wages by 60 percent, and there were 12 million people out of work.

In this crisis, a new president, Franklin Roosevelt, was elected. "I pledge you, I pledge myself, to a new deal for the American people," he said. He began his New Deal by employing people on public works paid for by the government. Thousands worked on great dams in the Tennessee Valley, which would irrigate farmland, prevent flooding, and provide electricity. Orders for schemes like this revived industry. The United States avoided total collapse, but it had not fully recovered by 1939. Only World War II pulled the United States out of depression.

Depression Spreads
The crash of the American economy meant that the United States stopped lending money to other countries and bought fewer imports. In the boom of the 1920s producers of cotton, coffee, sugar, wheat, and meat had found a ready market in the United States and western Europe. In the depression industrial countries could no longer buy their goods in the same quantities. Between June 1930 and

MUSSOLINI TAKES POWER
There was great unrest in Italy in the early 1920s. Many were unemployed, there were violent strikes, workers seized control of their factories, and peasants seized the landowners' land. Many people, particularly the frightened middle classes, looked for a strong leader and found one in Benito Mussolini. His Fascist squads, dressed in black shirts, attacked socialists, communists, and peasants who had seized land, and they broke up strikes. They were supported by businessmen and large sections of the police and army. Liberal leaders became convinced that Fascist mobs could be brought under control only by giving Mussolini a place in the government. Mussolini played for higher stakes. In October 1922 he planned a March on Rome with his supporters. This was a great bluff. Rome was defended by the regular army and the Fascists were poorly armed. They could easily have been crushed but the king, Victor Emmanuel, decided instead to give way and make Mussolini prime minister. The "March" never took place. Mussolini and his 25,000 supporters came to Rome by train and the Fascist rule of Italy began.

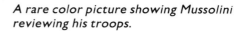

September 1931 the price of grain in world markets fell by 40 percent; Australian and Canadian exports dropped by 25 percent between 1929 and 1930, and those of Japan and Brazil by 30 percent.

Rise of the Nazis

German discontent went back to the Peace of Versailles in 1919, when Germany lost some of its territory. It had to accept responsibility for starting the war and had to pay huge sums of money (reparations) in compensation for damage caused during the war, particularly to France. Its army and navy were severely limited and its air force banned. When American loans ended, factories closed down and in 1933 a third of the workforce was unemployed. Terrible inflation made German money almost valueless. In these conditions extreme political parties thrived, most of all the National Socialists (Nazis). Their leader, Adolf Hitler, promised to end unemployment and to smash the Peace of Versailles. As the economic situation got worse the Nazis won more seats at elections. In January 1933 Hitler became chancellor of Germany, and was soon ruling without the *Reichstag* (parliament). It was the death of democracy. Hitler stamped out all opposition, banned other political parties and began public works, including *autobahns* (motorways), to provide jobs for the unemployed. Above all, German industry was helped to recover by his massive rearmament program, which the Peace of Versailles had forbidden.

A Greater Germany

In 1937 Hitler told his generals that Germany must be ready for war by 1943 at the latest. The first country to be added to Germany was Austria. Hitler forced the Austrian chancellor to resign; he was replaced by a Nazi, who invited the Germans in. *Anschluss* (union with Germany), forbidden at Versailles, took place without any fighting and was popular with the German people.

Nearly 3 million Germans lived in the Sudetenland of Czechoslovakia. Hitler demanded that they be included in Germany. Both France and Russia had promised to defend Czechoslovakia, so it looked as though there might be another European war. Hitler, the British and French prime ministers, Chamberlain and Daladier, and Mussolini of Italy met at Munich. The Czechs (and Russians) were not invited. Czechoslovakia was forced to give up the Sudetenland and told that if it fought it would fight alone – France would not support it. "We have been disgracefully betrayed," said Benes, the Czech president. Chamberlain saw it differently. "This means peace in our time," he announced, and believed Hitler when he said "I have no more territorial claims to make in Europe."

Chamberlain realized his mistake when Hitler seized the rest of Czechoslovakia and took Memel from Lithuania. He guaranteed, as did France, to defend Poland if it were attacked. Hitler did not believe that Britain and France would go to war over Poland any more than they had done over Czechoslovakia, and so, making sure that he would not be attacked from the east by a pact with Russia, he invaded. At last Britain and France acted firmly. On September 3, 1939, they declared war on Germany.

THE SPANISH CIVIL WAR

The Civil War began with a revolt of right-wing army officers in Spanish Morocco in July 1936. They believed the liberal Spanish government was too weak and was likely to fall to a communist revolution. Morocco and northwest Spain were soon won by the rebels, supported by landowners and the church, but the Republican government controlled the main cities and the prosperous east, center, and south of Spain.

At first the rebels seemed certain to lose the war, but they were supported by Mussolini, who sent 50,000 troops, and Hitler, who supplied arms, planes, and pilots. The Republicans' only support came from Russia and the International Brigades, which were formed from volunteers from many countries. General Franco, the rebel Nationalist leader, gradually conquered the Republican areas. He was helped when the Republicans fought among themselves, liberals clashing with communists. The war ended on March 28, 1939, with the surrender of Madrid.

Adolf Hitler at a Nazi party rally.

The Second World War

The German and Italian, or Axis, powers and their dependents, and the greatest extent to which they overran Europe in 1942.

☐ Neutral	▦ Axis-occupied territory in November 1942
▨ Axis powers and dependents	☐

World War II was more of a world war than that of 1914–1918, as fighting on a large scale took place outside Europe. It was in fact two wars, one fought in Europe and along the coast of North Africa, the other in the Pacific. It was different from other wars in its scale and because 35 million out of 50 million casualties were civilians, including 20 million Russians, 6 million Jews and 4½ million Poles. At the end of the war European countries were bankrupt and western Russia was in ruins. Only the United States, whose people, money, and industry had played such a large part in the Allied victory, seemed to be in a strong position.

The War in the West

The war began with the German invasion of Poland on September 1, 1939. The Germans used *Blitzkrieg* (lightning war) tactics – their dive bombers attacked towns and railways and were followed by columns of tanks, which swept across the open countryside. Resistance ended in under four weeks. Russia meanwhile moved into eastern Poland and also seized the Baltic states of Latvia, Lithuania, and Estonia. Russia took some Finnish territory too, after a war in which the Finns resisted fiercely.

In April 1940 Germany attacked Denmark and Norway and soon overran both countries. Britain and France had taken little part in the war for the first eight months but in May Germany attacked Belgium and the Netherlands. German tanks smashed through French defenses in the Ardennes and then raced to the Channel coast. The French and British armies were cut in two, one part in Belgium, the other south of the German advance in France. The British retreated to Dunkirk and, helped by a courageous French rearguard action, evacuated 340,000 British and French troops. On June 14, Paris fell. The Germans occupied northern France and the Channel coast, and left the rest under Marshal Pétain.

Only Britain remained of Germany's enemies, but to invade it the Germans had to control the Channel and destroy the Royal Air Force. On August 13, the German *Luft-waffe* (airforce) began attacking southeast England, concentrating on British fighter bases. They had come close to destroying them when, on September 7, they switched to bombing London. This gave the Royal Air Force time to recover. Britain was saved, and on September 17, Hitler postponed his invasion.

CHRONOLOGY

1939	**Sept. 1 Germany invades Poland**
	Sept. 17 Russia invades Poland from the east
	Nov. Russia attacks Finland
1940	**April Germany attacks Denmark and Norway**
	May 10 Germany invades Belgium, the Netherlands, and Luxembourg
	May 26–June 4 British evacuated from Dunkirk
	June 10 Italy declares war against France and Britain
	Aug.–Sept. Battle of Britain
1941	**June Operation Barbarossa: Germany invades Russia**
	Dec. 7 Japanese attack on Pearl Harbor, the Philippines, Malaya, and Hong Kong
1942	**June Battle of Midway**
	Aug. U.S. marines land in Solomons and begin attack on Japanese-held islands in the Pacific
	Oct. Battle of El Alamein
1943	**Jan. Leningrad relieved after a 17-month siege**
	Feb. German army surrenders at Stalingrad
	Sept. Allies land in southern Italy
1944	**June Operation Overlord; Allies land on Normandy beaches**
	Oct. General MacArthur invades the Philippines
	Dec. Battle of the Bulge: last German offensive in the Ardennes, held up by the Americans at Bastogne
1945	**May 8 VE Day: Victory in Europe**
	Aug. 6 Atom bomb dropped on Hiroshima
	Aug. 8 Russia declares war on Japan
	Aug. 10 Japan surrenders

ICELAND

Messerschmidt fighter

ARCHANGEL

NORWAY
SWEDEN
FINLAND
Leningrad
ESTONIA
LATVIA
LITHUANIA Moscow
GREAT BRITAIN
NORTH SEA
BALTIC SEA
EIRE
DENMARK
UNION OF SOVIET SOCIALIST REPUBLICS
London
Berlin
Warsaw
ENGLISH CHANNEL
Dunkirk
POLAND
Vistula
NORMANDY
Bastogne
Stalingrad
Volga
Paris
GERMANY
Munich
CZECHOSLOVAKIA
ATLANTIC OCEAN
FRANCE
ALPS
Milan
Garonne
Marseilles
Danube
BLACK SEA
CAUCASUS MTS.
CASPIAN SEA
PORTUGAL
ITALY
Rome
Madrid
CORSICA
SPAIN
SARDINIA
Istanbul
TURKEY
MEDITERRANEAN SEA
SICILY
GREECE
CYPRUS
MOROCCO
ATLAS MTS.
ALGERIA
LIBYA
Sherman tank
El Alamein
EGYPT
Nile
URAL MTS.

War in the Desert

In 1940 Mussolini saw his chance to drive the British out of North Africa. He joined the war on the side of Germany and invaded Egypt from Libya. The British pushed the Italians back into Libya, but in turn were driven back to Egypt by German forces led by one of the most brilliant commanders in the war, Rommel. Finally, the British general Montgomery, supported by 300 Sherman tanks, defeated Rommel at El Alamein. Rommel, forced to retreat, was caught between Montgomery advancing from the east and an Allied force under the American Eisenhower which had landed in Morocco and Algeria. In May 1943 the last German and Italian forces were driven out of North Africa.

Operation Overlord

In 1943 the Allies invaded and conquered Sicily but met stiff German resistance in southern Italy. They had reached Rome in June 1944 when another Allied army invaded the Normandy beaches. British and American troops broke through the German defenses, and in August Paris was freed. France and Belgium were liberated, and despite desperate German fighting the Rhine was crossed in March 1945. A month later American and Russian troops met at Torgau on the Elbe. In the same month President Roosevelt died, Mussolini was shot by Italian supporters of the Allies, and Hitler committed suicide in his Berlin bunker. The Germans surrendered and the Allies celebrated VE Day (Victory in Europe Day) on May 8, 1945.

OPERATION BARBAROSSA

In June 1941 Hitler attacked Russia. He aimed to defeat it quickly in a three-pronged advance to Leningrad in the north, Moscow in the center, and the oilfields of the Caucasus in the south. "Operation Barbarossa" did not achieve any of its objectives, though the Germans reached the outskirts of Leningrad and Moscow before winter set in. In the spring of 1942 the Germans pushed on to the Caucasus but diverted many of their troops to Stalingrad, the great industrial and communications center on the Volga. The city was reduced to rubble but the Russians fought desperately in the sewers and among the ruins. The Germans were halted and then encircled, but Hitler forbade them to retreat. They were trapped and forced to surrender. This was a turning-point of the war. From now on the Russians continued their steady advance through eastern Europe to Berlin.

Right: Fighting in the snow outside Moscow in 1941. The bitterly cold Russian winter made it difficult for troops to maneuver, and froze their machinery. Soldiers are dressed in white as camouflage against the snow.

Center: The Pacific region.

Below: War in the air. In World War II, for the first time, control of the air was vitally important. These are Stirling bombers of the British Royal Air Force.

WAR IN THE PACIFIC

When the Japanese attacked Pearl Harbor on December 7, 1941, they gambled on destroying the American Pacific Fleet. They nearly succeeded; 18 American ships were sunk or destroyed and 349 planes put out of action, but America's most important ships, its aircraft carriers, were at sea. The Japanese attacked the Philippines too and by the end of May 1942, in a remarkable series of victories, had overrun Malaya, the Dutch East Indies, Burma, Hong Kong, and the Philippines.

The tide turned in June when the Japanese sent a fleet to capture the American base at Midway Island. In less than five minutes American dive bombers knocked out three Japanese carriers. The Japanese lost four aircraft carriers and a cruiser, the Americans one carrier and a destroyer. Before Midway Japan had never lost a battle in the Pacific: afterward it never won one.

In late 1943 the Americans began attacking Japanese islands. Once they captured Saipan they could bomb Tokyo and Japan's other wooden cities. Japanese resistance became more fanatical the nearer the Americans came to Japan. Okinawa, the last stronghold outside Japan, fell after 100,000 Japanese defenders had been killed. It seemed that millions of lives would be lost if Japan was invaded so President Truman gave permission for the dropping of an atomic bomb on Hiroshima. Three days later another atom bomb was dropped on Nagasaki and Russia declared war on Japan. The Japanese emperor announced Japan's surrender, which was accepted on September 2, 1945, by the Allied Supreme Commander, General MacArthur, on the USS *Missouri* in Tokyo Bay.

Mitsubishi Zero-Sen

Refugees flee from the fighting in a Vietnamese town. Refugees have proved an appalling problem from the mid-20th century on, with mass movements of people escaping from battle areas or from hostile regimes. International agencies do all they can to help look after the refugees and provide them with food and shelter until they can return home or be found a new place in which to live. Even so, many people spend years in crowded refugee camps.

The Cold War

World War II left two "superpowers" in the world, the United States of America and the Union of Soviet Socialist Republics (Russia). Germany, Italy, and Japan were defeated nations, while Britain and France were too weakened to play a leading role. The rivalry between these "superpowers" was known as the "Cold War." It was not a war in the true sense since Russian and American armies did not fight each other, though Americans did fight in Korea and Vietnam and there were several occasions when the "cold" war almost became a "hot" one.

The Cold War arose because the Soviet Union and the United States feared each other. The Russians thought that America, as the richest and strongest power in the world, would try to dominate Europe. The Americans watched as Russia set up communist governments in all the countries of eastern Europe, ending with Czechoslovakia in 1948, and thought this was the preparation for a communist assault on western Europe. Winston Churchill referred to the dividing line between the communist East and the democratic West as "the iron curtain."

Pacts and Organizations

At the end of World War II European countries had to rebuild their shattered industries. America made 15 billion dollars available as aid. The Western countries accepted this generous offer but Stalin would not let any communist country receive help from the Americans. Russia's answer was the Cominform, an organization of all communist parties, whose aim was to spread communism in theory and practice throughout the world.

In 1949 the Western powers joined forces to defend themselves against communism. The North Atlantic Treaty Organization (NATO) was formed by the United States, Canada, and ten West European countries. If one of them were attacked, the others would come to its aid. It was later joined by Greece, Turkey, and West Germany, and it may have saved western Europe from a Russian attack.

Russia's reply was the Warsaw Pact, made up of all the communist states in eastern Europe. The Soviet Union showed it would not allow any of these countries to go its own way. When there was a rising in Hungary in 1956 Russia sent in tanks to crush the revolt, as the Hungarians threatened to withdraw from the Warsaw Pact. Other revolts were crushed in a similar way.

CHRONOLOGY
1947   Mar. Truman Doctrine offers aid to "free peoples"
        Oct. Cominform set up
1948   June (to April 1949) Blockade of Berlin
1949   NATO formed
1950   Korean War (to 1953)
1954   March–May Battle of Dien Bien Phu – French defeated by Vietcong
        April–July Geneva Conference divides Vietnam into communist North and noncommunist South
        Sept. Southeast Asia Treaty Organization (SEATO) formed by U.S.A., Britain, France, Australia, New Zealand, Pakistan, the Philippines, and Thailand
1955   Warsaw Pact
1961   Berlin Wall built
1962   Cuban missile crisis
1963   Test Ban Treaty
1965   Vietnam War (to 1973)
1969   Death of Ho Chi Minh, leader of North Vietnam
1975   Vietnam is united as a communist country

The Korean War

In 1945 Korea had been divided into a communist north under Russian influence, and a noncommunist south which had American support. In 1950 the communists attacked the south and overran almost the whole country. South Korea appealed to the United Nations for help and soon an army, mainly American but provided by 15 countries, was fighting the north. It drove the communists right back to the Chinese border which alarmed China, which sent 150,000 "volunteers" to help the North Koreans. They were successful in pushing back the UN forces to the original border between north and south. After three years of fighting, peace was restored.

As a result of the Cold War in Asia the U.S.A. built up alliances, like the Southeast Asia Treaty Organization (SEATO), to stop the spread of communism.

The Cuban Missile Crisis

When Cuba became a communist state under Fidel Castro Russia had an ally only 160 kilometers (100 miles) from the United States. In 1962 American planes photographed Soviet nuclear missile sites on Cuba. President Kennedy demanded that the missile sites be demolished and ordered the American fleet to turn back 18 Soviet ships heading for Cuba. For several days there was danger of war, but on October 24, they turned for home. The Russian leader, Khrushchev, had backed down and war had been avoided.

This incident showed how easily a war could start, so a direct telephone link was set up in 1963 between Moscow and Washington to allow the leaders to discuss immediately any issues which might lead to war. In the same year Russia, America, and Britain signed the Test Ban Treaty, which stopped nuclear tests above ground. This was the beginning of "peaceful coexistence," the recognition by both sides that since nuclear war was too horrible to enter into, they had to live peacefully with one another. Differences must be sorted out by talking and not by war.

The Brandenburg Gate is in the Eastern sector of Berlin. This picture of it, taken in the Western zone, shows a notice which reads "Warning: You are now leaving West Berlin!" By 1961, more than 2 million people had fled from the communist East to West Berlin, and from there to West Germany. To stop this, the communists built a high wall across Berlin to prevent anyone crossing over – a permanent reminder of the city's divided state.

Vietnam

In 1954 the French left Vietnam which, like Korea, was divided into a communist north and a noncommunist south. The Americans believed in the "domino" theory, that is if one country became communist the country next to it would also become communist. They were determined to stop the communist advance and for the next 20 years supported weak governments in South Vietnam by providing them with money, arms, and later, troops.

The Vietcong (Vietnamese communists) waged guerilla warfare against the government in the south. It was easy for them to hide in the forests and the local peasants often supported them. The Americans sent in more and more of their own troops (over 500,000 by 1968). They began to bomb northern cities and use chemical weapons like napalm against the Vietcong. Many villages were destroyed and civilians killed. In the end the Americans, suffering 500 casualties a week, pulled out of a war they could not win, and in 1975 Saigon, the southern capital, fell to the Vietcong. Vietnam was united as a communist country, soon followed by the neighboring countries of Laos and Cambodia. This was the United States' biggest defeat in the Cold War.

BLOCKADE OF BERLIN

In 1945 Germany was divided into four occupation zones, British, French, American, and Russian. Berlin, 160 kilometers (100 miles) inside the Russian zone, was also divided into four parts. Stalin tried to force the Western powers out of the city. In June 1948 he closed all the roads and railways which led from Berlin to the west. If the allies had used their armies to break the blockade there would have been a major war, but if they allowed Russia to push them out of Berlin, they knew it might try to force them out of the rest of Germany. Instead they supplied Berlin by air. Over $1\frac{1}{2}$ million tons of supplies were flown in and over 300,000 flights made, two thirds by the United States Air Force, the rest by the British.

The winter of 1948–1949 was hard for the West Berliners. They were cold, as all coal had to come by plane and was strictly rationed. They were also hungry and lived off dried and tinned foods. But by May 1949 it was clear Stalin could not get what he wanted without a war, so he reopened the road and rail links to the West.

The blockade ended with the Americans and Russians giving up any ideas of uniting Germany. It left Berlin divided, as it is today: one part is the capital of the German Democratic Republic (East Germany), the other is in effect a part of West Germany.

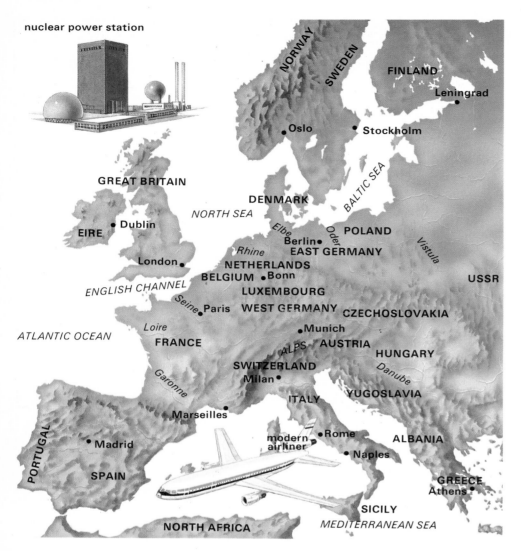

nuclear power station

NORWAY
SWEDEN
FINLAND
Leningrad
Oslo · Stockholm ·
GREAT BRITAIN
DENMARK
BALTIC SEA
NORTH SEA
EIRE · Dublin
POLAND
Elbe Berlin · Oder
London · EAST GERMANY
Rhine
NETHERLANDS
ENGLISH CHANNEL
BELGIUM · Bonn
Vistula
USSR
LUXEMBOURG
ATLANTIC OCEAN
Seine · Paris WEST GERMANY CZECHOSLOVAKIA
Loire · Munich
FRANCE
AUSTRIA
ALPS HUNGARY
SWITZERLAND Danube
Garonne
Milan ·
ITALY YUGOSLAVIA
· Marseilles
modern · Rome ALBANIA
PORTUGAL
airliner · Naples
· Madrid GREECE
SPAIN Athens ·
SICILY
NORTH AFRICA MEDITERRANEAN SEA

The Post-War West

In 1945 much of Europe was in ruins; 30 million people had been killed, 60 million were homeless and hundreds of towns had been destroyed. Homes, factories, roads, and railways had to be rebuilt. Fortunately, the United States came to Europe's aid with its Marshall Plan. Between 1948 and 1952 this made millions of dollars available for reconstruction. The Organization for European Economic Cooperation (OEEC) was set up to distribute this money.

The Common Market

After World War II there were only two great powers left, the United States and the USSR. Some people thought that if the peoples of western Europe could unite, instead of being divided into separate nations, they would create a power equal to either of the other two. The first step was taken in 1950 by the French foreign minister, Robert Schuman, who organized the European Coal and Steel Community (ECSC). Six nations –

France, West Germany, Italy, Belgium, the Netherlands, and Luxembourg – agreed to work out a joint plan to produce and sell iron, steel, and coal. Britain refused to join.

The ECSC was so successful that in 1957 the six member nations signed the Treaty of Rome, which set up the European Economic Community (EEC), generally known as the Common Market. They were to allow the free movement of goods, money, and people among the six, to have a common agricultural policy, and the same customs duties on imports.

Britain decided not to join, as it felt it had a "special relationship" with the United States and because of its trade links with the British Commonwealth. At the time three quarters of Britain's trade was with countries outside Europe. Instead it formed the European Free Trade Area (EFTA) with Norway, Denmark, Sweden, Austria, Portugal, and Switzerland to reduce customs duties between one another. From the start the Common Market was more successful than EFTA. Eventually Britain, Ireland (Eire), and Denmark were admitted to the Common Market in 1973. Greece joined in 1981, and Spain and Portugal in 1986.

The great achievement of western Europe since the war has been increased production. This has brought with it a rise in living standards for nearly everyone, far less unemployment and poverty, and far more prosperity than ever before.

Doctors and nurses of the British National Health Service carry out an operation. The Health Service was created by the Labor government, elected in 1945, as part of the welfare state. This aimed to care for the people "from the cradle to the grave." It provided free medical treatment, family allowances, and insurance to help people who were ill or unemployed.

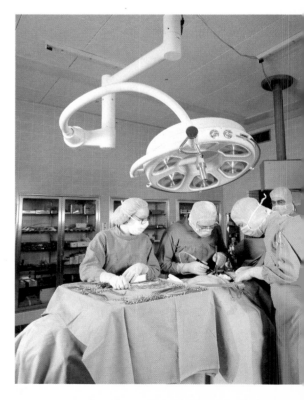

The German "Economic Miracle"

In 1949 the British, American, and French military occupied zones of Germany were joined together to create an independent Federal Republic of West Germany, with a parliament at Bonn. The Russian zone became the German Democratic Republic or East Germany. Neither side accepted that the division of Germany into two would be permanent.

Germany soon rebuilt its cities and recovered from the devastation of the war. With American aid new factories were built and equipped with the most modern machinery. The speed of the German recovery was astonishing. In 1946 production was a third of that before the war. By 1950 production was back to the prewar level, and Germany led Europe in the output of steel, electrical goods, and chemicals. By 1958 Germany had replaced Britain as the world's biggest exporter of manufactured goods after the United States. All this had been done by hard work, using the most up-to-date production methods, good design, and hard selling methods.

GENERAL DE GAULLE

Charles de Gaulle was one of the outstanding figures in the postwar West. After the fall of France in 1940 he escaped to England and led the "Free French" resistance to the Nazis. After the defeat of Germany he was elected president of France but resigned in ten weeks as the assembly would not give him the powers he wanted. For the next 12 years he lived in retirement, while weak governments followed one another.

By 1958 it appeared that army generals might try to seize power and that there would be civil war in France. De Gaulle was probably the only person who could prevent this. He returned as president and was given the powers he had wanted in 1945. He followed an independent foreign policy, withdrew France from NATO and became friendly with France's old enemy, Germany. Under de Gaulle there was settled government and French trade and industry did well. But people resented the high taxes needed to pay for France's nuclear bomb, while health, education, and the social services were neglected. There were student demonstrations and clashes with police in 1968, followed by nationwide strikes of workers. De Gaulle promised reforms and decided to appeal to the French people for a vote of confidence. Over 10 million voted in his favor, but 12 million voted against him. He resigned immediately and died a year later.

THE END OF DICTATORSHIPS

For more than 20 years after the war both Portugal and Spain were ruled by dictators. In 1974 a group of army officers seized power in Portugal, as they disliked the government's attempt to keep its African colonies. Civil war seemed likely, as conservative and radical groups in the army competed for control. This was avoided when a socialist government, with army support, took office after free elections in which no party gained a majority.

In 1975 General Franco, dictator of Spain since 1939, died. He had carefully prepared for Juan Carlos, grandson of the last king, to follow him as head of state. Soon political parties which opposed the government were allowed, and there were free elections for the first time in 40 years.

This picture of Hamburg shows how the largely ruined city has been rebuilt since World War II. The German economy has shown a similar rebirth.

Left: Charles de Gaulle, leader of the "Free French" and later president of France.

203

Communism since 1945

In 1939 the Soviet Union was the only communist country in the world. At the end of the war eastern Europe and North Korea became communist, as a result of Russian conquests. The greatest addition of all was China in 1949. At one stroke a quarter of all the people in the world had become communist. Communism spread farther in Southeast Asia to Vietnam, Laos, and Cambodia. Cuba became communist under Fidel Castro. In the 1970s African colonies fighting for independence, including Angola and Mozambique, were given aid and arms by Russia and Cuba.

The Soviet Union

No country suffered as much in World War II as the Soviet Union, where 8 million soldiers and 11 million civilians were killed. Much of industry and many cities were ruined. So in 1945 its leader, Stalin, wanted security against invasion. He gained this by taking over territory on Russia's western border and by setting up communist governments in eastern Europe – in Poland, East Germany, Romania, Hungary, and Bulgaria. In Yugoslavia a popular communist government arose under Marshal Tito out of the wartime resistance to Germany. Stalin did not like this, as Yugoslavia refused to take orders from him.

In Russia Stalin's dictatorship and purges continued (see page 187), but heavy industry was built up very quickly. By 1950 production was 40 percent more than in 1940. Then in 1953 Stalin died. At first power passed to the collective leadership of the *Politburo* (a small group at the top of the Communist party). Eventually Khrushchev appeared as the most important leader.

Agriculture was in a sorry state, so in 1954 Khrushchev announced his "Virgin Lands Scheme." Huge areas in Siberia and Kazakhstan were to be developed as state farms to grow wheat and maize, and half a million young people were to settle there. The scheme was a failure. There were good crops in 1956 and 1958 but in other years the harvest failed, as there was too little rainfall. Many of the "Virgin Lands" were allowed to return to pasture. Khrushchev was more successful with industry and production increased rapidly. Russia was also able to keep up with America in the space race; the first person in space was the Russian Yuri Gagarin.

Khrushchev was never a dictator like Stalin. He had to rely on the support of other members of the Politburo. He lost this support because of the failure of the "Virgin Lands Scheme," and because he backed down in the Cuban missile crisis (see page 201). In 1964 he was removed from office. The new leaders, Leonid Brezhnev and Alexei Kosygin, held their posts until Kosygin resigned in 1980 because of ill-health. When Brezhnev died in November 1982 he was followed by Andropov and Chernenko, both of whom soon died. It was then that Gorbachev took over, the fourth Russian leader in five years. The Soviet Union still has to buy huge quantities of wheat from the United States when harvests are bad. Soviet industry continued to grow and the standard of living to improve, as more consumer goods were produced. There was little freedom, but people were not shot if they criticized the government as in Stalin's time.

Eastern Europe

Russia took firm control of the communist states of eastern Europe and added Czechoslovakia after a communist coup in 1948. Their trade and industry were directed in Russia's interests by Comecon and their foreign policy by the Warsaw Pact (see page 202). Anyone suspected of being anti-Russian was ruthlessly dealt with. Between 1947 and 1952 all the communist parties of Eastern Europe were purged and many of their leaders executed. Discontent grew as the workers' living standards failed to get better. There were riots in 1953 in East Germany and in Poland in 1956. A rising in Hungary in 1956 was more serious. Thousands of political prisoners were released, and there was talk of allowing other political parties. Hungary threatened to withdraw from the Warsaw Pact and become a neutral state like Austria. The Russians crushed this rising savagely and showed that they would not allow any move to break away from the communist bloc.

The Russians felt threatened again in 1968 when Czechoslovakia's new leader, Alexander Dubcek, wanted communism "with a human face" and began far-reaching reforms. He said that Czechoslovakia would not leave the Warsaw Pact, but this did not save him. The Russians with their Warsaw Pact allies invaded Czechoslovakia and the reforms ended.

The latest expression of discontent in the communist bloc was in Poland in 1980, when shipyard workers at Gdansk went on strike and demanded free trade unions. They had much support, but in December 1982, the army clamped down, strikes were banned, and the workers lost their earlier gains.

CHRONOLOGY	
1948	Communist coup in Czechoslovakia
1953	Stalin dies
1954	Khrushchev begins the "Virgin Lands Scheme"
1956	Twentieth Party Congress in Russia: Khrushchev attacks Stalin. Riots in Poznam, Poland. Hungarian rising crushed by the Soviet Union
1957	Russia launches first *Sputnik*
1958	The Great Leap Forward in China
1960	Split between China and Russia
1961	First manned space flight by Russia
1964	Khrushchev is forced to retire
1966	The Cultural Revolution begins in China
1968	The "Prague Spring:" reforms of Dubcek in Czechoslovakia ended by Russian invasion
1976	Zhou En Lai and Mao Zedong die
1980	Workers strike in Gdansk, Poland, to gain free trade unions. Kosygin retires as Russian prime minister

A May Day parade in Moscow's Red Square, demonstrating the Soviet military strength.

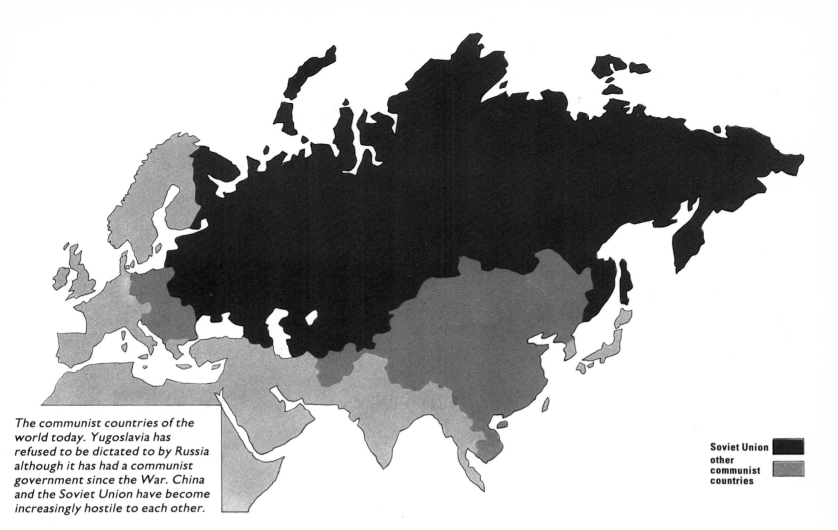

The communist countries of the world today. Yugoslavia has refused to be dictated to by Russia although it has had a communist government since the War. China and the Soviet Union have become increasingly hostile to each other.

Soviet Union ■
other communist countries ■

China

After the success of the communists in 1949 (see page 185) Mao Zedong began reorganizing China. Land was taken away from the rich landlords and given to the peasants. They were persuaded to join together in collective farms of 200 to 300 households. The Chinese followed the Soviet example of a Five-Year Plan and concentrated on heavy industry. Soon steel production had increased fourfold.

Mao was not satisfied. In 1958 he introduced the "Great Leap Forward," which aimed to help China to catch up with the West. The collective farms were joined together to form communes, each with about 25,000 people. These were to run not only agriculture but schools, medical services, a militia, and local industries. There was great enthusiasm and people worked hard digging canals and dams, but the movement got out of hand. Many people neglected their farming to build their own backyard furnaces, which produced steel of such poor quality that it could not be used.

In 1966 the Cultural Revolution again disrupted production, but in spite of this by 1973 China was the fifth largest steel producer in the world, and the third in coal. In 1976 Mao died. Soon Mao's wife and the rest of the "Gang of Four," who were responsible for some of the wildest ideas of the Cultural Revolution, were arrested. The new leaders set out to make China a more efficient country, and to improve relations with the West.

THE CULTURAL REVOLUTION

By 1966 Mao Zedong felt that party officials spent too much time giving orders and too little time working with the people. He wanted real equality, which meant that everybody, including university lecturers, scientists, students, and party officials, should spend part of each year working like a peasant on the land. There should be no privileges for the better educated. Schools and colleges were closed, factory managers replaced by revolutionary committees, and Communist party officials dismissed. In some areas there was chaos. By 1969 the movement had lost momentum but, in economic terms, it had done much harm and held up China's development.

Young Chinese bandsmen hold up little red books containing the Thoughts of Chairman Mao. Young people gave great support to Mao's Cultural Revolution.

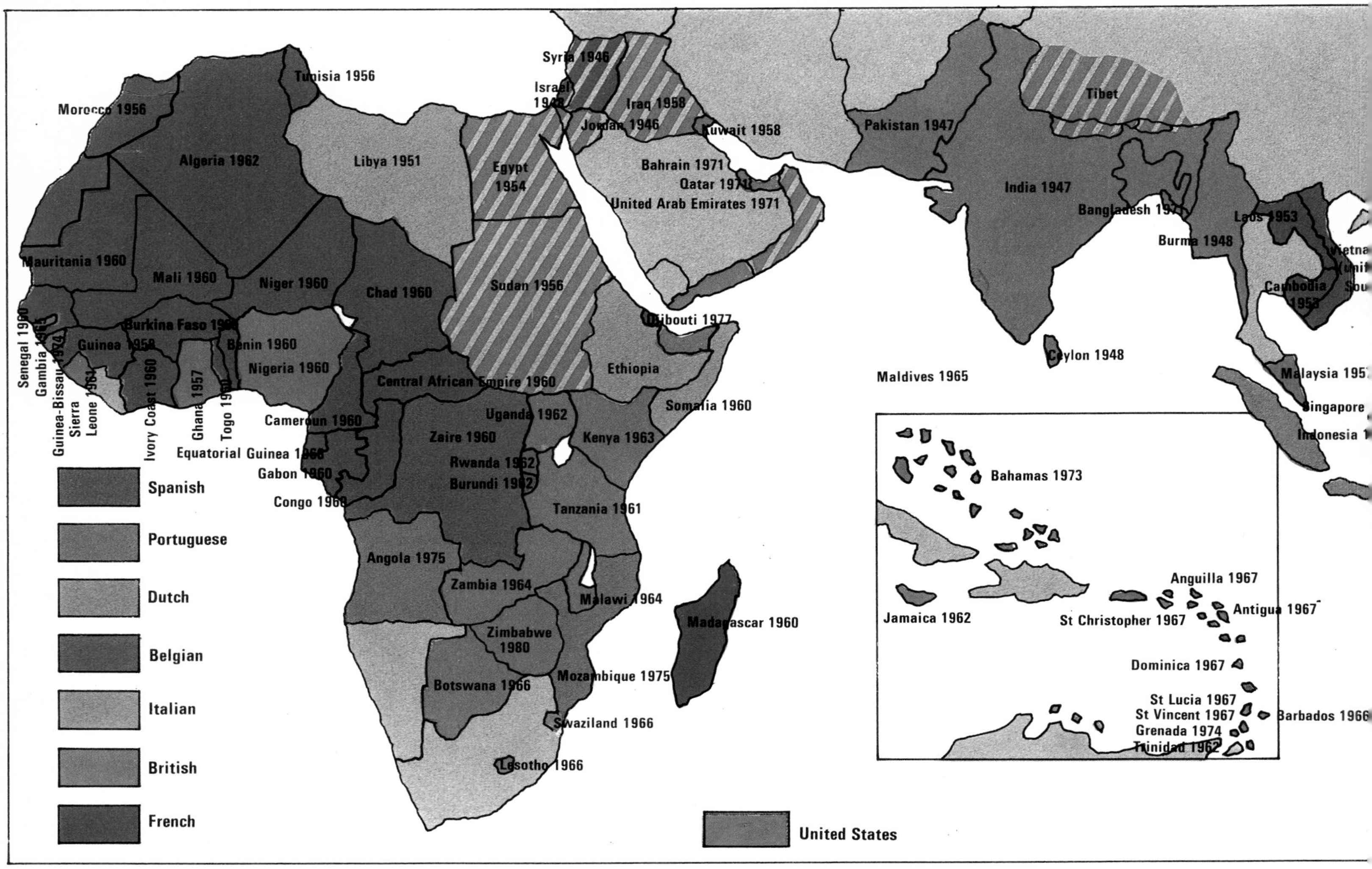
Morocco 1956
Tunisia 1956
Algeria 1962
Libya 1951
Egypt 1954
Syria 1946
Israel 1948
Iraq 1958
Jordan 1946
Kuwait 1958
Bahrain 1971
Qatar 1971
United Arab Emirates 1971
Pakistan 1947
Tibet
India 1947
Bangladesh 1971
Burma 1948
Laos 1953
Cambodia 1953
Mauritania 1960
Mali 1960
Niger 1960
Chad 1960
Sudan 1956
Djibouti 1977
Burkina Faso 1960
Benin 1960
Guinea 1958
Nigeria 1960
Ethiopia
Central African Empire 1960
Senegal 1960
Gambia 1965
Guinea-Bissau 1974
Sierra Leone 1961
Ivory Coast 1960
Ghana 1957
Togo 1960
Cameroun 1960
Uganda 1962
Somalia 1960
Zaire 1960
Kenya 1963
Equatorial Guinea 1968
Gabon 1960
Rwanda 1962
Burundi 1962
Congo 1960
Tanzania 1961
Angola 1975
Zambia 1964
Malawi 1964
Madagascar 1960
Zimbabwe 1980
Mozambique 1975
Botswana 1966
Swaziland 1966
Lesotho 1966
Maldives 1965
Ceylon 1948
Singapore
Bahamas 1973
Jamaica 1962
Anguilla 1967
St Christopher 1967
Antigua 1967
Dominica 1967
St Lucia 1967
St Vincent 1967
Grenada 1974
Trinidad 1962
Barbados 1966
Spanish
Portuguese
Dutch
Belgian
Italian
British
French
United States

Colonies Gain Independence

In 1939 Britain, France, the Netherlands, Italy, Belgium, Spain, and Portugal had colonies and intended to keep them. By 1975 these European empires had ceased to exist. Why did these colonies become independent so quickly? One reason was that in World War II Japan conquered the colonial territories of Malaya, Indochina, the Dutch East Indies, and Burma. By 1945 widely supported nationalist movements had grown up there which did not intend to allow the colonial powers to take back control. Though African colonies had not been overrun, nationalist movements grew up there too. Their leaders were Western-educated lawyers, civil servants, teachers, and clergymen. They had been trained in England or France to be democrats, but saw that there was no democracy in their own countries. As each colony became independent, it encouraged others to seek independence and persuaded European powers that there was no point in trying to hang on to their colonies.

India

Indian nationalists had long been pressing for independence, and after the war the British decided to grant it. The main problem was the Muslims who did not want to be part of an India ruled by Hindus. The viceroy, Lord Mountbatten, arranged that the land would be divided: India for the Hindus and Sikhs, Pakistan for the Muslims. In 1949 India and Pakistan became independent states. Appalling massacres of religious minorities immediately took place. Half a million people were killed and millions fled for safety, Hindus from Pakistan to India and Muslims to Pakistan.

CHRONOLOGY

1946	**Jordan and Syria and the Philippines independent**
1947	**India and Pakistan independent**
1948	**Ceylon (Sri Lanka) and Burma independent. State of Israel formed**
1949	**Dutch East Indies become new state of Indonesia**
1953	**Laos and Cambodia independent**
1954	**French withdraw from Vietnam, divided into Communist North and American-supported South**
1956	**Morocco, Tunisia, and Sudan independent**
1957	**Gold Coast (Ghana) and Malaya independent (Malaysia formed 1963)**
1960	**Independence of many former colonies in West and Central Africa now and in the next few years**
1963	**Nyasaland (Malawi) and Kenya independent**
1964	**Northern Rhodesia becomes Zambia Tanzania formed when Tanganyika and Zanzibar join**
1965	**Ian Smith declares independence of Rhodesia from Britain (UDI)**
1967	**Nigerian civil war (to 1970)**
1975	**End of Portuguese empire with independence of Angola and Mozambique**
1980	**Rhodesia gains independence as Zimbabwe**

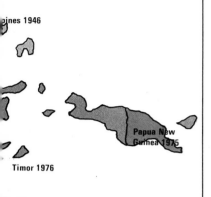

The newly independent countries, with their dates of independence. The colors show the former colonial powers; striped areas are those of colonial influence.

ɔines 1946

Papua New Guinea 1975

Timor 1976

The uniforms of the Bahamas police are a reminder of the island's years as a British colony. The islands of the West Indies have gained their independence peacefully since World War II, though efforts to group them in federations have proved unsuccessful.

Southeast Asia

The Japanese conquest of Southeast Asia had shown that the European colonists could be overthrown, and it soon became clear that the prewar pattern had been swept away for good. When the Dutch moved back into the East Indies they had to fight the nationalists. This was very expensive and not very successful, so in 1949 the 3,000 islands and 80 million people of the Dutch East Indies became the independent republic of Indonesia.

In Indochina the Japanese had been opposed by communists, led by Ho Chi Minh. When the French returned he fought a bitter war against them, ending with their defeat at Dien Bien Phu. In 1954 the Geneva Conference was called by Britain, France, the United States, and the Soviet Union. As a result Vietnam became independent, with a communist state in the north and a noncommunist one in the south. Laos and Cambodia, the rest of French Indochina, also became independent.

The Burmese National Army had helped the British to drive out the Japanese and in 1948 Burma gained independence. In Malaya, communist freedom fighters turned against the British after the war and fought against them and the other Malays until 1960. Meanwhile the British went ahead with plans for Malaya's independence which it gained in 1957.

Africa

In Africa, more than anywhere else, the boundaries of the colonies had been determined by the colonists. They had little to do with the histories of the regions, and many countries contained people with different languages and traditions. Tribal groups and languages spread across national borders. What gave the countries some sense of unity was their dislike of their foreign rulers. As a result the new political parties that were formed all demanded independence.

In many countries the colonial power began to grant the local people an increasing say in government. The British colonies in West Africa were prosperous and there

were many well-educated Africans. Ghana, Nigeria, and Sierra Leone were soon allowed internal self-government and moved on an agreed timetable toward independence.

In 1956 France, anxious to use its forces in the war against nationalists in Algeria, gave independence to Morocco and Tunisia. In 1958 de Gaulle offered the French colonies membership of the French Community. Guinea opted out and other countries quickly followed. By the end of 1960 all the French colonies in West and equatorial Africa were independent. Belgium hurriedly abandoned the Belgian Congo (Zaire) to civil war.

In other parts of Africa the situation was different. In some East and Central African colonies were white settlers who resisted a take-over by Africans. In Kenya nationalist fighters known as *Mau Mau* attacked white farmers and Africans who were loyal to them. Despite this, plans for independence went ahead, and in the early 1960s the British colonies in East and Central Africa became independent.

In Algeria too there were many French settlers, or *colons*. They refused to allow the Arabs any share in government and a terrible civil war broke out, with both sides torturing and murdering their opponents. It seemed as though the army, which took power in Algeria in 1958, might try to seize power in France itself. The French people turned to General de Gaulle, who became president. To end the war he settled with the Algerians and the country gained independence in 1962. The *colons* felt that he had betrayed them.

The first colonists of Africa, the Portuguese, were the last to give up their colonies, although these were very costly to defend against guerilla forces. But in 1974 the government in Portugal was overthrown by the army, which quickly gave the colonies of Guinea (Bissau), Angola, and Mozambique independence.

After independence the countries of Africa faced great problems of economic and political underdevelopment. These led in some countries to a series of coups, and in Nigeria to civil war. But in many other countries the leaders who brought their nations to independence are still securely in command.

The signing of the Rhodesia (Zimbabwe) ceasefire agreement in December 1979. On the right is Robert Mugabe, who became the first black prime minister in 1980. Rhodesia had had internal self-government since 1923. Its white rulers refused to agree to majority rule (which would obviously be black) and in 1965 declared their country independent. Britain could not agree. It was 15 years before international pressure and a guerilla war inside the country led to independence under a government elected by a majority of the people.

The World Today

The world is dominated by two "superpowers," Russia and the United States. Since 1945 they have competed for influence through the world and have built up a stock of nuclear arms which could destory the world. Europe is separated into the communist east under Russian control, and the democratic west where the Common Market has helped to bring prosperity to its members. Former colonies in Africa, Southeast Asia, and the West Indies have become independent. China has become communist (as have much of Southeast Asia and Cuba) but has disagreed with Russia. Japan is now third in the world in production. The wealth of the oil-producing countries of the Near East has increased enormously.

America The United States leads the West against communism, and through NATO and its nuclear weapons protects western
∾ Europe from communist attack. Much of Latin America is still poor, though some countries, such as Brazil, have great natural wealth.

Africa is almost wholly independent, though Southwest Africa (Namibia) is still ruled by South Africa. The whites in Zimbabwe (Rhodesia) have been forced to accept majority African rule and a black prime minister.

Europe The Common Market brings prosperity to most of its members. The east European states are communist and are dominated by Russia.

Russia's industry continues to grow but agriculture is less successful.

The Far East Japan is an economic "superpower," whose manufactured goods are sold all over the world. China is a communist state and the life of the ordinary peasant has grown better. Relations with the West have improved. The countries of Indochina – Laos, Cambodia, and Vietnam – are torn by terrible wars as the communists take over.

The Near East Saudi Arabia, a poor country 50 years ago, has larger oil deposits than any other country and is now very rich. The Jewish state of Israel survives, though surrounded by hostile Arab countries. Iran is in a troubled state after the overthrow of the shah and the setting up of an Islamic republic; in 1980 war breaks out with Iraq. Russian troops have occupied Afghanistan and set up their own communist puppet ruler.

Australia has grown prosperous through agriculture and by exploiting its great mineral wealth.

Finland

Union of Soviet Socialist Republics

Denmark

ermany
oland

W. Germany

Czechoslovakia
Hungary
Romania
slavia
Bulgaria

Mongolian People's Republic

Albania
Greece
Turkey

N. Korea
S. Korea
Japan

alta
Cyprus Lebanon
Israel Syria
Jordan Iraq
Iran
Afghanistan

China

ya
Egypt
Bahrain
Qatar
United Arab Emirates
Saudi Arabia
Oman

Pakistan

Nepal
Bhutan

Taiwan

Hong Kong

Guam

Sudan
Yemen
PDR
Djibouti

India

Bangladesh

Laos
Burma
Thailand
Vietnam
Kampuchea

Central
can Republic

Ethiopia

Sri Lanka

Philippines

Zaire Uganda
Rwanda Kenya
Burundi

Somali Republic

Malaysia
Singapore

Tanzania

Indonesia

Papua New Guinea
Solomon Is.

ola Malawi
Zambia
Zimbabwe
Botswana

Mozambique

Madagascar

Swaziland
h Africa Lesotho

Australia

New Zealand

Reference Tables

MAJOR WARS

Date	Name	Won by	Against
431–404 B.C.	Peloponnesian War	Peloponnesian League, led by Sparta, Corinth	Delian League, led by Athens
264–146 B.C.	Punic Wars	Rome	Carthage
1337–1453	Hundred Years' War	France	England
1455–1485	Wars of the Roses	House of Lancaster	House of York
1618–1648	Thirty Years' War	France, Sweden, German Protestant states	The Holy Roman Empire, Spain
1642–1648	English Civil War	Parliament	Charles I
1701–1713	War of the Spanish Succession	England, Austria, Prussia, Netherlands	France, Bavaria, Cologne, Mantua, Savoy
1740–1748	War of the Austrian Succession	Austria, Hungary, Britain, Holland	Bavaria, France, Poland, Prussia, Sardinia, Saxony, Spain
1756–1763	Seven Years' War	Britain, Prussia, Hanover	Austria, France, Russia, Sweden
1775–1783	American Revolutionary War	Thirteen Colonies	Britain
1792–1815	Napoleonic Wars	Austria, Britain, Prussia, Russia, Spain, Sweden	France
1812–1814	War of 1812	United States	Britain
1846–1848	Mexican-American War	United States	Mexico
1854–1856	Crimean War	Britain, France, Sardinia, Turkey	Russia
1861–1865	American Civil War	23 Northern states (the Union)	11 Southern states (the Confederacy)
1870–1871	Franco-Prussian War	Prussia and other German states	France
1894–1895	Chinese-Japanese War (1st)	Japan	China
1898	Spanish-American War	United States	Spain
1899–1902	Boer (South African) War	Britain	Boer Republics
1904–1905	Russo-Japanese War	Japan	Russia
1914–1918	World War I	Belgium, Britain and Empire, France, Italy, Japan, Russia, Serbia, United States	Austria-Hungary, Bulgaria, Germany, Ottoman Empire
1931–1933	Chinese-Japanese War (2nd)	Japan	China
1935–1936	Abyssinian War	Italy	Abyssinia (Ethiopia)
1936–1939	Spanish Civil War	Junta de Defensa Nacional (Fascists)	Republican government
1937–1945	Chinese-Japanese War (3rd)	China	Japan
1939–1945	World War II	Australia, Belgium, Britain, Canada, China, Denmark, France, Greece, Netherlands, New Zealand, Norway, Poland, Russia, South Africa, United States, Yugoslavia	Bulgaria, Finland, Germany, Hungary, Italy, Japan, Romania
1950–1953	Korean War	South Korea and United Nations forces	North Korea and Chinese forces
1957–1975	Vietnam War	North Vietnam	South Vietnam, United States
1967	Six-Day War	Israel	Egypt, Syria, Jordan, Iraq
1967–1970	Nigerian Civil War	Federal Government	Biafra
1971	Pakistani Civil War	East Pakistan (Bangladesh) and India	West Pakistan
1973·	Yom Kippur War	Ceasefire arranged by United Nations: fought by Israel against Egypt, Syria, Iraq, Jordan, Sudan, Saudi Arabia, Lebanon	

MAJOR BATTLES

GREEKS AND ROMANS

Marathon 490 B.C. Force of 10,000 Athenians and allies defeated 50,000 Persian troops, crushing a Persian invasion attempt.
Salamis 480 B.C. Greek fleet of 360 ships defeated Persian fleet of 1,000 ships. Persians had to withdraw from Greece.
Arbela 331 B.C. Alexander the Great's Greek army defeated a Persian force twice the size and conquered Persia.
Actium 31 B.C. Roman fleet of 400 ships under Octavian (later Emperor Augustus) defeated 500 ships, the combined fleet of Mark Antony and Cleopatra.
Châlons-sur-Marne 451 Romans and Visigoths defeated the Huns led by Attila.

EARLY EUROPE

Tours 732 The Franks under Charles Martel defeated the Saracens (Muslims), halting their advance in western Europe.
Lech 955 Emperor Otto the Great ended the Magyar threat in western Europe.
Hastings 1066 About 8,000 troops under Duke William of Normandy defeated an equal force under Saxon king Harold II. England soon came under Norman rule.
Crécy 1346 Invading army of 10,000 English defeated 20,000 French. English archers won the day.
Agincourt 1415 Henry V of England with 10,000 troops defeated 30,000 Frenchmen and recaptured Normandy.
Siege of Orléans 1428–1429 English troops began siege in October 1428, but in April 1429 Joan of Arc came to the aid of the city and forced the besiegers to withdraw.
Siege of Constantinople 1453 Ottoman Turkish army of more than 100,000 captured the city, held by 10,000 men.

WARS OF FAITH AND SUCCESSION

Lepanto 1571 Allied Christian fleet of 208 galleys defeated Ali Pasha's Turkish fleet of 230 galleys.
Armada 1588 Spanish invasion fleet defeated by the English.
Boyne 1690 William III of England with 35,000 troops routed his rival, James II, with 21,000 men.
Blenheim 1704 A British-Austrian army led by Duke of Marlborough and Prince Eugène defeated the French and Bavarians during the War of the Spanish Succession.

COLONIAL STRUGGLES

Plassey 1757 Robert Clive with an Anglo-Indian army of 3,000 defeated the Nawab of Bengal's army of 60,000, conquering Bengal and setting Britain on the road to domination in India.
Quebec 1759 British troops under James Wolfe made a night attack up the St. Lawrence River. They defeated the French forces under the Marquis de Montcalm. Montcalm and Wolfe were killed.

Yorktown 1781 8,000 British troops surrendered to a larger force under George Washington. American Revolutionary War ended.

AGE OF NAPOLEON
Trafalgar 1805 British fleet of 27 ships under Nelson shattered Franco-Spanish fleet of 33 ships. Nelson was killed. Napoleon's hopes of invading England ended.
Austerlitz 1805 Emperor Napoleon I with 65,000 French troops defeated an 83,000-strong Austro-Russian army under the Austrian and Russian emperors.
Jena and Auerstädt 1806 French forces routed the main Prussian armies on the same day (October 14), shattering Prussian power.
Waterloo 1815 A British, Dutch, and Belgian force of 67,000 fought off 74,000 French troops under Napoleon I until the arrival of Blücher's Prussian army. It ended Napoleon's final bid for power.

WORLD WAR I
Marne 1914 French and British armies halted German forces invading France.
First battle of Ypres 1914 German forces trying to reach Calais lost 150,000 men. British and French forces held off attack, losing more than 100,000 men.
Verdun 1916 In a six-month struggle French forces held off a major attack by German armies. French losses were 348,000; German losses 328,000.
Jutland 1916 British Grand Fleet fought German High Seas Fleet. The Germans did not again venture out to sea.
Somme 1916 In a 141-day battle following Verdun, the British and French captured 320 sq km (125 sq miles) of ground, losing 600,000 men. The German defenders lost almost 500,000 men.
Passchendaele 1917 British forces launched eight attacks over 102 days in heavy rain and through thick mud. They gained 8 km (5 miles) and lost 400,000 men.

WORLD WAR II
Britain 1940 A German air force of 2,500 planes launched an attack lasting 114 days to try to win air supremacy over Britain. The smaller Royal Air Force defeated the attack.
Midway 1942 A fleet of 100 Japanese ships was defeated in the Pacific by an American fleet half the size.
El Alamein 1942 Montgomery's British Eighth Army drove Rommel's German Afrika Korps out of Egypt and deep into Libya.
Stalingrad 1942–1943 Twenty-one German divisions tried to capture Stalingrad (now Volgograd), but siege was broken and more than 100,000 German troops surrendered.
Normandy 1944 Allied forces under Eisenhower invaded German-held northern France in biggest-ever seaborne attack. After a month of fighting Germans retreated.
Leyte Gulf 1944 United States 3rd and 7th fleets defeated a Japanese force, ending Japanese naval power in World War II.
Ardennes Bulge 1944–1945 Last German counter-attack in west through Ardennes Forest failed. Germans lost 100,000 casualties and 110,000 prisoners.

FAMOUS ROMAN EMPERORS

	Reigned		Reigned
Augustus (Octavian)	27 B.C.–A.D. 14	Diocletian	284–305
Tiberius	14–37	Maximian	286–305
Caligula (Gaius)	37–41	Constantine the Great	311–337
Claudius	41–54		
Nero	54–68	Valentinian I (in the West)	364–375
		Valens (in the East)	364–378
Vespasian	69–79		
Titus	79–81	Theodosius, the Great (in the East, and after 394, in the West)	379–395
Trajan	98–117		
Hadrian	117–138	Honorius (in the West)	395–423
Antoninus Pius	138–161		
Marcus Aurelius	161–180	Theodosius II (in the East)	408–450
		Valentinian III (in the West)	425–455
Septimius Severus	193–211		
		Zeno (in the East)	474–491
Alexander Severus	222–235	Romulus Augustulus (in the West)	475–476
Valerian	253–259		

HOLY ROMAN EMPERORS

FRANKISH KINGS AND EMPERORS (CAROLINGIAN)

	Reigned
Charlemagne	800–814
Louis I, the Pious	814–840
Lothair I	840–855
Louis II	855–875
Charles II, the Bald	875–877
Throne vacant	877–881
Charles III, the Fat	881–887
Throne vacant	887–891
Guido of Spoleto	891–894
Lambert of Spoleto (co-emperor)	892–898
Arnulf (rival)	896–901
Louis III of Provence	901–905
Berengar	905–924
Conrad I of Franconia (rival)	911–918

SAXON KINGS AND EMPERORS

Henry I, the Fowler	918–936
Otto I, the Great	936–973
Otto II	973–983
Otto III	983–1002
Henry II, the Saint	1002–1024

FRANCONIAN EMPERORS (SALIAN)

Conrad II, the Salian	1024–1039
Henry III, the Black	1039–1056
Henry IV	1056–1106
Rudolf of Swabia (rival)	1077–1080
Hermann of Luxemburg (rival)	1081–1093
Conrad of Franconia (rival)	1093–1101
Henry V	1106–1125
Lothair II	1125–1137

HOHENSTAUFEN KINGS AND EMPERORS

Conrad III	1138–1152
Frederick I Barbarossa	1152–1190
Henry VI	1190–1197
Otto IV	1198–1215
Philip of Swabia (rival)	1198–1208
Frederick II	1215–1250

	Reigned
Henry Raspe (rival)	1246–1247
William of Holland (rival)	1247–1256
Conrad IV	1250–1254
The Great Interregnum	1254–1273

RULERS FROM DIFFERENT HOUSES

Richard of Cornwall (rival)	1257–1272
Alfonso X of Castile (rival)	1257–1273
Rudolf I, Habsburg	1273–1291
Adolf I of Nassau	1292–1298
Albert I, Habsburg	1298–1308
Henry VII, Luxemburg	1308–1313
Louis IV of Bavaria	1314–1347
Frederick of Habsburg (co-regent)	1314–1325
Charles IV, Luxemburg	1347–1378
Wenceslas of Bohemia	1378–1400
Frederick III of Brunswick	1400
Rupert of the Palatinate	1400–1410
Sigismund, Luxemburg	1410–1437

HABSBURG EMPERORS

Albert II	1438–1439
Frederick III	1440–1493
Maximilian I	1493–1519
Charles V	1519–1558
Ferdinand I	1558–1564
Maximilian II	1564–1576
Rudolf II	1576–1612
Matthias	1612–1619
Ferdinand II	1619–1637
Ferdinand III	1637–1657
Leopold I	1658–1705
Joseph I	1507–1711
Charles VI	1711–1740
Charles VII of Bavaria	1742–1745

HABSBURG-LORRAINE EMPERORS

Francis I of Lorraine	1745–1765
Joseph II	1765–1790
Leopold II	1790–1792
Francis II	1792–1806

BRITISH RULERS

Rulers of England (to 1603)

Saxons

Egbert	827–839
Ethelwulf	839–858
Ethelbald	858–860
Ethelbert	860–865
Ethelred I	865–871
Alfred the Great	871–899
Edward the Elder	899–924
Athelstan	924–939
Edmund	939–946
Edred	946–955
Edwy	955–959
Edgar	959–975
Edward the Martyr	975–978
Ethelred II the Unready	978–1016
Edmund Ironside	1016

Danes

Canute	1016–1035
Harold I Harefoot	1035–1040
Hardicanute	1040–1042

Saxons

Edward the Confessor	1042–1066
Harold II	1066

House of Normandy

William the Conqueror	1066–1087
William II	1087–1100
Henry I	1100–1135
Stephen	1135–1154

House of Plantagenet

Henry II	1154–1189
Richard I	1189–1199
John	1199–1216
Henry III	1216–1272
Edward I	1272–1307
Edward II	1307–1327
Edward III	1327–1377
Richard II	1377–1399

House of Lancaster

Henry IV	1399–1413
Henry V	1413–1422
Henry VI	1422–1461

House of York

Edward IV	1461–1483
Edward V	1483
Richard III	1483–1485

House of Tudor

Henry VII	1485–1509
Henry VIII	1509–1547
Edward VI	1547–1553
Mary I	1553–1558
Elizabeth I	1558–1603

Rulers of Scotland (to 1603)

Malcolm II	1005–1034
Dunclan I	1034–1040
Macbeth	1040–1057
Malcolm III Canmore	1058–1093
Donald Bane	1093–1094
Duncan II	1094
Donald Bane (restored)	1094–1097
Edgar	1097–1107
Alexander I	1107–1124
David I	1124–1153
Malcolm IV	1153–1165
William the Lion	1165–1214
Alexander II	1214–1249
Alexander III	1249–1286
Margaret of Norway	1286–1290
John Baliol	1292–1296
Robert I (Bruce)	1306–1329
David II	1329–1371

House of Stuart

Robert II	1371–1390
Robert III	1390–1406
James I	1406–1437
James II	1437–1460
James III	1460–1488
James IV	1488–1513
James V	1513–1542
Mary	1542–1567
James VI (James I of England)	1567–1625

Rulers of Britain

House of Stuart

James I	1603–1625
Charles I	1625–1649
Commonwealth	1649–1660
Charles II	1660–1685
James II	1685–1688
William III ⎫ jointly	1689–1702
Mary II ⎭	1689–1694
Anne	1702–1714

House of Hanover

George I	1714–1727
George II	1727–1760
George III	1760–1820
George IV	1820–1830
William IV	1830–1837
Victoria	1837–1901

House of Saxe-Coburg

Edward VII	1901–1910

House of Windsor

George V	1910–1936
Edward VIII	1936
George VI	1936–1952
Elizabeth II	1952–

AMERICAN PRESIDENTS

F = Federalist; DR = Democratic-Republican; D = Democratic; W = Whig; R = Republican; U = Union

		Term
1	George Washington (F)	1789–1797
2	John Adams (F)	1797–1801
3	Thomas Jefferson (DR)	1801–1809
4	James Madison (DR)	1809–1817
5	James Monroe (DR)	1817–1825
6	John Quincy Adams (DR)	1825–1829
7	Andrew Jackson (D)	1829–1837
8	Martin Van Buren (D)	1837–1841
9	William H. Harrison* (W)	1841
10	John Tyler (W)	1841–1845
11	James K. Polk (D)	1845–1849
12	Zachary Taylor* (W)	1849–1850
13	Millard Fillmore (W)	1850–1853
14	Franklin Pierce (D)	1853–1857
15	James Buchanan (D)	1857–1861
16	Abraham Lincoln† (R)	1861–1865
17	Andrew Johnson (U)	1865–1869
18	Ulysses S. Grant (R)	1869–1877
19	Rutherford B. Hayes (R)	1877–1881
20	James A. Garfield† (R)	1881
21	Chester A. Arthur (R)	1881–1885
22	Grover Cleveland (D)	1885–1889
23	Benjamin Harrison (R)	1889–1893
24	Grover Cleveland (D)	1893–1897
25	William McKinley† (R)	1897–1901
26	Theodore Roosevelt (R)	1901–1909
27	William H. Taft (R)	1909–1913
28	Woodrow Wilson (D)	1913–1921
29	Warren G. Harding* (R)	1921–1923
30	Calvin Coolidge (R)	1923–1929
31	Herbert C. Hoover (R)	1929–1933
32	Franklin D. Roosevelt* (D)	1933–1945
33	Harry S. Truman (D)	1945–1953
34	Dwight D. Eisenhower (R)	1953–1961
35	John F. Kennedy† (D)	1961–1963
36	Lyndon B. Johnson (D)	1963–1969
37	Richard M. Nixon (R)	1969–1974
38	Gerald R. Ford (R)	1974–1977
39	Jimmy Carter (D)	1977–1981
40	Ronald Reagan (R)	1981–

*Died in office
†Assassinated in office

RULERS OF FRANCE

Hugh Capet	987–996
Robert II, the Pious	996–1031
Henri I	1031–1060
Philip I	1060–1108
Louis VI, the Fat	1108–1137
Louis VII, the Young	1137–1180
Philip II Augustus	1180–1223
Louis VIII	1223–1226
Louix IX, Saint Louis	1226–1270
Philip III, the Bold	1270–1285
Philip IV, the Fair	1285–1314
Louis X	1314–1316
John I	1316
Philip V	1316–1322
Charles IV	1322–1328
Philip VI	1328–1350
John II	1350–1364
Charles V	1364–1380
Charles VI	1380–1422
Charles VII	1422–1461
Louis XI	1461–1483
Charles VIII	1483–1498
Louis XII	1498–1515
François I	1515–1547
Henry II	1547–1559
François II	1559–1560
Charles IX	1560–1574
Henri III	1574–1589
Henri IV	1589–1610
Louis XIII	1610–1643
Louis XIV	1643–1715
Louis XV	1715–1774
Louis XVI	1774–1792
The First Republic	1792–1804
Napoleon I (Emperor)	1804–1814
Louis XVIII	1814–1824
Charles X	1824–1830
Louis Philippe	1830–1848
The Second Republic	1848–1852
Napoleon III (Emperor)	1852–1870

People in History

A

Agricola, Gnaeus Julius (A.D. 37–93) Roman soldier, governor of Britain 78–84. Carried Roman conquest to the farthest northern point of the empire, when he defeated Caledonians at Mt. Graupius near Aberdeen in 83.

Alaric (A.D. 370–410) Leader of the Visigoths, ravaged Thrace to the gates of Constantinople at the end of the 4th century. In 410 Alaric sacked Rome. He died soon after in southern Italy.

Alexander the Great (356–323 B.C.) Became king of Macedon at the age of 20 and then set out to conquer the world. By 323, his empire stretched from Greece to the Indus River in Northwest India and south to include Egypt. Perhaps the world's greatest military commander.

Archimedes (287–212 B.C.) Greek mathematician and engineer, discovered principles of buoyancy and the lever. Calculated accurate value of pi (ratio of circle's circumference to its diameter). His military defensive devices prolonged the siege of Syracuse by the Romans. He was reputedly killed by a Roman soldier because he would not stop the experiment upon which he was working when the Romans broke into the city.

Atatürk, Kemal (1881–1938) Turkish general and statesman, founder of modern Turkey. Atatürk was a general in World War I. He overthrew the Sultan and turned Turkey into a republic, becoming its president in 1923. He made Turkey secular, forbade the wearing of the fez (hat), and discouraged women from using the veil.

B

Baber (1483–1530) Mongol descendant of Genghis Khan, he became ruler at Kabul at the age of 21. From there set out upon the conquest of northern India to establish the Mughal empire, which lasted until the coming of the British to India in the 18th century.

Becket, Thomas à (1118–1170) Friend and Chancellor of Henry II. The king made him Archbishop of Canterbury, but he then quarreled with the king over the balance of church and state power. He was murdered in Canterbury Cathedral by followers of the king. Subsequently he was made a saint.

Bede, the Venerable (A.D. 673–735) English monk and scholar. His *History of the English Church and People*, written in medieval Latin, is one of the first source books of English history. It was translated into English by King Alfred the Great.

Bismarck, Prince Otto von (1815–1898) Prussian statesman, prime minister of Prussia and then Germany from 1862 to 1890. He is the creator of modern, united Germany. He was known as the "Iron Chancellor."

Boadicea (died A.D. 62) Queen of the Iceni tribe of Britain, she revolted against the Roman occupation. Only defeated after a major campaign that endangered Roman control of Britain.

Buddha (Siddhartha Gautama) (563–483 B.C.) Well-born Indian who renounced worldly pleasures and sat under a *bodhi* tree until mysteries of life were revealed to him. His followers are called Buddhists.

Burton, Sir Richard (1821–1890) Eccentric British traveler and explorer. One of first Europeans to enter Mecca, Islam's most holy city. Discovered Lake Tanganyika with John Speke. Wrote more than 50 books including a famous translation of the *Arabian Nights*.

C

Canute (994–1035) Son of Sweyn Forkbeard of Denmark. King of England from 1016 to his death. Strong king who restored order to the country after a period of weakness. The famous story of Canute telling the sea to stop has often been misunderstood. He wished to demonstrate the limit of kingly power to foolish courtiers, who said he could do anything.

Castro, Fidel (1927–) Cuban Marxist who overthrew President Batista in 1959 and became prime minister.

Catherine II, the Great (1729–1796) Deposed her mad husband Tsar Peter III of Russia and became empress in 1762. Strengthened power of nobility; captured Crimea, Black Sea coast, and much of Poland.

Charles V (1500–1558) Holy Roman emperor from 1519. King of Spain as Charles I from 1516. Ruled over more of Europe than any other Habsburg. Abdicated in 1556.

Charles Martel (A.D. 688–741) Frankish ruler of Austrasia from 715 to 741.

Halted Muslim advance into western Europe at battle of Tours in 732.

Cheops (c. 2600 B.C.) Egyptian King. He had the Great Pyramid built, the largest stone monument in the world. It contains 2,300,000 blocks of stone with an average weight of two-and-a-half tons each.

Chiang Kai-shek (1888–1975) Chinese Nationalist leader who succeeded Sun Yat-sen in 1925 as leader of the Kuomintang (Nationalist Party). He and his followers were forced from China by the victorious communists under Mao Tse-tung in 1949. He established a Nationalist government on Formosa (Taiwan).

Churchill, Winston S. (1874–1965) British soldier, statesman, and author. First Lord of Admiralty from 1911 to 1915 and from 1930 to 1940. Chancellor of Exchequer from 1924 to 1929. Britain's wartime prime minister from 1940 to 1945 and again from 1951 to 1955. He won the Nobel prize for literature in 1953.

Cleopatra VII (69–30 B.C.) Ptolemaic queen of Egypt from 51 to 30 B.C. Julius Caesar supported her against a rival claimant to the throne. She fell in love with Caesar and bore him a son. After Caesar's death, she became the wife of Marcus Antonius. She committed suicide in 30 B.C. Her great beauty is probably exaggerated, but she used it to keep her throne.

Clive, Robert (1725–1774) British soldier who did much to bring India under British control in the 18th century. Governor of Bengal from 1764 to 1767. On his return to England he was censured for misgovernment and corruption, and said that in retrospect he was astonished at his own moderation. Committed suicide.

Columbus, Christopher (1451–1506). Genoese navigator who discovered Cuba (the New World) in 1492. Made four trips to New World but never realized he had found a new continent. Died in poverty.

Confucius (K'ung Fu-tzu) (c. 561–479 B.C.) Chinese philosopher who preached absolute justice and moderation. The *Analeae* are his collected sayings. Confucianism has been the greatest influence upon Chinese thinking.

Cook, James (1728–1779) British navigator. First person to sail south of Antarctic Circle. Explored Pacific, charting coasts of New Zealand and Australia.

Cortes, Hernando (1485–1547) Greatest Spanish *Conquistadore*. He conquered Mexico (the Aztecs) in 1521 with only 550 men. He ruled as governor until 1530.

Cromwell, Oliver (1599–1658) Leader of the Roundhead (Parliamentary) faction in the civil war in England. Brilliant soldier and great statesman. Had Charles I executed and ruled as Lord Protector of England from 1653 to 1658.

Cyrus (600–529 B.C.) King of Persia and founder of the Persian empire. He overthrew Croesus and conquered Babylon, freeing the Jews from captivity there.

D

Danton, Georges Jacques (1759–1794) Lawyer and revolutionary who became a leader in the French Revolution of 1789. He helped organize the Reign of Terror and was himself guillotined by Robespierre.

Darwin, Charles Robert (1805–1882) English naturalist whose major work, *The Origin of Species*, proposed the theory of evolution by natural selection. This was utterly opposed to the ideas of the Church and caused major controversy.

Davy, Sir Humphry (1778–1829) English chemist who was also an inventor, best remembered for his miners' (Davy) lamp. Using electrolysis he isolated potassium, sodium, barium, strontium, and magnesium. Proved chlorine to be an element.

De Gaulle, Charles (1890–1970) French general and statesman. Only French soldier who successfully withstood the German panzer tank tactics of 1940. After the fall of France in 1940 he organized the Free French movement from London. President of France from 1945 to 1946 and during the important period from 1956 to 1969, with a new constitution (the Fifth Republic). Granted full independence to France's African colonies in 1960 and ended the war in Algeria in 1962.

Drake, Sir Francis (1541–1596) English adventurer who plundered Spanish settlements in America. Sailed around the world from 1577 to 1580. Burned a Spanish fleet at Cadiz in 1587 and helped to defeat the Spanish Armada in 1588. He died in the West Indies.

E

Edward the Black Prince (1330–1376) Son of Edward III, he won his spurs at the Battle of Crécy. Regarded as the greatest knight of his age. He died a year before his father, and his son became king of England as Richard II.

Einstein, Albert (1879–1955) German-born American physicist who made the greatest scientific advances since Newton over 200 years earlier. In 1905 used quantum theory to explain photoelectric effect, produced famous $E = mc^2$ equation relating mass to energy, explained Browning movement thus confirming atomic theory of matter, and expounded special theory of relativity. Published general theory of relativity in 1916 (replaced Newton's gravitational theory) and unified field theory in 1929. Became Swiss citizen in 1901; American, 1940 (as a Jew he could not work in Germany in the 1930s). Reluctantly persuaded President Roosevelt to begin atomic research in 1939. Fought for world peace. Won Nobel prize for physics in 1921.

Ericsson, Lief (c. A.D. 970–?) Viking explorer who crossed the northern Atlantic c. 1000 to found the colonies of "Woodland" and "Vinland" – possibly Newfoundland and Maryland.

Eugene of Savoy, Prince (1663–1736) Austrian general, born in France, who with Marlborough won many victories against the French in the War of the Spanish Succession. Napoleon considered him to be one of the greatest generals of all time.

F

Ford, Henry (1863–1947) American car manufacturer who pioneered methods of mass production to make inexpensive cars.

Fox, Charles James (1749–1806) British politician, arch opponent of George II. One of few British parliamentarians to support the French Revolution.

Franklin, Benjamin (1706–1790) American statesman and scientist and one of the founding fathers of the U.S.A. He invented bifocal glasses and the lightning conductor.

Frederick II, the Great (1712–1786) King of Prussia from 1740 and brilliant general. Fought Empress Maria Theresa in the War of the Austrian Succession. Skilled flautist.

Freud, Sigmund (1856–1939) Austrian psychiatrist whose theories of the conscious and subconscious mind and infantile sexuality have had a major influence upon modern psychiatry.

G

Gandhi, Mohandas Karamchand (1869–1948) Indian Lawyer, ascetic, and Hindu spiritual leader. Worked for independence from Britain, largely by nonviolent civil disobedience. Assassinated by a Hindu fanatic because he preached peace with Muslims. Known as *Mahatma*, great soul.

Garibaldi, Giuseppe (1807–1882) Italian patriot who played a major part in the struggle to bring about the unification of Italy in 1861. His most famous feat was the conquest of the kingdom of the Two Sicilies in 1860 with 1,000 men (Redshirts). Tried to conquer Rome in 1862 and 1867. Fought for France from 1870 to 1871. Member of Italian parliament 1874.

Gladstone, William Ewart (1809–1898) British Liberal statesman who was four times prime minister of Britain. Failed in several attempts to persuade Parliament to agree to Home Rule for Ireland. When, as an old man in 1894, he went to resign, Queen Victoria, who disliked him, kept him standing throughout the interview.

Goebbels, Joseph Paul (1897–1945) Chief of propaganda in Nazi Germany. He perfected a number of propaganda techniques. Close friend of Hitler. Committed suicide.

H

Hammurabi the Great (c. 1800 B.C.) Sixth king of the first Babylonian dynasty, he conquered all Mesopotamia. He was a great builder and his code of laws was not surpassed until Roman times.

Hannibal (247–183 B.C.) Great Carthaginian soldier and statesman. Crossed the Alps (with elephants) to invade Italy, where he defeated the Romans in many battles. He was defeated at Zama in 202 by the Romans and was later exiled. He committed suicide so as not to fall into Roman hands.

Hitler, Adolf (1889–1945) "Fuhrer" or leader of Germany during World War II. An ex-soldier, born in Vienna, Austria, he became leader of the Nazi party which came to power in 1933. Led Germany into war in 1939 and his armies conquered most of Europe before being defeated by the United States, France, Britain, and other Allies in 1945. Hitler killed himself in ruins of Berlin to avoid capture.

Homer (c. 850 B.C.) Greek poet, author of the *Iliad* and the *Odyssey*, though nothing certain is known of him.

I

Ivan IV, the Terrible (1530–1584) First tsar of all Russia. Became ruler in 1533, assumed personal power in 1546. Vicious and cruel, he had many people murdered and tortured. Developed religious mania, murdered eldest son, repented and became a monk on his death bed.

J

Jefferson, Thomas (1743–1826) Chief author of the Declaration of Independence and a great president (1801–1809). During Jefferson's first term of office he was responsible for the "Louisiana Purchase," the buying of a huge piece of French colonial territory stretching from the Mississippi to the northern Pacific border.

Joan of Arc (Jeanne d'Arc) (1412–1431) The peasant girl who led the French armies against the English in the Hundred Years' War. She was burned as a witch by the English.

Johnson, Samuel (1709–1784) English writer and debater who was renowned as a wit. He produced his *Dictionary* in 1755.

K

Kenyatta, Jomo (c. 1883–1978) Kenyan nationalist leader who spent much of his life campaigning for Kenyan independence from British rule. His book, *Facing Mount Kenya*, was a landmark in African nationalism. He became the first prime minister and then president of an independent Kenya in 1963. He died in office in 1978.

Kitchener, Horatio Herbert (1850–1916) Governor-general of Sudan, he recaptured Khartoum from Muslim fanatics. British soldier who won the battle of Omdurman in 1898. Became commander-in-chief in South Africa during the Boer War and was secretary of state for war in 1914. His features became famous on World War I poster, "Your Country Needs You."

L

Lawrence, Thomas Edward (1888–1935) British archeologist, soldier, and author who helped to organize the Arab revolt against Turkey in Arabia in 1917. Became famous (and lionized) as Lawrence of Arabia. Wrote *Seven Pillars of Wisdom* and *The Mint*.

Lenin, Vladimir (1870–1924) Russian revolutionary who was exiled from Russia from 1895 to 1917. He founded the Bolshevik (later the Communist) Party. Allowed across Germany in a sealed train after the February Revolution, he then led the October Revolution. Fell ill and lost control of government in 1922. Succeeded by Stalin in 1924.

Lincoln, Abraham (1809–1865) As sixteenth president of the United States, Lincoln led the Union to victory over the Confederate states in the Civil War. He declared all slaves free in 1863. Lincoln was famous for his honesty and noble speeches, such as the Gettysburg Address. He was assassinated five days after the end of the Civil War.

Livingstone, David (1813–1873) Scottish missionary and explorer of Africa who became a hero to Victorian England. After crossing the Kalahari Desert and traveling down the Zambesi River, he sought sources of Congo and Nile Rivers. Feared lost, he was found by the explorer, Henry Stanley. In a famous speech to Cambridge undergraduates, he called upon them to go out as missionaries to Africa, and a generation was to follow his advice.

M

Mao Zedong (1893–1976) Chinese Communist leader who defeated the Nationalists under Chiang Kai-shek in 1949. His revolutionary method was constantly to upset the Chinese establishment. After his death the Maoist notion of continuous cultural revolution was rejected.

Maria Theresa (1717–1780) Austrian empress of Holy Roman empire from 1740. Defended her right to the throne in the War of the Austrian Succession from 1740 to 1748. Her husband, Francis of Lorraine, was recognized as emperor in 1748.

Marx, Karl (1818–1883) German Jewish philosopher who in his writings laid the foundations of Communism. In 1848 (with Engels) he published *The Communist Manifesto*. His doctrine in *Das Kapital* (1867) revolutionized political thinking.

More, Sir Thomas (1478–1535) English lawyer and statesman who was made chancellor by Henry VIII. His *Utopia* describes an ideal society. He refused to recognize the king as head of the Church in England and was executed for treason. Declared a saint in 1935.

N

Nasser, Gamal Abdel (1918–1970) Egyptian revolutionary and army officer. Helped depose King Farouk in 1952. While president from 1956 tried to modernize country. Nationalized Suez Canal.

Nehru, Jawaharlal (1889–1964) Indian statesman who played a leading part in the nationalist struggle to gain independence from Britain. Prime minister of India from 1947 to 1964. He was one of the founders of the political movement known as Non-Alignment.

Nelson, Horatio (1758–1805) British naval hero, lost eye and arm in battle. Destroyed French fleet at Battle of Nile in 1798, won Battle of Copenhagen in 1801, destroyed another French fleet at Trafalgar in 1805, dying in moment of victory. Created viscount in 1801.

Nero (A.D. 37–68) Roman emperor from 54 to 68. Rebuilt Rome after the great fire and was wrongly depicted by later Christian writers as playing the lyre while Rome burned. He led a dissolute private life and committed suicide in 68.

Nightingale, Florence (1820–1910) English reformer and became nurse. Against great opposition she organized nursing reforms during the Crimean War when she became known as the "Lady with the Lamp." Her system of sanitary barrack hospitals was to be adopted worldwide.

Nkrumah, Kwame (1909–1972) Gold Coast nationalist, he founded the Convention People's Party and became the country's first prime minister at independence and then its first president when Ghana became a republic in 1960. He was ousted in a coup in 1966 and died in exile in Guinea. He was the author of several books, the most important of which was *I Speak of Freedom*.

P

Pasteur, Louis (1822–1895) French chemist who established bacteriology as science. Devised method of gentle heating (Pasteurization) to kill microorganisms in wine and beer. Showed that air contains spores of living organisms. Proposed germ theory of disease. Developed inoculation of animals against anthrax and rabies.

Pericles (495–429 B.C.) Greatest Athenian of its "golden age," he led Athens from 460 to 430 and was responsible for making Athens the "most beautiful city in the world." He died in 429 of the plague. Known as the "Father of Democracy."

Pizarro, Francisco (1474–1541) One of the greatest of the Spanish *Conquistadores*, he conquered the Inca empire of Peru in 1528 with only 180 men. Assassinated.

Plato (427–347) Greek philosopher who was a pupil of Socrates and teacher of Aristotle. Enshrined his philosophy in his *Dialogues*. Platonism, stressing idea of the good rather than material appearances, has had a profound influence upon philosophy.

Polo, Marco (1254–1324) Venetian merchant who traveled to the court of the great Mongol Emperor Kublai Khan in Cathay (China). Returned to Venice in 1295 after 24-year absence, a wealthy man. Described journeys in *Travels*, which astonished Europe of his day.

Ptolemy I Sotor (?–283 B.C.) Half-brother to Alexander the Great and one of his most trusted generals. Ptolemy took Egypt as his "share" of Alexander's empire when Alexander died, and founded the Ptolemaic line of pharaohs which lasted until the time of Julius Caesar.

R

Raleigh, Sir Walter (1552–1618) English soldier and courtier who established the first colony of Virginia and introduced the habit of smoking to England. Explored Guiana region of South America and was executed by James I after failing to find gold.

Rhodes, Cecil John (1853–1902) British statesman. As a young man went out to South Africa for his health. He made a fortune in diamonds, became prime minister of Cape colony, and created Rhodesia between 1890 and 1895. His dream was a Cape to Cairo railway through British-controlled territory in Africa. Disgraced over Jameson Raid in Transvaal in 1896.

Richelieu, Cardinal Armand Jean du Plessis (1585–1642) French statesman who became the first minister of Louis XIII from 1624 to 1642 and virtually ruled France. He curbed the old nobility, broke the independent power of the Huguenots, and extended France's borders and power in Europe.

Robespierre, Maximilien (1758–1794) Leader of the Jacobins in the French Revolution, became the most important figure in the "Reign of Terror." Almost a dictator for a time, he himself was denounced and guillotined.

Roosevelt, Franklin Delano (1884–1945) Four times president of the U.S.A., he was responsible for the New Deal in the 1930s to help end the Great Depression. He led his country through World War II until his death in 1945. He was a polio victim and spent his last years in a wheelchair.

S

Savonarola, Girolamo (1452–1498) Italian priest who denounced the corruption of Florentine society and led a rebellion against Pope Alexander VI. Captured and executed for sedition and heresy.

Shaka (1787–1828) He became king of the Zulus in 1818 and devised new military strategy and new weapons, creating a standing Zulu army of *impis* (regiments). His military conquests caused a dispersal of his people that had widespread effects throughout southern Africa.

Shakespeare, William (1564–1616) England's greatest writer. His plays and poetry have had a profound effect upon the English language and have been translated into most languages.

Smuts, Jan Christian (1870–1950) Boer general in the Boer War of 1899 to 1902, he was twice prime minister of South Africa and a supporter of the connection with Britain.

Stuart, Charles Edward (1720–1788) Known as the "Young Pretender" to the British crown. Son of James Edward Stuart and grandson of King James II. Led the unsuccessful 1745 invasion of Scotland in an attempt to bring about a Jacobite rebellion against the Hanoverian dynasty. Defeated at Culloden in 1746, lived the rest of his life in exile.

Sun Yat-sen (1866–1925) Chinese revolutionary who overthrew the Manchu dynasty and turned China into a republic. He was president of China from 1921 to his death.

T

Tamerlane (1336–1405) Name means Timur the Lame. He created a huge Mongol empire from Turkey to India and north to Moscow. A brilliant soldier, he was feared for his ruthlessness.

Toussaint L'Ouverture, Pierre Dominique (1743–1803) Haitian liberator, born of African slave parents, became leader of French republican rebels. Gained control of island and ruled well until overthrown by French military intervention in 1802.

Trotsky, Leon (Lev Davidovich Bronstein; 1879–1940) Russian revolutionary. Minister under Lenin in 1917. Organized Red Army in civil war of 1918 to 1921. Opposed Stalin and exiled in 1929. Assassinated by a Stalin agent in Mexico.

V

Victor Emmanuel II (1820–1878) King of Sardinia. Leader in war against Austria and struggle for unification of Italy. First king of Italy (from 1861) guided by Cavour, his chief minister.

W

Walpole, Sir Robert (1676–1745) Britain's first and one of her longest serving prime ministers from 1721 to 1742. His motto was, "Let sleeping dogs lie."

Washington, George (1732–1799) First president of the U.S.A. Led the American forces to victory in the Revolutionary War and became "Father of his Country."

Wilberforce, William (1759–1833). English reformer and evangelist who spent his life campaigning to end the slave trade and slavery. Achieved his goal in England in 1833.

Z

Zoroaster (Zarathustra; c. 660 B.C.) Persian who founded the religion of Zoroastrianism, and was said to have written its sacred book, *Avesta*.

Key Dates

BRITAIN

B.C.
c.4000	Farming develops in Britain
c.1300	Building of hill-forts begins

A.D.
43	Roman conquest begins
61	Rebellion of Boudica
122	Hadrian's Wall begun
367	Invasion of Picts and Scots
408	Roman troops finally withdraw
c.400–c.600	Angles, Saxons, and Jutes migrate and settle
563	St. Columba arrives at Iona
597	St. Augustine arrives in Kent
757–96	Reign of Offa of Mercia
865	Danes overrun East Anglia, Northumbria, and Eastern Mercia
871–99	Reign of Alfred of Wessex
899–939	Wessex kings reconquer Danelaw
1016–35	Reign of Cnut
1066	Norman Conquest
1086	Domesday Survey
1170	Thomas à Becket murdered
1215	Magna Carta
1264–5	Baron's War against Henry III; Simon de Montfort killed

EUROPE

B.C.
c.6500	Farming begins in Greece and the Aegean
c.2000–1200	Minoan and Mycenean civilization in Crete and Greece
c.750–c.550	Greek and Phoenicians colonize Mediterranean and Black Sea
490–479	Battles of the Persian Wars
431–404	Peloponnesian War
c.380–300	Work of Plato, Euclid and Aristotle
c.327–300	Main period of Roman expansion
27	Octavian takes title of Augustus: end of Roman republic

A.D.
284–305	Reign of Diocletian. Empire reorganized and divided into East and West
378	Valens defeated by Visigoths at Adrianople. Germanic peoples move into Europe
410	Sack of Rome
496	Baptism of Clovis, king of the Franks
535–40	Justinian reconquers Italy
568	Lombards settle in Italy
c.600	Slavs move into Balkans
711	Muslims invade Spain
732	Charles Martel defeats Arabs at Poitiers
800	Charlemagne crowned
843	Partition of Charlemagne's empire
886	Vikings besiege Paris
911	Vikings granted Duchy of Normandy
962	Otto I crowned emperor at Rome
1054	Break between Greek and Latin churches
1073–85	Quarrel between Holy Roman Empire and Papacy begins
1202–4	Philip II of France captures Normandy and Anjou

NEAR EAST AND NORTH AFRICA

B.C.
c.8000	Farming begins
c.4000–3500	Invention of wheel, plow and sail in Mesopotamia and Egypt
c.3500	Early writing in Mesopotamia and Egypt
c.2700–c.2200	Age of Pyramids in Egypt
c.2000–c.1200	Hittite civilization in Turkey
c.1200–c.650	Domination of Assyrian Empire
c.550–330	Achaemenid Empire in Persia
334–323	Campaigns of Alexander the Great
c.6	Birth of Jesus

A.D.
c.30	Crucifixion of Jesus, founder of Christianity
226–636	Sassanid Empire in Persia
313	Freedom of Christian worship in Roman Empire
429–44	Vandals occupy North Africa
533–4	Belisarius reconquers North Africa for Justinian
540	Persian-Byzantine war begins
622	Muhammad goes to Medina
636–43	Arab conquest of Syria, Egypt, and Persia
750	Abbasid caliphate established at Baghdad
969	Fatimids conquer Egypt
1055	Seljuk Turks capture Baghdad
1071	Seljuks defeat Byzantine army
1096–99	First Crusade; Kingdom of Jerusalem established
1187	Saladin overruns Kingdom of Jerusalem
1250	Mamluks seize power in Egypt
1258	Mongols sack Baghdad
1260	Mamluks defeat Mongols at Ain Jalut

ASIA AND AMERICA

B.C.
c.6000	Rice cultivation in Far East
c.2700–1750	Harappan civilization in Indus Valley
c.1750–1000	Shang dynasty in China
1000–c.500	Chou dynasty in China
c.320	Mauryan Empire in India
c.200 B.C.–c.A.D. 220	Han dynasty in China

A.D.
c.300–c.900	Mayan civilization in Central America
304–8	Huns invade China
c.320	Gupta Empire in Ganges Valley: "Golden Age" of Hindu culture
c.300–500	Main spread of Buddhism in China
c.520	Decimal system invented in India
618–906	T'ang dynasty in China
646	Taika reform in Japan
711–13	Muslims conquer Samarkand and Indus Valley
794	Japanese capital moves to Kyoto
?960–1280	Sung dynasty in China
c.1000	Greenland Vikings reach America
1206	Sultanate of Delhi founded. Tamujin (Genghis Khan) unites Mongol tribes
1206–80	Mongol conquests

BRITAIN		EUROPE		ASIA AND AFRICA		AMERICA AND AUSTRALASIA	
1277–83	Edward I annexes the Principality of Wales			1271–95	Travels of Marco Polo		
1296–1336	Anglo-Scottish Wars			c.1300	Ottoman Turkish expansion begins	c.1325–1520	Aztec civilization in Mexico
		1309–78	Papacy at Avignon				
1327	Edward II deposed and murdered	1337	Beginning of Hundred Years' War in France	1368–1644	Ming dynasty in China		
1348	Black Death in England	1347–50	Black Death	1380–1405	Career and conquests of Timur (Tamerlane)	c.1400–1525	Inca civilization in Andes
1381	Peasants' Revolt						
1399	Richard II deposed. Henry IV establishes Lancastrian dynasty	c.1450	Gutenberg starts printing				
1455–85	The Wars of the Roses	1450–53	English driven out of France				
		1453	Constantinople falls to Ottoman Turks				
		1505	Reign of Ivan III	1486–98	Voyages of Bartolomeu Dias and Vasco da Gama	1492	Columbus reaches America
1529–39	Henry VIII's Reformation Parliament and dissolution of the monasteries	1521	Condemnation of Martin Luther. Beginning of Protestantism	c.1500–1870	African slave trade	1519	Cortes begins conquest of Aztec Empire
		1526	Turks overrun Hungary	1522–1680	Mughal expansion in India	1532	Pizarro begins conquest of Inca Empire
1554–58	Brief Catholic restoration under Mary Tudor			c.1550–c.1650	Russians colonize Siberia	1608	French colonists found Quebec
1588	Spanish Armada dispersed			1619	Dutch found Batavia (Djakarta)	1620	*Mayflower* puritans (Pilgrim Fathers) settle in New England
c.1590–c.1613	Shakespeare writes his plays and sonnets	c.1600–1650	Scientific work of Kepler, Galileo, and Descartes	1630s	Japan isolates itself from rest of world		
1603	James VI of Scotland succeeds to English throne	1618–48	Thirty Years' War				
1642–48	Civil wars in England	1643–1715	Reign of Louis XIV	1644–1911	Manchu dynasty in China	1645	Tasman discovers New Zealand
1649	Charles I executed	1682–1725	Reign of Peter the Great, Tsar of Russia	1652	Dutch found Cape Colony		
1660	Monarchy restored under Charles II	1740–86	Reign of Frederick the Great, King of Prussia				
1688	James II deposed						
1707	Union of England and Scotland	1756–63	Seven Years' War	1757	Battle of Plassey; British defeat French in India	1776	American Declaration of Independence
c.1730	Wesley brothers found Methodism	1789	French Revolution begins			1788	British colony founded at Botany Bay, Australia
1800	Union of England and Ireland	1799	Napoleon seizes power in France	1805	Beginning of East India Company's dominance in India	1817–24	Careers of Simon Bolivar and José de San Martin
1825	Stockton–Darlington railway completed	1815	Battle of Waterloo; Congress of Vienna			1840	Britain annexes New Zealand
1845	Irish famine	1821–29	Greek War of Liberation	1839–42	Opium War; Britain takes Hong Kong		
		1848	Year of revolutions throughout Europe	1857–9	Indian Mutiny	1846–48	U.S.A.-Mexico War
1851	Great Exhibition, London	1854–6	Crimean War	1869	Suez Canal opened	1861–65	American Civil War
1863	First London underground built. Darwin's *On the Origin of Species*	1870–71	Franco-Prussian War	1880s	"Scramble for Africa"	1869	First transcontinental railroad completed in United States
		1885–95	Daimler and Benz work on automobile; Marconi's wireless	1900	Boxer Rebellion in China		
		1914	World War I begins	1899–1902	Boer War	1876	Alexander Bell patents telephone
		1917	Bolshevik revolution in Russia begins	1911	Republic established in China under Sun Yat-sen	1898	Spanish-American War
1922	Irish Free State established	1918	World War I ends	1920–38	Career of Mustapha Kemal, Atatürk	1903	Wright brothers: first powered flight
1926	General Strike	1922	Mussolini takes power in Italy	1937	Japan invades China	1911	Mexican Revolution
		1933	Hitler becomes German Chancellor	1941	Japanese attack Pearl Harbor	1914	Panama Canal opened
1940	Battle of Britain	1936–39	Spanish Civil War	1945	United States drops atomic bombs on Japan	1929	Wall Street Crash begins Great Depression
		1939	World War II begins	1947	India obtains independence	1941	United States enters World War II
		1941	Germany invades USSR	1948	State of Israel founded		
		1945	Defeat of Germany. Cold War begins	1949	Communist victory in China	1959	Cuban Revolution
		1957	USSR launches first space satellite. Treaty of Rome: formation of European Economic Community	1952–80	African states win independence	1963	President Kennedy assassinated
1973	Britain enters European Economic Community					1981	Neil Armstrong lands on the Moon
						1981	First space shuttle

Index

Page numbers in *italics* refer to illustrations.

PHOTOGRAPHIC ACKNOWLEDGEMENTS
The publishers wish to thank the following for supplying photographs for this book: Cover: *top right*, British Museum; *top middle*, National Gallery Washington; *top right*, Zefa; *middle right*, Greek Tourist Office; *bottom left*, Zefa; *bottom middle*, British Museum; *middle right*, Michael Holford/National Maritime Museum; title page: Science Museum; Page 4 *top middle left*, Mansell; *bottom left*, Sonia Halliday; *bottom middle right*, India Office Library; *right*, British Museum; 5 *top middle left*, Alan Hutchison; *top right*, Victoria & Albert Museum; *bottom left*, French Tourist Office; 6/7 Zefa; 8 *top left*, Mark Redknap; *bottom*, Ashmolean Museum; 9 *top left*, Middle East Archives; *top right*, British Museum; *bottom right*, British Tourist Authority; 11, Michael Holford; 12 *middle*, Michael Holford; *bottom*, Ellen Smart; *top right*, British Museum; 13 *bottom*, Palace Museum, Taiwan; *top right*, Zefa; *middle*, Michael Holford; 14 French Tourist Office; 15 *middle*, Jean Vertut; 16 British Museum; 17 British Museum; 18 *bottom left*, Peter Clayton; *top right*, Society for Anglo-Chinese Understanding; *middle & bottom right*, British Museum; 19 British Museum; 20 Nik Wheeler; 21 *top left*, British Museum; *bottom left*, Musées Nationaux Paris; *right*, Scala; 22 *middle bottom*, Louvre Paris; *top right*, Scala; *middle right*, Ronald Sheridan; 24 *top*, Robert Harding; *middle*, Peter Clayton; 25 *middle*, British Museum; *middle right*, Michael Holford; *bottom right*, Louvre Paris; 26 British Museum; 27 Robert Harding; 29 *middle left*, Michael Holford; *middle right*, Sonia Halliday; *bottom*, Ekdotike Athens; 32 *middle left & right*, British Museum; *middle*, Michael Holford; *middle right*, Ronald Sheridan; *bottom*, Air India; 33 *top*, Ellen Smart; *bottom*, British Museum; 35 *middle left*, Ronald Sheridan; *top right*, Sonia Halliday; 36 Zefa; 37 *top left*, British Museum; *bottom left*, Michael Holford; *middle right*, Ronald Sheridan; *right*, Sonia Halliday; 38 Josephine Powell; 39 Michael Holford; 40 *bottom left*, British Museum; *bottom right*, Louvre Paris; 41 *top left*, Sonia Halliday; *middle*, Peter Clayton; *bottom*, Musées Nationaux Paris; 42 Sonia Halliday; 43 *middle*, Michael Holford; *bottom*, Sonia Halliday; 44 Israel Tourist Office; 45 *top & middle*, British Museum; *bottom*, Musées Nationaux Paris; 46 *middle*, Peter Clayton; *bottom*, Robert Harding; 47 *top left & right*, Society for Anglo Chinese Understanding; *bottom*, Nelson Gallery, Atkins Museum; 49 *top left*, Zefa; *middle right*, British Tourist Authority; 50 British Museum; 52 Sonia Halliday; 53 Scala; 54 *middle*, Ashmolean Museum; *bottom*, Schleswig-Holstein Museum; 55 *top*, National Museum Copenhagen; *bottom*, British Museum; 56 *bottom left*, Dr. W. Bray; *middle right*, British Museum; 57 *middle*, Michael Holford; *bottom*, Robert Harding; 58 Robert Harding; 60 *top*, Salisbury Cathedral/Michael Holford; *bottom*, Bibliotheque Nationale, Paris; 61 *top*, Sonia Halliday; *bottom left*, Michael Holford; *bottom right*, British Museum; 63 Scala/Cividale, Museo Archaeologico; 64 *top*, Victoria & Albert Museum; *bottom*, Giraudon; *right*, Mansell Collection; 65 *top left*, BBC Hulton; *top right*, Bodleian Library; *bottom*, Scala Firenze/Museo dell'Opera del Duomo; 66 *top*, British Museum; *bottom*, Sonia Halliday; 67 *top*, Sonia Halliday; *bottom*, Scala/Bargello; 68 *right*, Georgina Herrmann; *bottom left*, Sonia Halliday; 69 *top right*, Middle East Archives; *middle left*, British Museum; *bottom*, British Museum; 70 *left*, Sonia Halliday; *right*, Michael Holford; 71 *left*, Bildarchiv Osterreichische Nationalbibliothek; *top right*, Giraudon; *bottom left*, Sonia Halliday; 72 *top right*, Victoria & Albert Museum; *left*, British Museum; 73 *top* Alan Hutchison; *bottom*, Bibliotheque Nationale; 75 *top*, Michael Holford; *bottom*, SACU; 76 Zefa; 77 *top*, Universitets Oldsaksamling, Oslo; *bottom*, Werner Foreman Archive; 79 Giraudon; 81 *bottom*, Louvre; 82–83 Courtesy of the Smithsonian Institution, Freer Gallery of Art, Washington DC; 83 *top*, Seattle Art Museum; *bottom*, Zefa; 84 Michael Holford; 85 *middle*, British Museum; *bottom*, Mary Evans Picture Library; 86 David Williamson; 87 *top right*,

Zefa; *bottom left*, Interfoto MTI Budapest; 88 *top left*, Alan Hutchison; *right*, Topkapi Museum, Istanbul; 89 Edinburgh University; 91 *top*, British Museum; *bottom*, Zefa; 92 Giraudon; 93 Sonia Halliday/Bibliotheque Nationale; *bottom*, Scala; 94 Sonia Halliday; 95 *top right*, Peter Clayton; *bottom left*, Sonia Halliday; *bottom right*, C. R. Warn; 96 Scala/Aquisgrana, Duomo; 97 *top*, Scala/Siena, Pinacoteca Nazionale; *bottom*, Sonia Halliday; 98 Michael Holford; 99 *top*, Zefa; *bottom*, Alan Hutchison; 100 Zefa; 101 *top right*, Sonia Halliday; *left*, Bildarchiv Preussischer Kulturbesitz; *bottom right*, Mansell; 102 *top*, M. Vautier; *bottom*, Alan Hutchison; 103 Robert Harding; 104 *right*, Scala/Museo dell'Opera del Duomo; 105 *top left*, Giraudon; *right*, Scala/Baptistery; 106 *bottom left*, Michael Holford; *top left*, British Museum; *bottom right*, J. Allan Cash; 107 British Museum; 108 Turkish Tourist Office; *bottom*, Sonia Halliday; 109 *top & bottom*, Sonia Halliday; 110/111 French Government Tourist Office; 112 National Gallery; 113 *top & bottom*, Michael Holford; 114 Science Museum, London; 115 *bottom*, National Maritime Museum; 117 *bottom right*, National Gallery of Art, Washington; 118 *bottom right*, British Museum; 119 Michael Holford; 121 *top*, Zefa; *bottom*, British Museum; 122 Mansell; 123 *top*, Scala; *bottom*, Mansell; 124 Zefa/Prado Madrid; 125 *top*, Sonia Halliday; *bottom*, National Maritime Museum; 127 *top*, reproduced by Gracious Permission of Her Majesty The Queen; *bottom*, Victoria & Albert Museum; 129 *top*, Victoria & Albert Museum; *bottom*, Sonia Halliday/Jane Taylor; 130 Alan Hutchison; 131 *top*, British Museum; *bottom*, National Maritime Museum; 132 *top*, Mansell; 133 *top*, Victoria & Albert Museum; *bottom*, Mary Evans; 134 Michael Holford; 135 *top & bottom right*, National Army Museum; *bottom left*, Mansell; 136 Bodleian Library; 137 *middle*, British Museum; *bottom*, Mary Evans; 138 Musées de la Ville de Strasburg; 139 National Maritime Museum; 141 *top*, Aldus Books; *bottom*, British Museum; 142 Aldus Books; 143 *top*, British Museum; *bottom*, Colour Library International; 145 Ian Hamilton; 146 *top left & bottom*, British Museum; 147 Mansell; 148 *top*, Stetens Museum fur Kunst, Copenhagen; *bottom*, Kungl Armemuseum, Stockholm; 149 Sonia Halliday; *bottom right*, Mansell; 152 *top*, Robert Harding; *middle*, British Museum; *bottom* Mary Evans Picture Library; 153 India Office Library; 154 *top*, Ronan Picture Library; *bottom*, Science Museum; 155 *top*, Science Museum; *bottom*, Mansell; 156 Mansell; 157 *middle*, Michael Holford; *bottom right*, Michael Holford/National Maritime Museum; *bottom left*, National Maritime Museum; 158/159 Robert Harding; 160 *top*, Fotomas; 161 *top*, United Nations; *bottom*, NASA; 162 *top right*, Mansell; 163 *bottom*, Mansell; 166 *bottom*, American Museum, Bath; 167 Peter Newark; 168 National Portrait Gallery, London; 169 *middle*, National Portrait Gallery, London; *bottom*, Bibliotheque Nationale, Paris; 171 *top*, Tony & Marion Morrison; *bottom*, Zefa; 175 *middle*, Mary Evans; *bottom*, Mansell; 176 BBC Hulton; 177 *top*, India Office Library; *bottom*, Axel Poignant; 178, Shell UK Ltd.; 179 *bottom*, Ford Motor Co.; 180 Mansell Collection; 181 Zefa; 182 Mary Evans; 183 *top*, Mansell; *bottom*, Alan Hutchison; 184 Mary Evans; 185 *top*, Victoria & Albert Museum; *bottom*, Mansell; 186 Victoria & Albert Museum; 187 *top*, Alan Hutchison; *bottom*, Novosti; 188 Sonia Halliday; 189 *top*, Keystone; *bottom*, Vision International/Paolo Koch; 190 *top*, Mary Evans; 191 *top*, Canadian Pacific Railway; *bottom*, Science Museum; 193 *top*, National Army Museum; *middle*, Imperial War Museum; 196 Zefa; 197 Robert Hunt Library; *bottom*, BBC Hulton; 199 *top*, Novosti; *bottom*, Imperial War Museum; 201 Zefa; 202 Siemens; 203 *top*, Zefa; *bottom*, Keystone; 204 Novosti; 205 Robert Harding; 207 *middle*, Bahamas Tourist office; *bottom*, Syndication International.

Picture Research: Penny J. Warn & Jackie Cookson.